Encountering the Real: Faith and Philosophical Enquiry

Saint Leo University

Louis Pojman
Michael Rea
Robert Solomon
Kathleen Higgins
Soren Kierkegaard

CENGAGE
Learning·

Australia • Brazil • Japan • Korea • Mexico • Singapore • Spain • United Kingdom • United States

Encountering the Real: Faith and Philosophical Enquiry Saint Leo University

Philosophy of Religion: An Anthology, Sixth Edition
Pojman / Rea
© 2012 Cengage Learning. All rights reserved.

The Big Questions: A Short Introduction to Philosophy, Eighth Edition
Solomon / Higgins
© 2010, 2006 Cengage Learning. All rights reserved.

Senior Project Development Manager:
 Linda deStefano

Market Development Manager:
 Heather Kramer

Senior Production/
Manufacturing Manager:
 Donna M. Brown

Production Editorial Manager:
 Kim Fry

Sr. Rights Acquisition Account Manager:
 Todd Osborne

For product information and technology assistance, contact us at
Cengage Learning Customer & Sales Support, 1-800-354-9706

For permission to use material from this text or product,
submit all requests online at **cengage.com/permissions**
Further permissions questions can be emailed to
permissionrequest@cengage.com

This book contains select works from existing Cengage Learning resources and was produced by Cengage Learning Custom Solutions for collegiate use. As such, those adopting and/or contributing to this work are responsible for editorial content accuracy, continuity and completeness.

Compilation © 2013 Cengage Learning

ISBN-13: 978-1-285-55349-8

ISBN-10: 1-285-55349-7

Cengage Learning
5191 Natorp Boulevard
Mason, Ohio 45040
USA

Cengage Learning is a leading provider of customized learning solutions with office locations around the globe, including Singapore, the United Kingdom, Australia, Mexico, Brazil, and Japan. Locate your local office at:
international.cengage.com/region.
Cengage Learning products are represented in Canada by Nelson Education, Ltd.
For your lifelong learning solutions, visit **www.cengage.com /custom.**
Visit our corporate website at **www.cengage.com.**

Printed at CLDPC,USA,09-19

A Little Logic

*The central problem of logic is the
classification of arguments, so that all those
that are bad are thrown into one division,
and those which are good into another.*

— Charles Sanders Peirce

Philosophy consists of ideas, grand theories, and visions, articulated in speech or in writing and presented in the clearest way possible. In the presentation, therefore, it is crucial to give **reasons** for your ideas, to *support* your theories with a variety of examples and considerations that will show that your philosophy is more persuasive than its alternatives (or at least as persuasive). Accordingly, the key to good philosophical presentation development is what we call an **argument.** In ordinary language, we sometimes think of an argument as a violent quarrel, filled with hostility and mutual resentment. This need not be the case, however; an argument is nothing more than the process of supporting what you believe with reasons. "I know that I am not dreaming right now because I never dream this vividly, I just pinched myself and, besides, if I were dreaming I'd probably be snoring right now." An argument ties your belief to other beliefs and helps persuade someone else to accept what you believe. A good argument can be presented in a perfectly coolheaded and amiable manner. Indeed, the best arguments are always defined by a process of careful thinking that we call **logic,** often described as the "science (and the process) of proper reasoning."

Philosophers use a variety of arguments and argument types. So, of course, do politicians, salespeople, television talk-show hosts, and each of us, every time we are trying to convince someone of something we believe or trying to think something through for ourselves. There are arguments by **example** ("Let's look at a particular case,") and arguments by **analogy** ("Life is like a novel. There is a beginning and an end; it can be dull or exciting; there will surely be conflicts and bad scenes; there is suspense; the plot thickens. Therefore, the most important thing in life is to live an interesting life, develop your character, and don't just play it safe."). There are arguments based on extensive scientific research, and there are arguments that are very abstract and largely verbal (concerned more with the words used to describe a phenomenon than with the phenomenon itself). There are arguments based on nothing more than a vicious attack on one's opponents, and there are arguments that—despite their appearance—are not really arguments at all. In general, we might divide arguments into two classes— good arguments and bad arguments—depending on the *relations* between various statements. (*Truth* and *falsity,* on the other hand, apply to the statements themselves, never to the arguments.)

What counts as a good or a bad argument depends upon what kind of an argument it is. As a useful way to understand arguments and what it is that makes them good or bad, it is convenient to divide them into two very general categories, to which philosophers and logicians (that is, those who study logic as their essential interest) apply the names **deduction** and **induction**.

Deduction

In a deductive argument, one argues for the truth of a conclusion by deducing a statement from a number of others. An example that might be familiar to you is any proof of a theorem you learned to formulate in high school geometry. Some statements are assumed to be true from the outset (for example, statements that are true by definition and statements so obviously true that they need not be proved at all, called **axioms**). Then, new statements are deduced, or **inferred,** by means of a number of established **rules of inference**—that is, the laws of thought, such as "A statement cannot be both true and false at the same time" or "If either *A* or *B,* but not *A,* then *B.*" A deductive argument is thus a progression from one true statement to another. The second statement is established as true, too; in fact, a deductive argument is sometimes defined as an argument whose final statement—or **conclusion**—is guaranteed to be true by the truth of the previous statements—or **premises.**

The best-known deductive arguments are called **syllogisms.** An example of a syllogism is:

> All philosophers are wise.
>
> Socrates is a philosopher.
> _____
> Therefore, Socrates is wise.

What is important in such arguments is the form of the component statements:

> All P's are Q's.
>
> S is a P.
> _____
> Therefore, S is a Q.

When a deductive argument proceeds correctly according to this form, we say that it is **deductively valid**, or simply **valid**. Arguments that are not valid are **invalid**. Deduction guarantees that our conclusions will be at least as certain as the premises. If the premises are certainly true, then the conclusions will certainly be true as well. But it is important to emphasize that an argument can be valid even if its premises and conclusion are false. For example, the following syllogism correctly follows the above form and is therefore valid:

> All cows are purple.
>
> Socrates is a cow.
> _____
>
> Therefore, Socrates is purple.

This is a valid argument, even though both the premises and the conclusion are false. But without true premises, even a valid argument cannot guarantee true conclusions. A good deductive argument must also have premises that are agreed to be true. Notice that, contrary to common usage, philosophers restrict their use of the words *valid* and *invalid* to talking about correct and incorrect arguments; the words *true* and *false* apply to the various statements that one makes in an argument—its premises and its conclusion. Thus, the claim that "3 + 2 = 8" is false, not invalid; and the argument "If Socrates is a man and all goats eat cabbage, then Socrates is a goat" is invalid, not false (whether or not its premises or conclusion are false). When an argument is both valid and has true premises (a good argument, in other words), it is called a **sound** argument. An argument is **unsound** (a bad deductive argument) if one or more of its premises are false, or if it is invalid. A good deductive argument, then, has two essential features:

1. It is a valid argument.

2. Its premises are true.

A detailed discussion of valid argument forms can be found in Appendix B.

Induction

Inductive arguments, on the other hand, do not guarantee the truth of their conclusions, even if all the premises are agreed to be true. The most familiar form of inductive argument is **generalization** from a number of particular cases—for example, noting that every animal we have seen with sharp front teeth eats meat and concluding that *all* animals with sharp front teeth eat meat. But notice that although we might be absolutely sure that we are correct about the particular cases—that every such animal we have seen does in fact eat meat—we might still be wrong in our generalization, our conclusion that *all* such animals are meat eaters. Thus, it is essential in any inductive argument to begin with a well-chosen number of particular cases and to make sure that they are as varied as possible (that is, to approximate what social scientists call a random sample). Inductive arguments can be **strong** or **weak**, depending on the weight of the evidence for the conclusion, the quality of the sample, and the plausibility of the generalization. Inductive arguments are not evaluated as valid or invalid; in fact, given the definition of validity as the guarantee that the conclusion is true if the premises are true, *no* inductive argument is ever deductively valid. (That is not a mark against it, of course. Inductive arguments have other functions; they are not supposed to be deductively valid.)

Deductive and Inductive Logic

Deductive logic guarantees the truth of the conclusion, *if* the premises are true.

Example: If Moriarty didn't do it, then the Spiderwoman did. We know that Moriarty was in prison at the time, so the Spiderwoman must have done it. (Premises: "If M didn't do it, S did," and "M was in prison at the time.")

Inductive logic does not guarantee the truth of the conclusion, but only makes it more reasonable for us to believe the conclusion (compared with other possible conclusions).

Example: The pipe tobacco is the same kind he uses, and the footprints match his shoes. He was seen in the neighborhood only an hour before the crime, and he was heard to say, "I'm going to get even with her if it's the last thing I do." The best explanation of the evidence in this case seems to be the conclusion that he is guilty.

Although generalization is the most familiar example of induction, inductive arguments can be used to support virtually every statement of fact. For example, if you believe that Julius Caesar was murdered in Rome on March 15, 44 BCE, that is a statement of fact that you cannot directly observe today. The argument for its truth must therefore be inductive, based on information you have read in history books, colored by imagery from a play by Shakespeare, to be further verified—if you are curious—by an investigation into the **evidence** available in chronicles of the period, records of Roman politics, and perhaps a few relics from the times.

In such inductive arguments, it is the **coherence** of the evidence that provides the argument—that is, the various elements of the argument fit together well. In a criminal trial, for instance, evidence is presented in favor of two contradictory statements of fact ("The defendant is guilty" versus "The defendant is not guilty"). The inductive question in the minds of the judge and the jury—and probably earlier in the minds of the detectives who worked on the case, too—is whether the evidence for conviction is more coherent than the evidence against. It is worth noting that what Sherlock Holmes and Dr. Watson continuously point to as Holmes's "amazing powers of deduction" are for the most part powers of *inductive* reasoning, drawing factual conclusions from scattered and sometimes barely noticeable evidence.

One of the most important ingredients in inductive reasoning is the **hypothesis,** the statement that an experiment is supposed to prove or disprove. You are probably familiar with hypotheses in science, but we use hypotheses throughout our lives. Induction would be a waste of time if we did not have some hypothesis in mind. Just as scientists try to organize their research around a particular topic and a specific claim, we organize our attention around particular concerns and specific hypotheses. "Who killed the judge? It must have been either Freddy or the thug. Which hypothesis is the more plausible?" Not only science but almost everything we know and want to know depends on hypotheses and inductive reasoning, from looking for the car keys in the morning ("Now, I probably left them somewhere near my books") to speculating on the existence and the nature of black holes in space.

From the preceding discussion, it should be clear that much of what passes for argument is not that at all. For example, many people seem to think that simply stating and restating their opinion—forcefully and with conviction—is the same thing as supporting it with arguments. It is not. Stating your opinion clearly is the essential preliminary to formulating an argument, but it is not the same thing. An argument goes beyond the opinion itself, supporting it by deduction from other statements or with evidence based on experience. Some people seem to think that a single example will serve as a complete argument, but, at most, a single example serves as *part* of an argument. Most inductive arguments require many examples, and they must deal with examples that *don't* fit the hypothesis, too. Every argument is bound to meet up with several counterarguments and objections, so even a single argument is rarely enough to make one's case.

Similarly, many people seem to think that an appeal to **authority** will settle the case, but in most philosophical disputes, it is the nature of authority itself that is in question. If someone insists that God exists because it says so in the Bible, the question immediately shifts to the authority of the Bible. (A person who does not believe in God will probably not accept the authority of the Bible either.) If someone defends a political position because his mother said so or, for that matter, because Thomas Jefferson said so, the question then moves to the authority of the arguer's mother or Jefferson. One of the main functions of philosophy is to let us question authority and see for ourselves what we should believe or not believe. Appeal to authority does not necessarily show respect for that authority, but it does show disrespect for ourselves. **Legitimate** authority has to be earned as well as respected.

Criticizing Arguments
꧅

One of the most crucial philosophical activities—but by no means the only one—is **criticism**. Criticism does not necessarily mean—as in everyday life— negative remarks about someone or something; it means carefully examining a statement, testing it out, seeing if in fact the arguments for it are good ones. But this does mean that, whether it is our own statements or other people's statements that are being examined, it is important to find out what is *wrong* with them so that they can be corrected or strengthened. One way to criticize a deductive argument, for example, is simply to show that its premises are not true; if it is an inductive argument, to show that the evidence on which it is based is falsified or distorted.

Another way to criticize an argument is to show that it consists of invalid deductive arguments or weak inductive generalizations. A particularly powerful way to do this is by the use of **counterexamples**. For instance, if someone claims, "All American men love football," he or she can be refuted if we can find a single American man who does not like football. Any claim that takes the form "All X's are Y's" or "No A's are B's" can be refuted if we can point out a single counterexample—that is, a single X that is not Y, or a single A that is a B. If a philosophy student says, "No one knows anything for certain," a familiar response might be to hold up your hand, stick out your thumb, and say, "Here is a thumb: I know *that* for certain." This may not be the end of the argument, but it is through such general claims and counterexamples to them that philosophical arguments are made more precise.

Even if all of its arguments seem to be sound, a philosophy can be shown to be in trouble if it is **inconsistent**, that is, if the conclusions of its different arguments **contradict** one another. In the same way, one can raise doubts about a philosophy's acceptability if it can be shown that it results in paradox and consequently must be thoroughly reexamined. For example, suppose a philosopher argues that God can do absolutely anything. For instance, God can create a mountain. He can move a mountain. But now a critical listener asks, "Can God create a mountain so large that even he can't move it?"—and we have a paradox. Either he can create such a mountain but then can't move it (and so cannot do everything) or he cannot create such a mountain (and so cannot do everything). The paradox forces us to reexamine the original claim that God can do absolutely anything. (Perhaps it can be revised to say something like, "God can do anything that is logically possible.") Notice that this is a form of *reductio ad absurdum* argument, a reduction to absurdity, in which a position is rejected because it results in a paradox.

Paradox

A **paradox** is a **self-contradictory** or seemingly absurd conclusion based on apparently good arguments. Sometimes the paradox is merely apparent and requires restating; on occasion a well-formulated paradox has brought about the total rethinking of the whole of a branch of science, philosophy, religion, or mathematics. Some examples are:

"This sentence is false." (If that is true, then it is false.)

"There is a barber who shaves everyone in town who does not shave himself." (Does he shave himself?)

"God is all-powerful, so he could create a mountain so huge that even he could not move it."

If Achilles shoots an arrow from point *A* toward point *B*, it first must cover distance *A–C*, which is half of *A–B*; then it must cover distance *C–D*, which is half of *C–B*, and then *D–E*, which is half of *D–B*, and so on, each moment covering half the distance it has covered in the moment before. The paradox is that if the arrow keeps moving forever, it will never reach point *B*.

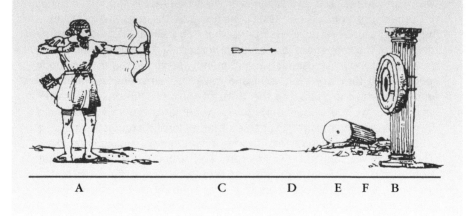

A philosophy that does not contain outright inconsistencies or lead to paradoxes may still be unsuccessful, however, if it is **incoherent**. This means that the various claims have virtually nothing to do with each other, or mean very little, or can be interpreted only in an absurd way. A philosophy can be accused of **begging the question**, repeating as a supposed solution the very problem that it is attempting to resolve. An example of begging the question is the argument, "Other people exist. I know because I've talked to them." And a philosophy can be accused of being silly or trivial, which is just about the most offensive thing you can say, indicating that it is not even worth your time to investigate it further. It is much better to say something false but interesting rather than silly or trivial. (A common way in which philosophical claims can turn out to be trivial is when they express what logicians call *tautologies*: for example, "A is A." A tautology is a statement that is so necessarily true, so obviously correct that a statement claiming the opposite would be self-contradictory.) An argument can be **ad hominem** (or **ad feminam**), aimed at the person but ignoring the issue completely. Accusing someone who disagrees of being an atheist, a communist, or a Nazi is an all-too-familiar example of an *ad hominem* argument. Such bad arguments, in general, are called **fallacies**, whether or not they are formally invalid. (A *formal* fallacy is one that violates the proper rules of inference. An *informal* fallacy may not break the rules of inference but "cheats" by sneaking in ambiguous terminology, biased language, evasion of the facts, and distraction.) A list and discussion of such fallacies can be found in Appendix C.

The Basic Concepts of Logic

An *argument* is a sequence of assertions, or statements to back up a viewpoint or idea. The *conclusion* is an assertion that is supported by all the other assertions. These assertions are thus the *reasons* for accepting the conclusion. Those assertions that are assumed to be true (for the sake of that argument) are called *premises*. Arguments can be either *deductive* or *inductive*: Deductive arguments *guarantee* the truth of their conclusion if they are both valid and have all true premises; inductive arguments do not guarantee the truth of their conclusions, no matter how impressive the evidence. Deductive arguments are said to be *valid* or *invalid*. (Arguments are never true or false.) Invalid arguments are also called *fallacies*. Individual assertions or statements are *true* or *false*. (They are never said to be valid or invalid.) A deductive argument that is both valid and has true premises is said to be *sound*. (Otherwise, it is *unsound*.) An inductive argument that is well supported by its evidence is called *strong*; a poorly supported argument is called *weak*. *Logic* is the use and the study of good arguments and the means of differentiating these from bad arguments.

In emphasizing criticism, it is important to point out, as a matter of balance, that philosophy is nevertheless an especially *cooperative* enterprise. Argumentation and criticism are not hostile or defensive. They are ways of making your ideas and their implications clear—clear to yourself as well as to other people. Socrates used to say that his truest friends were also his best critics.

Indeed, we would distrust a friend who was never critical and never argued. ("If you were really my friend, you would have told me!") Arguments and objections take place within an arena of shared interest and with a common concern for reaching the truth. But, just as important, arguments and objections and mutual respect between people who disagree are absolutely essential in a pluralistic democracy such as our own, in which everyone's opinion is respected and it is most unlikely that we will all agree. But to say that everyone's opinion is respected is not to say that everyone's opinion is of equal value; the depth of thinking and the quality of argument make some opinions better and more plausible than others. At the same time, cooperative respect, mutual concern for the importance of argument, and honest disagreement are indispensable to life as we want to live it.

In developing your own thoughts about the various questions of philosophy, you will inevitably find yourself using both deductive and inductive arguments, and it is perfectly normal to catch yourself—or your friends—using some incorrect arguments as well. What is important, however, is that you can recognize these forms when they appear and that you are aware—even in only a preliminary way—of what you are doing when you argue a position or an idea. Arguments aren't the whole of philosophy; an argument can't be interesting if the statements it is intended to support are trivial or uninteresting. But the best ideas in the world can be rendered ineffective and unheeded if there are no good arguments used to present them.

Tautology

A **tautology** is a trivially true statement. Some examples:

> A man is free if he is free.

> You can't know anything unless you know something.

> I wouldn't be here if I hadn't arrived.

What about the following? Are they tautologies?

> Business is business.

> Boys will be boys.

> "A rose is a rose is a rose." (Gertrude Stein)

> "Become who you are." (Friedrich Nietzsche)

Closing Questions

Examine the following arguments. Are they inductive or deductive arguments? Are they valid and sound? If they are invalid or unsound, why? Is there anything else wrong with them? (You may want to consult Appendixes B and C.)

1. The philosopher from northern Greece is a well-known homosexual. Therefore, his claim that the universe is ultimately made up of atoms should be ignored.

2. Every event in the world is caused by other events. Human actions and decisions are events in the world. Therefore, every human action and decision is caused by other events.

3. If God exists, then life has meaning. God does not exist. Therefore, life has no meaning.

4. All cows are purple. Socrates is purple. Therefore, Socrates is a cow.

5. William James and John Dewey both called themselves pragmatists. They are the leading American philosophers. Therefore, all American philosophers are pragmatists.

6. Believing in God makes people moral—that is, believers tend to do good and avoid evil.

7. If I try to doubt that I exist, I realize that I must exist if I am doing the doubting. Therefore, I must exist.

8. We haven't seen a fox all day. Therefore, there must be no foxes in the area.

9. If you don't agree with me, I'm going to hit you.

10. God must exist; the Bible says so.

11. He must be guilty; he has a criminal face.

12. If she were innocent, she would loudly proclaim her innocence. She is loudly proclaiming her innocence. Therefore, she must be innocent.

13. "The state is like a man writ large." (Plato)

14. "I have terrible news for you. Mary is going out with Frank. I called Mary on Saturday night, and she wasn't home. Then I tried to call Frank, and *he* wasn't home, either!"

Suggested Readings

Three good introductions to logic are Robert J. Fogelin and Walter Sinnott-Armstrong, *Understanding Arguments,* 7th ed. (Wadsworth, 2005); Patrick J. Hurley and Joseph P. DeMarco, *Learning Fallacies and Arguments* (Wadsworth, 2001); and Patrick J. Hurley, *A Concise Introduction to Logic,* 10th ed. (Wadsworth, 2007). The standard introductions to symbolic logic are Irving Copi, *Introduction to Logic,* 12th ed. (Pearson Education, 1961) and W. V. O. Quine, *Methods of Logic, 4th ed.* (Harvard University Press, 2006). A good and very practical book, with many good examples, is Merrillee Salmon, *Introduction to Logic and Critical Thinking,* 5th ed. (Wadsworth, 2006). A good discussion of fallacies is S. Morris Engel, *With Good Reason, 6th ed.* (St. Martin's, 1999). A wonderful student handbook on logic is Anthony Weston, *Rulebook for Arguments* (Hackett, 1987). An excellent introduction to critical thinking is Larry Wright, *Critical Thinking: An Introduction to Analytical Reading and Thinking* (Oxford University Press, 2001). Albert Einstein's "Religion and Science" appeared in the *New York Times Magazine,* November 9, 1930.

Appendix B
Deductive Logic Valid Argument Forms

I n "A Little Logic," we introduced the distinction between the truth (or falsity) of a statement and the validity (or invalidity) of a deductive argument. It is possible for an argument to be valid even if its premises and conclusion are false. For example:

> All dogs are green
>
> Socrates is a dog
> _____
>
> Therefore, Socrates is green.

This is a valid argument, even though both the premises and the conclusion are false. For a deductive argument to guarantee the truth of its conclusion, the premises must be true *and* the argument must be valid. Here we will say a little bit more about what it means for an argument to be valid.

A valid argument has the right *form;* invalid arguments do not. The right form of an argument is based on a list of basic rules of inference, such as the following:

The syllogistic form

> All P's are Q's.
>
> S is a P.
> _____
>
> Therefore, S is a Q.

is a valid form, as we saw above. But

> All P's are Q's.
>
> S is a Q.
> _____
>
> Therefore, S is a P.

is not. How do we know? Because the definition of a (valid) deductive argument is that the truth of the premises guarantees the truth of the conclusion, we try to find an argument that fits the form that does indeed have true premises and a false conclusion. If there is no such argument, the form is a valid argument form. If there is *any* such argument, then it is not a valid argument form. So, we know that the above form is invalid because we can make up an example such as:

> All lemons are yellow.
>
> Sam (the canary) is yellow.
> _____
> Therefore, Sam is a lemon.

When you suspect that an argument in philosophy is invalid, translate the argument into formal symbolism ("All P's are S's . . .") and then find another argument with true premises and a false conclusion that fits the form ("That's like arguing that . . ."). If even one such instance of an argument form is invalid, then the form itself is not a valid argument form.

The most familiar form of deductive argument, the form illustrated above, is the **categorical syllogism**. A syllogism consists of three lines—two premises and a conclusion—and contains three terms or categories. (The term that appears in both premises is called the middle term.) The form of the statements themselves is quantitative, preceded by "all," "some," "no . . . ," and "not all . . ."

But not all deductive arguments are syllogisms; others involve a variety of inferences and complexities. Two of the most frequently used and best-known have the Latin names ***modus ponens*** and ***modus tollens***. *Modus ponens* has the form:

> If P then Q.
>
> P.
> _____
> Therefore, Q.

For example,

> If Socrates keeps annoying people, he'll get in trouble.
>
> Socrates won't stop annoying people.
> _____
> Therefore, he'll get in trouble.

Modus tollens has the form:

> If P then Q.
>
> Not Q.
> _____
> Therefore, not P.

For example,

> If you care enough, you'll send the very best.
>
> You are not sending the very best.
> _____
> Therefore, you do not care enough.

Although any argument that fits one of these forms is valid, whether or not it is also sound depends on the truth of its premises.

There are two arguments that superficially look like *modus ponens* and *modus tollens* but are in fact invalid. They are:

If P then Q.	If P then Q.
Q.	Not P.
————	————
Therefore, P.	Therefore, not Q.

For example,

If you stay up too late, you'll miss breakfast.
You missed breakfast.
_____

Therefore, you stayed up too late.

If you stay up too late, you'll miss breakfast.
You didn't stay up too late.
_____

Therefore, you didn't miss breakfast.

These two fallacies are called the *fallacy of affirming the consequent* and *the fallacy of denying the antecedent*. They must always be avoided!

One type of argument, which is really a kind of *modus tollens*, is of special use in philosophy. It is called the **reductio ad absurdum** or "reduction to absurdity." One philosopher argues that P (for example, "Justice is whatever the strongest person insists on."). Her opponent argues that If P then Q (for example, "If justice is the will of the strongest, then it is just for the strongest to be unjust."). But Q in this case is obviously absurd and therefore false—so the original claim P must be false as well. (The example is a famous argument by Socrates.) One good way to attack a philosophical position is to show that regardless of the apparent logic, its consequences are absurd.

Hating Logic

There is one danger that we must guard against, Socrates said.

What sort of danger? I asked.

Of becoming misologic [hating logic], he said, in the sense that people become misanthropic. No greater misfortune could happen to anyone than that of developing a dislike for argument. Misology and misanthropy arise in just the same way. Misanthropy is induced by believing in somebody quite uncritically. You assume that a person is absolutely truthful and sincere and

(continued)

Hating Logic (*continued*)

reliable, and a little later you find that he is shoddy and unreliable. Then the same thing happens again. After repeated disappointments at the hands of the very people who might be supposed to be your nearest and most intimate friends, constant irritation ends by making you dislike everybody and suppose that there is no sincerity to be found anywhere . . .

The resemblance between arguments and human beings lies in this: that when one believes that an argument is true without reference to the art of logic, and then a little later decides rightly or wrongly that it is false, and the same thing happens again and again . . . they end by believing that they are wiser than anyone else, because they alone have discovered that there is nothing stable or dependable either in facts or in arguments, and that everything fluctuates just like the water in a tidal channel, and never stays at any point for any time . . .

But suppose that there is an argument which is true and valid but someone spent his life loathing arguments and so missed the chance of knowing the truth about reality—would that not be a deplorable thing?

— Plato, *Phaedo* 89d–90e, fourth century BCE

From: Hugh Tredennick, The Last Days of Socrates *(Harmondsworth, UK: Penguin, 1954).*

Rules of Inference

⊃ = if, then

~ = not

· = and

∨ = or

∴ = therefore

1. *Modus Ponens* (M.P.)

p ⊃ q

p

∴ q

2. *Modus Tollens* (M.T.)

p ⊃ q

~ q

∴ p

3. Hypothetical Syllogism (H.S.)

p ⊃ q

q ⊃ r

∴ p ⊃ r

4. *Disjunctive Syllogism* (D.S.)

p ∨ q

~ p

∴ q

5. *Constructive Dilemma* (C.D.)

$(p \supset q) \cdot (r \supset s)$

$p \lor r$

$\therefore q \lor s$

6. *Absorption* (Abs.)

$p \supset q$

$\therefore p \supset (p \cdot q)$

7. *Simplification* (Simp.)

$p \cdot q$

$\therefore p$

8. *Conjunction* (Conj.)

p

q

$\therefore p \cdot q$

10. *Addition* (Add.)

p

$\therefore p \lor q$

Irving Copi, Introduction to Logic, *7th ed. (New York: Macmillan, 1986),*
311–12.

Appendix C
Common Informal Fallacies

Informal Fallacies

Many intended arguments are fallacious even though they are, formally, valid arguments; that is, they do not violate the rules of inference and the proper forms of deductive argument. They are nevertheless bad arguments. A tautology, for example, is a straightforwardly valid argument ("If P, then P."). But obviously such an argument, in the context of a discussion or a philosophy paper, does nothing to further the point to be made. The following is a list of often made but almost always bad informal fallacies:

Mere Assertion

The fact that you accept a position is not sufficient for anyone else to believe it. Stating your view is not an argument for it, and unless you are just answering a public opinion survey, every opinion always deserves a supporting argument. There are statements, of course, that everyone would accept at face value, and you need not argue those. But that does not mean that they cannot be argued, for even the most obvious facts of common sense must be argued when challenged—this is what much of philosophy is about.

Begging the Question

Another fallacy is something that looks like an argument but simply accepts as a premise what is supposed to be argued for as a conclusion. For example, suppose you are arguing that one ought to be a Christian and your reason is that the Bible tells you so. This may in fact be conclusive for you, but if you are trying to convince someone who doesn't believe in Christ, he or she will probably not believe what the Bible says either. As an argument for becoming a Christian, therefore, referring to the Bible begs the question because it assumes the authority of the Bible, when this is in fact part of what you are trying to prove (the truth of Christianity and its sacred scripture). Question begging often consists of a reworded conclusion, as in "this book will improve your grades because it will help you to do better in your courses."

Vicious Circle

Begging the question is similar to another error, which is often called arguing in a vicious circle. Consider a more elaborate version of the above fallacy. A person claims to know God exists because she has had a religious vision. Asked how she knows that the vision was religious rather than just the effect of something she ate, she replies that such an elaborate and powerful experience could not have been caused by anyone or anything but God. Asked how she knows this, she replies that God himself told her—in the vision. Or, "He must be guilty because of the look on his face." "How do you know that he looks guilty rather than frightened or sad?" "Because he's the one who did it, that's why!" If you argue *A* because of *B,* and *B* because of *C,* but then *C* because of *A,* you have argued in a vicious circle. It is vicious because, as in begging the question, you have assumed just what you want to prove.

But this is worth remembering: ultimately, all positions may come full circle, depending upon certain beliefs that can be defended only if you accept the rest of a great many beliefs. Debates between religious people and atheists are often like this or arguments between free marketers and Marxists, where many hours of argument show quite clearly that each person accepts a large system of beliefs, all of which depend on the others. Some logicians call this a virtuous circle, but this does not mean that there are no vicious circles. A virtuous circle is the development of an entire worldview, and it requires a great deal of thinking and organizing. Vicious circles, like begging the question, are usually shortcuts to nowhere that result from careless thinking.

Irrelevancies

You have seen people who argue a point by arguing everything else, throwing up charts of statistics and complaining about the state of the universe and telling jokes—everything but getting to the point. This may be a technique of wearing out your opponent; it is not a way of persuading him or her to agree with you. No matter how brilliant an argument may be, it is no good to you unless it is relevant to the point you want to defend.

Ad Hominem Arguments

The most distasteful kind of irrelevancy is an attack on your opponent personally instead of arguing against his or her position. It may well be that the person you are arguing against is a liar, a sloppy dresser, ugly, too young to vote or too old to work, but the only question is whether what he or she says is to be accepted. Harping on the appearance, reputation, manners, intelligence, friends, or possessions of your opponent may sometimes give your readers insight into why he or she holds a certain position, but it does not prove or disprove the position itself. As insight into an opponent's motives or personal considerations may, in small doses, be appropriate. But more than a very small dose is usually offensive, and it will usually weigh more against you than against your opponent. Whenever possible, avoid this kind of argument completely. It usually indicates that you don't have any good arguments yourself.

Unclear or Shifting Conclusions

One of the most frustrating arguments to read is an argument that has a vague conclusion or that shifts conclusions with every paragraph. If something is worth defending at all, it is worth stating clearly and sticking with. If you argue that drug users should be punished but aren't clear about whether you mean people who traffic in heroin or people who take aspirin, you are not worth listening to. If you say that you mean illegal drug offenders, don't argue that "drugs" are bad for your body because this term applies to both legal and illegal drugs. If you say that you mean amphetamine users, then don't switch to talking about "illegal drugs" when someone explains to you the several medical uses of amphetamines. Know what you are arguing, or your arguments will have no point.

Changing Meanings

It is easy to miss a fallacy when the words seem to form a valid argument. For example, consider this:

People are free as long as they can think for themselves.

Prisoners in jail are free to think for themselves.

Therefore, prisoners in jail are free.

This paradoxical conclusion is due to the ambiguity of *free,* first used to refer to a kind of mental freedom, second to refer to physical freedom. An interesting example is the argument often attributed to the British philosopher John Stuart Mill: "Whatever people desire, that is what is desirable." But notice that this argument plays with an ambiguity in the English language. Not everything that is in fact desired (for example, alcohol by alcoholics) *should* be desired. (Mill makes the case, however, that the only evidence that *x* is desirable is that people in fact desire it.) Be careful that the key terms in your argument keep the same meaning throughout.

Distraction

Another familiar form of fallacy is the "red herring," the sometimes long-winded pursuit of an argument leading away from the point at issue. For example, in the middle of an argument about the relation between the mind and the brain, a neurologist may well enjoy telling you, in impressive detail, any number of odd facts about neurology, about brain operations he or she has performed, about silly theories that neurology-ignorant philosophers have defended in the past. But if these do not bear on the issue at hand; they are only pleasant ways of spending the afternoon, not steps to settling a difference of opinion. Distraction is a fallacy that is especially advantageous when the time for argument is limited. (For this reason, it is particularly prevalent in the classroom.)

Pseudoquestions

Sometimes fallacious reasoning begins with the very question being asked. For example, some philosophers have argued that asking such questions as "How is the mind related to the body?" or "Could God create a mountain so heavy that even he could not move it?" are pseudoquestions. In other words, they look like real questions—even profound questions—but are ultimately unanswerable because they are based on some hidden piece of nonsense. (In the first of these cases, it has been suggested that there is no legitimate distinction between mind and body, and therefore any question about how they are "related" is pointless; the second question presumes that God is omnipotent in the sense that he can do the logically impossible, which is absurd.) Pseudoquestions, like distractions, lead us down a lengthy path going nowhere, except that, with pseudoquestions, we start from nowhere as well.

Dubious Authority

We mentioned earlier that modern philosophy is based on the assumption that we have a right—and sometimes a duty—to question authority. Yet, most of our knowledge and opinions are based on appeals to authorities—whether scientists or "the people" are particularly wise or not. It would be extremely foolish, if not fatal, not to appeal to authorities, especially in a world that has grown so technologically and socially complicated. We ask an economist what will happen if interest rates fall. We ask Miss Manners which fork to use for the salad. The fallacy of dubious authority arises when we ask the wrong person, when we appeal to an expert who is not in fact an expert in the area of concern. For example, when physicians are asked questions about nuclear policy or physicists are asked questions about high school education, their expertise in one field does not necessarily transfer to the other. The authority behind opinions in books and newspapers depends on the expertise of the authors and publications in question. What is in print is not necessarily authoritative.

Slippery Slope

Metaphors often pervade arguments. One of the more common metaphors is the slippery slope, the greased incline that once trod inevitably carries us to the bottom. (In politics, it is sometimes called "the chilling effect" or "the domino theory.") For example, it is argued that any interference with free speech whatsoever, even forbidding someone to scream "Fire!" in a crowded auditorium, will sooner or later lead to the eradication of free speech of every kind, including informed, responsible political discussion. But is it the case that, by attacking an extreme instance, we thereby endanger an entire institution? Sometimes, this may be so. But more often than not, the slippery slope metaphor leads us to think that there is such inevitability when in fact there is no such thing.

Attacking a Straw Man

Real opponents with real arguments and objections are sometimes difficult to refute, and so the easy way out is to attack an unreal opponent with easily refutable arguments and objections. This is called attacking a straw man. For example, French existentialist Jean-Paul Sartre argued that human beings have absolute freedom, meaning that they could always find some alternative way of dealing with a difficult situation. But unsympathetic critics quickly interpreted his claim to mean that a person can do absolutely anything he wants to do—for example, fly to the moon by flapping his ears—believing they had refuted Sartre with such silly examples.

Pity (and Other Emotional Appeals)

Some forms of fallacy appeal to the better parts of us, even as they challenge our fragile logical abilities. The appeal to pity has always been such an argument. Photographs of suffering people may well be an incentive to social action, but the connection between our pity—which is an undeniable virtue—and the social action in question is not yet an argument. The appeal to pity—and all appeals to emotion—have a perfectly legitimate place in philosophical discussion, but such appeals are not yet themselves arguments for any particular position. An orator may make us angry, but what we are to do about the problem must be the product of further argument.

Appeal to Force

Physical might never makes philosophical right. Sometimes a person can be intimidated, but he or she is not thus refuted. Sometimes one has to back up a philosophical conviction with force, but it is never the force that justifies the conviction.

Inappropriate Arguments

The last fallacy we mention has to do with choice of methods. To insist on deductive arguments when there are powerful inductive arguments against you is a fallacy, too—not a fallacious argument, perhaps, but a mistake in logic all the same. For example, if you are arguing deductively that there cannot be any torture going on in a certain country because Mr. Q rules the country and Mr. Q is a good man (where the implicit premise is that "good men don't allow torture in their country"), you had better be willing to give up the argument when dozens of trustworthy eyewitnesses publicly describe the tortures they have seen or experienced. To continue with your deduction in the face of such information is foolish. This may not tell you where your argument has gone wrong: Perhaps Mr. Q is not such a good man. Or perhaps he has been overpowered. Or perhaps good men can't prevent torture if they aren't told about it. But in any case, the argument must now be given up.

The same may be true the other way around. Certain abstract questions seem to be answerable only by deduction. When arguing about religious questions, for example, looking for evidence upon which to build an inductive argument may be foolish. Evidence, in the sense of looking around for pertinent facts, may be irrelevant. What is at stake are your basic concepts of religion and their implications. Very abstract questions often require deductive arguments only.

To be caught in one of these fallacies is almost always embarrassing and damaging to your overall argument. If you have a case to make, then make it in the most powerfully persuasive way. An intelligent combination of deductive and inductive arguments, coupled with analogies and proper criticisms of alternative positions, is the most effective persuasion available. If you think your opinions are important, then they deserve nothing less than the best supporting arguments you can put together.

Informal Fallacy Examples

Changing meaning:

Power tends to corrupt (Lord Acton).

Knowledge is power (Francis Bacon).

Therefore knowledge tends to corrupt.

Begging the question:

She says that she loves me,
and she must be telling the truth,
because she certainly wouldn't lie to someone she loves.

Pity and other emotional appeals:

Mr. Scrooge, I certainly deserve a raise in pay.
I can hardly manage to feed my children on what
you are paying me. And my youngest child, Tim,
needs an operation if he is ever to walk without crutches.

Irving M. Copi, Informal Logic, *7th ed. (New York: Macmillan, 1986).*

VII.A.2

The Ethics of Belief

W. K. CLIFFORD

W. K. Clifford (1845–1879) was a British philosopher and mathematician. The selection that follows is perhaps his best known and most widely discussed philosophical essay. Clifford argues that there is an ethics to belief that makes it always wrong for anyone to believe anything on insufficient evidence. Pragmatic justifications are not justifications at all but counterfeits of genuine justifications, which must always be based on evidence.

A shipowner was about to send to sea an emigrant ship. He knew that she was old, and not over-well built at the first; that she had seen many seas and climes, and often had needed repairs. Doubts had been suggested to him that possibly she was not seaworthy. These doubts preyed upon his mind and made him unhappy; he thought that perhaps he ought to have her thoroughly overhauled and refitted, even though this should put him to great expense. Before the ship sailed, however, he succeeded in overcoming these melancholy reflections. He said to himself that she had gone safely through so many voyages and weathered so many storms that it was idle to suppose she would not come safely home from this trip also. He would put his trust in Providence, which could hardly fail to protect all these unhappy families that were leaving their fatherland to seek for better times elsewhere. He would dismiss from his mind all ungenerous suspicions about the honesty of builders and contractors. In such ways he acquired a sincere and comfortable conviction that his vessel was thoroughly safe and seaworthy; he watched her departure with a light heart, and benevolent wishes for the success of the exiles in their strange new home that was to be; and he got his insurance money when she went down in midocean and told no tales.

What shall we say of him? Surely this, that he was verily guilty of the death of those men. It is admitted that he did sincerely believe in the soundness of his ship; but the sincerity of his conviction can in no wise to help him, because he had no right to believe on such evidence as was before him. He had acquired his belief not by honestly earning it in patient investigation, but by stifling his doubts. And although in the end he may have felt so sure about it that he could not think otherwise, yet inasmuch as he had knowingly and willingly worked himself into that frame of mind, he must be held responsible for it.

Let us alter the case a little, and suppose that the ship was not unsound after all; that she made her voyage safely, and many others after it. Will that diminish the guilt of her owner? Not one jot. When an action is once done, it is right or wrong forever; no accidental failure of its good or evil fruits can possibly alter that. The man would not have been innocent, he would only have been not found out. The question of right or wrong has to do with the origin of his belief, not the matter of it; not what it was, but how he got it; not whether

Reprinted from W. K. Clifford, *Lecturers and Essays* (London: Macmillan, 1879).

it turned out to be true or false, but whether he had a right to believe on such evidence as was before him.

There was once an island in which some of the inhabitants professed a religion teaching neither the doctrine of original sin nor that of eternal punishment. A suspicion got abroad that the professors of this religion had made use of unfair means to get their doctrines taught to children. They were accused of wresting the laws of their country in such a way as to remove children from the care of their natural and legal guardians; and even of stealing them away and keeping them concealed from their friends and relations. A certain number of men formed themselves into a society for the purpose of agitating the public about this matter. They published grave accusations against individual citizens of the highest position and character, and did all in their power to injure those citizens in the exercise of their professions. So great was the noise they made, that a Commission was appointed to investigate the facts; but after the Commission had carefully inquired into all the evidence that could be got, it appeared that the accused were innocent. Not only had they been accused on insufficient evidence, but the evidence of their innocence was such as the agitators might easily have obtained, if they had attempted a fair inquiry. After these disclosures the inhabitants of that country looked upon the members of the agitating society, not only as persons whose judgment was to be distrusted, but also as no longer to be counted honorable men. For although they had sincerely and conscientiously believed in the charges they had made, yet they had no right to believe on such evidence as was before them. Their sincere convictions, instead of being honestly earned by patient inquiring, were stolen by listening to the voice of prejudice and passion.

Let us vary this case also, and suppose, other things remaining as before, that a still more accurate investigation proved the accused to have been really guilty. Would this make any difference in the guilt of the accusers? Clearly not; the question is not whether their belief was true or false, but whether they entertained it on wrong grounds. They would no doubt say, "Now you see that we were right

after all; next time perhaps you will believe us." And they might be believed, but they would not thereby become honorable men. They would not be innocent, they would only be not found out. Every one of them, if he chose to examine himself *in foro conscientiae*, would know that he had acquired and nourished a belief, when he had no right to believe on such evidence as was before him; and therein he would know that he had done a wrong thing.

It may be said, however, that in both of these supposed cases it is not the belief which is judged to be wrong, but the action following upon it. The shipowner might say, "I am perfectly certain that my ship is sound, but still I feel it my duty to have her examined, before trusting the lives of so many people to her." And it might be said to the agitator, "However convinced you were of the justice of your cause and the truth of your convictions, you ought not to have made a public attack upon any man's character until you had examined the evidence on both sides with the utmost patience and care."

In the first place, let us admit that, so far as it goes, this view of the case is right and necessary; right, because even when a man's belief is so fixed that he cannot think otherwise, he still has a choice in regard to the action suggested by it, and so cannot escape the duty of investigating on the ground of the strength of his convictions; and necessary, because those who are not yet capable of controlling their feelings and thoughts must have a plain rule dealing with overt acts.

But this being premised as necessary, it becomes clear that it is not sufficient, and that our previous judgment is required to supplement it. For it is not possible so to sever the belief from the action it suggests as to condemn the one without condemning the other. No man holding a strong belief on one side of a question, or even wishing to hold a belief on one side, can investigate it with such fairness and completeness as if he were really in doubt and unbiased; so that the existence of a belief not founded on fair inquiry unfits a man for the performance of this necessary duty.

Nor is that truly a belief at all which has not some influence upon the actions of him who holds it.

He who truly believes that which prompts him to an action has looked upon the action to lust after it, he has committed it already in his heart. If a belief is not realized immediately in open deeds, it is stored up for the guidance of the future. It goes to make a part of that aggregate of beliefs which is the link between sensation and action at every moment of all our lives, and which is so organized and compacted together that no part of it can be isolated from the rest, but every new addition modifies the structure of the whole. No real belief, however trifling and fragmentary it may seem, is ever truly insignificant; it prepares us to receive more of its like, confirms those which resembled it before, and weakens others; and so gradually it lays a stealthy train in our inmost thoughts, which may some day explode into overt action, and leave its stamp upon our character forever.

And no one man's belief is in any case a private matter which concerns himself alone. Our lives are guided by that general conception of the course of things which has been created by society for social purposes. Our words, our phrases, our forms and processes and modes of thought are common property, fashioned and perfected from age to age; an heirloom which every succeeding generation inherits as a precious deposit and a sacred trust to be handed on to the next one, not unchanged but enlarged and purified, with some clear marks of its proper handiwork. Into this, for good or ill, is woven every belief of every man who has speech of his fellows. An awful privilege, and an awful responsibility, that we should help to create the world in which posterity will live.

In the two supposed cases which have been considered, it has been judged wrong to believe on insufficient evidence, or to nourish belief by suppressing doubts and avoiding investigation. The reason of this judgment is not far to seek: it is that in both these cases the belief held by one man was of great importance to other men. But for as much as no belief held by one man, however seemingly trivial the belief, and however obscure the believer, is ever actually insignificant or without its effect on the fate of mankind, we have no choice but to extend our judgment to all cases of belief whatever. Belief, that sacred faculty which prompts the decisions of our will, and knits into harmonious working all the compacted energies of our being, is ours not for ourselves, but for humanity. It is rightly used on truths which have been established by long experience and waiting toil, and which have stood in the fierce light of free and fearless questioning. Then it helps to bind men together, and to strengthen and direct their common action. It is desecrated when given to unproved and unquestioned statements, for the solace and private pleasure of the believer; to add a tinsel splendor to the plain straight road of our life and display a bright mirage beyond it; or even to drown the common sorrows of our kind by a self-deception which allows them not only to cast down, but also to degrade us. Whoso would deserve well of his fellows in this matter will guard the purity of this belief with a very fanaticism of jealous care, lest at any time it should rest on an unworthy object, and catch a stain which can never be wiped away.

It is not only the leader of men, statesman, philosopher or poet, that owes this bounden duty to mankind. Every rustic who delivers in the village alehouse his slow, infrequent sentences, may help to kill or keep alive the fatal superstitions which clog his race. Every hard-worked wife of an artisan may transmit to her children beliefs which shall knit society together, or rend it in pieces. No simplicity of mind, no obscurity of station, can escape the universal duty of questioning all that we believe.

It is true that this duty is a hard one, and the doubt which comes out of it is often a very bitter thing. It leaves us bare and powerless where we thought that we were safe and strong. To know all about anything is to know how to deal with it under all circumstances. We feel much happier and more secure when we think we know precisely what to do, no matter what happens, than when we have lost our way and do not know where to turn. And if we have supposed ourselves to know all about anything, and to be capable of doing what is fit in regard to it, we naturally do not like to find that we are really ignorant and powerless, that we have to begin again at the beginning, and try to learn what the thing is and how it is to be dealt with—if indeed anything can be learned about it. It is the sense of power attached to a sense of knowledge that makes men desirous of believing, and afraid of doubting.

This sense of power is the highest and best of pleasures when the belief on which it is founded is a true belief, and has been fairly earned by investigation. For then we may justly feel that it is common property, and holds good for others as well as for ourselves. Then we may be glad, not that I have learned secrets by which I am safer and stronger, but that we men have got mastery over more of the world; and we shall be strong, not for ourselves, but in the name of Man and in his strength. But if the belief has been accepted on insufficient evidence, the pleasure is a stolen one. Not only does it deceive ourselves by giving us a sense of power which we do not really possess, but it is sinful, because it is stolen in defiance of our duty to mankind. That duty is to guard ourselves from such beliefs as from a pestilence, which may shortly master our own body and then spread to the rest of the town. What would be thought of one who, for the sake of a sweet fruit, should deliberately run the risk of bringing a plague upon his family and his neighbors?

And, as in other such cases, it is not the risk only which has to be considered; for a bad action is always bad at the time when it is done, no matter what happens afterwards. Every time we let ourselves believe for unworthy reasons, we weaken our powers of self-control, of doubting, of judicially and fairly weighing evidence. We all suffer severely enough from the maintenance and support of false beliefs and the fatally wrong actions which they lead to, and the evil born when one such belief is entertained is great and wide. But a greater and wider evil arises when the credulous character is maintained and supported, when a habit of believing for unworthy reasons is fostered and made permanent. If I steal money from any person, there may be no harm done by the mere transfer of possession; he may not feel the loss, or it may prevent him from using the money badly. But I cannot help doing this great wrong towards Man, that I make myself dishonest. What hurts society is not that it should lose its property, but that it should become a den of thieves; for then it must cease to be society. This is why we ought not to do evil that good may come; for at

any rate this great evil has come, that we have done evil and are made wicked thereby. In like manner, if I let myself believe anything on insufficient evidence, there may be no great harm done by the mere belief; it may be true after all, or I may never have occasion to exhibit it in outward acts. But I cannot help doing this great wrong toward Man, that I make myself credulous. The danger to society is not merely that it should believe wrong things, though that is great enough; but that it should become credulous, and lose the habit of testing things and inquiring into them; for then it must sink back into savagery.

The harm which is done by credulity in a man is not confined to the fostering of a credulous character in others, and consequent support of false beliefs. Habitual want of care about what I believe leads to habitual want of care in others about the truth of what is told to me. Men speak the truth to one another when each reveres the truth in his own mind and in the other's mind; but how shall my friend revere the truth in my mind when I myself am careless about it, when I believe things because I want to believe them, and because they are comforting and pleasant? Will he not learn to cry, "Peace," to me, when there is no peace? By such a course I shall surround myself with a thick atmosphere of falsehood and fraud, and in that must live. It may matter little to me, in my closed castle of sweet illusions and darling lies; but it matters much to Man that I have made my neighbors ready to deceive. The credulous man is father to the liar and the cheat; he lives in the bosom of this his family, and it is no marvel if he should become even as they are. So closely are our duties knit together, that whoso shall keep the whole law, and yet offend in one point, he is guilty of all.

To sum up: it is wrong always, everywhere and for anyone, to believe anything upon insufficient evidence.

If a man, holding a belief which he was taught in childhood or persuaded of afterwards, keeps down and pushes away any doubts which arise about it in his mind, purposely avoids the reading of books and the company of men that call in question or discuss it, and regards as impious those questions which cannot easily be asked without disturbing it—the life of that man is one long sin against mankind.

If this judgment seems harsh when applied to those simple souls who have never known better, who have been brought up from the cradle with a horror of doubt, and taught that their eternal welfare depends on what they believe, then it leads to the very serious question, Who hath made Israel to sin? ...

Inquiry into the evidence of a doctrine is not to be made once for all, and then taken as finally settled. It is never lawful to stifle a doubt; for either it can be honestly answered by means of the inquiry already made, or else it proves that the inquiry was not complete.

"But," says one, "I am a busy man; I have no time for the long course of study which would be necessary to make me in any degree a competent judge of certain questions, or even able to understand the nature of the arguments." Then he should have no time to believe....

Reprinted from William James, *The Will to Believe* (New York: Longmans Green & Co., 1897).

II.A.1

The Ontological Argument

ST. ANSELM

St. Anselm (1033–1109), Abbot of Bec and later Archbishop of Canterbury, is the originator of one of the most intriguing arguments ever devised by the human mind, the ontological argument for the existence of a supremely perfect being. After the short selection from Anselm's Proslogion, *there*

From *Monologion and Proslogion, with the replies of Gaunilo and Anselm*, trans. with introduction and notes by Thomas Williams. (Indianapolis, IN: Hackett Publishing Company, 1996.) © 1996 by Thomas Williams. Used with permission.

follows a brief selection from Gaunilo's reply, In Behalf of the Fool*, and a counterresponse by Anselm.*

[ST. ANSELM'S PRESENTATION]

Therefore, Lord, you who grant understanding to faith, grant that, insofar as you know it is useful for me, I may understand that you exist as we believe you exist, and that you are what we believe you to be. Now we believe that you are something than which nothing greater can be thought. So can it be that no such nature exists, since "The fool has said in his heart, 'There is no God'" (Psalm 14:1; 53:1)? But when this same fool hears me say "something than which nothing greater can be thought," he surely understands what he hears; and what he understands exists in his understanding,[1] even if he does not understand that it exists [in reality]. For it is one thing for an object to exist in the understanding and quite another to understand that the object exists [in reality]. When a painter, for example, thinks out in advance what he is going to paint, he has it in his understanding, but he does not yet understand that it exists, since he has not yet painted it. But once he has painted it, he both has it in his understanding and understands that it exists because he has now painted it. So even the fool must admit that something than which nothing greater can be thought exists at least in his understanding, since he understands this when he hears it, and whatever is understood exists in the understanding. And surely that than which a greater cannot be thought cannot exist only in the understanding. For if it exists only in the understanding, it can be thought to exist in reality as well, which is greater. So if that than which a greater cannot be thought exists only in the understanding, then that than which a greater *cannot* be thought is that than which a greater *can* be thought. But that is clearly impossible. Therefore, there is no doubt that something than which a greater cannot be thought exists both in the understanding and in reality....

This [being] exists so truly that it cannot be thought not to exist. For it is possible to think that something exists that cannot be thought not to exist, and such a being is greater than one that can be thought not to exist. Therefore, if that than which a greater cannot be thought can be thought not to exist, then that than which a greater cannot be thought is *not* that than which a greater cannot be thought; and this is a contradiction. So that than which a greater cannot be thought exists so truly that it cannot be thought not to exist.

And this is you, O Lord our God. You exist so truly, O Lord my God, that you cannot be thought not to exist. And rightly so, for if some mind could think something better than you, a creature would rise above the Creator and sit in judgment upon him, which is completely absurd. Indeed, everything that exists, except for you alone, can be thought not to exist. So you alone among all things have existence most truly, and therefore most greatly. Whatever else exists has existence less truly, and therefore less greatly. So then why did "the fool say in his heart, 'There is no God,'" when it is so evident to the rational mind that you among all beings exist most greatly? Why indeed, except because he is stupid and a fool?...

But how has he said in his heart what he could not think? Or how could he not think what he said in his heart, since to say in one's heart is the same as to think? But if he really—or rather, *since* he really—thought this, because he said it in his heart, and did not say it in his heart, because he could not think it, there must be more than one way in which something is "said in one's heart" or "thought." In one sense of the word, to think a thing is to think the word that signifies that thing. But in another sense, it is to understand what exactly the thing is. God can be thought not to exist in the first sense, but not at all in the second sense. No one who understands what God is can think that God does not exist, although he may say these words in his heart with no signification at all, or with some peculiar signification. For God is that than which a greater cannot be thought. Whoever understands this properly, understands that this being exists in such a way that he cannot, even in thought, fail to exist. So whoever understands that God exists in this way cannot think that he does not exist.

Thanks be to you, my good Lord, thanks be to you. For what I once believed through your grace, I now understand through your illumination, so that even if I did not want to *believe* that you exist, I could not fail to *understand* that you exist....

[GAUNILO'S CRITICISM]

"For example, there are those who say that somewhere in the ocean is an island, which, because of the difficulty—or rather, impossibility—of finding what does not exist, some call 'the Lost Island'. This island (so the story goes) is more plentifully endowed than even the Isles of the Blessed with an indescribable abundance of all sorts of riches and delights. And because it has neither owner nor inhabitant, it is everywhere superior in its abundant riches to all the other lands that human beings inhabit.

"Suppose someone tells me all this. The story is easily told and involves no difficulty, and so I understand it. But if this person went on to draw a conclusion, and say, 'You cannot any longer doubt that this island, more excellent than all others on earth, truly exists somewhere in reality. For you do not doubt that this island exists in your understanding, and since it is more excellent to exist not merely in the understanding, but also in reality, this island must also exist in reality. For if it did not, any land that exists in reality would be greater than it. And so this more excellent thing that you have understood would not in fact be more excellent.'–If, I say, he should try to convince me by, this argument that I should no longer doubt whether the island truly exists, either I would think he was joking, or I would not know whom I ought to think more foolish: myself, if I grant him his conclusion, or him, if he thinks he has

established the existence of that island with any degree of certainty, without first showing that its excellence exists in my understanding as a thing that truly and undoubtedly exists and not in any way like something false or uncertain."...

[ST. ANSELM'S REJOINDER]

But, you say, this is just the same as if someone were to claim that it cannot be doubted that a certain island in the ocean, surpassing all other lands in its fertility (which, from the difficulty—or rather, impossibility—of finding what does not exist, is called "the Lost Island"), truly exists in reality, because someone can easily understand it when it is described to him in words. I say quite confidently that if anyone can find for me something existing either in reality or only in thought to which he can apply this inference in my argument, besides that than which a greater cannot be thought, I will find and give to him that Lost Island, never to be lost again. In fact, however, it has already become quite clear that that than which a greater cannot be thought cannot be thought not to exist, since its existence is a matter of such certain truth. For otherwise it would not exist at all.

Finally, if someone says that he thinks it does not exist, I say that when he thinks this, either he is thinking something than which a greater cannot be thought, or he is not. If he is not, then he is not thinking that it does not exist, since he is not thinking it at all. But if he is, he is surely thinking something that cannot be thought not to exist. For if it could be thought not to exist, it could be thought to have a beginning and an end, which is impossible. Therefore, someone who is thinking it, is thinking something that cannot be thought not to exist. And of course someone who is thinking this does not think that that very thing does not exist. Otherwise he would be thinking something that cannot be thought. Therefore, that than which a greater cannot be thought cannot be thought not to exist....

NOTE

1. The word here translated "understanding" is "*intellectus*." The text would perhaps read better if I translated it as "intellect," but this would obscure the fact that it is from the same root as the verb "*intelligere*," "to understand." Some of what Anselm says makes a bit more sense if this fact is constantly borne in mind.

From Kant's *Critique of Pure Reason*, translated by J. M. D. Meiklejohn (New York: Colonial Press, 1900). Translation revised by Louis Pojman.

II.B.1

The Five Ways

THOMAS AQUINAS

The Dominican friar Thomas Aquinas (1225–1274) is considered by many to be the greatest theo-logian in Western religion. The five ways of showing the existence of God given in this selection are versions of the cosmological argument. The first way concerns the fact that there is change (or motion) and argues that there must be an Unmoved Mover that originates all change but itself is not moved. The second way is from the idea of causation and argues that there must be a first, uncaused cause to explain the existence of all other causes. The third way is from the idea of contingency. It argues that because there are dependent beings (e.g., humans), there must be an independent or necessary being on whom the dependent beings rely for their subsistence. The fourth way is from excellence, and it argues that because there are degrees of excellence, there must be a perfect being from whence all excellences come. The final way is from the harmony of things. There is a harmony of nature, which calls for an explanation. The only sufficient explanation is that there is a divine designer who planned this harmony.

ARTICLE 3: DOES GOD EXIST?

It seems that God does not exist:

Objection 1: If one of a pair of contraries were infinite, it would totally destroy the other contrary. But by the name 'God' one means a certain infinite good. Therefore, if God existed, there would be nothing evil. But there is evil in the world. Therefore, God does not exist.

Objection 2: What can be accomplished with fewer principles is not done through more principles. But it seems that everything that happens in the world could have been accomplished through other principles, even if God did not exist; for things that are natural are traced back to nature as a principle, whereas things that are purposeful are traced back to human reason or will as a principle. Therefore, there is no need to claim that God exists.

But contrary to this: Exodus 1:14 says under the personage of God, "I am Who am."

I respond: There are five ways to prove that God exists.

Printed with the permission of the translator, Alfred J. Freddoso. This translation is being published by Saint Augustine's Press.

The *first* and clearest way is that taken from motion:

It is certain, and obvious to the senses, that in this world some things are moved.

But everything that is moved is moved by another. For nothing is moved except insofar as it is in potentiality with respect to that actuality toward which it is moved, whereas something effects motion insofar as it is in actuality in a relevant respect. After all, to effect motion is just to lead something from potentiality into actuality. But a thing cannot be led from potentiality into actuality except through some being that is in actuality in a relevant respect; for example, something that is hot in actuality—say, a fire—makes a piece of wood, which is hot in potentiality, to be hot in actuality, and it thereby moves and alters the piece of wood. But it is impossible for something to be simultaneously in potentiality and in actuality with respect to same thing; rather, it can be in potentiality and in actuality only with respect to different things. For what is hot in actuality cannot simultaneously be hot in potentiality; rather, it is cold in potentiality. Therefore, it is impossible that something should be both mover and moved in the same way and with respect to the same thing, or, in other words, that something should move itself. Therefore, everything that is moved must be moved by another.

If, then, that by which something is moved is itself moved, then it, too, must be moved by another, and that other by still another. But this does not go on to infinity. For if it did, then there would not be any first mover and, as a result, none of the others would effect motion, either. For secondary movers effect motion only because they are being moved by a first mover, just as a stick does not effect motion except because it is being moved by a hand. Therefore, one has to arrive at some first mover that is not being moved by anything. And this is what everyone takes to be God.

The *second* way is based on the notion of an efficient cause:

We find that among sensible things there is an ordering of efficient causes, and yet we do not find—nor is it possible to find—anything that is an efficient cause of its own self. For if something

were an efficient cause of itself, then it would be prior to itself—which is impossible.

But it is impossible to go on to infinity among efficient causes. For in every case of ordered efficient causes, the first is a cause of the intermediate and the intermediate is a cause of the last—and this regardless of whether the intermediate is constituted by many causes or by just one. But when a cause is removed, its effect is removed. Therefore, if there were no first among the efficient causes, then neither would there be a last or an intermediate. But if the efficient causes went on to infinity, there would not be a first efficient cause, and so there would not be a last effect or any intermediate efficient causes, either—which is obviously false. Therefore, one must posit some first efficient cause—which everyone calls God.

The *third* way is taken from the possible and the necessary, and it goes like this:

Certain of the things we find in the world are able to exist and able not to exist; for some things are found to be generated and corrupted and, as a result, they are able to exist and able not to exist.

But it is impossible that everything should be like this; for that which is able not to exist is such that at some time it does not exist. Therefore, if everything is such that it is able not to exist, then at some time nothing existed in the world. But if this were true, then nothing would exist even now. For what does not exist begins to exist only through something that does exist; therefore, if there were no beings, then it was impossible that anything should have begun to exist, and so nothing would exist now—which is obviously false. Therefore, not all beings are able to exist [and able not to exist]; rather, it must be that there is something necessary in the world.

Now every necessary being either has a cause of its necessity from outside itself or it does not. But it is impossible to go on to infinity among necessary beings that have a cause of their necessity—in the same way, as was proved above, that it is impossible to go on to infinity among efficient causes. Therefore, one must posit something that is necessary *per se*, which does not have a cause of its necessity from outside itself but is instead a cause of necessity for the other [necessary] things. But this everyone calls God.

The *fourth* way is taken from the gradations that are found in the world:

In the world some things are found to be more and less good, more and less true, more and less noble, etc. But *more* and *less* are predicated of diverse things insofar as they approach in diverse ways that which is maximal in a given respect. For instance, the hotter something is, the closer it approaches that which is maximally hot. Therefore, there is something that is maximally true, maximally good, and maximally noble, and, as a result, is a maximal being; for according to the Philosopher in *Metaphysics* 2, things that are maximally true are maximally beings.

But, as is claimed in the same book, that which is maximal in a given genus is a cause of all the things that belong to that genus; for instance, fire, which is maximally hot, is a cause of all hot things. Therefore, there is something that is a cause for all beings of their *esse*, their goodness, and each of their perfections—and this we call God.

The *fifth* way is taken from the governance of things:

We see that some things lacking cognition, viz., natural bodies, act for the sake of an end. This is apparent from the fact that they always or very frequently act in the same way in order to bring about that which is best, and from this it is clear that it is not by chance, but by design, that they attain the end.

But things lacking cognition tend toward an end only if they are directed by something that has cognition and intelligence, in the way that an arrow is directed by an archer. Therefore, there is something intelligent by which all natural things are ordered to an end—and this we call God.

Reply to objection 1: As Augustine says in the *Enchiridion*, "Since God is maximally good, He would not allow any evil to exist in His works if He were not powerful enough and good enough to draw good even from evil." Therefore, it is part of God's infinite goodness that He should permit evils and elicit goods from them.

Reply to objection 2: Since it is by the direction of a higher agent that nature acts for the sake of a determinate end, those things that are done by nature must also be traced back to God as a first cause. Similarly, even things that are done by design must be traced back to a higher cause and not to human reason and will. For human reason and will are changeable and subject to failure, but, as was shown above, all things that can change and fail must be traced back to a first principle that is unmoved and necessary *per se*.

Reprinted from *A Discourse Concerning Natural Religion* (1705).

II.B.3

An Examination of the Cosmological Argument

WILLIAM ROWE

Brief biographical remarks about William Rowe appear before selection I.B.9. In the present selection, taken from the second edition of his Philosophy of Religion: An Introduction *(1993), Rowe begins by distinguishing between a priori and a posteriori arguments and setting the cosmological argument in historical perspective. Next, he divides the argument into two parts: that which seeks to prove the existence of a self-existent being and that which seeks to prove that this self-existent being is the God of theism. He introduces the principle of sufficient reason—"There must be an explanation (a) of the existence of any being and (b) of any positive fact whatever"—and shows its role in the cosmological argument. In the light of this principle, he examines the argument itself and four objections to it.*

STATING THE ARGUMENT

Arguments for the existence of God are commonly divided into *a posteriori* arguments and *a priori* arguments. An *a posteriori* argument depends on a principle or premise that can be known only by means of our experience of the world. An *a priori* argument, on the other hand, purports to rest on principles all of which can be known independently of our experience of the world, by just reflecting on and understanding them. Of the three major arguments for the existence of God—the Cosmological, the Teleological, and the Ontological—only the last of these is entirely *a priori*. In the Cosmological Argument one starts from some simple fact about the world, such as that it contains things which are caused to exist by other things. In the Teleological Argument a somewhat more complicated fact about the world serves as a starting point, the fact that the world exhibits order and design. In the Ontological Argument, however, one begins simply with a concept of God....

Before we state the Cosmological Argument itself, we shall consider some rather general points about the argument. Historically, it can be traced to the writings of the Greek philosophers, Plato and Aristotle, but the major developments in the argument took place in the thirteenth and in the eighteenth centuries. In the thirteenth century Aquinas put forth five distinct arguments for the existence of God, and of these, the first three are versions of the Cosmological Argument.[1] In the first of these he started from the fact that there are things in the world undergoing change and reasoned to the conclusion that there must be some ultimate cause of change that is itself unchanging. In the second he started from the fact that there are things in the world that clearly are caused to exist by other things and reasoned to the conclusion that there must be some ultimate cause of existence whose own existence is itself uncaused. And in the third argument he started from the fact that there are things in the world which need not have existed at all, things which do exist but which we can easily imagine might not, and reasoned to the conclusion that there must be some being that had to be, that exists and could not have failed to exist. Now it might be objected that even if Aquinas' arguments do prove beyond doubt the existence of an unchanging changer, an uncaused cause, and a being that could not have failed to exist, the arguments fail to prove the existence of the theistic God. For the theistic God, as we saw, is supremely good, omnipotent, omniscient, and creator of but separate from and independent of the world. How do we know, for example, that the unchanging changer isn't evil or slightly ignorant? The answer to this objection is that the Cosmological Argument has two parts. In the first part the effort is to prove the existence of a special sort of being, for example, a being that could not have failed to exist, or a being that causes change in other things but is itself unchanging. In the second part of the argument the effort is to prove that the special sort of being whose existence has been established in the first part has, and must have, the features—perfect goodness, omnipotence, omniscience, and so on—which go together to make up the theistic idea of God. What this means, then, is that Aquinas' three arguments are different versions of only the first part of the Cosmological Argument. Indeed, in later sections of his *Summa Theological* Aquinas undertakes to show that the unchanging changer, the uncaused cause of existence, and the being which had to exist are one and the same being and that this single being has all of the attributes of the theistic God.

We noted above that a second major development in the Cosmological Argument took place in the eighteenth century, a development reflected in the writings of the German philosopher, Gottfried

Leibniz (1646–1716), and especially in the writings of the English theologian and philosopher, Samuel Clarke (1675–1729). In 1704 Clarke gave a series of lectures, later published under the title *A Demonstration of the Being and Attributes of God*. These lectures constitute, perhaps, the most complete, forceful, and cogent presentation of the Cosmological Argument we possess. The lectures were read by the major skeptical philosopher of the century, David Hume (1711–1776), and in his brilliant attack on the attempt to justify religion in the court of reason, his *Dialogues Concerning Natural Religion*, Hume advanced several penetrating criticisms of Clarke's arguments, criticisms which have persuaded many philosophers in the modern period to reject the Cosmological Argument. In our study of the argument we shall concentrate our attention largely on its eighteenth-century form and try to assess its strengths and weaknesses in the light of the criticisms which Hume and others have advanced against it.

The first part of the eighteenth-century form of the Cosmological Argument seeks to establish the existence of a self-existent being. The second part of the argument attempts to prove that the self-existent being is the theistic God, that is, has the features which we have noted to be basic elements in the theistic idea of God. We shall consider mainly the first part of the argument, for it is against the first part that philosophers from Hume to Russell have advanced very important objections.

In stating the first part of the Cosmological Argument we shall make use of two important concepts, the concept of a *dependent being* and the concept of a *self-existent being*. By a *dependent being* we mean *a being whose existence is accounted for by the causal activity of other things*. Recalling Anselm's division into the three cases: "explained by another," "explained by nothing," and "explained by itself," it's clear that a dependent being is a being whose existence is explained by another. By a *self-existent being* we mean *a being whose existence is accounted for by its own nature*. This idea … is an essential element in the theistic concept of God. Again, in terms of Anselm's three cases, a self-existent being is a being whose existence is explained by itself. Armed with

these two concepts, the concept of a dependent being and the concept of a self-existent being, we can now state the first part of the Cosmological Argument.

1. Every being (that exists or ever did exist) is either a dependent being or a self-existent being.
2. Not every being can be a dependent being.

Therefore,

3. There exists a self-existent being.

DEDUCTIVE VALIDITY

Before we look critically at each of the premises of this argument, we should note that this argument is, to use an expression from the logician's vocabulary, *deductively valid*. To find out whether an argument is deductively valid, we need only ask the question: If its premises were true, would its conclusion have to be true? If the answer is yes, the argument is deductively valid. If the answer is no, the argument is deductively invalid. Notice that the question of the validity of an argument is entirely different from the question of whether its premises are in fact true. The following argument is made up entirely of false statements, but it is deductively valid.

1. Babe Ruth is the President of the United States.
2. The President of the United States is from Indiana.

Therefore,

3. Babe Ruth is from Indiana.

The argument is deductively valid because even though its premises are false, if they were true its conclusion would have to be true. Even God, Aquinas would say, cannot bring it about that the premises of this argument are true and yet its conclusion is false, for God's power extends only to what is possible, and it is an absolute impossibility that Babe Ruth be the President, the President be from Indiana, and yet Babe Ruth not be from Indiana.

The Cosmological Argument (that is, its first part) is a deductively valid argument. If its premises are or were true, its conclusion would have to be true. It's clear from our example about Babe Ruth, however, that the fact that an argument is deductively valid is insufficient to establish the truth of its conclusion. What else is required? Clearly that we know or have rational grounds for believing that the premises are true. If we know that the Cosmological Argument is deductively valid, and can establish that its premises are true, we shall thereby have proved that its conclusion is true. Are, then, the premises of the Cosmological Argument true? To this more difficult question we must now turn.

PSR AND THE FIRST PREMISE

At first glance the first premise might appear to be an obvious or even trivial truth. But it is neither obvious nor trivial. And if it appears to be obvious or trivial, we must be confusing the idea of a self-existent being with the idea of a being that is not a dependent being. Clearly, it is true that any being is either a dependent being (explained by other things) or it is not a dependent being (not explained by other things). But what our premise says is that any being is either a dependent being (explained by other things) or it is a self-existent being (explained by itself). Consider again Anselm's three cases.

a. explained by another
b. explained by nothing
c. explained by itself

What our first premise asserts is that each being that exists (or ever did exist) is either of sort *a* or of sort *c*. It denies that any being is of sort *b*. And it is this denial that makes the first premise both significant and controversial. The obvious truth we must not confuse it with is the truth that any being is either of sort *a* or not of sort *a*. While this is true it is neither very significant nor controversial.

Earlier we saw that Anselm accepted as a basic principle that whatever exists has an explanation of its existence. Since this basic principle denies that any thing of sort *b* exists or ever did exist, it's clear that Anselm would believe the first premise of our Cosmological Argument. The eighteenth-century proponents of the argument also were convinced of the truth of the basic principle we attributed to Anselm. And because they were convinced of its truth, they readily accepted the first premise of the Cosmological Argument. But by the eighteenth century, Anselm's basic principle had been more fully elaborated and had received a name, the *Principle of Sufficient Reason*. Since this principle (PSR, as we shall call it) plays such an important role in justifying the premises of the Cosmological Argument, it will help us to consider it for a moment before we continue our enquiry into the truth or falsity of the premises of the Cosmological Argument.

The Principle of Sufficient Reason, as it was expressed by both Leibniz and Samuel Clarke, is a very general principle and is best understood as having two parts. In its first part it is simply a restatement of Anselm's principle that there must be an explanation of the existence of any being whatever. Thus if we come upon a man in a room, PSR implies that there must be an explanation of the fact that that particular man exists. A moment's reflection, however, reveals that there are many facts about the man other than the mere fact that he exists. There is the fact that the man in question is in the room he's in, rather than somewhere else, the fact that he is in good health, and the fact that he is at the moment thinking of Paris, rather than, say, London. Now, the purpose of the second part of PSR is to require an explanation of these facts, as well. We may state PSR, therefore, as the principle that *there must be an explanation (a) of the existence of any being, and (b) of any positive fact whatever*. We are now in a position to study the role this very important principle plays in the Cosmological Argument.

Since the proponent of the Cosmological Argument accepts PSR in both its parts, it is clear that he will appeal to its first part, PSRa, as justification for the first premise of the Cosmological Argument. Of course, we can and should enquire into the deeper question of whether the proponent of the argument is rationally justified in accepting PSR itself. But we shall put this question aside for the moment. What we need to see first is whether he is correct in thinking that *if* PSR is true then both of the premises of the Cosmological Argument are true. And what we have just seen is that if only the first part of PSR, that is, PSRa, is true, the first premise of the Cosmological Argument will be true. But what of the second premise of the argument? For what reasons does the proponent think that it must be true?

THE SECOND PREMISE

According to the second premise, not every being that exists can be a dependent being, that is, can have the explanation of its existence in some other being or beings. Presumably, the proponent of the argument thinks there is something fundamentally wrong with the idea that every being that exists is dependent, that each existing being was caused by some other being which in turn was caused by some other being, and so on. But just what does he think is wrong with it? To help us in understanding his thinking, let's simplify things by supposing that there exists only one thing now, A_1, a living thing perhaps, that was brought into existence by something else, A_2, which perished shortly after it brought A_1 into existence. Suppose further that A_2 was brought into existence in similar fashion some time ago by A_3, and A_3 by A_4, and so forth back into the past. Each of these beings is a *dependent* being, it owes its existence to the preceding thing in the series. Now if nothing else ever existed but these beings, then what the second premise says would not be true. For if every being that exists or ever did exist is an A and was produced by a preceding A, then every being that exists or ever did exist would be dependent and, accordingly, premise two of the Cosmological Argument would be false. If the proponent of the Cosmological Argument is correct there must, then, be something wrong with the idea that

every being that exists or did exist is an A and that they form a causal series: A_1 caused by A_2, A_2 caused by A_3, A_3 caused by A_4, ... A_n caused by A_{n+1}. How does the proponent of the Cosmological Argument propose to show us that there is something wrong with this view?

A popular but mistaken idea of how the proponent tries to show that something is wrong with the view, that every being might be dependent, is that he uses the following argument to reject it.

1. There must be a *first* being to start any causal series.

2. If every being were dependent there would be no *first* being to start the causal series.

Therefore,

3. Not every being can be a dependent being.

Although this argument is deductively valid, and its second premise is true, its first premise overlooks the distinct possibility that a causal series might be *infinite*, with no first member at all. Thus if we go back to our series of A beings, where each A is dependent, having been produced by the preceding A in the causal series, it's clear that if the series existed it would have no first member, for every A in the series there would be a preceding A which produced it, *ad infinitum*. The first premise of the argument just given assumes that a causal series must stop with a first member somewhere in the distant past. But there seems to be no good reason for making that assumption.

The eighteenth-century proponents of the Cosmological Argument recognized that the causal series of dependent beings could be infinite, without a first member to start the series. They rejected the idea that every being that is or ever was is dependent not because there would then be no first member to the series of dependent beings, but because there would then be no explanation for the fact that there are and have always been dependent beings. To see their reasoning let's return to our simplification of the supposition that the only things that exist or ever did exist are dependent beings. In our simplification of that supposition only one of the dependent beings exists at a time, each one perishing as it produces the next in the series. Perhaps the first thing to note about this supposition is that there is no individual A in the causal series of dependent beings whose existence is unexplained—A_1 is explained by A_2, A_2 by A_3, and A_n by A_{n+1}. So the first part of PSR, PSRa, appears to be satisfied. There is no particular being whose existence lacks an explanation. What, then, is it that lacks an explanation, if every particular A in the causal series of dependent beings has an explanation? It is the *series itself* that lacks an explanation, or, as I've chosen to express it, *the fact that there are and have always been dependent beings*. For suppose we ask why it is that there are and have always been As in existence. It won't do to say that As have always been producing other As—we can't explain why there have always been As by saying there always have been As. Nor, on the supposition that only As have ever existed, can we explain the fact that there have always been As by appealing to something other than an A— for no such thing would have existed. Thus the supposition that the only things that exist or ever existed are dependent things leaves us with a fact for which there can be no explanation; namely, the fact that there are and have always been dependent beings.

QUESTIONING THE JUSTIFICATION OF THE SECOND PREMISE

Critics of the Cosmological Argument have raised several important objections against the claim that if every being is dependent the series or collection of those beings would have no explanation. Our understanding of the Cosmological Argument, as well as of its strengths and weaknesses, will be deepened by a careful consideration of these criticisms.

The first criticism is that the proponent of the Cosmological Argument makes the mistake of treating the collection or series of dependent beings as though it were itself a dependent being, and, therefore, requires an explanation of its existence. But, so the objection goes, the collection of dependent beings is not itself a dependent being any more than a collection of stamps is itself a stamp.

A second criticism is that the proponent makes the mistake of inferring that because each member of the collection of dependent beings has a cause, the collection itself must have a cause. But, as Bertrand Russell noted, such reasoning is as fallacious as to infer that the human race (that is, the collection of human beings) must have a mother because each member of the collection (each human being) has a mother.

A third criticism is that the proponent of the argument fails to realize that for there to be an explanation of a collection of things is nothing more than for there to be an explanation of each of the things making up the collection. Since in the infinite collection (or series) of dependent beings, each being in the collection does have an explanation—by virtue of having been caused by some preceding member of the collection—the explanation of the collection, so the criticism goes, has already been given. As David Hume remarked, "Did I show you the particular causes of each individual in a collection of twenty particles of matter, I should think it very unreasonable, should you afterwards ask me, what was the cause of the whole twenty. This is sufficiently explained in explaining the cause of the parts."[2]

Finally, even if the proponent of the Cosmological Argument can satisfactorily answer these objections, he must face one last objection to his ingenious attempt to justify premise two of the Cosmological Argument. For someone may agree that if nothing exists but an infinite collection of dependent beings, the infinite collection will have no explanation of its existence, and still refuse to conclude from this that there is something wrong with the idea that every being is a dependent being. Why, he might ask, should we think that everything has to have an explanation? What's wrong with admitting that the fact that there are and have always been dependent beings is a *brute fact*, a fact having no explanation whatever? Why does everything have to have an explanation anyway?

We must now see what can be said in response to these several objections.

Responses to Criticism

It is certainly a mistake to think that a collection of stamps is itself a stamp, and very likely a mistake to think that the collection of dependent beings is itself a dependent being. But the mere fact that the proponent of the argument thinks that there must be an explanation not only for each member of the collection of dependent beings but for the collection itself is not sufficient grounds for concluding that he must view the collection as itself a dependent being. The collection of human beings, for example, is certainly not itself a human being. Admitting this, however, we might still seek an explanation of why there is a collection of human beings, of why there are such things as human beings at all. So the mere fact that an explanation is demanded for the collection of dependent beings is no proof that the person who demands the explanation must be supposing that the collection itself is just another dependent being.

The second criticism attributes to the proponent of the Cosmological Argument the following bit of reasoning.

1. Every member of the collection of dependent beings has a cause or explanation.

Therefore,

2. The collection of dependent beings has a cause or explanation.

As we noted in setting forth this criticism, arguments of this sort are often unreliable. It would be a mistake to conclude that a collection of objects is light in weight simply because each object in the collection is light in weight, for if there were many objects in the collection it might be quite heavy. On the other hand, if we know that each marble weighs more than one ounce, we could infer validly that the collection of marbles weighs more than an ounce. Fortunately, however, we don't need to decide whether the inference from 1 to 2 is valid or invalid. We need not decide this question because

the proponent of the Cosmological Argument need not use this inference to establish that there must be an explanation of the collection of dependent beings. He need not use this inference because he has in PSR a principle from which it follows immediately that the collection of dependent beings has a cause or explanation. For according to PSR, every positive fact must have an explanation. If it is a fact that there exists a collection of dependent beings then, according to PSR, that fact too must have an explanation. So it is PSR that the proponent of the Cosmological Argument appeals to in concluding that there must be an explanation of the collection of dependent beings, and not some dubious inference from the premise that each member of the collection has an explanation. It seems, then, that neither of the first two criticisms is strong enough to do any serious damage to the reasoning used to support the second premise of the Cosmological Argument.

The third objection contends that to explain the existence of a collection of things is the same thing as to explain the existence of each of its members. If we consider a collection of dependent beings where each being in the collection is explained by the preceding member which caused it, it's clear that no member of the collection will lack an explanation of its existence. But, so the criticism goes, if we've explained the existence of every member of a collection, we've explained the existence of the collection—there's nothing left over to be explained. This forceful criticism, originally advanced by David Hume, has gained considerable support in the modern period. But the criticism rests on an assumption that the proponent of the Cosmological Argument would not accept. The assumption is that to explain the existence of a collection of things it is *sufficient* to explain the existence of every member in the collection. To see what is wrong with this assumption is to understand the basic issue in the reasoning by which the proponent of the Cosmological Argument seeks to establish that not every being can be a dependent being.

In order for there to be an explanation of the existence of the collection of dependent beings, it's clear that the eighteenth-century proponents would require that the following two conditions be satisfied:

C1. There is an explanation of the existence of each of the members of the collection of dependent beings.

C2. There is an explanation of why there are any dependent beings.

According to the proponents of the Cosmological Argument, if every being that exists or ever did exist is a dependent being—that is, if the whole of reality consists of nothing more than a collection of dependent beings—C1 will be satisfied, but C2 will not be satisfied. And since C2 won't be satisfied, there will be no explanation of the collection of dependent beings. The third criticism, therefore, says in effect that if C1 is satisfied, C2 will be satisfied, and, since in a collection of dependent beings each member will have an explanation in whatever it was that produced it, C1 will be satisfied, So, therefore, C2 will be satisfied and the collection of dependent beings will have an explanation.

Although the issue is a complicated one, I think it is possible to see that the third criticism rests on a mistake: the mistake of thinking that if C1 is satisfied C2 must also be satisfied. The mistake is a natural one to make for it is easy to imagine circumstances in which if C1 is satisfied C2 also will be satisfied. Suppose, for example that the whole of reality includes not just a collection of dependent beings but also a self-existent being. Suppose further that instead of each dependent being having been produced by some other dependent being, every dependent being was produced by the self-existent being. Finally, let us consider both the possibility that the collection of dependent beings is finite in time and has a first member, and the possibility that the collection of dependent beings is infinite in past time, having no first member. Using G for the self-existent being, the first possibility may be diagramed as follows:

G, we shall say, has always existed and always will. We can think of d_1 as some presently existing dependent being, d_2, d_3, and so forth as dependent beings that existed at some time in the past, and d_n as the first dependent being to exist. The second possibility may be portrayed as follows:

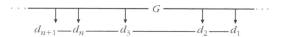

On this diagram there is no first member of the collection of dependent beings. Each member of the infinite collection, however, is explained by reference to the self-existent being G which produced it. Now the interesting point about both these cases is that the explanation that has been provided for the members of the collection of dependent beings carries with it, at least in part, an answer to the question of why there are any dependent beings at all. In both cases we may explain why there are dependent beings by pointing out that there exists a self-existent being that has been engaged in producing them. So once we have learned that the existence of each member of the collection of dependent beings has its existence explained by the fact that G produced it, we have already learned why there are dependent beings.

Someone might object that we haven't really learned why there are dependent beings until we also learn *why* G has been producing them. But, of course, we could also say that we haven't really explained the existence of a particular dependent being, say d_3, until we also learn not just that G produced it but *why* G produced it. The point we need to grasp, however, is that once we admit that every dependent being's existence is explained by G, we must admit that the fact that there are dependent beings has also been explained. So it is not unnatural that someone should think that to explain the existence of the collection of dependent beings is nothing more than to explain the existence of its members. For, as we've seen, to explain the collection's existence is to explain each member's existence and to explain why there are any dependent beings at all. And in the examples we've considered, in doing the one (explaining why each dependent being exists) we've already done the other (explained why there are any dependent beings at all). We must now see, however, that on the supposition that the whole of reality consists *only* of a collection of dependent beings, to give an explanation of each member's existence is not to provide an explanation of why there are dependent beings.

In the examples we've considered, we have gone outside of the collection of dependent beings in order to explain the members' existence. But if the only beings that exist or ever existed are dependent beings then each dependent being will be explained by some other dependent being, ad infinitum. This does not mean that there will be some particular dependent being whose existence is unaccounted for. Each dependent being has an explanation of its existence; namely, in the dependent being which preceded it and produced it. So C1 is satisfied: there is an explanation of the existence of each member of the collection of dependent beings. Turning to C2, however, we can see that it will not be satisfied. We cannot explain why there are (or have ever been) dependent beings by appealing to all the members of the infinite collection of dependent beings. For if the question to be answered is why there are (or have ever been) any dependent beings at all, we cannot answer that question by noting that there always have been dependent beings, each one accounting for the existence of some other dependent being. Thus on the supposition that every being is dependent, it seems there will be no explanation of why there are dependent beings. C2 will not be satisfied. Therefore, on the supposition that every being is dependent there will be no explanation of the existence of the collection of dependent beings.

THE TRUTH OF PSR

We come now to the final criticism of the reasoning supporting the second premise of the Cosmological Argument. According to the criticism, it is admitted that the supposition that every being is dependent implies that there will be a *brute fact* in the universe, a fact, that is, for which there can be no explanation whatever. For there will be no explanation of the fact that dependent beings exist and have always been in existence. It is this brute fact that the proponents of the argument were describing when they pointed out that if every being is dependent, the series or collection of dependent beings would lack an explanation of *its* existence. The final criticism asks what is wrong with admitting that the universe contains such a brute, unintelligible fact. In asking this question the critic challenges the fundamental principle, PSR, on which the Cosmological Argument rests. For, as we've seen, the first premise of the argument denies that there exists a being whose existence has no explanation. In support of this premise the proponent appeals to the first part of PSR. The second premise of the argument claims that not every being can be dependent. In support of this premise the proponent appeals to the second part of PSR, the part which states that there must be an explanation of any positive fact whatever.

The proponent reasons that if every being were a dependent being, then although the first part of PSR would be satisfied—every being would have an explanation—the second part would be violated; there would be no explanation for the positive fact that there are and have always been dependent beings. For first, since every being is supposed to be dependent, there would be nothing outside of the collection of dependent beings to explain the collection's existence. Second, the fact that each member of the collection has an explanation in some other dependent being is insufficient to explain why there are and have always been dependent beings. And, finally, there is nothing about the collection of dependent beings that would suggest that it is a self-existent collection. Consequently, if every being were dependent, the fact that there are and have always been dependent beings would have no explanation. But this violates the second part of PSR. So the second premise of the Cosmological Argument must be true: Not every being can be a dependent being. This conclusion, however, is no better than the principle, PSR, on which it rests. And it is the point of the final criticism to question the truth of PSR. Why, after all, should we accept the idea that every being and every positive fact must have an explanation? Why, in short, should we believe PSR? These are important questions, and any final judgment of the Cosmological Argument depends on how they are answered.

Most of the theologians and philosophers who accept PSR have tried to defend it in either of two ways. Some have held that PSR is (or can be) known *intuitively* to be true. By this they mean that if we fully understand and reflect on what is said by PSR we can see that it must be true. Now, undoubtedly, there are statements which are known intuitively to be true. "Every triangle has exactly three angles" or "No physical object can be in two different places in space at one and the same time" are examples of statements whose truth we can apprehend just by understanding and reflecting on them. The difficulty with the claim that PSR is intuitively true, however, is that a number of very able philosophers fail to apprehend its truth, and some even claim that the principle is false. It is doubtful, therefore, that many of us, if any, know intuitively that PSR is true.

The second way philosophers and theologians who accept PSR have sought to defend it is by claiming that although it is not known to be true, it is, nevertheless, a presupposition of reason, a basic assumption that rational people make, whether or not they reflect sufficiently to become aware of the assumption. It's probably true that there are some assumptions we all make about our world, assumptions which are so basic that most of us are unaware of them. And, I suppose, it might be true that PSR is such an assumption. What bearing would this view of PSR have on the Cosmological Argument? Perhaps the main point to note is that even if PSR is a presupposition we all share, the premises of the Cosmological Argument could still be false. For PSR itself could still be false. The fact, if it is a fact, that all of us *presuppose* that every existing being and every positive fact has an explanation does not imply that no being exists, and no positive fact obtains, without an explanation. Nature is not bound to satisfy our presuppositions. As the American philosopher William James once remarked in another connection, "In the great boarding house of nature, the cakes and the butter and the syrup seldom come out so even and leave the plates so clear."

Our study of the first part of the Cosmological Argument has led us to the fundamental principle on which its premises rest, the Principle of Sufficient Reason. Since we do not seem to know that PSR is true, we cannot reasonably claim to know that the premises of the Cosmological Argument are true. They might be true. But unless we do know them to be true they cannot *establish* for us the conclusion that there exists a being that has the explanation of its existence within its own nature. If it were shown, however, that even though we do not *know* that PSR is true we all, nevertheless, *presuppose* PSR to be true, then, whether PSR is true or not, to be consistent we should accept the Cosmological Argument. For, as we've seen, its premises imply its conclusion and its premises do seem to follow from PSR. But no one has succeeded in *showing* that PSR is an assumption that most or all of us share. So our final conclusion must be that although the Cosmological Argument might be a *sound* argument (valid with true premises), it does not provide us with good rational grounds for believing that among these beings that exist there is one whose existence is accounted for by its own nature. Having come to this conclusion, we may safely put aside the second part of the argument. For even if it succeeded in showing that a self-existent being would have the other attributes of the theistic God, the Cosmological Argument would still not provide us with good rational grounds for belief in God, having failed in its first part to provide us with good rational grounds for believing that there is a self-existent being.

NOTES

1. See St. Thomas Aquinas, *Summa Theologica, Ila.* 2, 3.

2. David Hume, *Dialogues Concerning Natural Religion,* Part IX, ed. H. D. Aiken (New York: Hafner Publishing Company, 1948), pp. 59–60.

II.C.1

The Watch and the Watchmaker

WILLIAM PALEY

William Paley (1743–1805), Archdeacon of Carlisle, was a leading evangelical apologist. His most important work is Natural Theology, or Evidences of the Existence and Attributes of the Deity Collected from the Appearances of Nature *(1802), the first chapter of which is reprinted here. Paley argues that just as we infer the existence of an intelligent designer to explain the presence of*

From William Paley, *Natural Theology, or Evidences of the Existence and Attributes of the Deity Collected from the Appearances of Nature* (1802).

a subtle and complex artifact like a watch, so too we must infer the existence of an intelligent Grand Designer to explain the existence of the works of nature, which are far more subtle, complex, and cleverly contrived than any human artifact.

STATEMENT OF THE ARGUMENT

In crossing a heath, suppose I pitched my foot against a stone, and were asked how the stone came to be there, I might possibly answer, that, for anything I knew to the contrary, it had lain there for ever; nor would it, perhaps, be very easy to show the absurdity of this answer. But suppose I found a watch upon the ground, and it should be inquired how the watch happened to be in that place, I should hardly think of the answer which I had given—that, for anything I knew, the watch might have always been there. Yet why should not this answer serve for the watch as well as for the stone? Why is it not as admissible in the second case as in the first? For this reason, and for no other; viz., that, when we come to inspect the watch, we perceive (what we could not discover in the stone) that its several parts are framed and put together for a purpose, e.g. that they are so formed and adjusted as to produce motion, and that motion so regulated as to point out the hour of the day; that, if the different parts had been differently shaped from what they are, if a different size from what they are, or placed after any other manner, or in any other order than that in which they are placed, either no motion at all would have been carried on in the machine, or none which would have answered the use that is now served by it. To reckon up a few of the plainest of these parts, and of their offices, all tending to one result:—We see a cylindrical box containing a coiled elastic spring, which, by its endeavor to relax itself, turns round the box. We next observe a flexible chain (artificially wrought for the sake of flexure) communicating the action of the spring from the box to the fusee. We then find a series of wheels, the teeth of which catch in, and apply to, each other, conducting the motion from the fusee to the balance, and from the balance to the pointer, and, at the same time, by the size and shape of those wheels,

so regulating that motion as to terminate in causing an index, by an equable and measured progression, to pass over a given space in a given time. We take notice that the wheels are made of brass, in order to keep them from rust; the springs of steel, no other metal being so elastic; that over the face of the watch there is placed a glass, a material employed in no other part of the work, but in the room of which, if there had been any other than a transparent substance, the hour could not be seen without opening the case. This mechanism being observed, (it requires indeed an examination of the instrument, and perhaps some previous knowledge of the subject, to perceive and understand it; but being once, as we have said, observed and understood,) the inference, we think, is inevitable, that the watch must have had a maker; that there must have existed, at some time, and at some place or other, an artificer or artificers who formed it for the purpose which we find it actually to answer; who comprehended its construction, and designed its use.

I. Nor would it, I apprehend, weaken the conclusion, that we had never seen a watch made; that we had never known an artist capable of making one; that we were altogether incapable of executing such a piece of workmanship ourselves, or of understanding in what manner it was performed; all this being no more than what is true of some exquisite remains of ancient art, of some lost and to the generality of mankind, of the more curious productions of modern manufacture. Does one man in a million know how oval frames are turned? Ignorance of this kind exalts our opinion of the unseen and unknown artist's skill, if he be unseen and unknown, but raises no doubt in our minds of the existence and agency of such an artist, at some former time, and in some place or other. Nor can I perceive that it varies at all the inference, whether the question arise concerning a human agent, or concerning an agent of a different species, or an agent possessing, in some respect, a different nature.

II. Neither, secondly, would it invalidate our conclusion, that the watch sometimes went wrong, or that it seldom went exactly right. The purpose of the machinery, the design, and the designer, might be evident, and, in the case supposed, would be evident, in whatever way we accounted for the irregularity of the movement, or whether we could account for it or not. It is not necessary that a machine be perfect, in order to show with what design it was made; still less necessary, where the only question is, whether it were made with any design at all.

III. Nor, thirdly, would it bring any uncertainty into the argument, if there were a few parts of the watch, concerning which we could not discover, or had not yet discovered, in what manner they conduced to the general effect; or even some parts, concerning which we could not ascertain whether they conduced to that effect in any manner whatever. For, as to the first branch of the case, if by the loss, or disorder, or decay of the parts in question, the movement of the watch were found in fact to be stopped, or disturbed, or retarded, no doubt would remain in our minds as to the utility or intention of these parts, although we should be unable to investigate the manner according to which, or the connection by which, the ultimate effect depended upon their action or assistance; and the more complex is the machine, the more likely is this obscurity to arise. Then, as to the second thing supposed, namely, that there were parts which might be spared without prejudice to the movement of the watch, and that he had proved this by experiment, these superfluous parts, even if we were completely assured that they were such, would not vacate the reasoning which we had instituted concerning other parts. The indication of contrivance remained, with respect to them, nearly as it was before.

IV. Nor, fourthly, would any man in his senses think the existence of the watch, with its various machinery, accounted for, by being told that it was one out of possible combinations of material forms; that whatever he had found in the place where he found the watch, must have contained some internal configuration or other; and that this configuration might be the structure now exhibited, viz., of the works of a watch, as well as a different structure.

V. Nor, fifthly, would it yield his inquiry more satisfaction, to be answered, that there existed in things a principle of order, which had disposed the parts of the watch into their present form and situation. He never knew a watch made by the principle of order; nor can he even form to himself an idea of what is meant by a principle of order, distinct from the intelligence of the watchmaker.

VI. Sixthly, he would be surprised to hear that the mechanism of the watch was no proof of contrivance, only a motive to induce the mind to think so.

VII. And not less surprised to be informed, that the watch in his hand was nothing more than the result of the laws of *metallic* nature. It is a perversion of language to assign any law as the efficient, operative cause of anything. A law presupposes an agent; for it is only the mode according to which an agent proceeds; it implies a power; for it is the order according to which that power acts. Without this agent, without this power, which are both distinct from itself, the *law* does nothing, is nothing. The expression, "the law of metallic nature," may sound strange and harsh to a philosophic ear; but it seems quite as justifiable as some others which are more familiar to him such as "the law of vegetable nature," "the law of animal nature," or, indeed, as "the law of nature" in general, when assigned as the cause of phenomena in exclusion of agency and power, or when it is substituted into the place of these.

VIII. Neither, lastly, would our observer be driven out of his conclusion, or from his confidence in its truth, by being told that he knew nothing at all about the matter. He knows enough for his argument: he knows the utility of the end: he knows the subserviency and adaptation of the means to the end. These points being known, his ignorance of other points, his doubts concerning other points, affect not the certainty of his reasoning. The consciousness of knowing little need not beget a distrust of that which he does know....

APPLICATION OF THE ARGUMENT

Every indication of contrivance, every manifestation of design, which existed in the watch, exists in the works of nature; with the difference, on the side of nature, of being greater and more, and that in a degree which exceeds all computation. I mean that the contrivances of nature surpass the contrivances of art, in the complexity, subtilty, and curiosity of the mechanism; and still more, if possible, do they go beyond them in number and variety; yet in a multitude of cases, are not less evidently mechanical, not less evidently contrivances, not less evidently accommodated to their end, or suited to their office, than are the most perfect productions of human ingenuity.

From David Hume, *Dialogue Concerning National Religion* (1779) London: Longman Green, 1878.

II.C.4

A Scientific Argument for the Existence of God

ROBIN COLLINS

Robin Collins (1961–   ) is professor of philosophy at Messiah College, and he has written several articles on the argument from design. The article included here presents a simplified version of an argument that he has developed in much more technical detail elsewhere. He begins by noting that life would have been impossible had certain laws of nature and fundamental physical constants (such as the gravitational constant) been even slightly different. He then argues that since this apparent "fine-tuning" of the laws and constants is significantly more probable on the assumption that the universe was designed to be hospitable for life than on the assumption that it was not designed at all, such apparent fine-tuning counts as evidence in favor of the existence of a designer.

I. INTRODUCTION

The Evidence of Fine-Tuning

Suppose we went on a mission to Mars, and found a domed structure in which everything was set up just right for life to exist. The temperature, for example, was set around 70° F and the humidity was at 50 percent; moreover, there was an oxygen recycling system, an energy gathering system, and a whole system for the production of food. Put simply, the domed structure appeared to be a fully functioning biosphere. What conclusion would we draw from finding this structure? Would we draw the conclusion that it just happened to form by chance? Certainly not. Instead, we would unanimously conclude that it was designed by some intelligent being. Why would we draw this conclusion? Because an intelligent designer appears to be the only plausible explanation for the existence of the structure. That is, the only alternative explanation we can think of—that the structure was formed by some natural process—seems extremely unlikely. Of course, it is *possible* that, for example, through some volcanic eruption various metals and other compounds could have formed, and then separated out in just the right way to produce the "biosphere," but such a scenario strikes us as extraordinarily unlikely, thus making this alternative explanation unbelievable.

The universe is analogous to such a "biosphere," according to recent findings in physics. Almost everything about the basic structure of the universe—for example, the fundamental laws and parameters of physics and the initial distribution of matter and energy—is balanced on a razor's edge for life to occur. As the eminent Princeton physicist Freeman Dyson notes, "There are many ... lucky accidents in physics. Without such accidents, water could not exist as liquid, chains of carbon atoms could not form complex organic molecules, and

From *Reason for the Hope Within*, Michael J. Murray, ed., © 1999, Wm. B. Eerdmans, Grand Rapids, MI. Used with permission.

hydrogen atoms could not form breakable bridges between molecules"[1]—in short, life as we know it would be impossible.

Scientists call this extraordinary balancing of the parameters of physics and the initial conditions of the universe the "fine-tuning of the cosmos." It has been extensively discussed by philosophers, theologians, and scientists, especially since the early 1970s, with hundreds of articles and dozens of books written on the topic. Today, it is widely regarded as offering by far the most persuasive current argument for the existence of God. For example, theoretical physicist and popular science writer Paul Davies—whose early writings were not particularly sympathetic to theism—claims that with regard to basic structure of the universe, "the impression of design is overwhelming."[2] Similarly, in response to the life-permitting fine-tuning of the nuclear resonances responsible for the oxygen and carbon synthesis in stars, the famous astrophysicist Sir Fred Hoyle declares that

> I do not believe that any scientists who examined the evidence would fail to draw the inference that the laws of nuclear physics have been deliberately designed with regard to the consequences they produce inside stars. If this is so, then my apparently random quirks have become part of a deep-laid scheme. If not then we are back again at a monstrous sequence of accidents.[3]

A few examples of this fine-tuning are listed below:

1. If the initial explosion of the big bang had differed in strength by as little as one part in 10^{60}, the universe would have either quickly collapsed back on itself, or expanded too rapidly for stars to form. In either case, life would be impossible. (As John Jefferson Davis points out, an accuracy of one part in 10^{60} can be compared to firing a bullet at a one-inch target on the other side of the observable universe, twenty billion light years away, and hitting the target.)[4]

2. Calculations indicate that if the strong nuclear force, the force that binds protons and neutrons together in an atom, had been stronger or weaker by as little as five percent, life would be impossible.[5]

3. Calculations by Brandon Carter show that if gravity had been stronger or weaker by one part in 10^{40}, then life-sustaining stars like the sun could not exist. This would most likely make life impossible.[6]

4. If the neutron were not about 1.001 times the mass of the proton, all protons would have decayed into neutrons or all neutrons would have decayed into protons, and thus life would not be possible.[7]

5. If the electromagnetic force were slightly stronger or weaker, life would be impossible, for a variety of different reasons.[8]

Imaginatively, one could think of each instance of fine-tuning as a radio dial: unless all the dials are set exactly right, life would be impossible. Or, one could think of the initial conditions of the universe and the fundamental parameters of physics as a dart board that fills the whole galaxy, and the conditions necessary for life to exist as a small one-foot-wide target: unless the dart hits the target, life would be impossible. The fact that the dials are perfectly set, or that the dart has hit the target, strongly suggests that someone set the dials or aimed the dart, for it seems enormously improbable that such a coincidence could have happened by chance.

Although individual calculations of fine-tuning are only approximate and could be in error, the fact that the universe is fine-tuned for life is almost beyond question because of the large number of independent instances of apparent fine-tuning. As philosopher John Leslie has pointed out, "Clues heaped upon clues can constitute weighty evidence despite doubts about each element in the pile."[9] What is controversial, however, is the degree to which the fine-tuning provides evidence for the existence of God. As impressive as the argument from fine-tuning seems to be, atheists have raised several significant objections to it. Consequently, those who are aware of these objections, or have thought of them on their own, often will find the argument unconvincing. This is not only true of atheists, but also many theists. I have known, for instance, both a committed Christian Hollywood filmmaker and a committed Christian biochemist who remained unconvinced because of certain atheist objections to the argument. This is unfortunate, particularly since the fine-tuning argument is probably the most powerful current argument for the existence of God. My goal in this chapter, therefore, is to make the fine-tuning argument as strong as possible. This will involve developing the argument in as objective and rigorous a way as I can, and then answering the major atheist objections to it. Before launching into this, however, I will need to make a preliminary distinction.

A Preliminary Distinction

To develop the fine-tuning argument rigorously, it is useful to distinguish between what I shall call the *atheistic single-universe hypothesis* and the *atheistic many-universes hypothesis*. According to the atheistic single-universe hypothesis, there is only one universe, and it is ultimately an inexplicable, "brute" fact that the universe exists and is fine-tuned. Many atheists, however, advocate another hypothesis, one which attempts to explain how the seemingly improbable fine-tuning of the universe could be the result of chance. We will call this hypothesis the *atheistic many-worlds hypothesis,* or *the atheistic many-universes hypothesis*. According to this hypothesis, there exists what could be imaginatively thought of as a "universe generator" that produces a very large or infinite number of universes, with each universe having a randomly selected set of initial conditions and values for the parameters of physics. Because this generator produces so many universes, just by chance it will eventually produce one that is fine-tuned for intelligent life to occur.

Plan of the Chapter

Below, we will use this distinction between the atheistic single-universe hypothesis and the atheistic many-universes hypothesis to present two separate arguments for theism based on the fine-tuning: one which argues that the fine-tuning provides strong reasons to prefer theism over the atheistic single-universe hypothesis and one which argues that we should prefer theism over the atheistic many-universes hypothesis. We will develop the argument against the atheistic single-universe hypothesis in section II below, referring to it as the core argument. Then we will answer objections to this *core* argument in section III, and finally develop the argument for preferring theism to the atheistic many-universes hypothesis in section IV. An appendix is also included that further elaborates and justifies one of the key premises of the core argument presented in section II.

II. CORE ARGUMENT RIGOROUSLY FORMULATED

General Principle of Reasoning Used

The Principle Explained   We will formulate the fine-tuning argument against the atheistic single-universe hypothesis in terms of what I will call the *prime principle of confirmation*. The prime principle of confirmation is a general principle of reasoning which tells us when some observation counts as evidence in favor of one hypothesis over another. *Simply put, the principle says that whenever we are considering two competing hypotheses, an observation counts as evidence in favor of the hypothesis under which the observation has the highest probability (or is the least improbable).* (Or, put slightly differently, the principle says that whenever we are considering two competing hypotheses, H_1 and H_2, an observation, O, counts as evidence in favor of H_1 over H_2 if O is more probable under H_1 than it is under H_2.) Moreover, the degree to which the evidence counts in favor of one hypothesis over another is proportional to the degree to which the observation is more probable under the one hypothesis than the other.[10] For example, the fine-tuning is much, much more probable under theism than under the atheistic single-universe hypothesis, so it counts as strong evidence for theism over this atheistic hypothesis. In the next major subsection, we will present a more formal and elaborated rendition of the fine-tuning argument in terms of the prime principle. First, however, let's look at a couple of illustrations of the principle and then present some support for it.

Additional Illustrations of the Principle   For our first illustration, suppose that I went hiking in the mountains, and found underneath a certain cliff a group of rocks arranged in a formation that clearly formed the pattern "Welcome to the mountains, Robin Collins." One hypothesis is that, by chance, the rocks just happened to be arranged in that pattern—ultimately, perhaps, because of certain initial conditions of the universe. Suppose the only viable alternative hypothesis is that my brother, who was in the mountains before me, arranged the rocks in this way. Most of us would immediately take the arrangements of rocks to be strong evidence in favor of the "brother" hypothesis over the "chance" hypothesis. Why? Because it strikes us as extremely *improbable* that the rocks would be arranged that way by chance, but *not improbable* at all that my brother would place them in that configuration. Thus, by the prime principle of confirmation we would conclude that the arrangement of rocks strongly supports the "brother" hypothesis over the chance hypothesis.

Or consider another case, that of finding the defendant's fingerprints on the murder weapon. Normally, we would take such a finding as strong evidence that the defendant was guilty. Why? Because we judge that it would be *unlikely* for these fingerprints to be on the murder weapon if the defendant was innocent, but *not unlikely* if the defendant was guilty. That is, we would go through the same sort of reasoning as in the above case.

Support for the Principle   Several things can be said in favor of the prime principle of confirmation. First, many philosophers think that this principle can be derived from what is known as the *probability calculus,* the set of mathematical rules that are typically assumed to govern probability. Second, there does not appear to be any case of recognizably good reasoning that violates this principle. Finally, the principle appears to have a wide range of applicability, undergirding much of our reasoning in science and everyday life, as the examples above illustrate. Indeed, some have even claimed that a slightly more general version of this principle undergirds all scientific reasoning. Because of all these reasons in favor of the principle, we can be very confident in it.

Further Development of Argument

To further develop the core version of the fine-tuning argument, we will summarize the argument by explicitly listing its two premises and its conclusion:

- *Premise 1.* The existence of the fine-tuning is not improbable under theism.

- *Premise 2.* The existence of the fine-tuning is very improbable under the atheistic single-universe hypothesis.

- *Conclusion*: From premises (1) and (2) and the prime principle of confirmation, it follows that the fine-tuning data provide strong evidence to favor the design hypothesis over the atheistic single-universe hypothesis.

At this point, we should pause to note two features of this argument. First, the argument does not say that the fine-tuning evidence proves that the universe was designed, or even that it is likely that the universe was designed. In order to justify these sorts of claims, we would have to look at the full range of evidence both for and against the design hypothesis, something we are not doing in this chapter. Rather, the argument merely concludes that the fine-tuning strongly *supports* theism *over* the atheistic single-universe hypothesis.

In this way, the evidence of the fine-tuning argument is much like fingerprints found on the gun: although they can provide strong evidence that the defendant committed the murder, one could not conclude merely from them alone that the defendant is guilty; one would also have to look at all the other evidence offered. Perhaps, for instance, ten reliable witnesses claimed to see the defendant at a party at the time of the shooting. In this case, the fingerprints would still count as significant evidence of guilt, but this evidence would be counterbalanced by the testimony of the witnesses. Similarly the evidence of fine-tuning strongly supports theism over the atheistic single-universe hypothesis, though it does not itself show that, everything considered, theism is the most plausible explanation of the world. Nonetheless, as I argue in the conclusion of this chapter, the evidence of fine-tuning provides a much stronger and more objective argument for theism (over the atheistic single-universe hypothesis) than the strongest atheistic argument does against theism.

The second feature of the argument we should note is that, given the truth of *the prime principle of confirmation*, the conclusion of the argument follows from the premises. Specifically, if the premises of the argument are true, then we are guaranteed that the conclusion is true: that is, the argument is what philosophers call *valid*. Thus, insofar as we can show that the premises of the argument are true, we will have shown that the conclusion is true. Our next task, therefore, is to attempt to show that the premises are true, or at least that we have strong reasons to believe them.

Support for the Premises

Support for Premise (1) Premise (1) is easy to support and fairly uncontroversial. One major argument in support of it can be simply stated as follows: *since God is an all good being, and it is good for intelligent, conscious beings to exist, it is not surprising or improbable that God would create a world that could support intelligent life.* Thus, the fine-tuning is not improbable under theism, as premise (1) asserts.

Support for Premise (2) Upon looking at the data, many people find it very obvious that the fine-tuning is highly improbable under the atheistic single-universe hypothesis. And it is easy to see why when we think of the fine-tuning in terms of the analogies offered earlier. In the dart board analogy, for example, the initial conditions of the universe and the fundamental parameters of physics are thought of as a dart board that fills the whole galaxy, and the conditions necessary for life to exist as a small one-foot-wide target. Accordingly, from this analogy it seems obvious that it would be highly improbable for the fine-tuning to occur under the atheistic single-universe hypothesis— that is, for the dart to hit the target by chance.

Typically, advocates of the fine-tuning argument are satisfied with resting the justification of premise (2), or something like it, on this sort of analogy. Many atheists and theists, however, question the legitimacy of this sort of analogy, and thus find the argument unconvincing. For these people, the appendix to this chapter offers a rigorous and objective justification of premise (2) using standard principles of probabilistic reasoning. Among other things, in the process of rigorously justifying premise (2), we effectively answer the common objection to the fine-tuning argument that because the universe is a unique, unrepeatable event, we cannot meaningfully assign a probability to its being fine-tuned.

III. SOME OBJECTIONS TO CORE VERSION

As powerful as the core version of the fine-tuning argument is, several major objections have been raised to it by both atheists and theists. In this section, we will consider these objections in turn.

Objection 1: More Fundamental Law Objection

One criticism of the fine-tuning argument is that, as far as we know, there could be a more fundamental law under which the parameters of physics *must* have the values they do. Thus, given such a law, it is not improbable that the known parameters of physics fall within the life-permitting range.

Besides being entirely speculative, the problem with postulating such a law is that it simply moves the improbability of the fine-tuning up one level, to that of the postulated physical law itself. Under this hypothesis, what is improbable is that of all the conceivable fundamental physical laws there could be, the universe just happens to have the one that constrains the parameters of physics in a life-permitting way. Thus, trying to explain the fine-tuning by postulating this sort of fundamental law is like trying to explain why the pattern of rocks below a cliff spell "Welcome to the mountains, Robin Collins" by postulating that an earthquake occurred and that all the rocks on the cliff face were arranged in just the right configuration to fall into the pattern in question. Clearly this explanation merely transfers the improbability up one level, since now it seems enormously improbable that of all the possible configurations the rocks could be in on the cliff face, they are in the one which results in the pattern "Welcome to the mountains, Robin Collins."

A similar sort of response can be given to the claim that the fine-tuning is not improbable because it might be *logically necessary* for the parameters of physics to have life-permitting values. That is, according to this claim, the parameters of physics must have life-permitting values in the same way 2 + 2 must equal 4, or the interior angles of a triangle must add up to 180 degrees in Euclidian geometry. Like the "more fundamental law" proposal above, however, this postulate simply transfers the improbability up one level: of all the laws and parameters of physics that conceivably could have been logically necessary, it seems highly improbable that it would be those that are life-permitting.[11]

Objection 2: Other Forms of Life Objection

Another objection people commonly raise to the fine-tuning argument is that as far as we know, other forms of life could exist even if the parameters of physics were different. So, it is claimed, the fine-tuning argument ends up presupposing that all forms of intelligent life must be like us. The answer to this objection is that most cases of fine-tuning do not make this presupposition. Consider, for instance, the case of the fine-tuning of the strong nuclear force. If it were slightly smaller, no atoms could exist other than hydrogen. Contrary to what one might see on *Star Trek*, an intelligent life-form cannot be composed merely of hydrogen gas: there

is simply not enough stable complexity. So, in general the fine-tuning argument merely presupposes that intelligent life requires some degree of stable, reproducible organized complexity. This is certainly a very reasonable assumption.

Objection 3: Anthropic Principle Objection

According to the weak version of the so-called *anthropic principle,* if the laws of nature were not fine-tuned, we would not be here to comment on the fact. Some have argued, therefore, that the fine-tuning is not really *improbable or surprising* at all under atheism, but simply follows from the fact that we exist. The response to this objection is to simply restate the argument in terms of our existence: our existence as embodied, intelligent beings is extremely unlikely under the atheistic single-universe hypothesis (since our existence requires fine-tuning), but not improbable under theism. Then, we simply apply the prime principle of confirmation to draw the conclusion that *our existence* strongly confirms theism over the atheistic single-universe hypothesis.

To further illustrate this response, consider the following "firing squad" analogy. As John Leslie points out, if fifty sharpshooters all miss me, the response "if they had not missed me I wouldn't be here to consider the fact" is not adequate. Instead, I would naturally conclude that there was some reason why they all missed, such as that they never really intended to kill me. Why would I conclude this? Because my continued existence would be very improbable under the hypothesis that they missed me by chance, but not improbable under the hypothesis that there was some reason why they missed me. Thus, by the prime principle of confirmation, my continued existence strongly confirms the latter hypothesis.[12]

Objection 4: The "Who Designed God?" Objection

Perhaps the most common objection that atheists raise to the argument from design, of which the fine-tuning argument is one instance, is that postulating the existence of God does not solve the problem of design, but merely transfers it up one level. Atheist George Smith, for example, claims that

> If the universe is wonderfully designed, surely God is even more wonderfully designed. He must, therefore, have had a designer even more wonderful than He is. If *God* did not require a designer, then there is no reason why such a relatively less wonderful thing as the universe needed one.[13]

Or, as philosopher J. J. C. Smart states the objection:

> If we postulate God in addition to the created universe we increase the complexity of our hypothesis. We have all the complexity of the universe itself, and we have in addition the at least equal complexity of God. (The designer of an artifact must be at least as complex as the designed artifact).... *If the theist can show the atheist that postulating God actually reduces the complexity of one's total world view, then the atheist should be a theist.*[14]

The first response to the above atheist objection is to point out that the atheist claim that the designer of an artifact must be as complex as the artifact designed is certainly not obvious. But I do believe that their claim has some intuitive plausibility: for example, in the world we experience, organized complexity seems only to be produced by systems that already possess it, such as the human brain/mind, a factory, or an organism's biological parent.

The second, and better, response is to point out that, at most, the atheist objection only works against a version of the design argument that claims that all organized complexity needs an explanation, and that God is the best explanation of the organized complexity found in the world. The version of the argument I presented against the atheistic single-universe hypothesis, however, only required that the fine-tuning be more probable under theism than under the atheistic single-universe hypothesis.

But this requirement is still met even if God exhibits tremendous internal complexity, far exceeding that of the universe. Thus, even if we were to grant the atheist assumption that the designer of an artifact must be as complex as the artifact, the fine-tuning would still give us strong reasons to prefer theism over the atheistic single-universe hypothesis.

To illustrate, consider the example of the "biosphere" on Mars presented at the beginning of this paper. As mentioned above, the existence of the biosphere would be much more probable under the .hypothesis that intelligent life once visited Mars than under the chance hypothesis. Thus, by the prime principle of confirmation, the existence of such a "biosphere" would constitute strong evidence that intelligent, extraterrestrial life had once been on Mars, even though this alien life would most likely have to be much more complex than the "biosphere" itself.

The final response theists can give to this objection is to show that a supermind such as God would *not* require a high degree of unexplained organized complexity to create the universe. Although I have presented this response elsewhere, presenting it here is beyond the scope of this chapter.

IV. THE ATHEISTIC MANY-UNIVERSES HYPOTHESIS

The Atheistic Many-Universes Hypothesis Explained

In response to the theistic explanation of fine-tuning of the cosmos, many atheists have offered an alternative explanation, what I will call the atheistic many-universes hypothesis. (In the literature it is more commonly referred to as the *many-worlds hypothesis,* though I believe this name is somewhat misleading.) According to this hypothesis, there are a very large—perhaps infinite—number of universes, with the fundamental parameters of physics varying from universe to universe.[15] Of course, in the vast majority of these universes the parameters of physics would not have life-permitting values.

Nonetheless, in a small proportion of universes they would, and consequently it is no longer improbable that universes such as ours exist that are fine-tuned for life to occur.

Advocates of this hypothesis offer various types of models for where these universes came from. We will present what are probably the two most popular and plausible, the so-called *vacuum fluctuation* models and the *oscillating big bang* models. According to the vacuum fluctuation models, our universe, along with these other universes, were generated by quantum fluctuations in a preexisting superspace.[16] Imaginatively, one can think of this preexisting superspace as an infinitely extending ocean full of soap, and each universe generated out of this superspace as a soap bubble which spontaneously forms on the ocean.

The other model, the oscillating big bang model, is a version of the big bang theory. According to the big bang theory, the universe came into existence in an "explosion" (that is, a "bang") somewhere between ten and fifteen billion years ago. According to the *oscillating* big bang theory, our universe will eventually collapse back in on itself (what is called the "big crunch") and then from that "big crunch" will arise another "big bang," forming a new universe, which will in turn itself collapse, and so on. According to those who use this model to attempt to explain the fine-tuning, during every cycle, the parameters of physics and the initial conditions of the universe are reset at random. Since this process of collapse, explosion, collapse, and explosion has been going on for all eternity, eventually a fine-tuned universe will occur, indeed infinitely many of them.

In the next section, we will list several reasons for rejecting the atheistic many-universes hypothesis.

Reasons for Rejecting the Atheistic Many-Universes Hypothesis

First Reason   The first reason for rejecting the atheistic many-universes hypothesis, and preferring the theistic hypothesis, is the following general rule: *everything else being equal, we should prefer hypotheses for which we have independent evidence or that are natural extrapolations from what we already know.* Let's first illustrate and support this principle, and then apply it to the case of the fine-tuning.

Most of us take the existence of dinosaur bones to count as very strong evidence that dinosaurs existed in the past. But suppose a dinosaur skeptic claimed that she could explain the bones by postulating a "dinosaur-bone-producing-field" that simply materialized the bones out of thin air. Moreover, suppose further that, to avoid objections such as that there are no known physical laws that would allow for such a mechanism, the dinosaur skeptic simply postulated that we have not yet discovered these laws or detected these fields. Surely, none of us would let this skeptical hypothesis deter us from inferring the existence of dinosaurs. Why? Because although no one has directly observed dinosaurs, we do have experience of other animals leaving behind fossilized remains, and thus the dinosaur explanation is a *natural extrapolation* from our common experience. In contrast, to explain the dinosaur bones, the dinosaur skeptic has invented a set of physical laws, and a set of mechanisms that are *not* a natural extrapolation from anything we know or experience.

In the case of the fine-tuning, we already know that minds often produce fine-tuned devices, such as Swiss watches. Postulating God—a supermind—as the explanation of the fine-tuning, therefore, is a natural extrapolation from what we already observe minds to do. In contrast, it is difficult to see how the atheistic many-universes hypothesis could be considered a natural extrapolation from what we observe. Moreover, unlike the atheistic many-universes hypothesis, we have some experiential evidence for the existence of God, namely religious experience. Thus, by the above principle, we should prefer the theistic explanation of the fine-tuning over the atheistic many-universes explanation, everything else being equal.

Second Reason

A second reason for rejecting the atheistic many-universes hypothesis is that the "many-universes generator" seems like it would need to be designed.

For instance, in all current worked-out proposals for what this "universe generator" could be—such as the oscillating big bang and the vacuum fluctuation models explained above—the "generator" itself is governed by a complex set of physical laws that allow it to produce the universes. It stands to reason, therefore, that if these laws were slightly different the generator probably would not be able to produce any universes that could sustain life. After all, even my bread machine has to be made just right in order to work properly, and it only produces loaves of bread, not universes! Or consider a device as simple as a mousetrap: it requires that all the parts, such as the spring and hammer, be arranged just right in order to function. It is doubtful, therefore, whether the atheistic many-universe theory can entirely eliminate the problem of design the atheist faces; rather, at least to some extent, it seems simply to move the problem of design up one level.[17]

Third Reason   A third reason for rejecting the atheistic many-universes hypothesis is that the universe generator must not only select the parameters of physics at random, but must actually randomly create or select the very laws of physics themselves. This makes this hypothesis seem even more far-fetched since it is difficult to see what possible physical mechanism could select or create laws.

The reason the "many-universes generator" must randomly select the laws of physics is that, just as the right values for the parameters of physics are needed for life to occur, the right set of laws is also needed. If, for instance, certain laws of physics were missing, life would be impossible. For example, without the law of inertia, which guarantees that particles do not shoot off at high speeds, life would probably not be possible.[18] Another example is the law of gravity: if masses did not attract each other, there would be no planets or stars, and once again it seems that life would be impossible. Yet another example is the *Pauli Exclusion Principle*, the principle of quantum mechanics that says that no two fermions—such as electrons or protons—can share the same quantum state. As prominent Princeton physicist Freeman Dyson points out,[19]

without this principle all electrons would collapse into the nucleus and thus atoms would be impossible.

Fourth Reason   The fourth reason for rejecting the atheistic many-universes hypothesis is that it cannot explain other features of the universe that seem to exhibit apparent design, whereas theism can. For example, many physicists, such as Albert Einstein, have observed that the basic laws of physics exhibit an extraordinary degree of beauty, elegance, harmony, and ingenuity. Nobel prize-winning physicist Steven Weinberg, for instance, devotes a whole chapter of his book *Dreams of a Final Theory*[20] explaining how the criteria of beauty and elegance are commonly used to guide physicists in formulating the right laws. Indeed, one of the most prominent theoretical physicists of this century, Paul Dirac, went so far as to claim that "it is more important to have beauty in one's equations than to have them fit experiment."[21]

Now such beauty, elegance, and ingenuity make sense if the universe was designed by God. Under the atheistic many-universes hypothesis, however, there is no reason to expect the fundamental laws to be elegant or beautiful. As theoretical physicist Paul Davies writes, "If nature is so 'clever' as to exploit mechanisms that amaze us with their ingenuity, is that not persuasive evidence for the existence of intelligent design behind the universe? If the world's finest minds can unravel only with difficulty the deeper workings of nature, how could it be supposed that those workings are merely a mindless accident, a product of blind chance?"[22]

Final Reason   This brings us to the final reason for rejecting the atheistic many-universes hypothesis, which may be the most difficult to grasp: namely, neither the atheistic many-universes hypothesis (nor the atheistic single-universe hypothesis) can at present adequately account for the improbable initial arrangement of matter in the universe required by the second law of thermodynamics. To see this, note that according to the second law of thermodynamics, the entropy of the universe is constantly increasing. The standard way of understanding this entropy increase is to say that the universe is going from a state of order to disorder. We observe this entropy increase all the time around us: things, such as a child's bedroom, that start out highly organized tend to "decay" and become disorganized unless something or someone intervenes to stop it.

Now, for purposes of illustration, we could think of the universe as a scrabble-board that initially starts out in a highly ordered state in which all the letters are arranged to form words, but which keeps getting randomly shaken. Slowly, the board, like the universe, moves from a state of order to disorder. The problem for the atheist is to explain how the universe could have started out in a highly ordered state, since it is extraordinarily improbable for such states to occur by chance.[23] If, for example, one were to dump a bunch of letters at random on a scrabble-board, it would be very unlikely for most of them to form into words. At best, we would expect groups of letters to form into words in a few places on the board.

Now our question is, Could the atheistic many-universes hypothesis explain the high degree of initial order of our universe by claiming that given enough universes, eventually one will arise that is ordered and in which intelligent life occurs, and so it is no surprise that we find ourselves in an ordered universe? The problem with this explanation is that it is overwhelmingly more likely for local patches of order to form in one or two places than for the whole universe to be ordered, just as it is overwhelmingly more likely for a few letters on the scrabble-board randomly to form words than for all the letters throughout the board randomly to form words. Thus, the overwhelming majority of universes in which intelligent life occurs will be ones in which the intelligent life will be surrounded by a small patch of order necessary for its existence, but in which the rest of the universe is disordered. Consequently, even under the atheistic many-universes hypothesis, it would still be enormously improbable for intelligent beings to find themselves in a universe such as ours which is highly ordered throughout.[24]

Conclusion

Even though the above criticisms do not definitively refute the atheistic many-universes hypothesis, they do show that it has some severe disadvantages relative to theism. This means that if atheists adopt the atheistic many-universes hypothesis to defend their position, then atheism has become much less plausible than it used to be. Modifying a turn of phrase coined by philosopher Fred Dretske: these are inflationary times, and the cost of atheism has just gone up.

V. OVERALL CONCLUSION

In the above sections I showed there are good, objective reasons for claiming that the fine-tuning provides strong evidence for theism. I first presented an argument for thinking that the fine-tuning provides strong evidence for preferring theism over the atheistic single-universe hypothesis, and then presented a variety of different reasons for rejecting the atheistic many-universes hypothesis as an explanation of the fine-tuning. In order to help one appreciate the strength of the arguments presented, I would like to end by comparing the strength of the *core* version of the argument from the fine-tuning to what is widely regarded as the strongest atheist argument against theism, the argument from evil.[25]

Typically, the atheist argument against God based on evil takes a similar form to the core version of the fine-tuning argument. Essentially, the atheist argues that the existence of the kinds of evil we find in the world is very improbable under theism, but not improbable under atheism. Thus, by the prime principle of confirmation, they conclude that the existence of evil provides strong reasons for preferring atheism over theism.

What makes this argument weak in comparison to the core version of the fine-tuning argument is that, unlike in the case of the fine-tuning, the atheist does not have a significant objective basis for claiming that the existence of the kinds of evil we find in the world is highly improbable under theism. In fact, their judgment that it is improbable seems largely to rest on a mistake in reasoning. To see this, note that in order to show that it is improbable, atheists would have to show that it is *unlikely* that the types of evils we find in the world are necessary for any morally good, greater purpose, since if they are, then it is clearly not at all unlikely that an all good, all powerful being would create a world in which those evils are allowed to occur. But how could atheists show this without first surveying all possible morally good purposes such a being might have, something they have clearly not done? *Consequently, it seems, at most the atheist could argue that since no one has come up with any adequate purpose yet, it is unlikely that there is such a purpose.* This argument, however, is very weak, as I will now show.

The first problem with this atheist argument is that it assumes that the various explanations people have offered for why an all good God would create evil—such as the free will theodicy—ultimately fail. But even if we grant that these theodicies fail, the argument is still very weak. To see why, consider an analogy. Suppose someone tells me that there is a rattlesnake in my garden, and I examine a portion of the garden and do not find the snake. I would only be justified in concluding that there was probably no snake in the garden if either: i) I had searched at least half the garden; or ii) I had good reason to believe that if the snake were in the garden, it would likely be in the portion of the garden that I examined. If, for instance, I were randomly to pick some small segment of the garden to search and did not find the snake, I would be unjustified in concluding from my search that there was probably no snake in the garden. Similarly, if I were blindfolded and did not have any idea of how large the garden was (e.g., whether it was ten square feet or several square miles), I would be unjustified in concluding that it was unlikely that there was a rattlesnake in the garden, even if I had searched for hours with my rattlesnake-detecting dogs. Why? Because I would not have any idea of what percentage of the garden I had searched.

As with the garden example, we have no idea of how large the realm is of possible greater purposes for evil that an all good, omnipotent being

could have. Hence we do not know what proportion of this realm we have actually searched. Indeed, considering the finitude of our own minds, we have good reason to believe that we have so far only searched a small proportion, and we do not have significant reason to believe that all the purposes God might have for allowing evil would be in the proportion we searched. Thus, we have little objective basis for saying that the existence of the types of evil we find in the world is highly improbable under theism.

From the above discussion, therefore, it is clear that the relevant probability estimates in the case of the fine-tuning are much more secure than those estimates in the probabilistic version of the atheist's argument from evil, since unlike the latter, we can provide a fairly rigorous, objective basis for them based on actual calculations of the relative range of life-permitting values for the parameters of physics. (See the appendix to this chapter for a rigorous derivation of the probability of the fine-tuning under the atheistic single-universe hypothesis.) *Thus, I conclude, the core argument for preferring theism over the probabilistic version of the atheistic single-universe hypothesis is much stronger than the atheist argument from evil.*[26]

APPENDIX

In this appendix, I offer a rigorous support for premise (2) of the main argument: that is, the claim that the fine-tuning is very improbable under the atheistic single-universe hypothesis. Support for premise (2) will involve three major subsections. The first subsection will be devoted to explicating the fine-tuning of gravity since we will often use this to illustrate our arguments. Then, in our second subsection, we will show how the improbability of the fine-tuning under the atheistic single-universe hypothesis can be derived from a commonly used, objective principle of probabilistic reasoning called the *principle of indifference*. Finally, in our third subsection, we will explicate what it could mean to say that the fine-tuning is improbable given that the universe is a unique, unrepeatable event as assumed by the atheistic single-universe hypothesis. The appendix will in effect answer the common atheist objection that theists can neither *justify* the claim that the fine-tuning is improbable under the atheistic single-universe hypothesis, nor can they provide an account of what it could possibly *mean* to say that the fine-tuning is improbable.

i. The Example of Gravity

The force of gravity is determined by Newton's law $F = Gm_1m_2/r^2$. Here G is what is known as the *gravitational constant*, and is basically a number that determines the force of gravity in any given circumstance. For instance, the gravitational attraction between the moon and the earth is given by first multiplying the mass of the moon (m_1) times the mass of the earth (m_2), and then dividing by the distance between them squared (r^2). Finally, one multiplies this result by the number G to obtain the total force. Clearly the force is directly proportional to G: for example, if G were to double, the force between the moon and the earth would double.

In the previous section, we reported that some calculations indicate that the force of gravity must be fine-tuned to one part in 10^{40} in order for life to occur. What does such fine-tuning mean? To understand it, imagine a radio dial, going from 0 to $2G_0$, where G_0 represents the current value of the gravitational constant. Moreover, imagine the dial being broken up into 10^{40}—that is, ten thousand, billion, billion, billion, billion—evenly spaced tick marks. To claim that the strength of gravity must be fine-tuned to one part in 10^{40} is simply to claim that, in order for life to exist, the constant of gravity cannot vary by even one tick mark along the dial from its current value of G_0.

ii. The Principle of Indifference

In the following subsections, we will use the *principle of indifference* to justify the assertion that the fine-tuning is highly improbable under the atheistic single-universe hypothesis.

a. The Principle Stated Applied to cases in which there is a finite number of alternatives, the principle of indifference can be formulated as the claim that we should assign the same probability to what are called *equipossible alternatives*, where two or more alternatives are said to be equipossible if we have no reason to prefer one of the alternatives over any of the others. (In another version of the principle, alternatives that are relevantly symmetrical are considered equipossible and hence the ones that should be assigned equal probability.) For instance, in the case of a standard two-sided coin, we have no more reason to think that the coin will land on heads than that it will land on tails, and so we assign them each an equal probability. Since the total probability must add up to one, this means that the coin has a 0.5 chance of landing on heads and a 0.5 chance of landing on tails. Similarly, in the case of a standard six-sided die, we have no more reason to think that it will land on one number, say a 6, than any of the other numbers, such as a 4. Thus, the principle of indifference tells us to assign each possible way of landing an equal probability—namely ⅙.

The above explication of the principle applies only when there are a finite number of alternatives, for example six sides on a die. In the case of the fine-tuning, however, the alternatives are not finite but form a continuous magnitude. The value of G, for instance, conceivably could have been any number between 0 and infinity. Now, continuous magnitudes are usually thought of in terms of ranges, areas, or volumes depending on whether or not we are considering one, two, three, or more dimensions. For example, the amount of water in an 8 oz. glass could fall anywhere within the *range* 0 oz. to 8 oz., such as 6.012345645 oz. Or, the exact position that a dart hits a dart board can fall anywhere within the *area* of the dart board. With some qualifications to be discussed below, the principle of indifference becomes in the continuous case the principle that *when we have no reason to prefer any one value of a parameter over another, we should, assign equal probabilities to equal ranges, areas, or volumes*. So, for instance, suppose one aimlessly throws a dart at a dart board. Assuming the dart hits the board, what is the probability it will hit within the bull's eye? Since the dart is thrown aimlessly, we have no more reason to believe it will hit one part of the dart board than any other part. The principle of indifference, therefore, tells us that the probability of its hitting the bull's eye is the same as the probability of hitting any other part of the dart board of equal area. This means that the probability of its hitting the bull's eye is simply the ratio of the area of the bull's eye to the rest of the dart board. So, for instance, if the bull's eye forms only 5 percent of the total area of the board, then the probability of its hitting the bull's eye will be 5 percent.

b. Application to Fine-Tuning In the case of the fine-tuning, we have no more reason to think that the parameters of physics will fall within the life-permitting range than within any other range, given the atheistic single-universe hypothesis. Thus according to the principle of indifference, equal ranges of these parameters should be assigned equal probabilities. As in the case of the dart board mentioned in the last section, this means that the probability of the parameters of physics falling within the life-permitting range under the atheistic single-universe hypothesis is simply the ratio of the range of life-permitting values (the "area of the bull's eye") to the total *relevant* range of possible values (the "relevant area of the dart board").

Now physicists can make rough estimates of the range of *life-permitting* values for the parameters of physics, as discussed above in the case of gravity, for instance. But what is the "total *relevant* range of possible values"? At first one might think that this range is infinite, since the values of the parameters could conceivably be anything. This, however, is not correct, for although the possible range of values could be infinite, for most of these values we have no way of estimating whether they are life-permitting or not. We do not truly know, for example, what would happen if gravity were 10^{60} times stronger than its current value: as far as we know, a new form of matter might come into existence that could sustain life. Thus, as far as we

know, there could be other life-permitting ranges far removed from the actual values that the parameters have. Consequently, all we can say is that the life-permitting range is very, very small *relative* to the limited range of values for which we can make estimates, a range that we will here-after refer to as the "*illuminated*" range.

Fortunately, however, this limitation does not affect the overall argument. The reason is that, based on the principle of indifference, we can still say that it is very improbable for the values for the parameters of physics to have fallen in the life-permitting range *instead* of some other part of the "illuminated" range.[27] And this *improbability* is all that is actually needed for our main argument to work. To see this, consider an analogy. Suppose a dart landed on the bull's eye at the center of a huge dart board. Further, suppose that this bull's eye is surrounded by a very large empty, bull's-eye-free, area. Even if there were many other bull's eyes on the dart board, we would still take the fact that the dart landed on the bull's eye instead of some other part of the large empty area surrounding the bull's eye as strong evidence that it was aimed. Why? Because we would reason that *given that the dart landed in the empty area*, it was very improbable for it to land in the bull's eye by chance but not improbable if it were aimed. Thus, by the prime principle of confirmation, we could conclude that the dart landing on the bull's eye strongly confirms the hypothesis that it was aimed over the chance hypothesis.

c. The Principle Qualified Those who are familiar with the principle of indifference, and mathematics, will recognize that one important qualification needs to be made to the above account of how to apply the principle of indifference. (Those who are not mathematically adept might want to skip this and perhaps the next paragraph.) To understand the qualification, note that the ratio of ranges used in calculating the probability is dependent on how one parameterizes, or writes, the physical laws. For example, suppose for the sake of illustration that the range of life-permitting values for the gravitational constant is 0 to G_0, and the "illuminated" range of possible values for G is 0 to $2G_0$. Then, the ratio of life-permitting values to the range of "illuminated" possible values for the gravitational constant will be ½. Suppose, however, that one writes the law of gravity in the mathematically equivalent form of $F = \sqrt{U m_1 m_2}/r^2$ instead of $F = G m_1 m_2/r^2$, where $U = G^2$. (In this way of writing Newton's law, U becomes the new gravitational constant.) This means that $U_0 = G_0^2$, where U_0, *like* G_0, represents the actual value of U in our universe. Then, the range of life-permitting values would be 0 to U_0, and the "illuminated" range of possible values would be 0 to $4U_0$ on the U scale (which is equivalent to 0 to $2G_0$ on the G scale). Hence, calculating the ratio of life-permitting values using the U scale instead of the G scale yields a ratio of ¼ instead of ½ Indeed, for almost any ratio one chooses—such as one in which the life-permitting range is about the same size as the "illuminated" range—there exist mathematically equivalent forms of Newton's law that will yield that ratio. So, why choose the standard way of writing Newton's law to calculate the ratio instead of one in which the fine-tuning is not improbable at all?

The answer to this question is to require that the proportion used in calculating the probability be between *real* physical ranges, areas, or volumes, not merely mathematical representations of them. That is, the proportion given by the scale used in one's representation must directly correspond to the proportions actually existing in physical reality. As an illustration, consider how we might calculate the probability that a meteorite will fall in New York state instead of somewhere else in the northern, contiguous United States. One way of doing this is to take a standard map of the northern, contiguous United States, measure the area covered by New York on the map (say 2 square inches) and divide it by the total area of the map (say 30 square inches). If we were to do this, we would get approximately the right answer because the proportions on a standard map directly correspond to the actual proportions of land areas in the United States.[28] On the other hand, suppose we had a map made by some lover of the east coast in

which, because of the scale used, the east coast took up half the map. If we used the proportions of areas as represented by this map we would get the wrong answer since the scale used would not correspond to real proportions of land areas. Applied to the fine-tuning, this means that our calculations of these proportions must be done using parameters that directly correspond to physical quantities in order to yield valid probabilities. In the case of gravity, for instance, the gravitational constant G directly corresponds to the force between two unit masses a unit distance apart, whereas U does not. (Instead, U corresponds to the square of the force.) Thus, G is the correct parameter to use in calculating the probability.[29]

d. Support for Principle   Finally, although the principle of indifference has been criticized on various grounds, several powerful reasons can be offered for its soundness if it is restricted in the ways explained in the last subsection. First, it has an extraordinarily wide range of applicability. As Roy Weatherford notes in his book, *Philosophical Foundations of Probability Theory*, "an astonishing number of extremely complex problems in probability theory have been solved, and usefully so, by calculations based entirely on the assumption of equiprobable alternatives [that is, the principle of indifference]."[30] Second, at least for the discrete case, the principle can be given a significant theoretical grounding in information theory, being derivable from Shannon's important and well-known measure of *information*, or *negative* entropy.[31] Finally, in certain everyday cases the principle of indifference seems the only justification we have for assigning probability. To illustrate, suppose that in the last ten minutes a factory produced the first fifty-sided die ever produced. Further suppose that every side of the die is (macroscopically) perfectly symmetrical with every other side, except for there being different numbers printed on each side. (The die we are imagining is like a fair six-sided die except that it has fifty sides instead of six.) Now, we all immediately know that upon being rolled the probability of the die coming up on any given side is one in fifty. Yet, we do not know this directly from experience with fifty-sided dice, since by hypothesis no one has yet rolled such dice to determine the relative frequency with which they come up on each side. Rather, it seems our only justification for assigning this probability is the principle of indifference: that is, given that every side of the die is relevantly macroscopically symmetrical with every other side, we have no reason to believe that the die will land on one side over any other side, and thus we assign them all an equal probability of one in fifty.[32]

iii. The Meaning of Probability

In the last section we used the principle of indifference to rigorously justify the claim that the fine-tuning is highly improbable under the atheistic single-universe hypothesis. We did not explain, however, what it could *mean* to say that it is improbable, especially given that the universe is a unique, unrepeatable event. To address this issue, we shall now show how the probability invoked in the fine-tuning argument can be straightforwardly understood either as what could be called *classical probability* or as what is known as *epistemic probability*.

Classical Probability The *classical conception of probability* defines probability in terms of the ratio of number of "favorable cases" to the total number of equipossible cases.[33] Thus, for instance, to say the probability of a die coming up "4" is one out of six is simply to say that the number of ways a die could come up "4" is one-sixth the number of equipossible ways it could come up. Extending this definition to the continuous case, classical probability can be defined in terms of the relevant ratio of ranges, areas, or volumes over which the principle of indifference applies. Thus, under this extended definition, to say that the probability of the parameters of physics falling into the life-permitting value is very improbable simply *means* that the ratio of life-permitting values to the range of possible values is very, very small. Finally, notice that this definition of probability implies the principle of indifference, and thus we can be certain

that the principle of indifference holds for classical probability.

Epistemic Probability *Epistemic probability* is a widely recognized type of probability that applies to claims, statements, and hypotheses—that is, what philosophers call propositions.[34] (A proposition is any claim, assertion, statement, or hypothesis about the world.) Roughly, the epistemic probability of a proposition can be thought of as the degree of credence—that is, degree of confidence or belief—we rationally should have in the proposition. Put differently, epistemic probability is a measure of our rational degree of belief under a condition of ignorance concerning whether a proposition is true or false. For example, when one says that the special theory of relativity is probably true, one is making a statement of epistemic probability. After all, the theory is actually either true or false. But, we do not know for sure whether it is true or false, so we say it is probably true to indicate that we should put more confidence in its being true than in its being false. It is also commonly argued that the probability of a coin toss is best understood as a case of epistemic probability. Since the side the coin will land on is determined by the laws of physics, it is argued that our assignment of probability is simply a measure of our rational expectations concerning which side the coin will land on.

Besides epistemic probability sumpliciter, philosophers also speak of what is known as the *conditional* epistemic probability of one proposition on another. The conditional epistemic probability of a proposition R on another proposition S—written as $P(R/S)$—can be defined as the degree to which the proposition S *of itself* should rationally lead us to expect that R is true. For example, there is a high conditional probability that it will rain today on the hypothesis that the weatherman has predicted a 100 percent chance of rain, whereas there is a low conditional probability that it will rain today on the hypothesis that the weatherman has predicted only a 2 percent chance of rain. That is, the hypothesis that the weatherman has predicted a 100 percent chance of rain today should strongly lead us to expect that it will rain, whereas the hypothesis that the weatherman has predicted a 2 percent chance should lead us to expect that it will not rain. Under the epistemic conception of probability, therefore, the statement that *the fine-tuning of the Cosmos is very improbable under the atheistic single-universe hypothesis* makes perfect sense: it is to be understood as making a statement about the degree to which the atheistic single-universe hypothesis would or should, of *itself*, rationally lead us to expect the cosmic fine-tuning.[35]

Conclusion

The above discussion shows that we have at least two ways of understanding improbability invoked in our main argument: as classical probability or epistemic probability. This undercuts the common atheist objection that it is meaningless to speak of the probability of the fine-tuning under the atheistic single-universe hypothesis since under this hypothesis the universe is not a repeatable event.

NOTES

1. Freeman Dyson, *Disturbing the Universe* (New York: Harper and Row, 1979), 251.

2. Paul Davies, *The Cosmic Blueprint: New Discoveries in Nature's Creative Ability to Order the Universe* (New York: Simon and Schuster, 1988), 203.

3. Fred Hoyle, in *Religion and the Scientists* (1959); quoted in *The Anthropic Cosmological Principle*, ed. John Barrow and Frank Tipler (Oxford: Oxford University Press, 1986), 22.

4. See Paul Davies, *The Accidental Universe* (Cambridge: Cambridge University Press, 1982), 90–91. John Jefferson Davis, "The Design Argument, Cosmic 'Fine-tuning,' and the Anthropic Principle," *The International Journal of Philosophy of Religion* 22 (1987): 140.

5. John Leslie, *Universes* (New York: Routledge, 1989), 4, 35; *Anthropic Cosmological Principle*, 322.

6. Paul Davies, *Superforce: The Search for a Grand Unified Theory of Nature* (New York: Simon and Schuster, 1984), 242.

7. Leslie, *Universes*, 39–40.

8. John Leslie, "How to Draw Conclusion from a Fine-Tuned Cosmos," in *Physics, Philosophy and Theology: A Common Quest for Understanding*, ed. Robert Russell et al. (Vatican City State: Vatican Observatory Press, 1988), 299.

9. Leslie, "How to Draw Conclusions," 300.

10. For those familiar with the probability calculus, a precise statement of the degree to which evidence counts in favor of one hypothesis over another can be given in terms of the odds form of Bayes's Theorem: that is, $P(H_1/E)/P(H_2/E) = [P(H_1/P$

$(H_2)] \times [P(E/H_1)/(E/H_2)]$. The general version of the principle stated here, however, does not require the applicability or truth of Bayes's Theorem.

11. Those with some training in probability theory will want to note that the kind of probability invoked here is what philosophers call *epistemic probability*, which is a measure of the rational degree of belief we should have in a proposition (see appendix, subsection iii). Since our rational degree of belief in a necessary truth can be less than 1, we can sensibly speak of it being improbable for a given law of nature to exist necessarily. For example, we can speak of an unproven mathematical hypothesis—such as Goldbach's conjecture that every even number greater than 6 is the sum of two odd primes—as being probably true or probably false given our current evidence, even though all mathematical hypotheses are either necessarily true or necessarily false.

12. Leslie, "How to Draw Conclusion," 304.

13. George Smith, "The Case Against God," reprinted in *An Anthology of Atheism and Rationalism*, ed. Gordon Stein (Buffalo: Prometheus Press, 1980), 56.

14. J. J. C. Smart, "Laws of Nature and Cosmic Coincidence," *The Philosophical Quarterly* 35 (July 1985): 275–76, italics added.

15. I define a "universe" as any region of space-time that is disconnected from other regions in such a way that the parameters of physics in that region could differ significantly from the other regions.

16. Quentin Smith, "World Ensemble Explanations," *Pacific Philosophical Quarterly* 67 (1986): 82.

17. Moreover, the advocate of the atheistic many-universes hypothesis could not avoid this problem by hypothesizing that the many universes always existed as "brute fact" without being produced by a universe generator. This would simply add to the problem: it would not only leave unexplained the fine-tuning or our own universe, but would leave unexplained the existence of these other universes.

18. Leslie, *Universes*, 59.

19. Dyson, *Disturbing the Universe*, 251.

20. Chapter 6, "Beautiful Theories."

21. Paul Dirac, "The Evolution of the Physicist's Picture of Nature," *Scientific American* (May 1963): 47.

22. Davies, *Superforce*, 235–36.

23. This connection between order and probability, and the second law of thermodynamics in general, is given a precise formulation in a branch of fundamental physics called *statistical mechanics*, according to which a state of high order represents a very improbable state, and a state of disorder represents a highly probable state.

24. See Lawrence Sklar, *Physics and Chance: Philosophical Issues in the Foundation of Statistical Mechanics* (Cambridge: Cambridge University Press, 1993), chapter 8, for a review of the nontheistic explanations for the ordered arrangement of the universe and the severe difficulties they face.

25. A more thorough discussion of the atheist argument from evil is presented in Daniel Howard-Snyder's chapter (pp. 76–115), and a discussion of other atheistic arguments is given in John O'Leary-Hawthorn's chapter (pp. 116–34).

26. This work was made possible in part by a Discovery Institute grant for the fiscal year 1997–1998.

27. In the language of probability theory, this sort of probability is known as a conditional probability. In the case of G, calculations indicate that this conditional probability of the fine-tuning would be less than 10^{-40} since the life-permitting range is less than 10^{-40} of the range 0 to $2G_0$, the latter range being certainly smaller than the total "illuminated" range for G.

28. I say "approximately right" because in this case the principle of indifference only applies to strips of land that are the same distance from the equator. The reason for this is that only strips of land equidistant from the equator are truly symmetrical with regard to the motion of the earth. Since the northern, contiguous United States are all about the same distance from the equator, equal land areas should be assigned approximately equal probabilities.

29. This solution will not always work since, as the well-known Bertrand Paradoxes illustrate (e.g., see Roy Weatherford, *Foundations of Probability Theory* [Boston: Routledge and Kegan Paul, 1982], 56), sometimes there are two equally good and conflicting parameters that directly correspond to a physical quantity and to which the principle of indifference applies. In these cases, at best we can say that the probability is somewhere between that given by the two conflicting parameters. This problem, however, typically does not seem to arise for most cases of fine-tuning. Also, it should be noted that the principle of indifference applies best to *classical* or *epistemic* probability, not other kinds of probability such as *relative frequency*. (See subsection iii below.)

30. Weatherford, *Probability Theory*, 35.

31. Sklar, *Physics and Chance*, 191; Bas van Fraassen, *Laws and Symmetry* (Oxford: Oxford University Press, 1989), 345.

32. Of course, one could claim that our experience with items such as coins and dice teaches us that whenever two alternatives are macroscopically symmetrical, we should assign them an equal probability, unless we have a particular reason not to. All this claim implies, however, is that we have experiential justification for the principle of indifference, and thus it does not take away from our main point that in certain practical situations we must rely on the principle of indifference to justify our assignment of probability.

33. See Weatherford, *Probability Theory*, ch. 2.

34. For an in-depth discussion of epistemic probability, see Richard Swinburne, *An Introduction to Confirmation Theory* (London: Methuen, 1973); Ian Hacking, *The Emergence of Probability: A Philosophical Study of Early Ideas About Probability, Induction and Statistical Inference* (Cambridge: Cambridge University Press, 1975); and Alvin Plantinga, *Warrant and Proper Function* (Oxford: Oxford University Press, 1993), chapters 8 and 9.

35. It should be noted here that this rational degree of expectation should not be confused with the degree to which one should expect the parameters of physics to fall within the life-permitting range if one believed the atheistic single-universe hypothesis. For even those who believe in this atheistic hypothesis should expect the parameters of physics to be life-permitting since this follows from the fact that we are alive. Rather, the conditional epistemic probability in this case is the degree to which the atheistic single-universe hypothesis *of itself* should lead us to expect parameters of physics to be life-permitting. This means that in assessing the conditional epistemic probability in this and other similar cases, one must exclude contributions to our expectations arising from other information we have, such as that we are alive. In the case at hand, one way of doing this is by means of the following sort of thought experiment. Imagine a disembodied being with mental capacities and a knowledge of physics comparable to that of the most intelligent physicists alive today, except that the being does not know whether the parameters of physics are within the life-permitting range. Further, suppose that this disembodied being believed in the atheistic single-universe hypothesis. Then, the degree that being should rationally expect the parameters of physics to be life-permitting will be equal to our conditional epistemic probability, since its expectation is solely a result of its belief in the atheistic single-universe hypothesis, not other factors such as its awareness of its own existence.

IV.B.1

Evil and Omnipotence

J. L. MACKIE

John L. Mackie (1917–1981) was born in Australia and taught at Oxford University until his death. He made important contributions to the fields of metaphysics, epistemology, ethics, and philosophy of religion. Among his works are The Cement of the Universe *(1974),* Ethics: Inventing Right and Wrong *(1977), and* The Miracle of Theism *(1982). In this essay, Mackie argues that the argument from evil demonstrates the incoherence of theism. If there is a God who is all-powerful and completely good, he will be able and willing to eliminate all evil in the world. But there is evil, so no God exists.*

The traditional arguments for the existence of God have been fairly thoroughly criticised by philosophers. But the theologian can, if he wishes, accept this criticism. He can admit that no rational proof of God's existence is possible. And he can still retain all that is essential to his position, by holding that God's existence is known in some other, nonrational way. I think, however, that a more telling criticism can be made by way of the traditional problem of evil. Here it can be shown, not that religious beliefs lack rational support, but that they are positively irrational, that the several parts of the essential theological doctrine are inconsistent with one another, so that the theologian can maintain his position as a whole only by a much more extreme rejection of reason than in the former case. He must now be prepared to believe, not merely what cannot be proved, but what can be *disproved* from other beliefs that he also holds.

The problem of evil, in the sense in which I shall be using the phrase, is a problem only for someone who believes that there is a God who is both omnipotent and wholly good. And it is a logical problem, the problem of clarifying and reconciling a number of beliefs: it is not a scientific problem that might be solved by further observations, or a practical problem that might be solved by a decision or an action. These points are obvious; I mention them only because they are sometimes ignored by theologians, who sometimes parry a statement of the problem with such remarks as "Well, can you solve the problem yourself?" or "This is a mystery which may be revealed to us later" or "Evil is something to be faced and overcome, not to be merely discussed."

In its simplest form the problem is this: God is omnipotent; God is wholly good; and yet evil exists. There seems to be some contradiction between these three propositions, so that if any two of them were true the third would be false. But at the same time all three are essential parts of most theological positions: the theologian, it seems, at once *must* adhere and *cannot consistently* adhere to all three. (The problem does not arise only for theists, but I shall discuss it in the form in which it presents itself for ordinary theism.)

However, the contradiction does not arise immediately; to show it we need some additional

From *Mind*, 64 (1955): 200–212. Reprinted by permission of Oxford University Press.

premises, or perhaps some quasi-logical rules connecting the terms "good, evil," and "omnipotent." These additional principles are that good is opposed to evil, in such a way that a good thing always eliminates evil as far as it can, and that there are no limits to what an omnipotent thing can do. From these it follows that a good omnipotent thing eliminates evil completely, and then the propositions that a good omnipotent thing exists, and that evil exists, are incompatible.

A. ADEQUATE SOLUTIONS

Now once the problem is fully stated it is clear that it can be solved, in the sense that the problem will not arise if one gives up at least one of the propositions that constitute it. If you are prepared to say that God is not wholly good, or not quite omnipotent, or that evil does not exist, or that good is not opposed to the kind of evil that exists, or that there are limits to what an omnipotent thing can do, then the problem of evil will not arise for you.

There are, then, quite a number of adequate solutions of the problem of evil, and some of these have been adopted, or almost adopted, by various thinkers. For example, a few have been prepared to deny God's omnipotence, and rather more have been prepared to keep the term "omnipotence" but severely to restrict its meaning, recording quite a number of things that an omnipotent being cannot do. Some have said that evil is an illusion, perhaps because they held that the whole world of temporal, changing things is an illusion, and that what we call evil belongs only to this world, or perhaps because they held that although temporal things are much as we see them, those that we call evil are not really evil. Some have said that what we call evil is merely the privation of good, that evil in a positive sense, evil that would really be opposed to good, does not exist. Many have agreed with Pope that disorder is harmony not understood, and that partial evil is universal good. Whether any of these views is true is, of course, another question. But each of them gives

an adequate solution of the problem of evil in the sense that if you accept it this problem does not arise for you, though you may, of course, have *other* problems to face.

But often enough these adequate solutions are only *almost* adopted. The thinkers who restrict God's power, but keep the term "omnipotence," may reasonably be suspected of thinking, in other contexts, that his power is really unlimited. Those who say that evil is an illusion may also be thinking, inconsistently, that this illusion is itself an evil. Those who say that "evil" is merely privation of good may also be thinking, inconsistently, that privation of good is an evil. (The fallacy here is akin to some forms of the "naturalistic fallacy" in ethics, where some think, for example, that "good" is just what contributes to evolutionary progress, and that evolutionary progress is itself good.) If Pope meant what he said in the first line of his couplet, that "disorder" is only harmony not understood, the "partial evil" of the second line must, for consistency, mean "that which, taken in isolation, falsely appears to be evil," but it would more naturally mean "that which, in isolation, really is evil." The second line, in fact, hesitates between two views, that "partial evil" isn't really evil, since only the universal quality is real, and that "partial evil" is really an evil, but only a little one.

In addition, therefore, to adequate solutions, we must recognise unsatisfactorily inconsistent solutions, in which there is only a half-hearted or temporary rejection of one of the propositions which together constitute the problem. In these, one of the constituent propositions is explicitly rejected, but it is covertly re-asserted or assumed elsewhere in the system.

B. FALLACIOUS SOLUTIONS

Besides these half-hearted solutions, which explicitly reject but implicitly assert one of the constituent propositions, there are definitely fallacious solutions which explicitly maintain all the constituent propositions, but implicitly reject at least one of them in the course of the argument that explains away the problem of evil.

There are, in fact, many so-called solutions which purport to remove the contradiction without abandoning any of its constituent propositions. These must be fallacious as we can see from the very statement of the problem, but it is not so easy to see in each case precisely where the fallacy lies. I suggest that in all cases the fallacy has the general form suggested above: in order to solve the problem one (or perhaps more) of its constituent propositions is given up, but in such a way that it appears to have been retained, and can therefore be asserted without qualification in other contexts. Sometimes there is a further complication: the supposed solution moves to and fro between, say, two of the constituent propositions, at one point asserting the first of these but covertly abandoning the second, at another point asserting the second but covertly abandoning the first. These fallacious solutions often turn upon some equivocation with the words "good" and "evil," or upon some vagueness about the way in which good and evil are opposed to one another, or about how much is meant by "omnipotence." I propose to examine some of these so-called solutions, and to exhibit their fallacies in detail. Incidentally, I shall also be considering whether an adequate solution could be reached by a minor modification of one or more of the constituent propositions, which would, however, still satisfy all the essential requirements of ordinary theism.

(1) "Good cannot exist without evil" or "Evil is necessary as a counterpart to good."

It is sometimes suggested that evil is necessary as a counterpart to good, that if there were no evil there could be no good either, and that this solves the problem of evil. It is true that it points to an answer to the question "Why should there be evil?" But it does so only by qualifying some of the propositions that constitute the problem.

First, it sets a limit to what God can do, saying that God *cannot* create good without simultaneously creating evil, and this means either that God is not omnipotent or that there are *some* limits to what an omnipotent thing can do. It may be replied that these limits are always presupposed, that omnipotence has never meant the power to do what is logically impossible, and on the present view the existence of good without evil would be a logical impossibility. This interpretation of omnipotence may, indeed, be accepted as a modification of our original account which does not reject anything that is essential to theism, and I shall in general assume it in the subsequent discussion. It is, perhaps, the most common theistic view, but I think that some theists at least have maintained that God can do what is logically impossible. Many theists, at any rate, have held that logic itself is created or laid down by God, that logic is the way in which God arbitrarily chooses to think. (This is, of course, parallel to the ethical view that morally right actions are those which God arbitrarily chooses to command, and the two views encounter similar difficulties.) And this account of logic is clearly inconsistent with the view that God is bound by logical necessities—unless it is possible for an omnipotent being to bind himself, an issue which we shall consider later, when we come to the Paradox of Omnipotence. This solution of the problem of evil cannot, therefore, be consistently adopted along with the view that logic is itself created by God.

But, secondly, this solution denies that evil is opposed to good in our original sense. If good and evil are counterparts, a good thing will not "eliminate evil as far as it can." Indeed, this view suggests that good and evil are not strictly qualities of things at all. Perhaps the suggestion is that good and evil are related in much the same way as great and small. Certainly, when the term "great" is used relatively as a condensation of "greater than so-and-so," and "small" is used correspondingly, greatness and smallness are counterparts and cannot exist without each other. But in this sense greatness is not a quality, not an intrinsic feature of anything; and it would be absurd to think of a movement in favour of greatness and against smallness in this sense. Such a movement would be self-defeating, since relative greatness can be promoted only by a simultaneous promotion of relative smallness. I feel sure that no theists would be content to regard God's goodness as analogous to this—as if what he supports were not the *good* but the *better*, and if he had the paradoxical aim that all things should be better than other things.

This point is obscured by the fact that "great" and "small" seem to have an absolute as well as a relative sense. I cannot discuss here whether there is absolute magnitude or not, but if there is, there could be an absolute sense for "great," it could mean of at least a certain size, and it would make sense to speak of all things getting bigger, of a universe that was expanding all over, and therefore it would make sense to speak of promoting greatness. But in *this* sense great and small are not logically necessary counterparts: either quality could exist without the other. There would be no logical impossibility in everything's being small or in everything's being great.

Neither in the absolute nor in the relative sense, then, of "great" and "small" do these terms provide an analogy of the sort that would be needed to support this solution of the problem of evil. In neither case are greatness and smallness *both* necessary counterparts *and* mutually opposed forces or possible objects for support and attack.

It may be replied that good and evil are necessary counterparts in the same way as any quality and its logical opposite: redness can occur, it is suggested, only if non-redness also occurs. But unless evil is merely the privation of good, they are not logical opposites, and some further argument would be needed to show that they are counterparts in the same way as genuine logical opposites. Let us assume that this could be given. There is still doubt of the correctness of the metaphysical principle that a quality must have a real opposite: I suggest that it is not really impossible that everything should be, say, red, that the truth is merely that if everything were red we should not notice redness, and so we should have no word "red"; we observe and give names to qualities only if they have real opposites. If so, the principle that a term must have an opposite would belong only to our language or to our thought, and would not be an ontological principle, and correspondingly, the rule that good cannot exist without evil would not state a logical

necessity of a sort that God would just have to put up with. God might have made everything good, though *we* should not have noticed it if he had.

But, finally, even if we concede that this is an ontological principle, it will provide a solution for the problem of evil only if one is prepared to say, "Evil exists, but only just enough evil to serve as the counterpart of good." I doubt whether any theist will accept this. After all, the ontological requirement that non-redness should occur would be satisfied even if all the universe, except for a minute speck, were red, and, if there were a corresponding requirement for evil as a counterpart to good, a minute dose of evil would presumably do. But theists are not usually willing to say, in all contexts, that all the evil that occurs is a minute and necessary dose.

(2) "Evil is necessary as a means to good."

It is sometimes suggested that evil is necessary for good not as a counterpart but as a means. In its simple form this has little plausibility as a solution of the problem of evil, since it obviously implies a severe restriction of God's power. It would be a *causal* law that you cannot have a certain end without a certain means, so that if God has to introduce evil as a means to good, he must be subject to at least some causal laws. This certainly conflicts with what a theist normally means by omnipotence. This view of God as limited by causal laws also conflicts with the view that causal laws are themselves made by God, which is more widely held than the corresponding view about the laws of logic. This conflict would, indeed, be resolved if it were possible for an omnipotent being to bind himself, and this possibility has still to be considered. Unless a favourable answer can be given to this question, the suggestion that evil is necessary as a means to good solves the problem of evil only by denying one of its constituent propositions, either that God is omnipotent or that "omnipotent" means what it says.

(3) "The universe is better with some evil in it than it could be if there were no evil."

Much more important is a solution which at first seems to be a mere variant of the previous one, that evil may contribute to the goodness of a whole in which it is found, so that the universe as a whole is better as it is, with some evil in it, than it would be if there were no evil. This solution may be developed in either of two ways. It may be supported by an aesthetic analogy, by the fact that contrasts heighten beauty, that in a musical work, for example, there may occur discords which somehow add to the beauty of the work as a whole. Alternatively, it may be worked out in connection with the notion of progress, that the best possible organization of the universe will not be static, but progressive, that the gradual overcoming of evil by good is really a finer thing than would be the eternal unchallenged supremacy of good.

In either case, this solution usually starts from the assumption that the evil whose existence gives rise to the problem of evil is primarily what is called physical evil, that is to say, pain. In Hume's rather half-hearted presentation of the problem of evil, the evils that he stresses are pain and disease, and those who reply to him argue that the existence of pain and disease makes possible the existence of sympathy, benevolence, heroism, and the gradually successful struggle of doctors and reformers to overcome these evils. In fact, theists often seize the opportunity to accuse those who stress the problem of evil of taking a low, materialistic view of good and evil, equating these with pleasure and pain, and of ignoring the more spiritual goods which can arise in the struggle against evils.

But let us see exactly what is being done here. Let us call pain and misery "first order evil" or "evil (1)." What contrasts with this, namely, pleasure and happiness, will be called "first order good" or "good (1)." Distinct from this is "second order good" or "good (2)" which somehow emerges in a complex situation in which evil (1) is a necessary component—logically not merely causally, necessary. (Exactly *how* it emerges does not matter: in the crudest version of this solution good (2) is simply the heightening of happiness by the contrast with misery, in other versions it includes sympathy with suffering, heroism in facing danger, and the gradual decrease of first order evil and increase of

first order good.) It is also being assumed that second order good is more important than first order good or evil, in particular that it more than outweighs the first order evil it involves.

Now this is a particularly subtle attempt to solve the problem of evil. It defends God's goodness and omnipotence on the ground that (on a sufficiently long view) this is the best of all logically possible worlds, because it includes the important second order goods, and yet it admits that real evils, namely first order evils, exist. But does it still hold that good and evil are opposed? Not, clearly, in the sense that we set out originally: good does not tend to eliminate evil in general. Instead, we have a modified, a more complex pattern. First order good (*e.g.* happiness) *contrasts with* first order evil (*e.g.* misery): these two are opposed in a fairly mechanical way; some second order goods (*e.g.* benevolence) try to maximize first order good and minimize first order evil; but God's goodness is not this, it is rather the will to maximize *second* order good. We might, therefore, call God's goodness an example of a third order goodness, or good (3). While this account is different from our original one, it might well be held to be an improvement on it, to give a more accurate description of the way in which good is opposed to evil, and to be consistent with the essential theist position.

There might, however, be several objections to this solution.

First, some might argue that such qualities as benevolence—and *a fortiori* the third order goodness which promotes benevolence—have a merely derivative value, that they are not higher sorts of good, but merely means to good (1), that is, to happiness, so that it would be absurd for God to keep misery in existence in order to make possible the virtues of benevolence, heroism, etc. The theist who adopts the present solution must, of course, deny this, but he can do so with some plausibility, so I should not press this objection.

Secondly, it follows from this solution that God is not in our sense benevolent or sympathetic: he is not concerned to minimize evil (1), but only to promote good (2); and this might be a disturbing conclusion for some theists.

But, thirdly, the fatal objection is this. Our analysis shows clearly the possibility of the existence of a *second* order evil, an evil (2) contrasting with good (2) as evil (1) contrasts with good (1). This would include malevolence, cruelty, callousness, cowardice, and states in which good (1) is decreasing and evil (1) increasing. And just as good (2) is held to be the important kind of good, the kind that God is concerned to promote, so evil (2) will, by analogy, be the important kind of evil, the kind which God, if he were wholly good and omnipotent, would eliminate. And yet evil (2) plainly exists, and indeed most theists (in other contexts) stress its existence more than that of evil (1). We should, therefore, state the problem of evil in terms of second order evil, and against this form of the problem the present solution is useless.

An attempt might be made to use this solution again, at a higher level, to explain the occurrence of evil (2); indeed the next main solution that we shall examine does just this, with the help of some new notions. Without any fresh notions, such a solution would have little plausibility: for example, we could hardly say that the really important good was a good (3), such as the increase of benevolence in proportion to cruelty, which logically required for its occurrence the occurrence of some second order evil. But even if evil (2) could be explained in this way, it is fairly clear that there would be third order evils contrasting with this third order good: and we should be well on the way to an infinite regress, where the solution of a problem of evil, stated in terms of evil (*n*), indicated the existence of an evil (*n* + 1), and a further problem to be solved.

(4)   "Evil is due to human free will."

Perhaps the most important proposed solution of the problem of evil is that evil is not to be ascribed to God at all, but to the independent actions of human beings, supposed to have been endowed by God with freedom of the will. This solution may be combined with the preceding one: first order evil (*e.g.* pain) may be justified as a logically necessary component in second order good (*e.g.* sympathy) while second order evil (*e.g.* cruelty) is not *justified*, but is so ascribed to human beings

that God cannot be held responsible for it. This combination evades my third criticism of the preceding solution.

The free will solution also involves the preceding solution at a higher level. To explain why a wholly good God gave men free will although it would lead to some important evils, it must be argued that it is better on the whole that men should act freely, and sometimes err, than that they should be innocent automata, acting rightly in a wholly determined way. Freedom that is to say, is now treated as a third order good, and as being more valuable than second order goods (such as sympathy and heroism) would be if they were deterministically produced, and it is being assumed that second order evils, such as cruelty, are logically necessary accompaniments of freedom, just as pain is a logically necessary precondition of sympathy.

I think that this solution is unsatisfactory primarily because of the incoherence of the notion of freedom of the will: but I cannot discuss this topic adequately here, although some of my criticisms will touch upon it.

First I should query the assumption that second order evils are logically necessary accompaniments of freedom. I should ask this: if God has made men such that in their free choices they sometimes prefer what is good and sometimes what is evil, why could he not have made men such that they always freely choose the good? If there is no logical impossibility in a man's freely choosing the good on one, or on several, occasions, there cannot be a logical impossibility in his freely choosing the good on every occasion. God was not, then, faced with a choice between making innocent automata and making beings who, in acting freely, would sometimes go wrong: there was open to him the obviously better possibility of making beings who would act freely but always go right. Clearly, his failure to avail himself of this possibility is inconsistent with his being both omnipotent and wholly good.

If it is replied that this objection is absurd, that the making of some wrong choices is logically necessary for freedom, it would seem that "freedom" must here mean complete randomness or indeterminacy, including randomness with regard to the alternatives good and evil, in other words that men's choices and consequent actions can be "free" only if they are not determined by their characters. Only on this assumption can God escape the responsibility for men's actions; for if he made them as they are, but did not determine their wrong choices, this can only be because the wrong choices are not determined by men as they are. But then if freedom is randomness, how can it be a characteristic of *will?* And, still more, how can it be the most important good? What value or merit would there be in free choices if these were random actions which were not determined by the nature of the agent?

I conclude that to make this solution plausible two different senses of "freedom" must be confused, one sense which will justify the view that freedom is a third order good, more valuable than other goods would be without it, and another sense, sheer randomness, to prevent us from ascribing to God a decision to make men such that they sometimes go wrong when he might have made them such that they would always freely go right.

This criticism is sufficient to dispose of this solution. But besides this there is a fundamental difficulty in the notion of an omnipotent God creating men with free will, for if men's wills are really free this must mean that even God cannot control them, that is, that God is no longer omnipotent. It may be objected that God's gift of freedom to men does not mean that he *cannot* control their wills, but that he always *refrains* from controlling their wills. But why, we may ask, should God refrain from controlling evil wills? Why should he not leave men free to will rightly, but intervene when he sees them beginning to will wrongly? If God could do this, but does not, and if he is wholly good, the only explanation could be that even a wrong free act of will is not really evil, that its freedom is a value which outweighs its wrongness, so that there would be a loss of value if God took away the wrongness and the freedom together. But this is utterly opposed to what theists say about sin in other contexts. The present solution of the problem of evil, then, can be maintained only in the form that God has made men so free that he *cannot* control their wills.

This leads us to what I call the Paradox of Omnipotence: can an omnipotent being make things which he cannot subsequently control? Or, what is practically equivalent to this, can an omnipotent being make rules which then bind himself? (These are practically equivalent because any such rules could be regarded as setting certain things beyond his control, and *vice versa*.) The second of these formulations is relevant to the suggestions that we have already met, that an omnipotent God creates the rules of logic or causal laws, and is then bound by them.

It is clear that this is a paradox: the questions cannot be answered satisfactorily either in the affirmative or in the negative. If we answer "Yes," it follows that if God actually makes things which he cannot control, or makes rules which bind himself, he is not omnipotent once he has made them: there are then things which he cannot do. But if we answer "No," we are immediately asserting that there are things which he cannot do, that is to say that he is already not omnipotent.

It cannot be replied that the question which sets this paradox is not a proper question. It would make perfectly good sense to say that a human mechanic has made a machine which he cannot control: if there is any difficulty about the question it lies in the notion of omnipotence itself.

This, incidentally, shows that although we have approached this paradox from the free will theory, it is equally a problem for a theological determinist. No one thinks that machines have free will, yet they may well be beyond the control of their makers. The determinist might reply that anyone who makes anything determines its ways of acting, and so determines its subsequent behaviour: even the human mechanic does this by his *choice* of materials and structure for his machine, though he does not know all about either of these: the mechanic thus determines, though he may not foresee, his machine's actions. And since God is omniscient, and since his creation of things is total, he both determines and foresees the ways in which his creatures will act. We may grant this, but it is beside the point. The question is not whether God *originally* determined the future actions of his creatures, but whether he can *subsequently* control their actions, or whether he was able in his original creation to put things beyond his subsequent control. Even on determinist principles the answers "Yes" and "No" are equally irreconcilable with God's omnipotence.

Before suggesting a solution of this paradox, I would point out that there is a parallel Paradox of Sovereignty. Can a legal sovereign make a law restricting its own future legislative power? For example, could the British parliament make a law forbidding any future parliament to socialise banking, and also forbidding the future repeal of this law itself? Or could the British parliament, which was legally sovereign in Australia in, say, 1899, pass a valid law, or series of laws, which made it no longer sovereign in 1933? Again, neither the affirmative nor the negative answer is really satisfactory. If we were to answer "Yes," we should be admitting the validity of a law which, if it were actually made, would mean that parliament was no longer sovereign. If we were to answer "No," we should be admitting that there is a law, not logically absurd, which parliament cannot validly make, that is, that parliament is not now a legal sovereign. This paradox can be solved in the following way. We should distinguish between first order laws, that is laws governing the actions of individuals and bodies other than the legislature, and second order laws, that is laws about laws, laws governing the actions of the legislature itself. Correspondingly, we should distinguish two orders of sovereignty, first order sovereignty (sovereignty (1)) which is unlimited authority to make first order laws, and second order sovereignty (sovereignty (2)) which is unlimited authority to make second order laws. If we say that parliament is sovereign we might mean that any parliament at any time has sovereignty (1), or we might mean that parliament has both sovereignty (1) and sovereignty (2) at present, but we cannot without contradiction mean both that the present parliament has sovereignty (2) and that every parliament at every time has sovereignty (1), for if the present parliament has sovereignty (2) it

may use it to take away the sovereignty (1) of later parliaments. What the paradox shows is that we cannot ascribe to any continuing institution legal sovereignty in an inclusive sense.

The analogy between omnipotence and sovereignty shows that the paradox of omnipotence can be solved in a similar way. We must distinguish between first order omnipotence (omnipotence (1)), that is unlimited power to act, and second order omnipotence (omnipotence (2)), that is unlimited power to determine what powers to act things shall have. Then we could consistently say that God all the time has omnipotence (1), but if so no beings at any time have powers to act independently of God. Or we could say that God at one time had omnipotence (2), and used it to assign independent powers to act to certain things, so that God thereafter did not have omnipotence (1). But what the paradox shows is that we cannot consistently ascribe to any continuing being omnipotence in an inclusive sense.

An alternative solution of this paradox would be simply to deny that God is a continuing being, that any times can be assigned to his actions at all. But on this assumption (which also has difficulties of its own) no meaning can be given to the assertion that God made men with wills so free that he could not control them. The paradox of omnipotence can be avoided by putting God outside time, but the free will solution of the problem of evil cannot be saved in this way, and equally it remains impossible to hold that an omnipotent God *binds himself* by causal or logical laws.

CONCLUSION

Of the proposed solutions of the problem of evil which we have examined, none has stood up to criticism. There may be other solutions which require examination, but this study strongly suggests that there is no valid solution of the problem which does not modify at least one of the constituent propositions in a way which would seriously affect the essential core of the theistic position.

Quite apart from the problem of evil, the paradox of omnipotence has shown that God's omnipotence must in any case be restricted in one way or another, that unqualified omnipotence cannot be ascribed to any being that continues through time. And if God and his actions are not in time, can omnipotence, or power of any sort, be meaningfully ascribed to him?

Reprinted from "The Problem of Evil and Some Varieties of Atheism," *American Philosophical Quarterly* 16 (1979) by permission. Footnotes edited.

IV.C.1

The Free Will Defense

ALVIN PLANTINGA

A brief biographical sketch of Alvin Plantinga appears before selection I.B.8. In the present selection, Plantinga argues that Mackie and other atheologians (those who argue against the existence of God) are mistaken in thinking that the existence of evil is inconsistent with the existence of a perfectly good and powerful God.

2. DOES THE THEIST CONTRADICT HIMSELF?

In a widely discussed piece entitled "Evil and Omnipotence" John Mackie makes this claim:

I think, however, that a more telling criticism can be made by way of the traditional problem of evil. Here it can be shown, not that religious beliefs lack rational support, but that they are positively irrational, that the several parts of the

From *God, Freedom, and Evil* by Alvin Plantinga (Harper & Row, 1974). Reprinted by permission of the author. Footnotes edited.

essential theological doctrine are *inconsistent* with one another....[1]

Is Mackie right? Does the theist contradict himself? But we must ask a prior question: just what is being claimed here? That theistic belief contains an inconsistency or contradiction, of course. But what, exactly, is an inconsistency or contradiction? There are several kinds. An *explicit* contradiction is a *proposition* of a certain sort—a conjunctive proposition, one conjunct of which is the denial or negation of the other conjunct. For example:

> Paul is a good tennis player, and it's false that Paul is a good tennis player.

(People seldom assert explicit contradictions.) Is Mackie charging the theist with accepting such a contradiction? Presumably not; what he says is

> In its simplest form the problem is this: God is omnipotent; God is wholly good; yet evil exists. There seems to be some contradiction between these three propositions, so that if any two of them were true the third would be false. But at the same time all three are essential parts of most theological positions; the theologian, it seems, at once *must* adhere and *cannot consistently* adhere to all three.

According to Mackie, then, the theist accepts a group or set of three propositions; this set is inconsistent. Its members, of course, are

(1)   God is omnipotent

(2)   God is wholly good

and

(3)   Evil exists.

Call this set *A*; the claim is that *A* is an inconsistent set. But what is it for a *set* to be inconsistent or contradictory? Following our definition of an explicit contradiction, we might say that a set of propositions is explicitly contradictory if one of the members is the denial or negation of another member. But then, of course, it is evident that the set we are discussing is not explicitly contradictory; the denials of (1), (2), and (3), respectively, are

(1′)   God is not omnipotent (or it's false that God is omnipotent)

(2′)   God is not wholly good

and

(3′)   There is no evil

none of which is in set *A*.

Of course many sets are pretty clearly contradictory, in an important way, but not explicitly contradictory. For example, set *B*:

(4)   If all men are mortal, then Socrates is mortal

(5)   All men are mortal

(6)   Socrates is not mortal.

This set is not explicitly contradictory; yet surely *some* significant sense of that term applies to it. What is important here is that by using only the rules of ordinary logic—the laws of propositional logic and quantification theory found in any introductory text on the subject—we can deduce an explicit contradiction from the set. Or to put it differently, we can use the laws of logic to deduce a proposition from the set, which proposition, when added to the set, yields a new set that is explicitly contradictory. For by using the law *modus ponens* (if *p,* then *q*; *p*; therefore *q*) we can deduce

(7)   Socrates is mortal

from (4) and (5). The result of adding (7) to *B* is the set {(4), (5), (6), (7)}. This set, of course, is explicitly contradictory in that (6) is the denial of (7). We might say that any set which shares this characteristic with set *B* is *formally* contradictory. So a formally contradictory set is one from whose members an explicit contradiction can be deduced by the laws of logic. Is Mackie claiming that set *A* is formally contradictory?

If he is, he's wrong. No laws of logic permit us to deduce the denial of one of the propositions in *A* from the other members. Set *A* isn't formally contradictory either.

But there is still another way in which a set of propositions can be contradictory or inconsistent. Consider set *C*, whose members are

(8)   George is older than Paul

(9)   Paul is older than Nick

and

(10)   George is not older than Nick.

This set is neither explicitly nor formally contradictory; we can't, just by using the laws of logic, deduce the denial of any of these propositions from the others. And yet there is a good sense in which it is inconsistent or contradictory. For clearly it is *not possible* that its three members all be true. It is *necessarily true* that

(11)   If George is older than Paul, and Paul is older than Nick, then George is older than Nick.

And if we add (11) to set *C*, we get a set that is formally contradictory; (8), (9), and (11) yield, by the laws of ordinary logic, the denial of (10).

I said that (11) is *necessarily true*; but what does *that* mean? Of course we might say that a proposition is necessarily true if it is impossible that it be false, or if its negation is not possibly true. This would be to explain necessity in terms of possibility. Chances are, however, that anyone who does not know what necessity is, will be equally at a loss about possibility; the explanation is not likely to be very successful. Perhaps all we can do by way of explanation is to give some examples and hope for the best. In the first place many propositions can be established by the laws of logic alone—for example,

(12)   If all men are mortal and Socrates is a man, then Socrates is mortal.

Such propositions are truths of logic; and all of them are necessary in the sense of question. But truths of arithmetic and mathematics generally are also necessarily true. Still further, there is a host of propositions that are neither truths of logic nor truths of mathematics but are nonetheless necessarily true; (11) would be an example, as well as

(13)   Nobody is taller than himself

(14)   Red is a color

(15)   No numbers are persons

(16)   No prime number is a prime minister

and

(17)   Bachelors are unmarried.

So here we have an important kind of necessity—let's call it "broadly logical necessity." Of course there is a correlative kind of *possibility*: a proposition *p* is possibly true (in the broadly logical sense) just in case its negation or denial is not necessarily true (in that same broadly logical sense). This sense of necessity and possibility must be distinguished from another that we may call *causal* or *natural* necessity and possibility. Consider

(18)   Henry Kissinger has swum the Atlantic.

Although this proposition has an implausible ring, it is not necessarily false in the broadly logical sense (and its denial is not necessarily true in that sense). But there is a good sense in which it is impossible: it is *causally* or *naturally* impossible. Human beings, unlike dolphins, just don't have the physical equipment demanded for this feat. Unlike Superman, furthermore, the rest of us are incapable of leaping tall buildings at a single bound or (without auxiliary power of some kind) traveling faster than a speeding bullet. These things are *impossible* for us—but not *logically* impossible, even in the broad sense.

So there are several senses of necessity and possibility here. There are a number of propositions, furthermore, of which it's difficult to say whether they are or aren't possible in the broadly logical sense; some of these are subjects of philosophical controversy. Is it possible, for example, for a person never to be conscious during his entire existence? Is it possible for a (human) person to exist *disembodied*? If that's possible, is it possible that there be a person who *at no time at all* during his entire existence has a body? Is it possible to see without eyes? These are propositions about whose possibility in that broadly logical sense there is disagreement and dispute.

Now return to set *C*.... What is characteristic of it is the fact that the conjunction of its members—the proposition expressed by the result of putting "and's" between (8), (9), and (10)—is necessarily false. Or we might put it like this: what characterizes set C is the fact that we can get a formally contradictory set by adding a necessarily true proposition—namely (11). Suppose we say that a set is *implicitly contradictory* if it resembles C in this respect. That is, a set S of propositions is implicitly contradictory if there is a necessary proposition p such that the result of adding p to S is a formally contradictory set. Another way to put it: S is implicitly contradictory if there is some necessarily true proposition p such that by using just the laws of ordinary logic, we can deduce an explicit contradiction from p together with the members of S. And when Mackie says that set A is contradictory, we may properly take him, I think, as holding that it is implicitly contradictory in the explained sense. As he puts it:

> However, the contradiction does not arise immediately; to show it we need some additional premises, or perhaps some quasi-logical rules connecting the terms "good" and "evil" and "omnipotent." These additional principles are that good is opposed to evil, in such a way that a good thing always eliminates evil as far as it can, and that there are no limits to what an omnipotent thing can do. From these it follows that a good omnipotent thing elimi-nates evil completely, and then the propositions that a good omnipotent thing exists, and that evil exists, are incompatible.[2]

Here Mackie refers to "additional premises"; he also calls them "additional principles" and "quasi-logical rules"; he says we need them to show the contradiction. What he means, I think, is that to get a formally contradictory set we must add some more propositions to set A; and if we aim to show that set A is implicitly contradictory, these propositions must be necessary truths—"quasi-logi-cal rules" as Mackie calls them. The two additional principles he suggests are

(19) A good thing always eliminates evil as far as it can

and

(20) There are no limits to what an omnipotent being can do.

And, of course, if Mackie means to show that set A is implicitly contradictory, then he must hold that (19) and (20) are not merely *true* but *necessarily true*.

But, are they? What about (20) first? What does it mean to say that a being is omnipotent? That he is *all-powerful*, or *almighty*, presumably. But are there no limits at all to the power of such a being? Could he create square circles, for example, or married bachelors? Most theologians and theistic philosophers who hold that God is omnipotent, do not hold that He can create round squares or bring it about that He both exists and does not exist. These theologians and philosophers may hold that there are no *nonlogical* limits to what an omnipotent being can do, but they concede that not even an omnipotent being can bring about logically impossible states of affairs or cause necessarily false propositions to be true. Some theists, on the other hand—Martin Luther and Descartes, perhaps—have apparently thought that God's power is unlimited even by the laws of logic. For these theists the question whether set A is contradictory will not be of much interest. As theists they believe (1) and (2), and they also, presumably, believe (3). But they remain undisturbed by the claim that (1), (2), and (3) are jointly inconsistent—because, as they say, God can do what is logically impossible. Hence He can bring it about that the members of set A are all true, even if that set is contradictory (concentrating very intensely upon this suggestion is likely to make you dizzy). So the theist who thinks that the power of God isn't *limited at all*, not even by the laws of logic, will be unimpressed by Mackie's argument and won't find any difficulty in the contradiction set A is alleged to contain. This view is not very popular, however, and for good reason; it is quite incoherent. What the theist typically means when he says that God is omnipotent is not that there are *no* limits to God's power, but at most that there are no nonlogical limits to what He can do; and given this qualification, it is perhaps initially plausible to suppose that (20) is necessarily true.

But what about (19), the proposition that every good thing eliminates every evil state of affairs that it can eliminate? Is that necessarily true? Is it true at all? Suppose, first of all, that your friend Paul unwisely goes for a drive on a wintry day and runs out of gas on a deserted road. The temperature dips to −10°, and a miserably cold wind comes up. You are sitting comfortably at home (twenty-five miles from Paul) roasting chestnuts in a roaring blaze. Your car is in the garage; in the trunk there is the full five-gallon can of gasoline you always keep for emergencies. Paul's discomfort and danger are certainly an evil, and one which you could eliminate. You don't do so. But presumably you don't thereby forfeit your claim to being a "good thing"—you simply didn't know of Paul's plight. And so (19) does not appear to be necessary. It says that every good thing has a certain property— the property of eliminating every evil that it can. And if the case I described is possible—a good person's failing through ignorance to eliminate a certain evil he can eliminate—then (19) is by no means necessarily true.

But perhaps Mackie could sensibly claim that if you *didn't know* about Paul's plight, then in fact you were not, at the time in question, able to eliminate the evil in question; and perhaps he'd be right. In any event he could revise (19) to take into account the kind of case I mentioned:

(19a) Every good thing always eliminates every evil that *it knows about* and can eliminate.

{(1), (2), (3), (20), (19a)}, you'll notice is not a formally contradictory set—to get a formal contradiction we must add a proposition specifying that God *knows about* every evil state of affairs. But most theists do believe that God is omniscient or all-knowing; so if this new set—the set that results when we add to set *A* the proposition that God is omniscient—is implicitly contradictory then Mackie should be satisfied and the theist confounded. (And, henceforth, set *A* will be the old set *A* together with the proposition that God is omniscient.)

But is (19a) necessary? Hardly. Suppose you know that Paul is marooned as in the previous example, and you also know another friend is similarly marooned fifty miles in the opposite direction. Suppose, furthermore, that while you can rescue one or the other, you simply can't rescue both. Then each of the two evils is such that it is within your power to eliminate it; and you know about them both. But you can't eliminate *both*; and you don't forfeit your claim to being a good person by eliminating only one—it wasn't within your power to do more. So the fact that you don't doesn't mean that you are not a good person. Therefore (19a) is false; it is not a necessary truth or even a truth that every good thing eliminates every evil it knows about and can eliminate.

We can see the same thing another way. You've been rock climbing. Still something of a novice, you've acquired a few cuts and bruises by inelegantly using your knees rather than your feet. One of these bruises is fairly painful. You mention it to a physician friend, who predicts the pain will leave of its own accord in a day or two. Meanwhile, he says, there's nothing he can do, short of amputating your leg above the knee, to remove the pain. Now the pain in your knee is an evil state of affairs. All else being equal, it would be better if you had no such pain. And it is within the power of your friend to eliminate this evil state of affairs. Does his failure to do so mean that he is not a good person? Of course not; for he could eliminate this evil state of affairs only by bringing about another, much worse evil. And so it is once again evident that (19a) is false. It is entirely possible that a good person fail to eliminate an evil state of affairs that he knows about and can eliminate. This would take place, if, as in the present example, he couldn't eliminate the evil without bringing about a *greater* evil.

A slightly different kind of case shows the same thing. A really impressive good state of affairs G will outweigh a trivial E—that is, the conjunctive state of affairs G and E is itself a good state of affairs. And surely a good person would not be obligated to eliminate a given evil if he could do so only by eliminating a good that outweighed it. Therefore (19a) is not necessarily true; it can't be used to show that set *A* is implicitly contradictory.

These difficulties might suggest another revision of (19); we might try

(19b) A good being eliminates every evil *E* that it knows about and that it can eliminate without either bringing about a greater evil or eliminating a good state of affairs that outweighs *E*.

Is this necessarily true? It takes care of the second of the two difficulties afflicting (19a) but leaves the first untouched. We can see this as follows. First, suppose we say that a being *properly eliminates* an evil state of affairs if it eliminates that evil without either eliminating an outweighing good or bringing about a greater evil. It is then obviously possible that a person find himself in a situation where he could properly eliminate an evil *E* and could also properly eliminate another evil *E′*, but couldn't properly eliminate them *both*. You're rock climbing again, this time on the dreaded north face of the Grand Teton. You and your party come upon Curt and Bob, two mountaineers stranded 125 feet apart on the face. They untied to reach their cigarettes and then carelessly dropped the rope while lighting up. A violent, dangerous thunderstorm is approaching. You have time to rescue one of the stranded climbers and retreat before the storm hits; if you rescue both, however, you and your party and the two climbers will be caught on the face during the thunderstorm, which will very likely destroy your entire party. In this case you can eliminate one evil (Curt's being stranded on the face) without causing more evil or eliminating a greater good; and you are also able to properly eliminate the other evil (Bob's being thus stranded). But you can't properly eliminate them *both*. And so the fact that you don't rescue Curt, say, even though you could have, doesn't show that you aren't a good person. Here, then, each of the evils is such that you can properly eliminate it; but you can't properly eliminate them both, and hence can't be blamed for failing to eliminate one of them.

So neither (19a) nor (19b) is necessarily true. You may be tempted to reply that the sort of counterexamples offered—examples where someone is able to eliminate an evil *A* and also able to eliminate a different evil *B*, but unable to eliminate them both—are irrelevant to the case of a being who, like God, is both omnipotent and omniscient.

That is, you may think that if an omnipotent and omniscient being is able to eliminate each of two evils, it follows that he can eliminate them *both*. Perhaps this is so; but it is not strictly to the point. The fact is the counterexamples show that (19a) and (19b) are not necessarily true and hence can't be used to show that set *A* is implicitly inconsistent. What the reply does suggest is that perhaps the atheologian will have more success if he works the properties of omniscience and omnipotence into (19). Perhaps he could say something like

(19c) An omnipotent and omniscient good being eliminates every evil that it can properly eliminate.

And suppose, for purposes of argument, we concede the necessary truth of (19c). Will it serve Mackie's purposes? Not obviously. For we don't get a set that is formally contradictory by adding (20) and (19c) to set *A*. This set (call it *A′*) contains the following six members:

(1)   God is omnipotent

(2)   God is wholly good

(2′)   God is omniscient

(3)   Evil exists

(19c) An omnipotent and omniscient good being eliminates every evil that it can properly eliminate

and

(20)   There are no nonlogical limits to what an omnipotent being can do.

Now if *A′* were formally contradictory, then from any five of its members we could deduce the denial of the sixth by the laws of ordinary logic. That is, any five would *formally entail* the denial of the sixth. So if *A′* were formally inconsistent, the denial of (3) would be formally entailed by the remaining five. That is, (1), (2), (2′), (19c), and (20) would formally entail

(3′)   There is no evil.

But they don't; what they formally entail is not that there is no evil *at all* but only that

(3″) There is no evil that God can properly eliminate.

So (19c) doesn't really help either—not because it is not necessarily true but because its addition [with (20)] to set A does not yield a formally contradictory set.

Obviously, what the atheologian must add to get a formally contradictory set is

(21) If God is omniscient and omnipotent, then he can properly eliminate every evil state of affairs.

Suppose we agree that the set consisting in A plus (19c), (20), and (21) is formally contradictory. So if (19c), (20), and (21) are all necessarily true, then set A is implicitly contradictory. We've already conceded that (19c) and (20) are indeed necessary. So we must take a look at (21). Is this proposition necessarily true?

No. To see this let us ask the following question. Under what conditions would an omnipotent being be unable to eliminate a certain evil E without eliminating an outweighing good? Well, suppose that E is *included in* some good state of affairs that outweighs it. That is, suppose there is some good state of affairs G so related to E that it is impossible that G obtain or be actual and E fail to obtain. (Another way to put this: a state of affairs S includes S' if the conjunctive state of affairs S but not S' is impossible, or if it is necessary that S' obtains if S does.) Now suppose that some good state of affairs G includes an evil state of affairs E that it outweighs. Then not even an omnipotent being could eliminate E without eliminating G. But are there any cases where a good state of affairs includes, in this sense, an evil that it outweighs?[3] Indeed there are such states of affairs. To take an artificial example, let's suppose that E is Paul's suffering from a minor abrasion and G is your being deliriously happy. The conjunctive state of affairs, G *and* E—the state of affairs that obtains if and only if both G and E obtain—is then a good state of affairs: it is better, all else being equal, that you be intensely happy and Paul suffer a mildly annoying abrasion than that this state of affairs not obtain. So G *and* E is a good state of affairs. And clearly G *and* E includes E: obviously it is

necessarily true that if you are deliriously happy and Paul is suffering from an abrasion, then Paul is suffering from an abrasion.

But perhaps you think this example trivial, tricky, slippery, and irrelevant. If so, take heart; other examples abound. Certain kinds of values, certain familiar kinds of good states of affairs, can't exist apart from evil of some sort. For example, there are people who display a sort of creative moral heroism in the face of suffering and adversity—a heroism that inspires others and creates a good situation out of a bad one. In a situation like this the evil, of course, remains evil; but the total state of affairs—someone's bearing pain magnificently, for example—may be good. If it is, then the good present must outweigh the evil; otherwise the total situation would not be *good*. But, of course, it is not possible that such a good state of affairs obtain unless some evil also obtain. It is a necessary truth that if someone bears pain magnificently, then someone is in pain.

The conclusion to be drawn, therefore, is that (21) is not necessarily true. And our discussion thus far shows at the very least that it is no easy matter to find necessarily true propositions that yield a formally contradictory set when added to set A.[4] One wonders, therefore, why the many atheologians who confidently assert that this set is contradictory make no attempt whatever to *show* that it is. For the most part they are content just to *assert* that there is a contradiction here. Even Mackie, who sees that some "additional premises" or "quasi-logical rules" are needed, makes scarcely a beginning towards finding some additional premises that are necessarily true and that together with the members of set A formally entail an explicit contradiction.

3. CAN WE SHOW THAT THERE IS NO INCONSISTENCY HERE?

To summarize our conclusions so far: although many atheologians claim that the theist is involved in contradiction when he asserts the members of set *A*, this set, obviously, is neither *explicitly nor formally* contradictory; the claim, presumably, must be that it is *implicitly* contradictory. To make good this claim the atheologian must find some necessarily true proposition *p* (it could be a conjunction of several propositions) such that the addition of *p* to set *A* yields a set that is formally contradictory. No atheologian has produced even a plausible candidate for this role, and it certainly is not easy to see what such a proposition might be. Now we might think we should simply declare set *A* implicitly consistent on the principle that a proposition (or set) is to be presumed consistent or possible until proven otherwise. This course, however, leads to trouble. The same principle would impel us to declare the atheologian's claim—that set *A* is inconsistent—possible or consistent. But the claim that a given set of propositions is implicitly contradictory, is itself either necessarily true or necessarily false; so if such a claim is *possible*, it is not necessarily false and is, therefore, true (in fact, necessarily true). If we followed the suggested principle, therefore, we should be obliged to declare set *A* implicitly consistent (since it hasn't been shown to be otherwise), but we should have to say the same thing about the atheologian's claim, since we haven't shown *that* claim to be inconsistent or impossible. The atheologian's claim, furthermore, is necessarily true if it is possible. Accordingly, if we accept the above principle, we shall have to declare set *A* both implicitly consistent and implicitly inconsistent. So all we can say at this point is that set *A* has not been shown to be implicitly inconsistent.

Can we go any further? One way to go on would be to try to *show* that set *A* is implicitly consistent or possible in the broadly logical sense. But what is involved in showing such a thing? Although there are various ways to approach this matter, they all resemble one another in an important respect. They all amount to this: to show that a set *S* is consistent you think of a *possible state of affairs* (it needn't *actually obtain*) which is such that if it were actual, then all of the members of *S* would be true. This procedure is sometimes called *giving a model of S.* For example, you might construct an axiom set and then show that it is consistent by giving a model of it; this is how it was shown that the denial of Euclid's parallel postulate is formally consistent with the rest of his postulates.

There are various special cases of this procedure to fit special circumstances. Suppose, for example, you have a pair of propositions *p* and *q* and wish to show them consistent. And suppose we say that a proposition *p*1 entails a proposition *p*2 if it is impossible that *p*1 be true and *p*2 false—if the conjunctive proposition *p*1 and not *p*2 is necessarily false. Then one way to show that *p* is consistent with *q* is to find some proposition *r* whose conjunction with *p* is both possible, in the broadly logical sense, and entails *q*. A rude and unlettered behaviorist, for example, might hold that thinking is really nothing but movements of the larynx; he might go on to hold that

P   Jones did not move his larynx after April 30 is inconsistent (in the broadly logical sense) with

Q   Jones did some thinking during May.

By way of rebuttal, we might point out that *P* appears to be consistent with

R   While convalescing from an April 30 laryngotomy, Jones whiled away the idle hours by writing (in May) a splendid paper on Kant's *Critique of Pure Reason.*

So the conjunction of *P* and *R* appears to be consistent; but obviously it also entails *Q* (you can't write even a passable paper on Kant's *Critique of Pure Reason* without doing some thinking); so *P* and *Q* are consistent.

We can see that this is a special case of the procedure I mentioned above as follows. This proposition *R* is consistent with *P*; so the proposition *P and R* is possible, describes a possible state of affairs. But *P and R* entails *Q*; hence if *P and R* were true, *Q* would also be true, and hence both *P* and *Q* would be true. So this is really a case of producing a possible state of affairs such that, if it were actual, all the members of the set in question (in this case the pair set of *P* and *Q*) would be true.

How does this apply to the case before us? As follows, let us conjoin propositions (1), (2), and (2′) and henceforth call the result (1):

(1)   God is omniscient, omnipotent, and wholly good.

The problem, then, is to show that (1) and (3) (evil exists) are consistent. This could be done, as we've seen, by finding a proposition *r* that is consistent with (1) and such that (1) and (*r*) together entail (3). One proposition that might do the trick is

(22)   God creates a world containing evil and has a good reason for doing so.

If (22) is consistent with (1), then it follows that (1) and (3) (and hence set *A*) are consistent. Accordingly, one thing some theists have tried is to show that (22) and (1) are consistent.

One can attempt this in at least two ways. On the one hand, we could try to apply the same method again. Conceive of a possible state of affairs such that, if it obtained, an omnipotent, omniscient, and wholly good God would have a good reason for permitting evil. On the other, someone might try to specify *what God's reason is* for permitting evil and try to show, if it is not obvious, that it is a good reason. St. Augustine, for example, one of the greatest and most influential philosopher-theologians of the Christian Church, writes as follows:

… some people see with perfect truth that a creature is better if, while possessing free will, it remains always fixed upon God and never sins; then, reflecting on men's sins, they are grieved, not because they continue to sin, but because they were created. They say: He should have made us such that we never willed to sin, but always to enjoy the unchangeable truth.

They should not lament or be angry. God has not compelled men to sin just because He created them and gave them the power to choose between sinning and not sinning. There are angels who have never sinned and never will sin.

Such is the generosity of God's goodness that He has not refrained from creating even that creature which He foreknew would not only sin, but remain in the will to sin. As a runaway horse is better than a stone which does not run away because it lacks self-movement and sense perception, so the creature is more excellent which sins by free will than that which does not sin only because it has no free will.[5]

In broadest terms Augustine claims that God could create a better, more perfect universe by permitting evil than He could by refusing to do so:

Neither the sins nor the misery are necessary to the perfection of the universe, but souls as such are necessary, which have the power to sin if they so will, and become miserable if they sin. If misery persisted after their sins had been abolished, or if there were misery before there were sins, then it might be right to say that the order and government of the universe were at fault. Again, if there were sins but no consequent misery, that order is equally dishonored by lack of equity.[6]

Augustine tries to tell us *what God's reason is* for permitting evil. At bottom, he says, it's that God can create a more perfect universe by permitting evil. A really top-notch universe requires the existence of free, rational, and moral agents; and some of the free creatures He created went wrong. But the universe with the free creatures it contains and the evil they commit is better than it would have been had it contained neither the free creatures nor this evil. Such an attempt to specify God's reason for permitting evil is what I earlier called a *theodicy*; in the words of John Milton it is an attempt to "justify the ways of God to man," to show that God is just in permitting evil. Augustine's kind of theodicy might be called a Free Will Theodicy, since the idea of rational creatures with free will plays such a prominent role in it.

A theodicist, then, attempts to tell us why God permits evil. Quite distinct from a Free Will

Theodicy is what I shall call a Free Will Defense. Here the aim is not to say what God's reason *is*, but at most what God's reason *might possibly be*. We could put the difference like this. The Free Will Theodicist and Free Will Defender are both trying to show that (1) is consistent with (22), and of course if so, then set *A* is consistent. The Free Will Theodicist tries to do this by finding some proposition *r* which in conjunction with (1) entails (22); he claims, furthermore, that this proposition is true, not just consistent with (1). He tries to tell us what God's reason for permitting evil *really is*. The Free Will Defender, on the other hand, though he also tries to find a proposition *r* that is consistent with (1) and in conjunction with it entails (22), does *not* claim to know or even believe that *r* is true. And here, of course, he is perfectly within his rights. His aim is to show that (1) is consistent with (22); all he need do then is find an *r* that is consistent with (1) and such that (1) and (*r*) entail (22); whether *r* is true is quite beside the point.

So there is a significant difference between a Free Will Theodicy and a Free Will Defense. The latter is sufficient (if successful) to show that set *A* is consistent; in a way a Free Will Theodicy goes beyond what is required. On the other hand, a theodicy would be much more satisfying, if possible to achieve. No doubt the theist would rather know what God's reason is for permitting evil than simply that it's possible that He has a good one. But in the present context (that of investigating the consistency of set A), the latter is all that's needed. Neither a defense or a theodicy, of course, gives any hint to what God's reason for some *specific* evil—the death or suffering of someone close to you, for example—might be. And there is still another function[7]—a sort of pastoral function—in the neighborhood that neither serves. Confronted with evil in his own life or suddenly coming to realize more clearly than before the *extent* and *magnitude* of evil, a believer in God may undergo a crisis of faith. He may be tempted to follow the advice of Job's "friends"; he may be tempted to "curse God and die." Neither a Free Will Defense nor a Free Will Theodicy is designed to be of much help or comfort to one suffering from such a storm in the soul (although in a specific case, of course, one or the other could prove useful). Neither is to be thought of first of all as a means of pastoral counseling. Probably neither will enable someone to find peace with himself and with God in the face of the evil the world contains. But then, of course, neither is intended for that purpose.

4. THE FREE WILL DEFENSE

In what follows I shall focus attention upon the Free Will Defense. I shall examine it more closely, state it more exactly, and consider objections to it; and I shall argue that in the end it is successful. Earlier we saw that among good states of affairs there are some that not even God can bring about without bringing about evil: those goods, namely, that *entail* or *include* evil states of affairs. The Free Will Defense can be looked upon as an effort to show that there may be a very different kind of good that God can't bring about without permitting evil. These are good states of affairs that don't include evil; they do not entail the existence of any evil whatever; nonetheless God Himself can't bring them about without permitting evil.

So how does the Free Will Defense work? And what does the Free Will Defender mean when he says that people are or may be free? What is relevant to the Free Will Defense is the idea of *being free with respect to an action*. If a person is free with respect to a given action, then he is free to perform that action and free to refrain from performing it; no antecedent conditions and/or causal laws determine that he will perform the action, or that he won't. It is within his power, at the time in question, to take or perform the action and within his power to refrain from it. Freedom so conceived is not to be confused with unpredictability. You might be able to predict what you will do in a given situation even if you are free, in that situation, to do something else. If I know you well, I may be able to predict what action you will take in response to a certain set of conditions; it does not follow that you are not free with respect to that action. Secondly, I shall say that an action is *morally significant*, for a given person, if it would be wrong for him to perform the action but right to refrain or vice versa. Keeping a promise, for example, would ordinarily be morally significant for a person, as would refusing induction into the army. On the other hand, having Cheerios for breakfast (instead of Wheaties) would not normally be morally significant. Further, suppose we say that a person is *significantly free*, on a given occasion, if he is then free with respect to a morally significant action. And finally we must distinguish between *moral evil* and *natural evil*. The former is evil that results from free human activity; natural evil is any other kind of evil.[8]

Given these definitions and distinctions, we can make a preliminary statement of the Free Will Defense as follows. A world containing creatures who are significantly free (and freely perform more good than evil actions) is more valuable, all else being equal, than a world containing no free creatures at all. Now God can create free creatures, but He can't *cause* or *determine* them to do only what is right. For if He does so, then they aren't significantly free after all; they do not do what is right *freely*. To create creatures capable of *moral good*, therefore, He must create creatures capable of moral evil; and He can't give these creatures the freedom to perform evil and at the same time prevent them from doing so. As it turned out, sadly enough, some of the free creatures God created went wrong in the exercise of their freedom; this is the source of moral evil. The fact that free creatures sometimes go wrong, however, counts neither against God's omnipotence nor against His goodness; for He could have forestalled the occurrence of moral evil only by removing the possibility of moral good.

I said earlier that the Free Will Defender tries to find a proposition that is consistent with

(1)   God is omniscient, omnipotent, and wholly good

and together with (1) entails that there is evil. According to the Free Will Defense, we must find this proposition somewhere in the above story. The heart of the Free Will Defense is the claim that it is *possible* that God could not have created a universe containing moral good (or as much moral good as this world contains) without creating one that also contained moral evil. And if so, then it is possible that God has a good reason for creating a world containing evil.

Now this defense has met with several kinds of objections. For example, some philosophers say that *causal determinism* and *freedom*, contrary to what we might have thought, are not really incompatible.[9] But if so, then God could have created free creatures who were free, and free to do what is wrong, but nevertheless were causally determined to do only what is right. Thus He could have created creatures who were free to do what was wrong, while nevertheless preventing them from ever performing any wrong actions—simply by seeing to it that they were causally determined to do only what is right. Of course this contradicts the Free Will Defense, according to which there is inconsistency in supposing that God determines free creatures to do only what is right. But is it really possible that all of a person's actions are causally determined while some of them are free? How could that be so? According to one version of the doctrine in question, to say that George acts freely on a given occasion is to say only this: *if George had chosen to do otherwise, he would have done otherwise.* Now George's action A is causally determined if some event E— some event beyond his control—has already occurred, where the state of affairs consisting in E's occurrence conjoined with George's *refraining* from performing A, is a causally impossible state of affairs. Then one can consistently hold both that all of a man's actions are causally determined and that some of them are free in the above sense. For suppose that all of a man's actions are causally determined and that he *couldn't*, on any occasion, have made any choice or performed any action different from the ones he did make and perform. It could still be true that if he *had* chosen to do otherwise, he would have done otherwise. Granted, he couldn't have chosen to do otherwise; but this is consistent with saying that *if* he had, things would have gone differently.

This objection to the Free Will Defense seems utterly implausible. One might as well claim that being in jail doesn't really limit one's freedom on the grounds that if one were *not* in jail, he'd be free to come and go as he pleased. So I shall say no more about this objection here.[10]

A second objection is more formidable. In essence it goes like this. Surely it is possible to do only what is right, even if one is free to do wrong. It is *possible*, in that broadly logical sense, that there would be a world containing free creatures who always do what is right. There is certainly no *contradiction* or *inconsistency* in this idea. But God is omnipotent; his power has no nonlogical limitations. So if it's possible that there be a world containing creatures who are free to do what is wrong but never in fact do so, then it follows that an omnipotent God could create such a world. If so, however, the Free Will Defense must be mistaken in its insistence upon the possibility that God is omnipotent but unable to create a world containing moral good without permitting moral evil.). J. L. Mackie … states this objection:

> If God has made men such that in their free choices they sometimes prefer what is good and sometimes what is evil, why could he not have made men such that they always freely choose the good? If there is no logical impossibility in a man's freely choosing the good on one, or on several occasions, there cannot be a logical impossibility in his freely choosing the good on every occasion. God was not, then, faced with a choice between making innocent automata and making beings who, in acting freely, would sometimes go wrong; there was open to him the obviously better possibility of making beings who would act freely but always go right. Clearly, his failure to avail himself of this possibility is inconsistent with his being both omnipotent and wholly good.[11]

Now what, exactly, is Mackie's point here? This. According to the Free Will Defense, it is possible both that God is omnipotent and that He was unable to create a world containing moral good without creating one containing moral evil. But,

replies Mackie, this limitation on His power to create is inconsistent with God's omnipotence. For surely it's *possible* that there be a world containing perfectly virtuous persons—persons who are significantly free but always do what is right. Surely there are *possible worlds* that contain moral good but no moral evil. But God, if He is omnipotent, can create any possible world He chooses. So it is *not* possible, contrary to the Free Will Defense, both that God is omnipotent and that He could create a world containing moral good only by creating one containing moral evil. If He is omnipotent, the only limitations of His power are *logical* limitations; in which case there are no possible worlds He could not have created.

This is a subtle and important point. According to the great German philosopher G. W. Leibniz, *this* world, the actual world, must be the best of all possible worlds. His reasoning goes as follows. Before God created anything at all, He was confronted with an enormous range of choices; He could create or bring into actuality any of the myriads of different possible worlds. Being perfectly good, He must have chosen to create the best world He could; being omnipotent, He was able to create any possible world He pleased. He must, therefore, have chosen the best of all possible worlds; and hence *this* world, the one He did create, must be the best possible. Now Mackie, of course, agrees with Leibniz that God, if omnipotent, could have created any world He pleased and would have created the best world he could. But while Leibniz draws the conclusion that this world, despite appearances, must be the best possible, Mackie concludes instead that there is no omnipotent, wholly good God. For, he says, it is obvious enough that this present world is not the best of all possible worlds.

The Free Will Defender disagrees with both Leibniz and Mackie. In the first place, he might say, what is the reason for supposing that there is such a thing as the best of all possible worlds? No matter how marvelous a world is—containing no matter how many persons enjoying unalloyed bliss—isn't it possible that there be an even better world containing even more persons enjoying even more unalloyed bliss? But what is really characteristic and central to the Free Will Defense is the claim that God, though omnipotent, could not have actualized just any possible world He pleased.

5. WAS IT WITHIN GOD'S POWER TO CREATE ANY POSSIBLE WORLD HE PLEASED?

This is indeed the crucial question for the Free Will Defense. If we wish to discuss it with insight and authority, we shall have to look into the idea of *possible worlds*. And a sensible first question is this: what sort of thing is a possible world? The basic idea is that a possible world is *a way things could have been*; it is a *state of affairs* of some kind. Earlier we spoke of states of affairs, in particular of good and evil states of affairs. Suppose we look at this idea in more detail. What sort of thing is a state of affairs? The following would be examples:

Nixon's having won the 1972 election

7 + 5's being equal to 12

All men's being mortal

and

Gary, Indiana's, having a really nasty pollution problem.

These are *actual* states of affairs: states of affairs that do in fact obtain. And corresponding to each such actual state of affairs there is a true proposition—in the above cases, the corresponding propositions would be *Nixon won the 1972 presidential election, 7 + 5 is equal to 12, all men are mortal, and Gary, Indiana, has a really nasty pollution problem.* A proposition *p corresponds* to a state of affairs s_1, in this sense, if it is impossible that *p* be true and s_1 fail to obtain and impossible that s_1 obtain and *p* fail to be true.

But just as there are false propositions, so there are states of affairs that do *not* obtain or are *not* actual. *Kissinger's having swum the Atlantic* and *Hubert Horatio Humphrey's having run a mile in four minutes* would be examples. Some states of affairs that do not obtain are impossible: e.g., *Hubert's having drawn a square circle, 7 + 5's being equal to 75,* and *Agnew's having a brother who was an only child.* The propositions corresponding to these states of affairs, of course, are necessarily false. So there are states of affairs that *obtain* or are *actual* and also states of affairs that don't obtain. Among the latter some are *impossible* and others are possible. And a possible world is a possible state of affairs. Of course not every possible state of affairs is a possible world; *Hubert's having run a mile in four minutes* is a possible state of affairs but not a possible world. No doubt it is an *element* of many possible worlds, but it isn't itself inclusive enough to be one. To be a possible world, a state of affairs must be very large—so large as to be *complete* or *maximal.*

To get at this idea of completeness we need a couple of definitions. As we have already seen … a state of affairs *A includes* a state of affairs *B* if it is not possible that *A* obtain and *B* not obtain or if the conjunctive state of affairs *A but not B*—the state of affairs that obtains if and only if *A* obtains and *B* does not—is not possible. For example, *Jim Whittaker's being the first American to climb Mt. Everest* includes *Jim Whittaker's being an American.* It also includes *Mt. Everest's being climbed, something's being climbed, no American's having climbed Everest before Whittaker did,* and the like. *Inclusion* among states of affairs is like *entailment* among propositions; and where a state of affairs *A* includes a state of affairs *B,* the proposition corresponding to *A* entails the one corresponding to *B.* Accordingly, *Jim Whittaker is the first American to climb Everest* entails *Mt. Everest has been climbed, something has been climbed,* and *no American climbed Everest before Whittaker did.* Now suppose we say further that a state of affairs *A precludes* a state of affairs *B* if it is not possible that *both* obtain, or if the conjunctive state of affairs *A and B* is impossible. Thus *Whittaker's being the first American to climb Mt. Everest* precludes *Luther Jerstad's being the first American to climb Everest,* as well as Whittaker's never having climbed any mountains. If *A* precludes *B,* than *A's* corresponding proposition entails the denial of the one corresponding to *B.* Still further, let's say that the *complement* of a state of affairs is the state of affairs that obtains just in case *A* does not obtain. [Or we might say that the complement (call it $\bar{A}$) of A is the state of affairs corresponding to the *denial* or *negation* of the proposition corresponding to A.] Given these definitions, we can say what it is for a state of affairs to be *complete*: A is a complete state of affairs if and only if for every state of affairs B, either A *includes* B or A *precludes* B. (We could express the same thing by saying that if A is a complete state of affairs, then for every state of affairs B, either A includes B or A includes $\bar{B}$, the complement of B.) And now we are able to say what a possible world is: a possible world is any possible state of affairs that is complete. If A is a possible world, then it says something about everything; every state of affairs S is either included in or precluded by it.

Corresponding to each possible world W, furthermore, there is a set of propositions that I'll call the book on W. A proposition is in the book on W just in case the state of affairs to which it corresponds is included in W. Or we might express it like this. Suppose we say that a proposition P *is true in a world* W if and only if P *would have been true if W had been actual*—if and only if, that is, it is not possible that W be actual and P be false. Then the book on W is the set of propositions true in W. Like possible worlds, books are *complete*; if B is a book, then for any proposition P, either P or the denial of P will be a member of B. A book is a *maximal consistent set* of propositions; it is so large that the addition of another proposition to it always yields an explicitly inconsistent set.

Of course, for each possible world there is exactly one book corresponding to it (that is, for a given world W there is just one book B such that each member of B is true in M; and for each book there is just one world to which it corresponds). So every world has its book.

It should be obvious that exactly one possible world is actual. At *least* one must be, since the set of true propositions is a maximal consistent set and hence a book. But then it corresponds to a possible world, and the possible world corresponding to this set of propositions (since it's the set of *true* propositions) will be actual. On the other hand there is at *most* one actual world. For suppose there were two:

W and W'. These worlds cannot include all the very same states of affairs; if they did, they would be the very same world. So there must be at least one state of affairs S such that W includes S and W' does not. But a possible world is maximal; W', therefore, includes the complement $\bar{S}$ of S. So if both W and W' were actual, as we have supposed, then both S and $\bar{S}$ would be actual—which is impossible. So there can't be more than one possible world that is actual.

Leibniz pointed out that a proposition p is necessary if it is true in every possible world. We may add that p is possible if it is true in one world and impossible if true in none. Furthermore, p *entails* q if there is no possible world in which p is true and q is false, and p *is consistent with* q if there is at least one world in which both p and q are true.

A further feature of possible worlds is that people (and other things) exist in them. Each of us exists in the actual world, obviously; but a person also exists in many worlds distinct from the actual world. It would be a mistake, of course, to think of all of these worlds as somehow "going on" at the same time, with the same person reduplicated through these worlds and actually existing in a lot of different ways. This is not what is meant by saying that the same person exists in different possible worlds. What is meant, instead, is this: a person Paul exists in each of those possible worlds W which is such that, if W *had been actual*, Paul would have existed—actually existed. Suppose Paul had been an inch taller than he is, or a better tennis player. Then the world that does in fact obtain would not have been actual; some other world—W', let's say—would have obtained instead. If W' had been actual, Paul would have existed; so Paul exists in W'. (Of course there are still other possible worlds in which Paul does not exist—worlds, for example, in which there are no people at all.) Accordingly, when we say that Paul exists in a world W, what we mean is that Paul *would have* existed had W been actual. Or we could put it like this: Paul exists in each world W that includes the state of affairs consisting in Paul's existence. We can put this still more simply by saying that Paul exists in those worlds whose books contain the proposition *Paul exists*.

But isn't there a problem here? *Many* people are named "Paul": Paul the apostle, Paul J. Zwier, John Paul Jones, and many other famous Pauls. So who goes with "Paul exists"? Which Paul? The answer has to do with the fact that books contain *propositions*—not sentences. They contain the sort of thing sentences are used to express and assert. And the same sentence—"Aristotle is wise," for example—can be used to express many different propositions. When Plato used it, he asserted a proposition predicating wisdom of his famous pupil; when Jackie Onassis uses it, she asserts a proposition predicating wisdom of her wealthy husband. These are distinct propositions (we might even think they differ in truth value); but they are expressed by the same sentence. Normally (but not always) we don't have much trouble determining which of the several propositions expressed by a given sentence is relevant in the context at hand. So in this case a given person, Paul, exists in a world *W* if and only if *W'* book contains the proposition that says that *he*— that particular person—exists. The fact that the sentence we use to express this proposition can also be used to express *other* propositions is not relevant.

After this excursion into the nature of books and worlds we can return to our question. Could God have created just any world He chose? Before addressing the question, however, we must note that God does not, strictly speaking, *create* any possible worlds or states of affairs at all. What He creates are the heavens and the earth and all that they contain. But He has not created states of affairs. There are, for example, the state of affairs consisting in God's existence and the state of affairs consisting in His nonexistence. That is, there is such a thing as the state of affairs consisting in the existence of God, and there is also such a thing as the state of affairs consisting in the nonexistence of God, just as there are the two propositions *God exists* and *God does not exist*. The theist believes that the first state of affairs is actual and the first proposition true; the atheist believes that the second state of affairs is actual and the second proposition true. But, of course, both propositions *exist*, even though just one is true. Similarly, there are two states of affairs

here, just one of which is actual. So both states of affairs *exist*, but only one *obtains*. And God has not created either one of them since there never was a time at which either did not exist. Nor has he created the state of affairs consisting in the earth's existence; there was a time when *the earth* did not exist, but none when the state of affairs consisting in the earth's existence didn't exist. Indeed, God did not bring into existence any states of affairs at all. What He did was to perform actions of a certain sort— creating the heavens and the earth, for example— which resulted in the *actuality* of certain states of affairs. God *actualizes* states of affairs. He actualizes the possible world that does in fact obtain; He does not create it. And while He has created Socrates, He did not create the state of affairs consisting in Socrates' existence.[12]

Bearing this in mind, let's finally return to our question. Is the atheologian right in holding that if God is omnipotent, then he could have actualized or created any possible world He pleased? Not obviously. First, we must ask ourselves whether God is a *necessary* or a *contingent* being. A necessary being is one that exists in every possible world— one that would have existed no matter which possible world had been actual; a contingent being exists only in some possible worlds. Now if God is not a necessary being (and many, perhaps most, theists think that He is not), then clearly enough there will be many possible worlds He could not have actualized—all those, for example, in which He does not exist. Clearly, God could not have created a world in which He doesn't even exist.

So, if God is a contingent being then there are many possible worlds beyond His power to create. But this is really irrelevant to our present concerns. For perhaps the atheologian can maintain his case if he revises his claim to avoid this difficulty; perhaps he will say something like this: if God is omnipotent, then He could have actualized any of these possible worlds *in which He exists*. So if He exists and is omnipotent, He could have actualized (contrary to the Free Will Defense) any of those possible worlds in which He exists and in which there exist free creatures who do no wrong. He could have actualized worlds containing moral good but no moral evil. Is this correct?

Let's begin with a trivial example. You and Paul have just returned from an Australian hunting expedition: your quarry was the elusive double-waffled cassowary. Paul captured an aardvark, mistaking it for a cassowary. The creature's disarming ways have won it a place in Paul's heart; he is deeply attached to it. Upon your return to the States you offer Paul $500 for his aardvark, only to be rudely turned down. Later you ask yourself, "What would he have done if I'd offered him $700?" Now what is it, exactly, that you are asking? What you're really asking in a way is whether, under a *specific set of conditions*, Paul would have sold it. These conditions include your having offered him $700 rather than $500 for the aardvark, everything else being as much as possible like the conditions that did in fact obtain. Let S' be this set of conditions or state of affairs. S' includes the state of affairs consisting in your offering Paul $700 (instead of the $500 you did offer him); of course it does not include his *accepting* your offer, and it does not include his *rejecting* it; for the rest, the conditions it includes are just like the ones that did obtain in the actual world. So, for example, S' includes Paul's being free to accept the offer and free to refrain; and if in fact the going rate for an aardvark was $650, then S' includes the state of affairs consisting in the going rate's being $650. So we might put your question by asking which of the following conditionals is true:

(23) If the state of affairs S' had obtained, Paul would have accepted the offer

(24) If the state of affairs S' had obtained, Paul would not have accepted the offer.

It seems clear that at least one of these conditionals is true, but naturally they can't both be; so exactly one is.

Now since S' includes neither Paul's accepting the offer not his rejecting it, the antecedent of (23) and (24) does not entail the consequent of either. That is,

(25) S' *obtains* does not entail either

(26) Paul accepts the offer

or

(27) Paul does not accept the offer.

So there are possible worlds in which both (25) and (26) are true, and other possible worlds in which both (25) and (27) are true.

We are now in a position to grasp an important fact. Either (23) or (24) is in fact true; and either way there are possible worlds God could not have actualized. Suppose, first of all, that (23) is true. Then it was beyond the power of God to create a world in which (1) Paul is free to sell his aardvark and free to refrain, and in which the other states of affairs included in S' obtain, and (2) Paul does not sell. That is, it was beyond His power to create a world in which (25) and (27) are both true. There is at least one possible world like this, but God, despite His omnipotence, could not have brought about its actuality. For let W be such a world. To actualize W, God must bring it about that Paul is free with respect to this action, and that the other states of affairs included in S' obtain. But (23), as we are supposing, is true; so if God had actualized S' and left Paul *free* with respect to this action, he would have sold: in which case W would not have been actual. If, on the other hand, God had *brought it about* that Paul didn't sell or had *caused him to* refrain from selling, then Paul would not have been free with respect to this action; then S' would not have been actual (since S' includes Paul's being free with respect to it), and W would not have been actual since W includes S'.

Of course if it is (24) rather than (23) that is true, then another class of worlds was beyond God's power to actualize—those, namely, in which S' obtains and Paul *sells* his aardvark. These are the worlds in which both (25) and (26) are true. But either (23) or (24) is true. Therefore, there are possible worlds God could not have actualized. If we consider whether or not God could have created a world in which, let's say, both (25) and (26) are true, we see that the answer depends upon a peculiar kind of fact; it depends upon what Paul would have freely chosen to do in a certain situation. So there are any number of possible worlds such that it is partly up to Paul whether God can create them.[13]

That was a past tense example. Perhaps it would be useful to consider a future tense case, since this might seem to correspond more closely to God's situation in choosing a possible world to actualize. At some time t in the near future Maurice will be free with respect to some insignificant action—having freeze-dried oatmeal for breakfast, let's say. That is, at time t Maurice will be free to have oatmeal but also free to take something else—shredded wheat, perhaps. Next, suppose we consider S', a state of affairs that is included in the actual world and includes Maurice's being free with respect to taking oatmeal at time t. That is, S' includes Maurice's being free at time t to take oatmeal and free to reject it. S' does not include Maurice's taking oatmeal, however; nor does it include his rejecting it. For the rest S' is as much as possible like the actual world. In particular there are many conditions that do in fact hold at time t and are *relevant* to his choice—such conditions, for example, as the fact that he hasn't had oatmeal lately, that his wife will be annoyed if he rejects it, and the like; and S' includes each of these conditions. Now God no doubt knows what Maurice will do at time t, if S obtains; He knows which action Maurice would freely perform if S were to be actual. That is, God knows that one of the following conditionals is true:

(28)   If S' were to obtain, Maurice will freely take the oatmeal

or

(29)   If S' were to obtain, Maurice will freely reject it.

We may not know which of these is true, and Maurice himself may not know; but presumably God does.

So either God knows that (28) is true, or else He knows that (29) is. Let's suppose it is (28). Then there is a possible world that God, though omnipotent, cannot create. For consider a possible world W' that shares S' with the actual world (which for ease of reference I'll name "Kronos") and in which Maurice does not take oatmeal. (We know there is such a world, since S' does not include Maurice's taking the oatmeal.) S' obtains in W' just as it does in Kronos. Indeed, everything in W' is just as it is in Kronos up to time t. But whereas in Kronos Maurice takes oatmeal at time t, in W' he does not. Now W' is a perfectly possible world; but it is not within God's power to create it or bring about its actuality. For to do so He must actualize S'. But (28) is in fact true. So if God actualizes S' (as He must to create W') and leaves Maurice free with respect to the action in question, then he will take the oatmeal; and then, of course, W' will not be actual. If, on the other hand, God causes Maurice to *refrain* from taking the oatmeal, then he is not free to take it. That means, once again, that W' is not actual; for in W' Maurice is free to take the oatmeal (even if he doesn't do so). So if (28) is true, then this world W' is one that God can't actualize, it is not within His power to actualize it even though He is omnipotent and it is a possible world.

Of course, if it is (29) that is true, we get a similar result; then too there are possible worlds that God can't actualize. These would be worlds which share S' with Kronos and in which Maurice *does* take oatmeal. But either (28) or (29) is true; so either way there is a possible world that God can't create. If we consider a world in which S' obtains and in which Maurice freely chooses oatmeal at time t, we see that whether or not it is within God's power to actualize it depends upon what Maurice would do if he were free in a certain situation. Accordingly, there are any number of possible worlds such that it is partly up to Maurice whether or not God can actualize them. It is, of course, up to God whether or not to create Maurice and also up to God whether or not to make him free with respect to the action of taking oatmeal at time t. (God could, if He chose, cause him to succumb to the dreaded *equine obsession*, a condition shared by some people and most horses, whose victims find it *psychologically impossible* to refuse oats or oat products.) But if He creates Maurice and creates him free with respect to this action, then whether or not he actually performs the action is up to Maurice—not God.[14]

Now we can return to the Free Will Defense and the problem of evil. The Free Will Defender, you recall, insists on the possibility that it is not within God's power to create a world containing moral good without creating one containing moral evil. His atheological opponent—Mackie, for example—agrees with Leibniz in insisting that *if* (as the theist holds) God is omnipotent, then it *follows* that He could have created any possible world He pleased. We now see that this contention—call it "Leibniz' Lapse"—is a mistake. The atheologian is right in holding that there are many possible worlds containing moral good but no moral evil; his mistake lies in endorsing Leibniz' Lapse. So one of his premises—that God, if omnipotent, could have actualized just any world He pleased—is false.

6. COULD GOD HAVE CREATED A WORLD CONTAINING MORAL GOOD BUT NO MORAL EVIL?

Now suppose we recapitulate the logic of the situation. The Free Will Defender claims that the following is possible:

(30)   God is omnipotent, and it was not within His power to create a world containing moral good but no moral evil.

By way of retort the atheologian insists that there are possible worlds containing moral good but no moral evil. He adds that an omnipotent being could have actualized any possible world he chose. So if God is omnipotent, it follows that He could have actualized a world containing moral good but no moral evil, hence (30), contrary to the Free Will Defender's claim, is not possible. What we have seen so far is that his second premise—Leibniz' Lapse—is false.

Of course, this does not settle the issue in the Free Will Defender's favor. Leibniz' Lapse (appropriately enough for a lapse) is false; but this doesn't show that (30) is possible. To show this latter we must demonstrate the possibility that among the worlds God could not have actualized are all the worlds containing moral good but no moral evil. How can we approach this question?

Instead of choosing oatmeal for breakfast or selling an aardvark, suppose we think about a morally significant action such as taking a bribe. Curley Smith, the mayor of Boston, is opposed to the proposed freeway route; it would require destruction of the Old North Church along with some other antiquated and structurally unsound buildings. L. B. Smedes, the director of highways, asks him whether he'd drop his opposition for $1 million. "Of course," he replies. "Would you do it for $2?" asks Smedes. "What do you take me for?" comes the indignant reply. "That's already established," smirks Smedes; "all that remains is to nail down your price." Smedes then offers him a bribe of $35,000; unwilling to break with the fine old traditions of Bay State politics, Curley accepts. Smedes then spends a sleepless night wondering whether he could have bought Curley for $20,000.

Now suppose we assume that Curley was free with respect to the action of taking the bribe— free to take it and free to refuse. And suppose, furthermore, that he would have taken it. That is, let us suppose that

(31)   If Smedes had offered Curley a bribe of $20,000, he would have accepted it.

If (31) is true, then there is a state of affairs S' that (1) includes Curley's being offered a bribe of $20,000; (2) does not include either his accepting the bribe or his rejecting it; and (3) is otherwise as much as possible like the actual world. Just to make sure S' includes every relevant circumstance, let us suppose that it is a *maximal world segment*. That is, add to S' any state of affairs compatible with but not included in it, and the result will be an entire possible world. We could think of it roughly like this: S' is included in at least one world W in which Curley takes the bribe and in at least one world W'

in which he rejects it. If S' is a maximal world segment, then S' is what remains of W when *Curley's taking the bribe* is deleted; it is also what remains of W' when *Curley's rejecting the bribe* is detected. More exactly, if S' is a maximal world segment, then every possible state of affairs that includes S', but isn't included by S', is a possible world. So if (31) is true, then there is a maximal world segment S' that (1) includes Curley's being offered a bribe of $20,000; (2) does not include either his accepting the bribe or his rejecting it; (3) is otherwise as much as possible like the actual world—in particular, it includes Curley's being free with respect to the bribe; and (4) is such that if it were actual then Curley would have taken the bribe. That is

(32) if S' were actual, *Curley would have accepted the bribe* is true.

Now, of course, there is at least one possible world W' in which S' is actual and Curley does not take the bribe. But God could not have created W'; to do so, he would have been obliged to actualize S', leaving Curley free with respect to the action of taking the bribe. But under these conditions Curley, as (32) assures us, would have accepted the bribe, so that the world thus created would not have been S'.

Curley, as we see, is not above a bit of Watergating. But there may be worse to come. Of course, there are possible worlds in which he is significantly free (i.e., free with respect to a morally significant action) and never does what is wrong. But the sad truth about Curley may be this. Consider W', any of these worlds: in W' Curley is significantly free, so in W' there are some actions that are morally significant for him and with respect to which he is free. But at least one of these actions—call it A— has the following peculiar property. There is a maximal world segment S' that obtains in W' and is such that (1) S' includes Curley's being free *re A* but neither his performing A nor his refraining from A; (2) S' is otherwise as much as possible like W' and (3) if S' had been actual, Curley would have gone wrong with respect to A.[15] (Notice that this third condition holds in fact, in the actual world; it does not hold in that world W'.)

This means, of course, that God could not have actualized W'. For to do so He'd have been obliged to bring it about that S' is actual; but then Curley would go wrong with respect to A. Since in W' he always does what is right, the world thus actualized would not be W'. On the other hand, if God *causes* Curley to go right with respect to A or *brings it about* that he does so, then Curley isn't free with respect to A; and so once more it isn't W' that is actual. Accordingly God cannot create W'. But W' was just any of the worlds in which Curley is significantly free but always does only what is right. It therefore follows that it was not within God's power to create a world in which Curley produces moral good but no moral evil. Every world God can actualize is such that if Curley is significantly free in it, he takes at least one wrong action.

Obviously Curley is in serious trouble. I shall call the malady from which he suffers transworld depravity. (I leave as homework the problem of comparing transworld depravity with what Calvinists call "total depravity.") By way of explicit definition:

(33) A person P *suffers from transworld depravity* if and only if the following holds: for every world W such that P is significantly free in W and P does only what is right in W, there is an action A and a maximal world segment S' such that

(1) S' includes A's being morally significant for P

(2) S' includes P's being free with respect to A

(3) S' is included in W and includes neither P's performing A nor P's refraining from performing A

and

(4) If S' were actual, P would go wrong with respect to A.

(In thinking about this definition, remember that (4) is to be true in fact, in the actual world—not in that world W.)

What is important about the idea of transworld depravity is that if a person suffers from it, then it wasn't within God's power to actualize any world in which that person is significantly free but does no wrong—that is, a world in which he produces moral good but no moral evil.

We have been here considering a crucial contention of the Free Will Defender: the contention, namely, that

(30)   God is omnipotent, and it was not within His power to create a world containing moral good but no moral evil.

How is transworld depravity relevant to this? As follows. Obviously it is possible that there be persons who suffer from transworld depravity. More generally, it is possible that *everybody* suffers

from it. And if this possibility were actual, then God, though omnipotent, could not have created any of the possible worlds containing just the persons who do in fact exist, and containing moral good but no moral evil. For to do so He'd have to create persons who were significantly free (otherwise there would be no moral good) but suffered from transworld depravity. Such persons go wrong with respect to at least one action in any world God could have actualized and in which they are free with respect to morally significant actions; so the price for creating a world in which they produce moral good is creating one in which they also produce moral evil.

NOTES

1. John Mackie, "Evil and Omnipotence," in *The Philosophy of Religion*, ed. Basil Mitchell (London Oxford University Press:, 1971), p. 92. [See previous reading.]

2. Ibid., p. 93. [*Philosophy of Religion: Selected Readings, Second Edition*, p. 224.]

3. More simply, the question is really just whether any good state of affairs includes an evil; a little reflection reveals that no good state of affairs can include an evil that it does not outweigh.

4. In Plantinga, *God and Other Minds* (Ithaca, N.Y.: Cornell University Press, 1967), chap. 5, I explore further the project of finding such propositions.

5. *The Problem of Free Choice*, Vol. 22 of *Ancient Christian Writers* (Westminster, Md.: The Newman Press, 1955), bk. 2, pp. 14–15.

6. Ibid., bk. 3, p. 9.

7. I am indebted to Henry Schuurman (in conversation) for helpful discussion of the difference between this pastoral function and those served by a theodicy or a defense.

8. This distinction is not very precise (how, exactly, are we to construe "results from"?), but perhaps it will serve our present purposes.

9. See, for example, A. Flew, "Divine Omnipotence and Human Freedom," in *New Essays in Philosophical Theology*, eds. A. Flew and A. MacIntyre (London SCM:, 1955), pp. 150–53.

10. For further discussion of it see Plantinga, *God and Other Minds*, pp. 132–35.

11. Mackie, in *The Philosophy of Religion*, pp. 100–101.

12. Strict accuracy demands, therefore, that we speak of God as actualizing rather than creating possible worlds. I shall continue to use both locutions, thus sacrificing accuracy to familiarity. For more about possible worlds see my book *The Nature of Necessity* (Oxford The Clarendon Press:, 1974), chaps. 4–8.

13. For a fuller statement of this argument see Plantinga, *The Nature of Necessity*, chap. 9, secs. 4–6.

14. For a more complete and more exact statement of this argument see Plantinga, *The Nature of Necessity*, chap. 9, secs. 4–6.

15. A person goes wrong with respect to an action if he either wrongfully performs it or wrongfully fails to perform it.

IV.C.2

Evil and Soul-Making

JOHN HICK

John Hick (1922–   ) was for many years professor of theology at the University of Bir-
mingham in England and, until his retirement, was professor of philosophy at Claremont
Graduate School. His book Evil and the God of Love *(1966), from which the following*
selection is taken, is considered one of the most thorough treatises on the problem of evil.
"Evil and Soul-Making" is an example of a theodicy argument that is based on the free will
defense. Theodicies can be of two differing types depending on how they justify the ways of
God in the face of evil. The Augustinian position is that God created humans without sin
and set them in a sinless, paradisical world. However, humanity fell into sin through the
misuse of free will. God's grace will save some of us, but others will perish everlastingly. The
second type of theodicy stems from the thinking of Irenaeus (120–202), of the Greek
Church. The Irenaean tradition views Adam not as a free agent rebelling against God but as
more akin to a small child. The fall is humanity's first faulty step in the direction of freedom.
God is still working with humanity in order to bring it from undeveloped life (bios) to a state
of self-realization in divine love, spiritual life (zoe). This life is viewed as the "vale of soul-
making." Hick favors this version and develops it in this reading.

Fortunately there is another and better way. As well as the "majority report" of the Augustinian tradition, which has dominated Western Christendom, both Catholic and Protestant, since the time of Augustine himself, there is the "minority report" of the Irenaean tradition. This latter is both older and newer than the other, for it goes back to Sr. Irenaeus and others of the early Hellenistic Fathers of the Church in the two centuries prior to St. Augustine, and it has flourished again in more developed forms during the last hundred years.

Instead of regarding man as having been created by God in a finished state, as a finitely perfect being fulfilling the divine intention for our human level of existence, and then falling disastrously away from this, the minority report sees man as still in process of creation. Irenaeus himself expressed the point in terms of the (exegetically dubious) distinction between the "image" and the "likeness" of God referred to in Genesis i.26: "Then God said, Let us make man in our image, after our likeness." His view was that man as a personal and moral being already exists in the image, but has not yet been formed into the finite likeness of God. By this "likeness" Irenaeus means something more than personal existence as such; he means a certain valuable quality of personal life which reflects finitely the divine life. This represents the perfecting of man, the fulfillment of God's purpose for humanity, the "bringing of many sons to glory," the creating of "children of God" who are "fellow heirs with Christ" of his glory.

And so man, created as a personal being in the image of God, is only the raw material for a further and more difficult stage of God's creative work. This is the leading of men as relatively free and autonomous persons, through their own dealings with life in the world in which He has placed them, towards that quality of personal existence that is the finite likeness of God. The features of this likeness are revealed in the person of Christ, and the process of man's creation into it is the work of the Holy Spirit. In St. Paul's words, "And we all, with unveiled faces, beholding the glory of the Lord, are being changed into his likeness (εἰκών) from one degree of glory to another; for this comes from the Lord who is the Spirit";[1] or again, "For God knew his own before ever they were, and also ordained that they should be shaped to the likeness (εἰκών) of his Son."[2] In Johannine terms, the movement from the image to the likeness is a transition from one level of existence, that of animal life (*Bios*), to another and higher level, that of eternal life (*Zoe*), which includes but transcends the first. And the fall of man was seen by Irenaeus as a failure within the second phase of this creative process, a failure that has multiplied the perils and complicated the route of the journey in which God is seeking to lead mankind.

In the light of modern anthropological knowledge some form of two-stage conception of the creation of man has become an almost unavoidable Christian tenet. At the very least we must acknowledge as two distinguishable stages the fashioning of *homo sapiens* as a product of the long evolutionary process, and his sudden or gradual spiritualization as a child of God. But we may well extend the first stage to include the development of man as a rational and responsible person capable of personal relationship with the personal Infinite who has created him. This first stage of the creative process was, to our anthropomorphic imaginations, easy for divine omnipotence. By an exercise of creative power God caused the physical universe to exist, and in the course of countless ages to bring forth within it organic life, and finally to produce out of organic

life personal life; and when man had thus emerged out of the evolution of the forms of organic life, a creature had been made who has the possibility of existing in conscious fellowship with God. But the second stage of the creative process is of a different kind altogether. It cannot be performed by omnipotent power as such. For personal life is essentially free and self-directing. It cannot be perfected by divine fiat, but only through the uncompelled responses and willing co-operation of human individuals in their actions and reactions in the world in which God has placed them. Men may eventually become the perfected persons whom the New Testament calls "children of God," but they cannot be created ready-made as this.

The value-judgment that is implicitly being invoked here is that one who has attained to goodness by meeting and eventually mastering temptations, and thus by rightly making responsible choices in concrete situations, is good in a richer and more valuable sense than would be one created *ab initio* in a state either of innocence or of virtue. In the former case, which is that of the actual moral achievements of mankind, the individual's goodness has within it the strength of temptation overcome, a stability based upon an accumulation of right choices, and a positive and responsible character that comes from the investment of costly personal effort. I suggest, then, that it is an ethically reasonable judgment, even though in the nature of the case not one that is capable of demonstrative proof, that human goodness slowly built up through personal histories of moral effort has a value in the eyes of the Creator which justifies even the long travail of the soul-making process.

The picture with which we are working is thus developmental and teleological. Man is in process of becoming the perfected being whom God is seeking to create. However, this is not taking place—it is important to add—by a natural and inevitable evolution, but through a hazardous adventure in individual freedom. Because this is a pilgrimage within the life of each individual, rather than a racial evolution, the progressive fulfillment of God's purpose does not entail any corresponding progressive improvement in the moral state of the world. There is no doubt a development in man's ethical situation from generation to generation through the building of individual choices into public institutions, but this involves an accumulation of evil as well as of good. It is thus probable that human life was lived on much the same moral plane two thousand years ago or four thousand years ago as it is today. But nevertheless during this period uncounted millions of souls have been through the experience of earthly life, and God's purpose has gradually moved towards its fulfillment within each one of them, rather than within a human aggregate composed of different units in different generations.

If, then, God's aim in making the world is "the bringing of many sons to glory," that aim will naturally determine the kind of world that He has created. Antitheistic writers almost invariably assume a conception of the divine purpose which is contrary to the Christian conception. They assume that the purpose of a loving God must be to create a hedonistic paradise; and therefore to the extent that the world is other than this, it proves to them that God is either not loving enough or not powerful enough to create such a world. They think of God's relation to the earth on the model of a human being building a cage for a pet animal to dwell in. If he is humane he will naturally make his pet's quarters as pleasant and healthful as he can. Any respect in which the cage falls short of the veterinarian's ideal, and contains possibilities of accident or disease, is evidence of either limited benevolence or limited means, or both. Those who use the problem of evil as an argument against belief in God almost invariably think of the world in this kind of way. David Hume, for example, speaks of an architect who is trying to plan a house that is to be as comfortable and convenient as possible. If we find that "the windows, doors, fires, passages, stairs, and the whole economy of the building were the source of noise, confusion, fatigue, darkness, and the extremes of heat and cold" we should have no hesitation in blaming the architect. It would be in vain for him to prove that if this or that defect were corrected greater ills would result: "still you would assert in general, that, if the architect had had skill and good

intentions, he might have formed such a plan of the whole, and might have adjusted the parts in such a manner, as would have remedied all or most of these inconveniences."[3]

But if we are right in supposing that God's purpose for man is to lead him from human *Bios*, or the biological life of man, to that quality of *Zoe*, or the personal life of eternal worth, which we see in Christ, then the question that we have to ask is not, Is this the kind of world that an all-powerful and infinitely loving being would create as an environment for his human pets? or, Is the architecture of the world the most pleasant and convenient possible? The question that we have to ask is rather, Is this the kind of world that God might make as an environment in which moral beings may be fashioned, through their own free insights and responses, into "children of God"?

Such critics as Hume are confusing what heaven ought to be, as an environment for perfected finite beings, with what this world ought to be, as an environment for beings who are in process of becoming perfected. For if our general conception of God's purpose is correct the world is not intended to be a paradise, but rather the scene of a history in which human personality may be formed towards the pattern of Christ. Men are not to be thought of on the analogy of animal pets, whose life is to be made as agreeable as possible, but rather on the analogy of human children, who are to grow to adulthood in an environment whose primary and overriding purpose is not immediate pleasure but the realizing of the most valuable potentialities of human personality.

Needless to say, this characterization of God as the heavenly Father is not a merely random illustration but an analogy that lies at the heart of the Christian faith. Jesus treated the likeness between the attitude of God to man, and the attitude of human parents at their best towards their children, as providing the most adequate way for us to think about God. And so it is altogether relevant to a Christian understanding of this world to ask, How does the best parental love express itself in its influence upon the environment in which children are to grow up? I think it is clear that a parent who loves his children, and wants them to become the best human beings that they are capable of becoming, does not treat pleasure as the sole and supreme value. Certainly we seek pleasure for our children, and take great delight in obtaining it for them; but we do not desire for them unalloyed pleasure at the expense of their growth in such even greater values as moral integrity, unselfishness, compassion, courage, humour, reverence for the truth, and perhaps above all the capacity for love. We do not act on the premise that pleasure is the supreme end of life; and if the development of these other values sometimes clashes with the provision of pleasure, then we are willing to have our children miss a certain amount of this, rather than fail to come to possess and to be possessed by the finer and more precious qualities that are possible to the human personality. A child brought up on the principle that the only or the supreme value is pleasure would not be likely to become an ethically mature adult or an attractive or happy personality. And to most parents it seems more important to try to foster quality and strength of character in their children than to fill their lives at all times with the utmost possible degree of pleasure. If, then, there is any true analogy between God's purpose for his human creatures, and the purpose of loving and wise parents for their children, we have to recognize that the presence of pleasure and the absence of pain cannot be the supreme and overriding end for which the world exists. Rather, this world must be a place of soul-making. And its value is to be judged, not primarily by the quantity of pleasure and pain occurring in it at any particular moment, but by its fitness for its primary purpose, the purpose of soul-making.

In all this we have been speaking about the nature of the world considered simply as the God given environment of man's life. For it is mainly in this connection that the world has been regarded in Irenaean and in Protestant thought. But such a way of thinking involves a danger of anthropocentrism from which the Augustinian and Catholic tradition has generally been protected by its sense of the relative insignificance of man within the totality of the created universe. Man was dwarfed within the medieval worldview by the innumerable hosts of angels and archangels above him—unfallen rational natures which rejoice in the immediate presence of God, reflecting His glory in the untarnished mirror of their worship. However, this higher creation has in our modern world lost its hold upon the imagination. Its place has been taken, as the minimizer of men, by the immensities of outer space and by the material universe's unlimited complexity transcending our present knowledge. As the spiritual environment envisaged by Western man has shrunk, his physical horizons have correspondingly expanded. Where the human creature was formerly seen as an insignificant appendage to the angelic world, he is now seen as an equally insignificant organic excrescence, enjoying a fleeting moment of consciousness on the surface of one of the planets of a minor star. Thus the truth that was symbolized for former ages by the existence of the angelic hosts is today impressed upon us by the vastness of the physical universe, countering the egoism of our species by making us feel that this immense prodigality of existence can hardly all exist for the sake of man—though, on the other hand, the very realization that it is not all for the sake of man may itself be salutary and beneficial to man!

However, instead of opposing man and nature as rival objects of God's interest, we should perhaps rather stress man's solidarity as an embodied being with the whole natural order in which he is embedded. For man is organic to the world; all his acts and thoughts and imaginations are conditioned by space and time; and in abstraction from nature he would cease to be human. We may, then, say that the beauties and sublimities and powers, the microscopic intricacies and macroscopic vastnesses, the wonders and the terrors of the natural world and of the life that pulses through it, are willed and valued by their Maker in a creative act that embraces man together with nature. By means of matter and living flesh God both builds a path and weaves a veil between Himself and the creature made in His image. Nature thus has permanent significance; for God has set man in a creaturely environment, and the final fulfilment of our nature in relation to God will accordingly take the form of an embodied life within "a new heaven and a new earth." And as in the present age man moves slowly towards that fulfillment through the pilgrimage of his earthly life, so also "the whole creation" is "groaning in travail," waiting for the time when it will be "set free from its bondage to decay."

And yet however fully we thus acknowledge the permanent significance and value of the natural order, we must still insist upon man's special character as a personal creature made in the image of God; and our theodicy must still centre upon the soul-making process that we believe to be taking place within human life.

This, then, is the starting-point from which we propose to try to relate the realities of sin and suffering to the perfect love of an omnipotent Creator. And as will become increasingly apparent, a theodicy that starts in this way must be eschatological in its ultimate bearings. That is to say, instead of looking to the past for its clue to the mystery of evil, it looks to the future, and indeed to that ultimate future to which only faith can look. Given the conception of a divine intention working in and through human time towards a fulfilment that lies in its completeness beyond human time, our theodicy must find the meaning of evil in the part that it is made to play in the eventual outworking of that purpose; and must find the justification of the whole process in the magnitude of the good to which it leads. The good that outshines all ill is not a paradise long since lost but a kingdom which is yet to come in its full glory and permanence.

NOTES

1. II Corinthians iii. 18.
2. Romans viii. 29. Other New Testament passages expressing a view of man as undergoing a process of spiritual growth within God's purpose are: Ephesians ii. 21, iii. 16; Colossians ii. 19; I John iii. 2; II Corinthians iv. 16.
3. *Dialogues Concerning Natural Religion*, pt. xi. Kemp-Smith's ed. (Oxford: Clarendon Press, 1935), p.251.

Reprinted from Peter van Inwagen, ed, *Christian Faith and the Problem of Evil* (Grand Rapids, Mich.: Wm. B. Eerdmans, 2009), pp. 1–25. Used by permission of Wm. B. Eerdmans.

IV.B.2

The Inductive Argument from Evil against the Existence of God

WILLIAM ROWE

A short biographical sketch of William Rowe appears before selection I.B.9. In the present selection, Rowe argues that an inductive or probabilistic version of the argument from evil justifies atheism. He concedes that deductive arguments against the existence of God on the basis of evil, such as J. L. Mackie uses (Reading IV. B. 1), do not succeed. Nevertheless, he says it is reasonable to believe that there is no God. In the last part of his essay, Rowe defines his position as "friendly atheism" since he admits that a theist may be justified in rejecting the probabilistic argument from evil.

This paper is concerned with three interrelated questions. The first is: Is there an argument for atheism based on the existence of evil that may rationally justify someone in being an atheist? To this first question I give an affirmative answer and try to support that answer by setting forth a strong argument for atheism based on the existence of evil.[1] The second question is: How can the theist best defend his position against the argument for atheism based on the existence of evil? In response to this question I try to describe what may be an adequate rational defense for theism against any argument for atheism based on the existence of evil. The final question is: What position should

the informed atheist take concerning the rationality of theistic belief? Three different answers an atheist may give to this question serve to distinguish three varieties of atheism: unfriendly atheism, indifferent atheism, and friendly atheism. In the final part of the paper I discuss and defend the position of friendly atheism.

Before we consider the argument from evil, we need to distinguish a narrow and a broad sense of the terms "theist," "atheist," and "agnostic." By a "theist" in the narrow sense I mean someone who believes in the existence of an omnipotent, omniscient, eternal, supremely good being who created the world. By a "theist" in the

Reprinted from "The Problem of Evil and Some Varieties of Atheism," *American Philosophical Quarterly* 16 (1979) by permission. Footnotes edited.

broad sense I mean someone who believes in the existence of some sort of divine being or divine reality. To be a theist in the narrow sense is also to be a theist in the broad sense, but one may be a theist in the broad sense—as was Paul Tillich—without believing that there is a supremely good, omnipotent, omniscient, eternal being who created the world. Similar distinctions must be made between a narrow and a broad sense of the terms "atheist" and "agnostic." To be an atheist in the broad sense is to deny the existence of any sort of divine being or divine reality. Tillich was not an atheist in the broad sense. But he was an atheist in the narrow sense, for he denied that there exists a divine being that is all-knowing, all-powerful and perfectly good. In this paper I will be using the terms "theism," "theist," "atheism," "atheist," "agnosticism," and "agnostic" in the narrow sense, not in the broad sense.

I

In developing the argument for atheism based on the existence of evil, it will be useful to focus on some particular evil that our world contains in considerable abundance. Intense human and animal suffering, for example, occurs daily and in great plenitude in our world. Such intense suffering is a clear case of evil. Of course, if the intense suffering leads to some greater good, a good we could not have obtained without undergoing the suffering in question, we might conclude that the suffering is justified, but it remains an evil nevertheless. For we must not confuse the intense suffering in and of itself with the good things to which it sometimes leads or of which it may be a necessary part. Intense human or animal suffering is in itself bad, an evil, even though it may sometimes be justified by virtue of being a part of, or leading to, some good which is unobtainable without it. What is evil in itself may sometimes be good as a means because it leads to something that is good in itself. In such a case, while remaining an evil in itself, the intense human or animal suffering is, nevertheless, an evil which someone might be morally justified in permitting.

Taking human and animal suffering as a clear instance of evil which occurs with great frequency in our world, the argument for atheism based on evil can be stated as follows:

1. There exist instances of intense suffering which an omnipotent, omniscient being could have prevented without thereby losing some greater good or permitting some evil equally bad or worse.[2]

2. An omniscient, wholly good being would prevent the occurrence of any intense suffering it could, unless it could not do so without thereby losing some greater good or permitting some evil equally bad or worse.

3. There does not exist an omnipotent, omniscient, wholly good being.

What are we to say about this argument for atheism, an argument based on the profusion of one sort of evil in our world? The argument is valid; therefore, if we have rotational grounds for accepting its premises, to that extent we have rational grounds for accepting atheism. Do we, however, have rational grounds for accepting the premises of this argument?

Let's begin with the second premise. Let s_1 be an instance of intense human or animal suffering which an omniscient, wholly good being could prevent. We will also suppose that things are such that s_1 will occur unless prevented by the omniscient, wholly good (OG) being. We might be interested in determining what would be a sufficient condition of OG failing to prevent s_1. But, for our purpose here, we need only try to state a necessary condition for OG failing to prevent s_1. That condition, so it seems to me, is this:

Either

(i)   there is some greater good, G, such that G is obtainable by OG only if OG permits s_1,

or

(ii)   there is some greater good, G, such that G is obtainable by OG only if OG permits either s_1 or some evil equally bad or worse,

or

(iii) s_1 is such that it is preventable by OG only if OG permits some evil equally bad or worse.

It is important to recognize that (iii) is not included in (i). For losing a good greater than s_1 is not the same as permitting an evil greater than s_1. And this because the *absence* of a good state of affairs need not itself be an evil state of affairs. It is also important to recognize that s_1 might be such that it is preventable by OG *without* losing G (so condition (i) is not satisfied) but also such that if OG did prevent it, G would be lost unless OG permitted some evil equal to or worse than s_1. If this were so, it does not seem correct to require that OG prevent s_1. Thus, condition (ii) takes into account an important possibility not encompassed in condition (i).

Is it true that if an omniscient, wholly good being permits the occurrence of some intense suffering it could have prevented, then either (i) or (ii) or (iii) obtains? It seems to me that it is true. But if it is true then so is premise (2) of the argument for atheism. For that premise merely states in more compact form what we have suggested must be true if an omniscient, wholly good being fails to prevent some intense suffering it could prevent. Premise (2) says that an omniscient, wholly good being would prevent the occurrence of any intense suffering it could, unless it could not do so without thereby losing some greater good or permitting some evil equally bad or worse. This premise (or something not too distant from it) is, I think, held in common by many atheists and nontheists. Of course, there may be disagreement about whether something is good, and whether, if it is good, one would be morally justified in permitting some intense suffering to occur in order to obtain it. Someone might hold, for example, that no good is great enough to justify permitting an innocent child to suffer terribly. Again, someone might hold that the mere fact that a given good

outweighs some suffering and would be lost if the suffering were prevented, is not a morally sufficient reason for permitting the suffering. But to hold either of these views is not to deny (2). For (2) claims only that *if* an omniscient, wholly good being permits intense suffering *then* either there is some greater good that would have been lost, or some equally bad or worse evil that would have occurred, had the intense suffering been prevented. (2) does not purport to describe what might be a *sufficient* condition for an omniscient, wholly good being to permit intense suffering, only what is a *necessary* condition. So stated, (2) seems to express a belief that accords with our basic moral principles, principles shared by both theists and nontheists. If we are to fault the argument for atheism, therefore, it seems we must find some fault with its first premise.

Suppose in some distant forest lightning strikes a dead tree, resulting in a forest fire. In the fire a fawn is trapped, horribly burned, and lies in terrible agony for several days before death relieves its suffering. So far as we can see, the fawn's intense suffering is pointless. For there does not appear to be any greater good such that the prevention of the fawn's suffering would require either the loss of that good or the occurrence of an evil equally bad or worse. Nor does there seem to be any equally bad or worse evil so connected to the fawn's suffering that it would have had to occur had the fawn's suffering been prevented. Could an omnipotent, omniscient being have prevented the fawn's apparently pointless suffering? The answer is obvious, as even the theist will insist. An omnipotent, omniscient being could have easily prevented the fawn from being horribly burned, or, given the burning, could have spared the fawn the intense suffering by quickly ending its life, rather than allowing the fawn to lie in terrible agony for several days. Since the fawn's intense suffering was preventable and, so far as we can see, pointless, doesn't it appear that premise (1) of the argument is true, that there do exist instances of intense suffering which an omnipotent, omniscient being could have prevented without thereby losing some greater good or permitting some evil equally bad or worse?

It must be acknowledged that the case of the fawn's apparently pointless suffering does not prove that (1) is true. For even though we cannot see how the fawn's suffering is required to obtain some greater good (or to prevent some equally bad or worse evil), it hardly follows that it is not so required. After all, we are often surprised by how things we thought to be unconnected turn out to be intimately connected. Perhaps, for all we know, there is some familiar good outweighing the fawn's suffering to which that suffering is connected in a way we do not see. Furthermore, there may well be unfamiliar goods, goods we haven't dreamed of, to which the fawn's suffering is inextricably connected. Indeed, it would seem to require something like omniscience on our part before we could lay claim to *knowing* that there is no greater good connected to the fawn's suffering in such a manner than an omnipotent, omniscient being could not have achieved that good without permitting that suffering or some evil equally bad or worse. So the case of the fawn's suffering surely does not enable us to *establish* the truth of (1).

The truth is that we are not in a position to prove that (1) is true. We cannot know with certainty that instances of suffering of the sort described in (1) do occur in our world. But it is one thing to *know* or *prove* that (1) is true and quite another thing to have *rational grounds* for believing (1) to be true. We are often in the position where in the light of our experience and knowledge it is rational to believe that a certain statement is true, even though we are not in a position to prove or to know with certainty that the statement is true. In the light of our past experience and knowledge it is, for example, very reasonable to believe that neither Goldwater nor McGovern will ever be elected President, but we are scarcely in the position of knowing with certainty that neither will ever be elected President. So, too, with (1), although we cannot know with certainty that it is true, it perhaps can be rationally supported, shown to be a rational belief.

Consider again the case of the fawn's suffering. Is it reasonable to believe that there is some greater good so intimately connected to that suffering that even an omnipotent, omniscient being could not have obtained that good without permitting that suffering or some evil at least as bad? It certainly does not appear reasonable to believe this. Nor does it seem reasonable to believe that there is some evil at least as bad as the fawn's suffering such that an omnipotent being simply could not have prevented it without permitting the fawn's suffering. But even if it should somehow be reasonable to believe either of these things of the fawn's suffering, we must then ask whether it is reasonable to believe either of these things of *all* the instances of seemingly pointless human and animal suffering that occur daily in our world. And surely the answer to this more general question must be no. It seems quite unlikely that all the instances of intense suffering occurring daily in our world are intimately related to the occurrence of greater goods or the prevention of evils at least as bad; and even more unlikely, should they somehow all be so related, that an omnipotent, omniscient being could not have achieved at least some of those goods (or prevented some of those evils) without permitting the instances of intense suffering that are supposedly related to them. In the light of our experience and knowledge of the variety and scale of human and animal suffering in our world, the idea that none of this suffering could have been prevented by an omnipotent being without thereby losing a greater good or permitting an evil at least as bad seems an extraordinary absurd idea, quite beyond our belief. It seems then that although we cannot prove that (1) is true, it is, nevertheless, altogether *reasonable* to believe that (1) is true, that (1) is a *rational* belief.

Returning now to our argument for atheism, we've seen that the second premise expresses a basic belief common to many theists and nontheists. We've also seen that our experience and knowledge of the variety and profusion of suffering in our world provides *rational support* for the first premise. Seeing that the conclusion, "There does not exist an omnipotent, omniscient, wholly good being" follows from these two premises, it does seem that we have *rational support* for atheism, that it is reasonable for us to believe that the theistic God does not exist.

II

Can theism be rationally defended against the argument for atheism we have just examined? If it can, how might the theist best respond to that argument? Since the argument from (1) and (2) to (3) is valid, and since the theist, no less than the nontheist, is more than likely committed to (2), it's clear that the theist can reject this atheistic argument only by rejecting its first premise, the premise that states that there are instances of intense suffering which an omnipotent, omniscient being could have prevented without thereby losing some greater good or permitting some evil equally bad or worse. How, then, can the theist best respond to this premise and the considerations advanced in its support?

There are basically three responses a theist can make. First, he might argue not that (1) is false or probably false, but only that the reasoning given in support of it is in some way *defective*. He may do this either by arguing that the reasons given in support of (1) are *in themselves* insufficient to justify accepting (1), or by arguing that there are other things we know which, when taken in conjunction with these reasons, do not justify us in accepting (1). I suppose some theists would be content with this rather modest response to the basic argument for atheism. But given the validity of the basic argument and the theist's likely acceptance of (2), he is thereby committed to the view that (1) is false, not just that we have no good reasons for accepting (1) as true. The second two responses are aimed at showing that it is reasonable to believe that (1) is false. Since the theist is committed to this view, I shall focus the discussion on these two attempts, attempts which we can distinguish as "the direct attack" and "the indirect attack."

By a direct attack, I mean an attempt to reject (1) by pointing out goods, for example, to which suffering may well be connected, goods which an omnipotent, omniscient being could not achieve without permitting suffering. It is doubtful, however, that the direct attack can succeed. The theist may point out that some suffering leads to moral and spiritual development impossible without suffering. But it's reasonably clear that suffering often occurs in a degree far beyond what is required for character development. The theist may say that some suffering results from free choices of human beings and might be preventable only by preventing some measure of human freedom. But, again, it's clear that much intense suffering occurs not as a result of human free choices. The general difficulty with this direct attack on premise (1) is twofold. First, it cannot succeed; for the theist does not know what greater goods might be served, or evils prevented, by each instance of intense human or animal suffering. Second, the theist's own religious tradition usually maintains that in this life it is not given to us to know God's purpose in allowing particular instances of suffering. Hence, the direct attack against premise (1) cannot succeed and violates basic beliefs associated with theism.

The best procedure for the theist to follow in rejecting premise (1) is the indirect procedure. This procedure I shall call "the G. E. Moore shift," so-called in honor of the twentieth century philosopher G. E. Moore, who used it to great effect in dealing with the arguments of the skeptics. Skeptical philosophers such as David Hume have advanced ingenious arguments to prove that no one can know of the existence of any material object. The premises of their arguments employ plausible principles, principles which many philosophers have tried to reject directly, but only with questionable success. Moore's procedure was altogether different. Instead of arguing directly against the premises of the skeptic's arguments, he simply noted that the premises implied, for example, that he (Moore) did not know of the existence of a pencil. Moore then proceeded indirectly against the skeptic's premises by arguing:

I do know that this pencil exists.

If the skeptic's principles are correct I cannot know of the existence of this pencil.

∴. The skeptic's principles (at least one) must be incorrect.

Moore then noted that his argument is just as valid as the skeptic's, that both of their arguments contain the premise "If the skeptic's principles are correct Moore cannot know of the existence of this pencil," and concluded that the only way to choose between the two arguments (Moore's and the skeptic's) is by deciding which of the first premises it is more rational to believe—Moore's premise "I do know that this pencil exists" or the skeptic's premise asserting that his skeptical principles are correct. Moore concluded that his own first premise was the more rational of the two.

Before we see how the theist may apply the G. E. Moore shift to the basic argument of atheism, we should note the general strategy of the shift. We're given an argument: *p, q,* therefore, *r.* Instead of arguing directly against *p,* another argument is constructed not-*r, q,* therefore, not-*p*—which begins with the denial of the conclusion of the first argument, keeps its second premise, and ends with the denial of the first premise as its conclusion. Compare, for example, these two:

I. *p*   II. not-*r*

$$\frac{q}{r} \qquad \frac{q}{\text{not-}p}$$

It is a truth of logic that if I is valid II must be valid as well. Since the arguments are the same so far as the second premise is concerned, any choice between them must concern their respective first premises. To argue against the first premise (*p*) by constructing the counter argument II is to employ the G. E. Moore shift.

Applying the G. E. Moore shift against the first premise of the basic argument for atheism, the theist can argue as follows:

not-3. There exists an omnipotent, omniscient, wholly good being.

2. An omniscient, wholly good being would prevent the occurrence of any intense suffering it could, unless it could not do so without thereby losing some greater good or permitting some evil equally bad or worse.

therefore,

not-1. It is not the case that there exist instances of intense suffering which an omnipotent, omniscient being could have prevented without thereby losing some greater good or permitting some evil equally bad or worse.

We now have two arguments: the basic argument for atheism from (1) and (2) to (3), and the theist's best response, the argument from (not-3) and (2) to (not-1). What the theist then says about (1) is that he has rational grounds for believing in the existence of the theistic God (not-3), accepts (2) as true, and sees that (not-1) follows from (not-3) and (2). He concludes, therefore, that he has rational grounds for rejecting (1). Having rational grounds for rejecting (1), the theist concludes that the basic argument for atheism is mistaken.

III

We've had a look at a forceful argument for atheism and what seems to be the theist's best response to that argument. If one is persuaded by the argument for atheism, as I find myself to be, how might one best view the position of the theist? Of course, he will view the theist as having a false belief, just as the theist will view the atheist as having a false belief. But what position should the atheist take concerning the *rationality* of the theist's belief? There are three major positions an atheist might take, positions which we may think of as some varieties of atheism. First, the atheist may believe that no one is rationally justified in believing that the theistic God exists. Let us call this position "unfriendly atheism." Second, the atheist may hold no belief concerning whether any theist is or isn't rationally justified in believing that the theistic God exists. Let us call this view "indifferent atheism." Finally, the atheist may believe that some theists are rationally justified in believing that the theistic God exists. This view we shall call "friendly atheism." In this final part of the paper I propose to discuss and defend the position of friendly atheism.

If no one can be rationally justified in believing a false proposition then friendly atheism is a paradoxical, if not incoherent position. But surely the truth of a belief is not a necessary condition of someone's being rationally justified in having that belief. So in holding that someone is rationally justified in believing that the theistic God exists, the friendly atheist is not committed to thinking that the theist has a true belief. What he is committed to is that the theist has rational grounds for his belief, a belief the atheist rejects and is convinced he is rationally justified in rejecting. But is this possible? Can someone, like our friendly atheist, hold a belief, be convinced that he is rationally justified in holding that belief, and yet believe that someone else is equally justified in believing the opposite? Surely this is possible. Suppose your friends see you off on a flight to Hawaii. Hours after take-off they learn that your plane has gone down at sea. After a twenty-four hour search, no survivors have been found. Under these circumstances they are rationally justified in believing that you have perished. But it is hardly rational for you to believe this, as you bob up and down in your life vest, wondering why the search planes have failed to spot you. Indeed, to amuse yourself while awaiting your fate, you might very well reflect on the fact that your friends are rationally justified in believing that you are now dead, a proposition you disbelieve and are rationally justified in disbelieving. So, too, perhaps an atheist may be rationally justified in his atheistic belief and yet hold that some theists are rationally justified in believing just the opposite of what he believes.

What sort of grounds might a theist have for believing that God exists? Well, he might endeavor to justify his belief by appealing to one or more of the traditional arguments: Ontological, Cosmological, Teleological, Moral, etc. Second, he might appeal to certain aspects of religious experience, perhaps even his own religious experience. Third, he might try to justify theism as a plausible theory in terms of which we can account for a variety of phenomena. Although an atheist must hold that the theistic God does not exist, can he not also believe, and be justified in so believing, that some of these "justifications of theism" do actually rationally justify some theists in their belief that there exists a supremely good, omnipotent, omniscient being? It seems to me that he can.

If we think of the long history of theistic belief and the special situations in which people are sometimes placed, it is perhaps as absurd to think that no one was ever rationally justified in believing that the theistic God exists as it is to think that no one was ever justified in believing that human beings would never walk on the moon. But in suggesting that friendly atheism is preferable to unfriendly atheism, I don't mean to rest the case on what some human beings might reasonably have believed in the eleventh or thirteenth century. The more interesting question is whether some people in modern society, people who are aware of the usual grounds for belief and disbelief and are acquainted to some degree with modern science, are yet rationally justified in accepting theism. Friendly atheism is a significant position only if it answers this question in the affirmative.

It is not difficult for an atheist to be friendly when he has reason to believe that the theist could not reasonably be expected to be acquainted with the grounds for disbelief that he (the atheist) possesses. For then the atheist may take the view that some theists are rationally justified in holding to theism, but would not be so were they to be acquainted with the grounds for disbelief—those grounds being sufficient to tip the scale in favor of atheism when balanced against the reasons the theist has in support of his belief.

Friendly atheism becomes paradoxical, however, when the atheist contemplates believing that the theist has all the grounds for atheism that he, the atheist, has, and yet is rationally justified in maintaining his theistic belief. But even so excessively friendly a view as this perhaps can be held by the atheist if he also has some reason to think that the grounds for theism are not as telling as the theist is justified in taking them to be.

In this paper I've presented what I take to be a strong argument for atheism, pointed out what I think is the theist's best response to that argument, distinguished three positions an atheist might take concerning the rationality of theistic belief, and made some remarks in defense of the position called "friendly atheism." I'm aware that the central points of the paper are not likely to be warmly received by many philosophers. Philosophers who are atheists tend to be tough minded—holding that there are no good reasons for supposing that theism is true. And theists tend either to reject the view that the existence of evil provides rational grounds for atheism or to hold that religious belief has nothing to do with reason and evidence at all. But such is the way of philosophy.

NOTES

1. Some philosophers have contended that the existence of evil is *logically inconsistent* with the existence of the theistic God. No one, I think, has succeeded in establishing such an extravagant claim. Indeed, granted incompatibilism, there is a fairly compelling argument for the view that the existence of evil is logically consistent with the existence of the theistic God. (For a lucid statement of this argument see Alvin Plantinga, *God, Freedom, and Evil* (New York, 1974), 29-59.) There remains, however, what we may call the *evidential* form—as opposed to the *logical* form—of the problem of evil; the view that the variety and profusion of evil in our world, although perhaps not logically inconsistent with the existence of the theistic God, provides, nevertheless, *rational support* for atheism. In this paper I shall be concerned solely with the evidential form of the problem, the form of the problem which, I think, presents a rather severe difficulty for theism. William L. Rowe,

   "The Problem of Evil and Some Varieties of Atheism," first published in *American Philosophical Quarterly*, 16 (1979), pp. 335-41. Used with permission.

2. If there is some good, G, greater than any evil, (1) will be false for the trivial reason that no matter what evil, E, we pick the conjunctive good state of affairs consisting of G and E will outweigh E and be such that an omnipotent being could not obtain it without permitting E. (See Alvin Plantinga, *God and Other Minds* (Ithaca, 1967), 167.) To avoid this objection we may insert "unreplaceable" into our premises (1) and (2) between "some" and "greater." If E isn't required for G, and G is better than G plus E, then the good conjunctive state of affairs composed of G and E would be replaceable by the greater good of G alone. For the sake of simplicity, however, I will ignore this complication both in the formulation and discussion of premises (1) and (2).

VII.A.1

The Wager

BLAISE PASCAL

Blaise Pascal (1623–1662) was a renowned French physicist and mathematician. In 1654, at the age of 31, Pascal had an intense religious experience that completely changed his life. After this experience, he devoted himself to prayer and the study of Scripture, abandoned his mathematical and scientific endeavors, and set himself to the task of writing a defense of the Christian faith. The book was never finished, but the present selection is taken from Pascal's notes, compiled under the title Pensées. Here he argues that if we do a cost–benefit analysis of the matter, we find that it is eminently reasonable to take steps to put ourselves in a position to believe that God exists, regardless of whether we now have good evidence for that belief.

Infinite—nothing.—Our soul is cast into a body, where it finds number, time, dimension. Thereupon it reasons, and calls this nature, necessity, and can believe nothing else.

Unity joined to infinity adds nothing to it, no more than one foot to an infinite measure. The finite is annihilated in the presence of the infinite, and becomes a pure nothing. So our spirit before God, so our justice before divine justice. There is not so great disproportion between our justice and that of God, as between unity and infinity.

The justice of God must be vast like His compassion. Now, justice to the outcast is less vast, and ought less to offend our feelings than mercy towards the elect.

We know that there is an infinite, and are ignorant of its nature. As we know it to be false that numbers are finite, it is therefore true that there is an infinity in number. But we do not know what it is. It is false that it is even, it is false that it is odd; for the addition of a unit can make no change in its nature. Yet it is a number, and every number is odd or even (this is certainly true of every finite number). So we may well

know that there is a God without knowing what He is. Is there not one substantial truth, seeing there are so many things which are not the truth itself?

We know then the existence and nature of the finite, because we also are finite and have extension. We know the existence of the infinite, and are ignorant of its nature, because it has extension like us, but not limits like us. But we know neither the existence nor the nature of God, because He has neither extension nor limits.

But by faith we know His existence; in glory we shall know His nature. Now, I have already shown that we may well know the existence of a thing, without knowing its nature.

Let us now speak according to natural lights.

If there is a God, He is infinitely incomprehensible, since, having neither parts nor limits, He has no affinity to us. We are then incapable of knowing either what He is or if He is. This being so, who will dare to undertake the decision of the question? Not we, who have no affinity to Him.

Who then will blame Christians for not being able to give a reason for their belief, since they

---

Reprinted from Blaise Pascal, *Thoughts*, translated by W. F. Trotter (New York: Collier & Son, 1910).

profess a religion for which they cannot give a reason? They declare, in expounding it to the world, that it is a foolishness, *stultitiam*; and then you complain that they do not prove it! If they proved it, they would not keep their words; it is in lacking proofs, that they are not lacking in sense. "Yes, but although this excuses those who offer it as such, and takes away from them the blame of putting it forward without reason, it does not excuse those who receive it." Let us then examine this point, and say, "God is, or He is not." But to which side shall we incline? Reason can decide nothing here. There is an infinite chasm which separates us. A game is being played at the extremity of this infinite distance where heads or tails will turn up. What will you wager? According to reason, you can do neither the one thing nor the other, according to reason, you can defend neither of the propositions.

Do not then reprove for error those who have made a choice; for you know nothing about it. "No, but I blame them for having made, not this choice, but a choice; for again both he who chooses heads and he who chooses tails are equally at fault, they are both in the wrong. The true course is not to wager at all."

—Yes; but you must wager. It is not optional. You are embarked. Which will you choose then; let us see. Since you must choose, let us see which interests you least. You have two things to lose, the true and the good; and two things to stake, your reason and your will, your knowledge and your happiness; and your nature has two things to shun, error and misery. Your reason is no more shocked in choosing one rather than the other, since you must of necessity choose. This is one point settled. But your happiness? Let us weigh the gain and the loss in wagering that God is. Let us estimate these two chances. If you gain, you gain all; if you lose, you lose nothing. Wager them without hesitation that He is.—"That is very fine. Yes, I must wager; but I may perhaps wager too much."—Let us see.

Since there is an equal risk of gain and of loss, if you had only to gain two lives, instead of one, you might still wager. But if there were three lives to gain, you would have to play (since you are under the necessity of playing), and you would be imprudent, when you are forced to play, not to chance your life to gain three at a game where there is an equal risk of loss and gain. But there is an eternity of life and happiness. And this being so, if there were an infinity of chances, of which one only would be for you, you would still be right in wagering one to win two, and you would act stupidly, being obliged to play, by refusing to stake one life against three at a game in which out of an infinity of an infinitely happy life to gain. But there is here an infinity of an infinitely happy life to gain a chance of gain against a finite number of chances of loss, and what you stake is infinite. It is all divided; wherever the infinite is and there is not an infinity of chances of loss against that of gain, there is no time to hesitate, you must give all. And thus, when one is forced to play, he must renounce reason to preserve his life, rather than risk it for infinite gain, as likely to happen as the loss of nothingness.

For it is no use to say it is uncertain if we will gain, and it is certain that we risk, and that the infinite distance between the *certainty* of what is staked and the *uncertainty* of what will be gained, equals the finite good which is certainly staked against the uncertain infinite. It is not so, as every player stakes a certainty to gain an uncertainty, and yet he stakes a finite certainty to gain a finite uncertainty, without transgressing against reason. There is not an infinite distance between the certainty staked and the uncertainty of the gain; that is untrue. In truth, there is an infinity between the certainty of gain and the certainty of loss. But the uncertainty of the gain is proportioned to the certainty of the stake according to the proportion of the chances of gain and loss. Hence it comes that, if there are as many risks on one side as on the other, the course is to play even; and then the certainty of the stake is equal to the uncertainty of the gain, so far is it from the fact that there is an infinite distance between them. And so our proposition is of infinite force, when there is the finite to stake in a game where there are equal risks of gain and loss, and the infinite to gain. This is demonstrable; and if men are capable of any truths, this is one.

VII.A.3

The Will to Believe

WILLIAM JAMES

William James (1842–1910) was a philosopher and psychologist, the elder brother of novelist Henry James, and one of the central figures in the American pragmatist school of philosophy. Among his more important works are The Varieties of Religious Experience *(1902),* Pragmatism *(1907), and* The Meaning of Truth *(1909). In the present essay James argues, against W. K. Clifford, that sometimes practical considerations force us to make decisions on propositions for which we do not yet and, indeed, may never have sufficient evidence.*

I

Let us give the name of hypothesis to anything that may be proposed to our belief; and just as the electricians speak of live and dead wires, let us speak of any hypothesis as either *live* or *dead*. A live hypothesis is one which appeals as a real possibility to him to whom it is proposed. If I ask you to believe in the Mahdi, the notion makes no electric connection with your nature—it refuses to scintillate with any credibility at all. As an hypothesis it is completely dead. To an Arab, however (even if he be not one of the Mahdi's followers), the hypothesis is among the mind's possibilities: It is alive. This shows that deadness and liveness in an hypothesis are not intrinsic properties, but relations to the individual thinker. They are measured by his willingness to act. The maximum of liveness in an hypothesis means willingness to act irrevocably. Practically, that means belief; but there is some believing tendency wherever there is willingness to act at all.

Reprinted from William James, *The Will to Believe* (New York: Longmans Green & Co., 1897).

Next, let us call the decision between two hypotheses an option. Options may be of several kinds. They maybe first, *living* or *dead*; secondly, *forced* or *avoidable*; thirdly, *momentous* or *trivial*; and for our purposes we may call an option a *genuine* option when it is of a forced, living, and momentous kind.

1. A living option is one in which both hypotheses are live ones. If I say to you: "Be a theosophist or be a Mohammedan," it is probably a dead option, because for you neither hypothesis is likely to be alive. But if I say: "Be an agnostic or be a Christian," it is otherwise: trained as you are, each hypothesis makes some appeal, however small, to your belief.

2. Next, if I say to you: "Choose between going out with your umbrella or without it," I do not offer you a genuine option, for it is not forced. You can easily avoid it by not going out at all. Similarly, if I say, "Either love me or hate me," "Either call my theory true or call it false," your option is avoidable. You may remain indifferent to me, neither loving nor hating, and you may decline to offer any judgment as to my theory. But if I say, "Either accept this truth or go without it," I put on you a forced option, for there is no standing place outside of the alternative. Every dilemma based on a complete logical disjunction, with no possibility of not choosing, is an option of this forced kind.

3. Finally, if I were Dr. Nansen and proposed to you to join my North Pole expedition, your option would be momentous; for this would probably be your similar opportunity, and your choice now would either exclude you from the North Pole sort of immortality altogether or put at least the chance of it into your hands. He who refuses to embrace a unique opportunity loses the prize as surely as if he tried and failed. Per contra, the option is trivial when the opportunity is not unique, when the stake is insignificant, or when the decision is reversible if it later proves unwise. Such trivial options abound in the scientific life. A chemist finds an hypothesis live enough to spend a year in its verification: he believes in it to that extent. But if his experiments prove inconclusive either way, he is quit for his loss of time, no vital harm being done.

It will facilitate our discussion if we keep all these distinctions well in mind.

II

The next matter to consider is the actual psychology of human opinion. When we look at certain facts, it seems as if our passional and volitional nature lay at the root of all our convictions. When we look at others, it seems as if they could do nothing when the intellect had once said its say. Let us take the latter facts up first.

Does it not seem preposterous on the very face of it to talk of our opinions being modifiable at will? Can our will either help or hinder our intellect in its perceptions of truth? Can we, by just willing it, believe that Abraham Lincoln's existence is a myth, and that the portraits of him in *McClure's Magazine* are all of some one else? Can we, by any effort of our will, or by any strength of wish that it were true, believe ourselves well and about when we are roaring with rheumatism in bed, or feel certain that the sum of the two one-dollar bills in our pocket must be a hundred dollars? We can say any of these things, but we are absolutely impotent to believe them; and of just such things is the whole fabric of the truths that we do believe in made up—matters of fact, immediate or remote, as Hume said, and relations between ideas, which are either there or not there for us if we see them so, and which if not there cannot be put there by any action of our own.

In Pascal's *Thoughts* there is a celebrated passage known in literature as Pascal's Wager. In it he tries to force us into Christianity by reasoning as if our concern with truth resembled our concern with the stakes in a game of chance. Translated freely his words are these: You must either believe or not believe that God is—which will you do? Your human reason cannot say. A game is going on between you and the nature of things which at the day of judgment will bring out either heads or tails. Weigh what your gains and your losses would be if you should stake all you have on heads, or God's existence: if you win in such case you gain eternal beatitude; if you lose, you lose nothing at all. If there were an infinity of chances and only one for God in this wager, still you ought to stake your all on God; for though you surely risk a finite loss by this procedure, any finite loss is reasonable, even a certain one is reasonable, if there is but the possibility of infinite gain. Go then, and take holy water, and have masses said: belief will come and stupefy your scruples.... Why should you not? At bottom, what have you to lose?

You probably feel that when religious faith expresses itself thus, in the language of the gaming-table, it is put to its last trumps. Surely Pascal's own personal belief in masses and holy water had far other springs; and this celebrated page of his is but an argument for others, a last desperate snatch at a weapon against the hardness of the unbelieving heart. We feel that a faith in masses and holy water adopted wilfully after such a mechanical calculation would lack the inner soul of faith's reality; and if we were ourselves in the place of the Deity, we should probably take particular pleasure in cutting off believers of this pattern from their infinite reward. It is evident that unless there be some preexisting tendency to believe in masses and holy water, the option offered to the will by Pascal is not a living option. Certainly no Turk ever took to masses and holy water on its account and even to us Protestants these means of salvation seem such foregone impossibilities that Pascal's logic, invoked for them specifically, leaves us unmoved. As well might the Mahdi write to us saying, "I am the Expected One whom God has created in his effulgence. You shall be infinitely happy if you confess me; otherwise you shall be cut off from the light of the sun. Weigh, then, your infinite gain if I am genuine against your finite sacrifice if I am not!" His logic would be that of Pascal; but he would vainly use it on us, for the hypothesis he offers us is dead. No tendency to act on it exists in us to any degree.

The talk of believing by our volition seems, then from one point of view, simply silly. From another point of view it is worse than silly, it is vile. When one turns to the magnificent edifice of the physical sciences, and sees how it was reared; what thousands of disinterested moral lives of men lie buried in its mere foundations; what patience and postponement, what choking down of preference, what submission to the icy laws of outer fact are wrought into its very stones and mortar; how absolutely impersonal it stands in its vast augustness—then how besotted and contemptible seems every little sentimentalist who comes blowing his voluntary smoke-wreaths, and pretending to decide things from out of his private dream! Can we wonder if those bred in the rugged and manly school of science should feel like spewing such subjectivism out of their mouths? The whole system of loyalties which grow up in the schools of science go dead against its toleration; so that it is only natural that those who have caught the scientific fever should pass over to the opposite extreme, and write sometimes as if the incorruptibly truthful intellect ought positively to prefer bitterness and unacceptableness to the heart in its cup.

> *It fortifies my soul to know*
> *That though I perish, truth is so*

sings Clough, while Huxley exclaims: "My only consolation lies in the reflection that, however bad our posterity may become, so far as they hold by the plain rule of not pretending to believe what they have no reason to believe, because it may be to their advantage so to pretend [the word "pretend" is surely here redundant], they will not have reached the lowest depths of immorality." And that delicious *enfant terrible* Clifford writes: "Belief is desecrated when given to unproved and unquestioned statements for the solace and private pleasure of the believer.... Whoso would deserve well of his fellows in this matter will guard the purity of his belief with a very fanaticism of jealous care, lest at any time it should rest on an unworthy object, and catch a stain which can never be wiped away.... If [a] belief has been accepted on insufficient evidence [even though the belief be true, as Clifford on the same page explains] the pleasure is a stolen one…. It is sinful because it is stolen in defiance of our duty to mankind. That duty is to guard ourselves from such beliefs as from a pestilence which may shortly master our own body and then spread to the rest of the town…. It is wrong always, everywhere, and for every one, to believe anything upon insufficient evidence."

III

All this strikes one as healthy, even when expressed, as by Clifford, with somewhat too much of robustious pathos in the voice. Free will and simple wishing do seem, in the matter of our credences, to be only fifth wheels to the coach. Yet if any one should thereupon assume that intellectual insight is what remains after wish and will and sentimental preference have taken wing, or that pure reason is what then settles our opinions, he would fly quite as directly in the teeth of the facts.

It is only our already dead hypotheses that our willing nature is unable to bring to life again. But what has made them dead for us is for the most part a previous action of our willing nature of an antagonistic kind. When I say "willing nature," I do not mean only such deliberate volitions as may have set up habits of belief that we cannot now escape from—I mean all such factors of belief as fear and hope, prejudice and passion, imitation and partisanship, the circumpressure of our caste and set. As a matter of fact we find ourselves believing, we hardly know how or why. Mr. Balfour gives the name of "authority" to all those influences, born of the intellectual climate, that make hypotheses possible or impossible for us, alive or dead. Here in this room, we all of us believe in molecules and the conservation of energy, in democracy and necessary progress, in Protestant Christianity and the duty of fighting for "the doctrine of the immortal Monroe," all for no reasons worthy of the name. We see into these matters with no more inner clearness, and probably with much less, than any disbeliever in them might possess. His unconventionality would probably have

some grounds to show for its conclusions; but for us, not insight, but the *prestige* of the opinions, is what makes the spark shoot from them and light up our sleeping magazines of faith. Our reason is quite satisfied, in nine hundred and ninety-nine cases out of every thousand of us, if it can find a few arguments that will do to recite in case our credulity is criticized by some one else. Our faith is faith in some one else's faith, and in the greatest matters this is the most the case. Our belief in truth itself, for instance, that there is a truth, and that our minds and it are made for each other,—what is it but a passionate affirmation of desire, in which our social system backs us up? We want to have a truth; we want to believe that our experiments and studies and discussions must put us in a continually better and better position towards it; and on this line we agree to fight out our thinking lives. But if a pyrrhonistic sceptic asks *us how we know* all this, can our logic find a reply? No! certainly it cannot. It is just one volition against another,—we willing to go in for life upon a trust or assumption which he, for his part, does not care to make.

As a rule we disbelieve all facts and theories for which we have no use. Clifford's cosmic emotions find no use for Christian feelings. Huxley belabors the bishops because there is no use for sacerdotalism in his scheme of life. Newman, on the contrary, goes over to Romanism, and finds all sorts of reasons good for staying there, because a priestly system is for him an organic need and delight. Why do so few "scientists" even look at the evidence for telepathy, so called? Because they think, as a leading biologist, now dead, once said to me, that even if such a thing were true, scientists ought to band together to keep it suppressed and concealed. It would undo the uniformity of Nature and all sorts of other things without which scientists cannot carry on their pursuits. But if this very man had been shown something which as a scientist he might *do* with telepathy, he might not only have examined the evidence, but even have found it good enough.

This very law which the logicians would impose upon us—if I may give the name of logicians to those who would rule out our willing nature here—is based on nothing but their own natural wish to exclude all elements for which they, in their professional quality of logicians, can find no use.

Evidently, then, our non-intellectual nature does influence our convictions. There are passional tendencies and volitions which run before and others which come after belief, and it is only the latter that are too late for the fair; and they are not too late when the previous passional work has been already in their own direction. Pascal's argument, instead of being powerless, then seems a regular clincher, and is the last stroke needed to make our faith in masses and holy water complete. The state of things is evidently far from simple; and pure insight and logic, whatever they might do ideally, are not the only things that really do produce our creeds.

IV

Our next duty, having recognized this mixed up state of affairs, is to ask whether it be simply reprehensible and pathological, or whether, on the contrary, we must treat it as a normal element in making up our minds. The thesis I defend is, briefly stated, this: *Our passional nature not only lawfully may, but must, decide an option between propositions, whenever it is a genuine option that cannot by its nature be decided on intellectual grounds; for to say, under such circumstances, "Do not decide, but leave the question open," is itself a passional decision—just like deciding yes or no—and is attended with the same risk of losing the truth....*

VII

One more point, small but important, and our preliminaries are done. There are two ways of looking at our duty in the matter of opinion—ways entirely different, and yet ways about whose difference the theory of knowledge seems hitherto to have shown very little concern. *We must know the truth; and we must avoid error*—these are our first and great commandments as would-be knowers; but they are not two ways of stating an identical commandment, they are two separable laws. Although it may indeed happen that when we believe the truth A, we escape as an incidental consequence from believing the falsehood B, it hardly ever happens that by merely disbelieving B we necessarily believe A. We may in escaping B fall into believing other falsehoods, C or D, just as bad as B; or we may escape B by not believing anything at all, not even A.

Believe truth! Shun error!—these, we see, are two materially different laws; and by choosing between them we may end by coloring differently our whole intellectual life. We may regard the chase for truth as paramount, and the avoidance of error as secondary; or we may, on the other hand, treat the avoidance of error as more imperative, and let truth take its chance. Clifford, in the instructive passage which I have quoted, exhorts us to the latter course. Believe nothing, he tells us, keep your mind in suspense forever, rather than by closing it on insufficient evidence incur the awful risk of believing lies. You, on the other hand, may think that the risk of being in error is a very small matter when compared with the blessings of real knowledge, and be ready to be duped many times in your investigation rather than postpone indefinitely the chance of guessing true. I myself find it impossible to go with Clifford. We must remember that these feelings of our duty about either truth or error are in any case only expressions of our passional life. Biologically considered, our minds are as ready to grind out falsehood as veracity, and he who says, "Better go without belief forever than believe a lie!" merely shows his own preponderant private horror of becoming a dupe. He may be critical of many of his desires and fears, but this fear he slavishly obeys. He cannot imagine any one questioning its binding force. For my own part, I have also a horror of being duped; but I can believe that worse things than being duped may happen to a man in this world; so Clifford's exhortation has to my ears a thoroughly fantastic sound. It is like a general informing his soldiers that it is better to keep out of battle forever than to risk a single wound. Not so are victories either over enemies or over nature gained. Our errors are surely not such awfully solemn things. In a world where we are so certain to incur them in spite of all our caution, a certain lightness of heart seems healthier than this excessive nervousness on their behalf. At any rate, it seems the fittest thing for the empiricist philosopher.

VIII

And now, after all this introduction, let us go straight at our question. I have said, and now repeat it, that not only as a matter of fact do we find our passional nature influencing us in our opinions, but that there are some options between opinions in which this influence must be regarded both as an inevitable and as a lawful determinant of our choice.

I fear here that some of you my hearers will begin to scent danger, and lend an inhospitable ear. Two first steps of passion you have indeed had to admit as necessary—we must think so as to avoid dupery, and we must think so as to gain truth; but the surest path to those ideal consummations, you will probably consider, is from now onwards to take no further passional step.

Well, of course, I agree as far as the facts will allow. Wherever the option between losing truth and gaining it is not momentous, we can throw the chance of *gaining truth* away, and at any rate save ourselves from any chance of *believing falsehood*, by not making up our minds at all till objective evidence has come. In scientific questions, this is almost always the case; and even in human affairs in general, the need of acting is seldom so urgent that a false belief to act on is better than no belief at all. Law courts, indeed, have to decide on the best evidence attainable for the moment, because a judge's duty is to make law as well as to ascertain it, and (as a learned judge once said to me) few cases are worth spending much time over: the great thing is to have them decided on *any* acceptable principle,

and got out of the way. But in our dealings with objective nature we obviously are recorders, not makers, of the truth; and decisions for the mere sake of deciding promptly and getting on to the next business would be wholly out of place. Throughout the breadth of physical nature facts are what they are quite independently of us, and seldom is there any such hurry about them that the risks of being duped by believing a premature theory need be faced. The questions here are always trivial options, the hypotheses are hardly living (at any rate not living for us spectators), the choice between believing truth or falsehood is seldom forced. The attitude of sceptical balance is therefore the absolutely wise one if we would escape mistakes. What difference, indeed, does it make to most of us whether we have or have not a theory of the Röntgen rays, whether we believe or not in mind-stuff, or have a conviction about the causality of conscious states? It makes no difference. Such options are not forced on us. On every account it is better not to make them, but still keep weighing reasons *pro et contra* with an indifferent hand.

I speak, of course, here of the purely judging mind. For purposes of discovery such indifference is to be less highly recommended, and science would be far less advanced than she is if the passionate desires of individuals to get their own faiths confirmed had been kept out of the game. See for example the sagacity which Spencer and Weismann now display. On the other hand, if you want an absolute duffer in an investigation, you must, after all, take the man who has no interest whatever in its results: he is the warranted incapable, the positive fool. The most useful investigator, because the most sensitive observer, is always he whose eager interest in one side of the question is balanced by an equally keen nervousness lest he become deceived.[1] Science has organized this nervousness into a regular *technique*, her so-called method of verification; and she has fallen so deeply in love with the method that one may even say she has ceased to care for truth by itself at all. It is only truth as technically verified that interests her. The truth of truths might come in merely affirmative form, and she would decline to touch it. Such truth as that, she might repeat with Clifford, would be stolen in defiance of her duty to mankind. Human passions, however, are stronger than technical rules. *"Le cœur a ses raisons,"* as Pascal says, *"que la raison ne connait pas";*[2] and however indifferent to all but the bare rules of the game the umpire, the abstract intellect, may be, the concrete players who furnish him the materials to judge of are usually, each one of them, in love with some pet "live hypothesis" of his own. Let us agree, however, that wherever there is no forced option, the dispassionately judicial intellect with no pet hypothesis, saving us, as it does, from dupery at any rate, ought to be our ideal.

The question next arises: Are there not somewhere forced options in our speculative questions, and can we (as men who may be interested at least as much in positively gaining truth as in merely escaping dupery) always wait with impunity till the coercive evidence shall have arrived? It seems *a priori* improbable that the truth should be so nicely adjusted to our needs and powers as that. In the great boarding-house of nature, the cakes and the butter and the syrup seldom come out so even and leave the plates so clean. Indeed, we should view them with scientific suspicion if they did.

IX

Moral questions immediately present themselves as questions whose solution cannot wait for sensible proof. A moral question is a question not of what sensibly exists, but of what is good, or would be good if it did exist. Science can tell us what exists; but to compare the *worths*, both of what exists and of what does not exist, we must consult not science, but what Pascal calls our heart....

Turn now from these wide questions of good to a certain class of questions of fact, questions concerning personal relations, states of mind between one man and another. *Do you like me or not?*—for example. Whether you do or not depends, in countless instances, on whether I meet you halfway, am willing to assume that you must like me, and show you trust and expectation. The previous faith on my part in your liking's

existence is in such cases what makes your liking come. But if I stand aloof, and refuse to budge an inch until I have objective evidence, until you shall have done something apt, as the absolutists say, *ad extorquendum assensum meum,* ten to one your liking never comes. How many women's hearts are vanquished by the mere sanguine insistence of some man that they must love him! He will not consent to the hypothesis that they cannot. The desire for a certain kind of truth here brings about that special truth's existence; and so it is in innumerable cases of other sorts.... *And where faith in a fact can help create the fact,* that would be an insane logic which should say that faith running ahead of scientific evidence is the "lowest kind of immorality" into which a thinking being can fall. Yet such is the logic by which our scientific absolutists pretend to regulate our lives!

X

In truths dependent on our personal action, then faith based on desire is certainly a lawful and possibly an indispensable thing.

But now, it will be said, these are all childish human cases, and have nothing to do with great cosmical matters, like the question of religious faith. Let us then pass on to that. Religions differ so much in their accidents that in discussing the religious question we must make it very generic and broad. What then do we now mean by the religious hypothesis? Science says things are; morality says some things are better than other things; and religion says essentially two things.

First, she says that the best things are the more eternal things, the overlapping things, the things in the universe that throw the last stone, so to speak and say the final word. "Perfection is eternal"—this phrase of Charles Secrétan seems a good way of putting this first affirmation of religion, an affirmation which obviously cannot yet be verified scientifically at all.

The second affirmation of religion is that we are better off even now if we believe her first affirmation to be true.

Now, let us consider what the logical elements of this situation are *in case the religious hypothesis in both its branches be really true.* (Of course, we must admit that possibility at the outset. If we are to discuss the question at all, it must involve a living option. If for any of you religion be a hypothesis that cannot, by any living possibility, be true, then you need go no farther. I speak to the "saving remnant" alone.) So proceeding, we see, first, that religion offers itself as a *momentous* option. We are supposed to gain, even now, by our belief, and to lose by our non-belief, a certain vital good. Secondly religion is a *forced* option, so far as that good goes. We cannot escape the issue by remaining sceptical and waiting for more light, because, although we do avoid error in that way *if religion be untrue*, we lose the good, *if it be true*, just as certainly as if we positively chose to disbelieve. It is as if a man should hesitate indefinitely to ask a certain woman to marry him because he was not perfectly sure that she would prove an angel after he brought her home. Would he not cut himself off from that particular angel-possibility as decisively as if he went and married some one else? Scepticism, then, is not avoidance of option; it is option of a certain particular kind of risk. *Better risk loss of truth than chance of error*—that is your faith-vetoer's exact position. He is actively playing his stake as much as the believer is; he is backing the field against the religious hypothesis, just as the believer is backing the religious hypothesis against the field. To preach scepticism to us as a duty until "sufficient evidence" for religion to be found is tantamount therefore to telling us, when in presence of the religious hypothesis, that to yield to our fear of its being error is wiser and better than to yield to our hope that it may be true. It is not intellect against all passions, then; it is only intellect with one passion laying down its law. And by what, forsooth, is the supreme wisdom of this passion warranted? Dupery for dupery, what proof is there that dupery through hope is so much worse than dupery through fear? I, for one, can see no proof; and I simply refuse obedience to the scientist's command to imitate his kind of option, in a case where my own stake is important enough to give me the right to choose my own form of risk. If religion be true and the evidence for it be still insufficient, I do not wish, by putting your extinguisher upon my nature (which feels to me as if it had after all some business in this matter), to forfeit my sole chance in life of getting upon the winning side—that chance depending, of course, on my willingness to run the risk of acting as if my passional need of taking the world religiously might be prophetic and right.

All this is on the supposition that it really may be prophetic and right, and that, even to us who are discussing the matter, religion is a live hypothesis which may be true. Now, to most of us religion comes in a still further way that makes a veto on our active faith even more illogical. The more perfect and more eternal aspect of the universe is represented in our religions as having personal form. The universe is no longer a mere *It* to us, but a *Thou*, if we are religious; and any relation that may be possible from person to person might be possible here. For instance, although in one sense we are passive portions of the universe, in another we show a curious autonomy, as if we were small active centers on our own account. We feel, too, as if the appeal of religion to us were made to our own active goodwill, as if evidence might be forever withheld from us unless we met the hypothesis halfway to take a trivial illusion; just as a man who in a company of gentlemen made no advances, asked a warrant for every concession, and believed no one's word without proof, would cut himself off by such churlishness from all the social rewards that a more trusting spirit would earn—so here, one who should shut himself up in snarling logicality and try to make the gods extort his recognition willy-nilly, or not get it at all, might cut himself off forever from his only opportunity of making the gods' acquaintance. This feeling, forced on us we know not whence that by obstinately believing that there are gods (although not to do so would be so easy both for our logic and our life) we are doing the universe the deepest service we can, seems part of the living essence of the religious hypothesis. If the hypothesis were true in all its parts, including this one, then pure intellectualism, with its veto on our making willing advances, would be an absurdity; and some participation of our sympathetic nature would be logically required. I therefore, for one, cannot see my way to accepting the agnostic rules for truth-seeking, or wilfully agree to keep my willing nature out of the game. I cannot do so for this plain reason, that *a rule of thinking which would absolutely prevent me from acknowledging certain kinds of truth if those kinds of truth were really there, would be an irrational rule.* That for me is the long and short of the formal logic of the situation, no matter what the kinds of truth might materially be.

I confess I do not see how this logic can be escaped. But sad experience makes me fear that some of you may still shrink from radically saying with me, *in abstracto*, that we have the right to believe at our own risk any hypothesis that is live enough to tempt our will. I suspect, however, that if this is so, it is because you have got away from the abstract logical point of view altogether, and are thinking (perhaps without realizing it) of some particular religious hypothesis which for you is dead. The freedom to "believe what we will" you apply to the case of some patent superstition; and the faith you think of is the faith defined by the schoolboy when he said, "Faith is when you believe something that you know ain't true." I can only repeat that this is misapprehension. *In concreto*, the freedom to believe can only cover living options which the intellect of the individual cannot by itself resolve; and living options never seem absurdities to him who has them to consider. When I look at the religious question as it really puts itself to concrete men, and when I think of all the possibilities which both practically and theoretically it involves, then this command that we shall put a stopper on our heart, instincts, and courage, and *wait*—acting of course meanwhile more or less as if religion were not true[3]—till doomsday, or till such time as our intellect and senses working together may have raked in evidence enough—this command, I say, seems to me the queerest idol ever manufactured in the philosophic cave. Were we scholastic absolutists, there might be more excuse. If we had an infallible intellect with its objective certitudes, we might feel ourselves disloyal to such a perfect organ or knowledge in not trusting to it exclusively, in not

waiting for its releasing word. But if we are empiricists, if we believe that no bell in us tolls to let us know for certain when truth is in our grasp, then it seems a piece of idle fantasticality to preach so solemnly our duty of waiting for the bell. Indeed we may wait if we will—I hope you do not think that I am denying that—but if we do so, we do so at our peril as much as if we believed. In either case we act, taking our life in our hands. No one of us ought to issue vetoes to the other, nor should we bandy words of abuse. We ought, on the contrary, delicately and profoundly to respect one another's mental freedom: then only shall we bring about the intellectual republic; then only shall we have that spirit of inner tolerance without which all our outer tolerance is soulless, and which is empiricism's glory; then only shall we live and let live, in speculative as well as in practical things.

I began by a reference to Fitz-James Stephen; let me end by a quotation from him. "What do you think of yourself? What do you think of the world? … These are questions with which all must deal as it seems good to them. They are riddles of the Sphinx, and in some way or other we must deal with them…. In all important transactions of life we have to take a leap in the dark…. If we decide to leave the riddles unanswered, that is a choice; if we waver in our answer, that, too, is a choice: but whatever choice we make, we make it at our peril. If a man chooses to turn his back altogether on God and the future no one can prevent him; no one can show beyond reasonable doubt that he is mistaken. If a man thinks otherwise and acts as he thinks, I do not see that any one can prove that he is mistaken. Each must act as he thinks best; and if he is wrong, so much the worse for him. We stand on a mountain pass in the midst of whirling snow and blinding mist, through which we get glimpses now and then of paths which may be deceptive. If we stand still we shall be frozen to death. If we take the wrong road we shall be dashed to pieces. We do not certainly know whether there is any right one. What must we do? 'Be strong and of a good courage.' Act for the best, hope for the best, and take what comes…. If death ends all, we cannot meet death better."

NOTES

1. Compare Wilfrid Ward's Essay "The Wish to Believe," in his *Witnesses to the Unseen* (Macmillan & Co., 1893).

2. "The heart has its reasons which reason does not know."

3. Since belief is measured by action, he who forbids us to believe religion to be true, necessarily also forbids us to act as we should if we did believe it to be true. The whole defence of religious faith hinges upon action. If the action required or inspired by the religious hypothesis is in no way different from that dictated by the naturalistic hypothesis, then religious faith is a pure superfluity, better pruned away, and controversy about its legitimacy is a piece of idle trifling, unworthy of serious minds. I myself believe, of course, that the religious hypothesis gives to the world an expression which specifically determines our reactions, and makes them in a large part unlike what they might be on a purely naturalistic scheme of belief.

VII.B.3

Rational Religious Belief Without Arguments

MICHAEL BERGMANN

Michael Bergmann (1964–) is professor of philosophy at Purdue University and works primarily in the fields of epistemology and philosophy of religion. In this chapter, Bergmann explains and defends the view (held by Alvin Plantinga and other so-called "Reformed epistemologists") that religious beliefs—like the belief that God exists—can be rational even if they are not based on arguments.

There have been many different attempts, by philosophers and others, to show that religious belief of various kinds is irrational. And there have been at least as many attempts by religious people to defend the rationality of their beliefs. Perhaps the most common religious belief to be attacked and defended in this way is belief in God—an omniscient, omnipotent, immaterial, eternal, perfectly good, wholly loving person on whom everything else depends. It will be convenient to focus our attention on belief in God, though much of our discussion will be relevant to other religious beliefs as well. Believers in God (theists) have for centuries now offered a variety of arguments for God's existence: they've argued that there must be a first cause (an uncaused cause) of the existence of things; they've argued that there must be a designer to account for the apparent design found in the natural world; they've argued that we can't make sense of morality without appealing to the existence of God; they've even argued that simply by reflecting on the concept of God we can see that God exists because such reflection reveals that God is the sort of being that *must* exist. The goal of these arguments is, at least in part, to show

that belief in God is rational. Reliance on these sorts of arguments is supposed by many to be what *makes* belief in God rational. In fact, it is commonly thought that belief in God *couldn't* be rational unless it is held on the basis of such arguments. But is that last thought right? Could a person's belief in God be rational even if it is not held on the basis of any of these alleged theistic proofs? Could there be rational religious belief without arguments?

For the past few decades, a prominent position within the philosophy of religion literature is that belief in God *can* be rational even if it isn't based on any arguments. This position is often called "Reformed Epistemology" to signify its roots in the writings of John Calvin (1509–1564), the great Protestant theologian and the main source of the Reformed tradition within Christendom. But one can find developments of the same idea in the writings of earlier figures such as Aquinas, Augustine, and even the apostle Paul. The central thesis of Reformed Epistemology is simply that religious belief, including belief in God, can be rational (sensible, reasonable, justified) even if it is not inferred from any other beliefs—even if it is not held on the basis of any argument at all. In what follows, I will

This essay was commissioned for the 6th edition of this anthology, and is published here for the first time.

explain this view in greater detail and then consider and respond to a number of objections to it.

I. UNDERSTANDING REFORMED EPISTEMOLOGY

A. A Little Background in Epistemology

In order to understand Reformed Epistemology, it will be helpful to begin with a little background in epistemology, which is the study of knowledge and rational belief. Epistemologists typically aren't concerned with religious belief in particular. Their concern is more general. They are trying to understand the nature of knowledge and rationality as these concepts apply to any belief whatsoever, regardless of the belief's topic or the means by which it was produced.

Let's begin by highlighting two distinctions. The first, which we've already been employing, is the distinction between rational and irrational beliefs. This is an *evaluative* distinction insofar as rational beliefs are, by definition, epistemically *better* than irrational beliefs. The second distinction is between basic beliefs and nonbasic beliefs. A basic belief is a belief that is not based on or inferred from another belief. A nonbasic belief is a belief that *is* based on or inferred from another belief. This is a *psychological* distinction, not an evaluative one. It has to do with how the beliefs are formed. Let's consider some examples of basic and nonbasic beliefs. Suppose you're visiting your doctor after being in a minor car accident and she is trying to determine the extent of your injuries. She gently presses on various parts of your back and neck, asking if it hurts when she does so. At one point you feel a very sharp pain and you tell her that it hurts. You tell her that because you *believe* that it hurts. That belief isn't inferred from other beliefs you have. (You don't first believe that you flinched when she pressed that spot and then infer that, because you flinch only when you're in pain, you must be in pain now). Instead, that belief is an automatic

noninferential response to the feeling of pain you experience; it is based on that experience, even though it isn't based on another belief. Because it is not based on another belief of yours, it is a basic (or noninferential) belief. Nonbasic (or inferential) beliefs are different. Suppose you want to figure out in your head what 9×53 equals. To do this, you typically will come first to believe that $9 \times 50 = 450$, that $9 \times 3 = 27$, and that $450 + 27 = 477$. Then you infer from those beliefs the further belief that $9 \times 53 = 477$. Since that last belief is inferred from other beliefs, it is a nonbasic belief.

An important question that has been of interest to philosophers as early as Aristotle (384–322 BCE) is whether any basic beliefs are rational. It's natural to think that for a belief to be rational, you must have a reason for holding it, where your reason is another belief of yours. But to hold a belief for a reason is to base it on or infer it from that other belief that is your reason. These considerations might incline a person to endorse *Inferentialism*, the view that a belief can be rational only if it's inferred from another belief. But there is a powerful and influential objection to Inferentialism, first proposed by Aristotle (*Posterior Analytics*, Book I, Chapters 2–3). This objection starts by noting that it's implausible to think that a belief can be rational in virtue of being inferred from an *irrational belief*. Hence, Inferentialism implies that a belief is rational only if it's inferred from another *rational* belief. But according to Inferentialism, for that second belief to be rational, it too must be inferred from another belief—which also must be rational. And so on. Thus, Inferentialism implies that in order for a belief to be rational, you must either base it on an infinite chain of reasoning or else reason in a circle. But it's obvious that reasoning in a circle cannot make a belief rational. And none of us is able to carry out an infinite chain of reasoning. (And even if we could, an infinite chain of reasoning cannot, by itself, make a belief rational without some original rationality to be transferred along the chain.) The upshot is that if Inferentialism is true, then it's impossible to have rational beliefs. Given that most philosophers think that it isn't impossible to have rational beliefs, it's widely believed that

Inferentialism is false: basic beliefs can be, and often are, rational. These rational basic beliefs are often called "properly basic beliefs."

Not just any basic belief is *properly* basic (i.e., both rational and noninferential). The reckless gambler who is having a run of terrible luck in the casino and who believes on a whim, not on the basis of any other beliefs, that his luck is about to improve, is thereby forming an irrational basic belief. Unlike your basic belief that you're in pain (when the doctor presses on your neck), the gambler's basic belief is not *properly* basic. So although some basic beliefs are properly basic, not all of them are. Which of our basic beliefs *are* properly basic? The answer to this question has to do with which belief-forming abilities we have. We humans have the ability to tell, without inference, that we're in pain. But we don't have the ability to tell, without inference, that our gambling luck is about to improve. We also have the ability to tell, without inference, what our own thoughts are. But we don't have the ability to tell, without inference, what others are thinking. Likewise, we have the ability to tell just by looking, without inference from other beliefs, that there's a book on the table in front of us. But we don't have the ability to tell in complete darkness, without inference, that there's a pillar six feet in front of us (though if we had the echolocation abilities that bats have, we could reasonably form such basic beliefs in the darkness). So which beliefs can be properly basic for us depends on which noninferential belief-forming abilities we have.

Which noninferential belief-forming abilities do we have? Which of our basic beliefs can be rational? There is wide agreement that we can tell noninferentially via introspection what we're thinking and feeling. In addition, there's wide agreement that we can tell noninferentially via rational intuition that one thing is logically implied by another, though this ability is limited for most people to very simple logical implications. (For example, we can tell noninferentially via rational intuition that if Jack and Jill are at the party then it logically follows that Jack is at the party.) Suppose that those were the only sorts of

properly basic beliefs we had and that the only way for us to have rational beliefs in addition to beliefs of those kinds would be to draw inferences from them. The famous philosopher René Descartes (1596–1650) began with only those sorts of basic belief—i.e., those formed via introspection and rational intuition—and tried from there to see what he could learn by inference. He thought that in that way, starting from those meager foundations, he could prove that God exists and that there is a physical world surrounding us. Most philosophers think that he failed in this attempt and that the problem had a lot to do with the fact that he allowed so few beliefs to count as properly basic. Today, most epistemologists think that in addition to the ability to form noninferential beliefs via introspection and rational intuition, we also have the ability to form noninferential beliefs via perception and memory. When, upon glancing at a nearby basketball, I believe there's a ball in front of me, I don't do this via inference: I don't first notice that it visually appears to me as if there's a ball there and that such appearances are good indicators that there is a ball there and from this infer that there's a ball in front of me. I can just tell noninferentially via perception that there's a ball in front of me. Likewise, I can tell noninferentially via memory that I had orange juice at breakfast. I don't infer this from the fact that there's a glass on the kitchen counter that looks as if it contained orange juice a few hours ago and that no one else in the house likes orange juice. Thus, it's very common for epistemologists to think we have the ability to form noninferential beliefs via perception, memory, introspection, and rational intuition. Because we have these abilities, the beliefs so produced are properly basic (i.e., noninferentially rational). And from these starting points, we can make inferences via good reasoning to the many other beliefs we hold; these other beliefs are then inferentially rational.

It's important to emphasize that although these properly basic beliefs aren't inferred from other beliefs, it doesn't follow that they are groundless or that we hold them without any evidence. Take for example the belief that you are in pain. It's true you don't infer that from other beliefs. But it's not groundless. Instead, it's based on your experience of pain. It's that experience, not another belief, which is the ground of your belief that you're in pain—that experience is your evidence for that belief. Other introspective beliefs are also based on experiences (such as the belief that you're happy or sad, which is based on your experience of feeling happy or sad).[1] Likewise, although perceptual beliefs aren't inferred from other beliefs, they aren't lacking in grounds or evidence. My belief that there's a ball in front of me is based on my visual experience at the moment (not on the belief that I'm having such a visual experience—I typically don't form such beliefs about my visual experience). That visual experience is my evidence—it is the ground of that visual belief. In the case of beliefs formed via memory or rational intuition, it's more difficult to say what they are based on. According to one common way of thinking about memory beliefs, they are based on memory seemings. It seems to me—in a remembering sort of way—that I had orange juice for breakfast. On the basis of that seeming (that memory seeming) I hold the memory belief that I had orange juice for breakfast. Similarly, beliefs in simple logical truths, formed via rational intuition are based on rational intuitions. I can just *see* (intellectually) that one thing logically follows from another. This "seeing" is a sort of insight, a rational intuition; it's an experience of something's seeming to me a certain way—it's an experience of its seeming obvious to me that this thing logically follows from that thing. And my belief that the one thing follows from the other is based on this rational intuition. Both the memory seeming and the rational intuition are experiences. They aren't themselves beliefs. So beliefs based on them still count as basic.

The resulting picture, widely endorsed by contemporary epistemologists, is the following. Some beliefs are rational and some are not. Those that are rational are either basic or not. The rational beliefs that aren't basic are inferred from other rational beliefs. These inference chains are ultimately traced back to properly basic beliefs—i.e., rational beliefs that aren't based on any other beliefs. What makes a basic belief rational has to do with which noninferential belief-forming abilities we have. At the very least, we humans seem to have the ability to form beliefs via perception, memory, rational intuition, and introspection. And the beliefs produced by these noninferential belief-forming abilities are based not on other beliefs but on experiences of various kinds—perceptual experiences, memory seemings, rational intuitions, and introspectable experiences such as pain, pleasure, happiness, sadness, etc.

There is one further "background epistemology" question that often gets discussed by philosophers and which will be relevant to our discussion of religious belief. The question is this: can a belief be properly basic for a person who has never thought at all about the epistemology of such beliefs in anything like the way we just have? For example, can a sad child be rational in remembering that his mother left the room a moment ago even if the child has no idea that that belief is based on a memory seeming? The answer, it seems, is "yes." One can be rational in forming noninferential beliefs via memory even if one has never thought about how memory works or what memory beliefs are based on or whether memory beliefs are basic or nonbasic.

However, given that rationality seems to rule out haphazard or careless belief formation, some might be tempted by a contrary view that we can call "Confirmationalism," which requires for a belief's rationality that we confirm that it was produced in the right way:

> *Confirmationalism:* In order for a belief to be rational, the person holding it needs a further belief that the first belief has an adequate basis.

So, for example, Confirmationalism would say that I can't be rational in my memory belief that I was in Florida last year unless I have an additional belief that that memory belief of mine has an adequate basis. Of course that second belief—required to confirm the adequacy of the first belief's basis—must itself be rational. But according to Confirmationalism, that second belief (like any other belief) is rational only if the person holding it has yet another belief that the second belief has an adequate basis. And that third belief must be rational too, which will require a fourth belief confirming the adequacy of its basis. And so on. Thus, Confirmationalism implies that in order for a simple belief—such as the belief that *there is a ball in front of me*—to be rational, I need to have an infinite number of other beliefs, each of which is about the previous belief having an adequate basis. (Because each belief is about the previous belief, this chain of beliefs will not circle back on itself.) But people aren't able to have an infinite number of extra beliefs for each of the simple beliefs they hold. Given Confirmationalism, this implies that people aren't able to have any rational beliefs. For this reason, most epistemologists reject Confirmationalism.[2]

B. Reformed Epistemology

Let us turn now to the task of trying to gain a better understanding of Reformed Epistemology, the view that belief in God can be rational even if it is not inferred from any other beliefs. Our background reflections in epistemology will benefit us as our discussion proceeds.

A helpful way to begin our more careful examination of Reformed Epistemology is to consider the context in which it was introduced into the contemporary philosophy of religion literature. A prominent twentieth-century objection to the rationality of belief in God runs as follows:

The Evidentialist Objection

1. *The Evidentialist Thesis*: Belief in God is rational only if it is inferred from other rational beliefs via good arguments.

2. But there aren't any good arguments for God's existence.

3. Therefore, belief in God is irrational.

The reason this objection is called "The Evidentialist Objection" is that it relies on the Evidentialist Thesis as its first premise.[3] According to that premise, theistic belief is rational only if it is based on good evidence in the form of good theistic arguments. The proponent of this objection to theism will, of course, endorse the Evidentialist Thesis but will not believe in God. Let's call such a proponent a "Nontheistic Evidentialist." For most of the twentieth century, the most common response to this argument, by those who wanted to defend theistic belief, was the response given by Theistic Evidentialists. Like Nontheistic Evidentialists, they accept the first premise, the Evidentialist Thesis. But they reject the second premise. They think there *are* good arguments for God's existence. And they spend a lot of time devising such arguments and defending those arguments against objections. It was in just this context of disagreement (between Theistic Evidentialists and Nontheistic Evidentialists over whether there are good theistic arguments) that a second theistic response to the Evidentialist Objection was offered, this time by Reformed Epistemologists. They turned their sights on the first premise, the Evidentialist Thesis itself. Their claim was that belief in God—like the belief that I had orange juice for breakfast or the belief that there's a ball in front of me—can be properly basic. (As for the second premise, some Reformed Epistemologists join Nontheistic Evidentialists in accepting it; others join Theistic Evidentialists in rejecting it. But all Reformed Epistemologists reject the first premise; and that is what they tend to focus on in responding to the Evidentialist Objection.)

Given that Reformed Epistemologists think belief in God is properly basic (and in light of our background excursion into epistemology in the previous section), you would expect Reformed Epistemologists to also think that we have a noninferential belief-forming ability enabling us to tell, without inference, that God exists. And that's just what we find in their writings. Alvin Plantinga, perhaps the most prominent of contemporary Reformed Epistemologists, suggests that we have a "sense of divinity" enabling us to form properly basic beliefs about God. And just as noninferential beliefs formed via perception and memory are not groundless but instead based on experience, so also properly basic beliefs about God are, according to the Reformed Epistemologist, not groundless but based on experience. Plantinga gives some examples of the sort of experiential grounds on which noninferential beliefs about God are based:

> [T]here is in us a disposition to believe propositions of the sort *this flower was created by God* or *this vast and intricate universe was created by God* when we contemplate the flower or behold the starry heavens or think about the vast reaches of the universe.... Upon reading the Bible, one may be impressed with a deep sense that God is speaking to him. Upon having done what I know is cheap, or wrong, or wicked I may feel guilty in God's sight and form the belief *God disapproves of what I've done*. Upon confession and repentance, I may feel forgiven, forming the belief *God forgives me for what I've done*. A person in grave danger may turn to God asking for his protection and help; and of course he or she then forms the belief that God is indeed able to hear and help if he sees fit. When life is sweet and satisfying, a spontaneous sense of gratitude may well up within the soul; someone in this condition may thank and praise the Lord for his goodness, and will of course form the accompanying belief that indeed the Lord is to be thanked and praised.[4]

The proposal here is that experiences of awe, guilt, forgiveness, fear, and gratitude can operate as grounds for beliefs about God. The beliefs so formed aren't usually of the form "God exists." They're more often of the form "God does this" or "God has done that" or "God is able to do such and such." In this way, they're like our more ordinary beliefs about the world around us. We typically don't form beliefs like "that lake exists." Instead, we think "that lake is cold" or "that lake is beautiful" or some such thing. But it's a short step from the belief about the lake (or God) to the further belief that the lake (or God) exists.[5]

It's important to emphasize (because it's so common for people to mistakenly think otherwise)

that Reformed Epistemologists hold that ordinary unsophisticated religious believers who know nothing of the epistemological views discussed in this paper can have properly basic belief in God. As I already noted, most epistemologists (whether religious or not) think that a child's memory-produced belief that his mother left the room a few moments ago is rational even if the child can give no account of what that memory belief is based on or why it is rational. What matters for the rationality of that memory belief is that the child *has* the ability to form beliefs using his memory, not whether the child can give an account of the epistemology of memory beliefs. Likewise, Reformed Epistemologists say that what matters for properly basic belief in God is that the believer *has* the ability to form beliefs via the sense of divinity, not that the person can give an account of the epistemology of noninferential theistic beliefs. So a belief in God can be rational even if the person holding it doesn't have the further belief that her belief in God has an adequate basis via the sense of divinity. Some objectors will insist that your belief via this alleged sense of divinity won't be rational without a further belief, based on good reasons, that the experiences on which you base your belief in God provide an adequate basis for such a belief. In response, the Reformed Epistemologist will point out that this complaint seems to rely on an appeal to Confirmationalism discussed above—a principle which most philosophers reject, and for good reason.

Here is a simple way to think of the Reformed Epistemologist's position: *belief in God is more like belief in other people than it is like belief in electrons.* We are able to form properly basic beliefs that there are people around us because, by using our vision, we can tell noninferentially that there are people nearby. But we aren't able to tell noninferentially, just by looking, that there are electrons nearby. We don't have that sort of ability. Instead, humans arrived at the belief in electrons via inference: we inferred their existence because it provided the best explanation of all the experimental evidence collected by scientists. According to the Evidentialist Thesis, belief in God—like belief in electrons—is rational only if we infer it as the best explanation of the available evidence (in the case of belief in God, the evidence in question is what gets cited in the premises of theistic arguments). But according to the Reformed Epistemologist, belief in God is more like belief in other people.[6] We don't first notice that it visually appears to us as if there are other people and then conclude that the best explanation of these visual appearances is that there really are other people that are the causes of these visual appearances. Rather, we just have the visual experiences and believe on the basis of them, without inference, that there are people around us. Likewise, the Reformed Epistemologist thinks that for many people, belief in God is not an inferred explanatory hypothesis but a noninferential response to experience. It's worth noting that it wouldn't be surprising for a loving God who wants all people to believe in him to give us the ability to believe in him noninferentially through a sense of divinity. That way of believing in God seems to be easier and less affected by differences in intelligence than inferential belief-formation, which requires an expertise (that isn't widely shared) in formulating and evaluating arguments.

As I signaled at the beginning of this essay, the Reformed Epistemologist's views don't apply only to the belief that God exists. Other religious beliefs as well can be rational in a similar way—beliefs in specific doctrines of this or that religion. There are a number of accounts of how these other religious beliefs are formed.[7] But ultimately it comes down to something very much like the views described above concerning properly basic belief in God.

II. OBJECTIONS TO REFORMED EPISTEMOLOGY

Let's turn now to some objections to Reformed Epistemology and consider what sorts of response are available.

Objection 1: Religious Interpretation of Experiential Evidence Needs Defense. The Reformed Epistemologist says that beliefs about God are based on experiences such as feeling forgiven after confession and repentance. On the basis of such an experience a person believes "God forgives me for what I've done." But this is to *interpret* the experience within a particular theological framework—it's to impose one interpretation among many possible ones on a raw experience consisting of a feeling of being forgiven replacing a feeling of guilt. In order for the belief about God's forgiveness to be rational, one needs some reason for favoring that particular theological interpretation over some other nontheistic interpretation of that same raw experience.

Consider a parallel complaint lodged against perceptual beliefs: "When you believe, on the basis of visual experience, that there is a chair and a desk nearby, you are imposing one interpretation among many possible interpretations on the raw experience consisting of a visual appearance that seems to be of a chair and desk nearby. You've adopted the "standard" interpretation according to which there really is a chair and a desk nearby causing you to have that visual appearance. But perhaps you are dreaming. Or perhaps you are the victim of an experiment in which computers are connected to your brain causing you to have that visual appearance. You aren't rational in believing there really is a chair and desk nearby unless you first have a reason for favoring the standard interpretation over the dreaming interpretation and the computer–simulation interpretation."

How have epistemologists responded to this parallel complaint about perception? One common response is to note the following things. First, if this complaint were legitimate, then most people wouldn't be rational in their beliefs about the world around them since most people simply don't have any reasons they could produce for favoring the standard interpretation of perceptual experience. Second, epistemologists have worked very hard for centuries trying to come up with good reasons for preferring the standard interpretation of perceptual experience to its rivals and have yet to come up with an argument acknowledged to be convincing. Because of this failure, it is widely believed that there is no good argument for preferring the standard interpretation of perceptual experience that doesn't itself rely on perceptual experience to tell us about the world around us.[8] Third, it seems that, in looking around us and forming visual beliefs about our environment, we don't first have a visual experience and then consider various ways to interpret it, ultimately selecting the standard interpretation. Instead, the world seems to present itself to us in visual experience as if the standard interpretation is true—the standard interpretation comes along unbidden with the visual experience. In light of all this, many epistemologists conclude that our perceptual beliefs are rational not because we've got a good reason for preferring the standard interpretation of our perceptual experience but because the rational response to having such experiences is to form beliefs, without inference, in accord with the standard interpretation.

The Reformed Epistemologist will say similar things about belief in God based on things such as an experience of feeling forgiven.[9] Many who believe, on the basis of such an experience, that God has forgiven them don't have any arguments available for favoring a theistic interpretation of that experience over a nontheistic one. Moreover, in many cases, they don't first have the experience and then consider various ways of interpreting it, ultimately selecting the theistic interpretation. Instead, that theistic interpretation comes along unbidden with that experience of feeling forgiven. And just as the rational response to perceptual experience is to form noninferential beliefs in the objects one takes oneself to see nearby, so also (says the Reformed Epistemologist) the rational response to the experience of feeling forgiven is to believe, without inference, that God is as one takes God to be on the basis of that experience.

Objection 2: The Great Pumpkin Objection. The Reformed Epistemologist's strategy for defending the rationality of religious belief is seriously problematic because the same strategy could be used to defend any

bizarre belief you like, including Linus's belief (in the Charlie Brown comics) that the gift-delivering Great Pumpkin rises each Halloween over the most sincere pumpkin patch. When challenged to give reasons for their belief, Great Pumpkinites could simply point out that their belief is properly basic so they don't need to give any arguments for it. The fact that this strategy can be used to defend such a bizarre view reveals the bankruptcy of the strategy. But it seems that the Reformed Epistemologist, in endorsing this sort of strategy for defending the rationality of her belief in God, cannot offer any principled objection to this same strategy used by others in defense of silly views like belief in the Great Pumpkin.

Here too we can consider a parallel complaint, this time against those who think introspective beliefs are rational. Suppose you tell me that you're feeling a little hungry and I ask you what your argument is for that claim. You tell me that you don't need an argument in order to be rational in believing that claim; you have the ability to tell, just by thinking about it, what sorts of feelings you are having. In response I say "Oh really? Well, with that sort of reasoning, you could have no objection to a person who claimed to be a mind-reader with the special ability to tell, just by thinking about it, what those around her are thinking and feeling." Notice what I would be suggesting by that response. I'd be suggesting that because you claim to be able to tell *one* thing without argument (namely, what sorts of feelings you're having), you can have no objection to a person who claims to be able to tell *another* thing without argument (namely, what those around her are thinking and feeling). But that suggestion of mine would be silly. It's perfectly sensible to say there are some things people can tell without argument and other things they can't tell without argument.

Reformed Epistemologists respond to the Great Pumpkin Objection in a similar manner.

They think there are some things people can tell without argument and other things people can't tell without argument. They think people can tell without argument that God exists but they can't tell without argument that the Great Pumpkin exists. There is nothing remarkable about the suggestion that people have abilities to tell some things, but not others, without inference. We already know that people can tell, just by looking and without inference, that there are people around them; but they can't tell just by looking and without inference that there are electrons. People can also tell, just by thinking about it and without inference, what thoughts they are having; but they can't in the same way tell, without inference, what thoughts others are having. They can, without inference, remember what happened in the recent past; but they can't in the same way tell, without inference, what is going to happen in the future. The Reformed Epistemologist's claim—that we have the ability to tell noninferentially that God exists but we don't have any such ability with respect to the Great Pumpkin—is just another claim of this sort. The "strategy" of claiming to have an ability to know something noninferentially can be employed in defending the rationality of a belief even by those who think there are many things we don't have the ability to know noninferentially. So Reformed Epistemologists aren't committed to approving of others who use the same sort of strategy to defend all sorts of silly views.

Objection 3: Why Doesn't Everyone Believe in God? The previous two responses have compared basic belief in God to properly basic perceptual beliefs or properly basic introspective beliefs. But this ignores a very important difference between basic belief in God, on the one hand, and basic perceptual and introspective beliefs, on the other: pretty much everybody forms basic beliefs about their surroundings via perception and basic beliefs about their thoughts and feelings via introspection; but there are many people who don't believe in God at all. That's an important

difference. If we have the ability to tell, without inference, that God exists, why are there so many people who don't believe in God?

The first thing to note here is that belief in some sort of deity is very widespread throughout human history, across many different cultures.[10] This of course doesn't prove that it's true. But it's important to keep in mind that it's not as if only a small minority of the world's population believes in God. Nevertheless, there are many people who don't seem to have any belief in God, and this is strikingly different from what we see when we compare basic belief in God with basic perceptual belief in the world around us or introspective belief in our mental states. What does the Reformed Epistemologist have to say about this?

The natural thing to say is that the *sense of divinity* isn't working equally well in all people. It is either damaged or hindered in its operation in many people and this has been so for a long time. It would be as if all humans had their vision damaged or otherwise hindered from normal operation and this condition of humanity lasted for many centuries. If that were to happen, some humans wouldn't be able to see at all and others would have only distorted or unclear vision. It might then happen that some who could see better than others would believe that the moon existed, but those who were blind or couldn't see as well, might not believe that the moon existed. Of course this analogy breaks down after a while.[11] But the main point of it, according to Reformed Epistemologists, is just that the sense of divinity is more damaged in some people than it is in others, and this explains why some people don't have properly basic belief in God whereas others do.[12]

Objection 4: Sinfulness Doesn't Explain Atheism. In responding to the last objection, Reformed Epistemologists say that the sense of divinity is more damaged in some people than in others. But what is it that causes this damage? A common suggestion by some Reformed Epistemologists is that "sinfulness" is the cause of this damage. But that's both insulting and implausible. It's easy to give examples of nontheists and theists where the nontheists are, morally speaking, much better behaved than the theists.

It's true that many in the Reformed tradition say that operational deficiencies in the sense of divinity are caused by sinfulness. And it's also clear that some morally well-behaved people are nontheists and that some theists behave terribly (the Bible itself points to fallen angels as well as to many humans in giving examples of badly behaved theists). So how can anyone take seriously the suggestion that sinfulness explains why many people don't believe in God?

What follows is one possible way to make sense of the suggestion that sinfulness can explain lack of belief in God. (Notice that the goal here isn't to prove the truth of the explanation of unbelief in terms of sinfulness or of this particular way of making sense of it. Rather, it's to show how explaining unbelief by pointing to sinfulness can be consistent with the observation that nontheists often seem to be better behaved than theists.) We first need to distinguish inherited sinfulness from willful sinfulness. Ever since humans fell into sin, the result (according to Christians, including those in the Reformed tradition) has been that *all* of their descendents have been born with an inherited tendency to selfishness and pride.[13] This inherited tendency seems to come in various degrees. Because it is inherited, this tendency is not something we've chosen. Nor did we choose how severe it is in our own case.[14] In addition to inherited sinfulness, which we don't choose, there is also willful sinfulness. This occurs when we freely choose to act in a way that is contrary to our conscience. We are responsible for our willful sinfulness even though we aren't responsible for our inherited sinfulness. The explanation I want to consider for why not all people believe in God appeals, in part, to both inherited sinfulness and willful sinfulness.

There are really two things that need explaining: how sinfulness can keep people from believing

in God and why, despite that first explanation, there isn't a tight correlation between one's belief status (as theist or nontheist) and one's moral status (as well-behaved or badly behaved). As for the first explanation, there are two ways sinfulness can hinder belief in God: it can hinder it in a way for which the unbeliever is *not* to blame; and it can hinder it in a way for which the unbeliever *is* to blame. Let's consider how it might hinder it in ways for which the unbeliever is not to blame. For starters, the inherited tendency to selfishness and pride damages the sense of divinity in all people so that it doesn't work as it was originally intended.[15] It's as if all of us have blurred vision when it comes to detecting God noninferentially. And because our inherited sinfulness comes in varying degrees, the damage it causes to the sense of divinity also comes in varying degrees. On top of that, due to both the inherited and willful sinfulness of those in our family and our larger society, our upbringing can cause further damage or hindrance to the operation of the sense of divinity in us. Here too, the resulting damage will come in varying degrees, depending on what has happened in our family and society, on what damage was caused by our own inherited sinfulness, and on how those two kinds of damage interact. All of these sin-caused effects on our sense of divinity hinder belief in God in a way for which the unbeliever is *not* to blame.

But, in addition to the above-mentioned things that affect what we might think of as our unchosen "starting point," there are other things that hinder belief in God. These other things affect how we progress from our starting point either further from or closer to belief in God. One contributor here could be willful sinfulness. By choosing to go against my conscience, I can perhaps further contribute to the damage to my sense of divinity. This is a case in which I am partially to blame for the way in which sin hinders my belief in God. But there are other possible contributors as well. God may choose to give experiential evidence for theistic belief to some people and not to others— evidence on which a properly basic belief in God can be based without inference.[16] (This might involve giving experiences to a person that the person wouldn't otherwise have had. Or it might involve correcting damage to the sense of divinity so that the person treats as evidence for belief about God experiences that the person wouldn't otherwise have treated in that way.) God's decision to give or delay giving such evidence might be based on the willful sinfulness of the person in question. But it might be based on other things as well. Perhaps God thinks the person isn't yet ready to respond correctly to such evidence. Or perhaps God has a reason for wanting this person to progress further morally than others before coming to believe in God. And there may be other good reasons God has for delay in giving evidence, reasons that we don't know of.

In light of the above explanation for how sinfulness can hinder belief in God, we can see why it might be that there isn't a tight correlation between one's theistic-belief status and one's moral-behavior status. For, as we've just noted, though unbelief may be due to sinfulness in the ways described, God might give or delay giving evidence for properly basic belief in God on the basis of considerations that aren't correlated with how well-behaved the person is. And we aren't well placed to discern why there is unbelief in a particular case.

Moreover, appearances can be deceiving when we consider the moral goodness of those around us. It's natural to think that if God existed and were just and fair, he would judge people based on how well they did with the moral resources they were given. Consider two people, one of whom is given the opportunities of a naturally pleasant and cooperative personality and excellent moral training in her home and society while the other naturally has a more irritable and stubborn personality and is raised in a terrible home environment and influenced by a morally depraved society. It's easy to see how it might turn out that the person with the less fortunate background *might* be judged by God to have done much better, morally speaking, with what she was given than the more fortunate person; and this could be so even though the more fortunate person appears in many ways to behave better than the one with the less fortunate background. The point

here is just that we really aren't able to tell how people are to be judged unless we can look into their hearts and backgrounds to see how well they are doing with what they were given, something we are rarely, if ever, able to do with much accuracy. This point is reinforced when we consider that motives matter tremendously. A person may perform many seemingly kind and generous actions but be doing them from motives of selfishness and pride. Again, it seems that if God existed and were to judge us fairly, he would take that into account. Because we can't always tell how good people are (in terms of their motives or how well they've done with what they've been given), we aren't well placed to draw conclusions about how belief in God is in fact correlated with goodness in people. There might be more of a correlation there than meets the eye. But even if there isn't (and Reformed Epistemologists certainly aren't committed to thinking there is), there are the other considerations noted above explaining why there needn't be any such correlation even if sinfulness (both inherited and willful) does go some way toward explaining why people don't believe in God.

Objection 5: Religious Disagreement as a Reason for Doubt. In addition to the problem of people who don't believe in God, there's the problem of people who do believe in God but hold very different views about God. If each of them is relying on the sense of divinity and yet getting such different beliefs as a result, doesn't that give a person good reason to mistrust this alleged belief-forming ability in herself, especially given that many don't seem to have it at all? This problem is especially disconcerting when we consider that intelligent, thoughtful people who are sincerely seeking the truth discuss their disagreements about theism at length, explaining their evidence to each other, and yet continue to disagree.

There are three points to make in response to this objection.[17] The first has to do with the principle on which the objection seems to be based. The principle focuses on disagreement with someone who is intellectually virtuous (let's say a person is intellectually virtuous when he or she is intelligent, thoughtful, and sincerely seeking the truth). The basic idea seems to be that when someone who is intellectually virtuous disagrees with you, especially if you recognize that this person is about as intellectually virtuous as you are, then you thereby have a good reason to give up your belief. We can call this principle on which this objection seems to rely "the Withholding Principle." It can be formulated as follows:

> *Withholding Principle:* If an intellectually virtuous person (whom you realize is about as intellectually virtuous as you are) disagrees with you on a controversial topic even after each of you has tried your best to disclose all your relevant evidence to the other (where this evidence falls short of being a knockdown proof that every intelligent thoughtful truth-seeker would accept), then to be rational each of you should give up your contentious belief on this topic and, instead, withhold judgment on the matter.

The problem is that intelligent, thoughtful truth-seekers disagree about the Withholding Principle itself. Some think you should withhold judgment whenever you're in the circumstances described in the principle; but others think that's not so. Moreover, those who endorse the Withholding Principle don't have a knockdown proof for the principle, one that every intelligent, thoughtful truth-seeker would accept. The result is that if the principle is true, then rationality requires you to reject it—since you can't *prove* the principle's truth to intelligent, thoughtful truth-seekers who think it's false. And that means that the principle is self-undermining, saying about itself that it's irrational to accept it.

A second thing worth pointing out is that the Reformed Epistemologist can distinguish internal rationality from external rationality, conceding the former but not the latter to those who disagree about religious matters. This distinction highlights the fact that there are two stages in the formation of noninferential beliefs based on experiential evidence rather than on arguments. The first stage is where the person comes to have the experiential evidence; the second stage is where the person bases the noninferential belief in question on that experiential evidence. The belief so based is *internally rational* if it is an appropriate (reasonable, sensible) response for a person to have to that sort of experiential evidence. One way to put this point is to say that, in the formation of an internally rational belief, all is going well *downstream* from (i.e., in response to) the experience on which it is based. The belief is *externally* rational if, in addition to being internally rational, it's also the case that all is going well *upstream* from that experience—that is to say, the experiential evidence arises in the right way in the person who has it and is not due, for example, to any sort of cognitive malfunction. With this distinction in hand, the Reformed Epistemologist can point out that those who disagree with her may well be internally rational even if they aren't externally rational. Thus, for example, a Jewish theist who denies the divinity of Christ and who endorses the Reformed Epistemologist approach[18] can say (i) the Christian is internally rational in believing, on the basis of her experiential evidence in support of the doctrine, that *Jesus is God incarnate* and (ii) the atheist who lacks any experiential evidence in support of belief in God is internally rational in believing there is no God. But the Jewish believer can go on to add that the Christian is externally *irrational* because it is only due to some sort of cognitive malfunction that the Christian has that experiential evidence supporting the doctrine that Jesus is God incarnate; likewise, the Jewish believer can say that the atheist is externally irrational in believing there is no God because it is only due to some sort of cognitive malfunction (affecting the sense of divinity) that the atheist lacks any experiential evidence in support of belief in God.[19] In this way, those who endorse the Reformed Epistemologist approach can recognize that there is a sense in which the intelligent, thoughtful truth-seekers who disagree with them may be rational—they may be internally rational. But the Reformed Epistemologist can also explain why her beliefs are epistemically better than the religious beliefs of those who disagree—her own beliefs are externally rational whereas the beliefs of those who disagree with her are externally irrational.

The third point to make is that there seem to be examples where it is entirely appropriate to say—of intelligent, thoughtful truth-seekers whose views you disagree with but can't prove wrong—that their contrary views are externally irrational and mistaken whereas yours are externally rational and correct. Consider a case of moral disagreement about how to evaluate the following very disturbing behavior of Jack's. Jack takes pleasure in torturing and killing children, and he has found a way to do this without getting caught. I assume that you think this behavior of Jack's is morally wrong (extremely so). But you have a friend—who, like you, is an intelligent, thoughtful truth-seeker—who disagrees. She is a moral nihilist, someone who thinks it's false that Jack's behavior is morally wrong because there are no moral facts and nothing is morally wrong—or morally right. Like you, this friend is utterly disgusted by Jack's behavior and very strongly wishes that Jack wouldn't engage in it. But, unlike you, your friend doesn't think it is morally wrong. Now suppose you and your friend try to share with each other all your evidence for your opposing views. You point to your properly basic belief (based on some sort of intuitive seeming[20]) that actions of the sort Jack performs are morally wrong, which shows that moral nihilism is false. Your friend points to her properly basic belief (also based on some sort of intuitive seeming) in a key premise used to support her belief in moral nihilism—a view implying that Jack's behavior is neither morally wrong nor morally right. Unfortunately, even after you each try your best to share your relevant evidence, the disagreement persists. Does rationality require that, upon learning of this persistent disagreement with your friend, you should give up your belief that Jack's behavior is wrong? No. Instead of being moved to doubt the reliability of our own beliefs on this topic, we are sensibly moved to feel badly for the friend who disagrees with us and to be glad that we are fortunate enough not to lack the moral insight we have or to have the misleading moral views that our moral nihilist friend has.

Moreover, you can acknowledge that your moral nihilist friend may be *internally* rational in thinking Jack's behavior isn't wrong. After all, your friend has strong experiential evidence (i.e., *her* intuitive seemings) in support of that noninferential belief in the premise supporting moral nihilism. And your friend doesn't have the additional evidence you have which would outweigh this—namely, stronger experiential evidence (i.e., *your* intuitive seemings) in support of the view that Jack's behavior is wrong. You can concede that the right response to the evidence your friend has may be to believe in moral nihilism; so all may be going well downstream from your friend's experiential evidence. But you will insist that your friend isn't externally rational because something has gone wrong upstream from her experiential evidence. The very fact that moral nihilism seems intuitively more plausible to your friend than the claim that Jack's behavior is morally wrong shows that your friend is suffering from some sort of cognitive malfunction or problem, despite your friend's intelligence, thoughtfulness, and sincere interest in discovering the truth.[21]

The Reformed Epistemologist can, therefore, insist that, in the above scenario, it is appropriate for you to think Jack's behavior is wrong despite the fact that your intelligent, thoughtful, and truth-seeking friend continues to disagree with you about this, even after you share all your evidence. Moreover, it seems sensible for you to think that your friend is mistaken and externally irrational in her moral nihilist view that Jack's behavior is not wrong, though you could allow that that view of hers may be internally rational. And the Reformed Epistemologist can then point out that something similar is going on in the case of religious disagreement. Those who disagree with her religious beliefs might be *internally* rational in their beliefs in a different religion or against all religions. But the beliefs of those who disagree with her are both mistaken and *externally* irrational, despite the fact that they are held by intelligent, thoughtful truth-seekers. The point here is most definitely *not* that there is any connection between rejecting moral nihilism and endorsing a religious view. Rather, the point is that *if*—in the case of your belief that Jack's behavior is wrong—you can sensibly think your friend is mistaken and externally irrational despite the fact that she's also an internally rational, intelligent, thoughtful truth-seeker, *then* there is, in principle, no bar to your sensibly thinking something similar of a friend in the case of a religious disagreement. In addition, the fact that you and your friend are both relying on intuitive seemings in arriving at your opposing views about the morality of Jack's behavior doesn't show that you rationally ought to give up all views you have that are based on intuitive seemings. Likewise, the fact that you and someone else differ in your views about God even though you both rely on the sense of divinity doesn't show that you rationally ought to give up all your views based on the sense of divinity.

Of course, it's true that the nontheist will be inclined to think that her nontheistic beliefs are externally rational and that it's the *theist* that is externally irrational. But why think this should be a problem for the theist? After all, your moral nihilist friend will be inclined to think that she is externally rational and that *you* are externally irrational in thinking Jack's behavior is morally wrong. Should the fact that the moral nihilist views you this way lead you to give up your view that you, not her, are the one that is holding the externally rational belief on this matter? It seems not. Even if your moral nihilist friend thinks that of you, it seems perfectly reasonable for you to continue holding your belief and thinking that you are externally rational in doing so.[22] In the same way, even if the nontheist will be inclined to view the theist as externally irrational, it doesn't follow that the theist should give up her view that she, and not the nontheist, is externally rational.

CONCLUSION

We've considered in this paper the Reformed Epistemologist's position that belief in God can be rational even if it is not based on any argument. We've tried to understand what her view is—the sense in which she thinks belief in God is more like belief in other people like belief in electrons. And we've considered several challenging objections to the Reformed Epistemologist's proposal. There is a lot more that could be said in explaining and trying to make plausible the Reformed Epistemologist's position, especially as it applies to religious beliefs other than belief in God. And more should also be said in response to the above objections and to others besides.[23] Nevertheless, I hope what has been said here helps the reader to appreciate why many people take this sort of view seriously.[24]

NOTES

1. What about your introspective beliefs about what you're thinking? What are they based on? They're based on your experience of having those thoughts. They aren't inferred from other beliefs of yours.

2. Confirmationalism is similar to Inferentialism; in fact, it seems to be one version of Inferentialism.

3. Notice, by the way, that the Evidentialist Thesis is different from Inferentialism. The latter says that *no* belief can be rational unless it is inferred from other rational beliefs; the former says merely that *belief in* *God* cannot be rational unless it is inferred from other beliefs.

4. Plantinga (1983:80).

5. For this reason, Plantinga suggests (1983:81–82) that it is beliefs about what God does or is like, not the belief that God exists, that are properly basic. But for simplicity's sake, I'll speak as if he and others think belief in God is properly basic.

6. Interestingly, current research in the cognitive science of religion has arrived at a similar conclusion in its attempts to explain the origins of

religious belief (which is widespread across times and cultures). One common theme in this research is that belief in God is a natural and instinctive reaction to a variety of stimuli; it is not the result of inferences or arguments. See Clark and Barrett (2010) for a summary of this research and a discussion of how it compares to the views of Reformed Epistemologists.

7. See Plantinga (2000) for one prominent example.

8. See Alston (1993) where this point is defended at length.

9. See, for example, Alston (1983).

10. For an extended explanation, from the perspective of cognitive science, of why this is so, see Barrett (2004).

11. Some might think that the analogy breaks down because vision can be cross-checked with other perceptual faculties such as sense of touch whereas we can't cross-check the sense of divinity in that same way. But see Alston (1991, ch. 5) for a discussion of how something like the sense of divinity might be subject to cross-checking.

12. Additional explanations for differences between properly basic religious belief and properly basic perceptual belief are given in Alston (1983) and Alston (1991).

13. Must one believe in a literal reading of early Genesis to believe that there was a time that humans fell into sin? And doesn't that literal reading conflict with the well-established theory of evolution? A literal reading of early Genesis does seem to conflict with evolutionary theory. But many religious people who accept the teachings of the Bible as authoritative think that (i) early Genesis is not best interpreted in that literal way, (ii) evolutionary theory is true, and (iii) one thing we can learn from early Genesis is that humanity fell into sin in some way or other, even if not in the precise way described there. For a discussion of how inherited sinfulness can be combined with an evolutionary account of human origin, see Collins (2003).

14. Is it fair for Gold to let the immoral choices of our ancestors cause us to have this inherited tendency? This is just an instance of the more general question: is it fair for God to let the wrong choices of some people negatively affect the lives of others? It's not implausible to think that, so long as God has some justifying reason for doing so (one that treats those negatively affected with love and respect), it is fair for God to do that.

15. How does selfishness and pride cause damage to the sense of divinity? This might happen in any number of ways: perhaps selfishness and pride make one less inclined to believe in a being to whom they owe worship and service; or perhaps the sense of divinity works by way of divine blessing that is withheld from those who are selfish and proud; or perhaps the damage to the sense of divinity caused by selfishness and pride comes about in some other way.

16. Recall that, although basic beliefs are ones that are not inferred from other beliefs, they might still be based on evidence of some kind.

17. These three points are developed at greater length in a different context in Bergmann (2009).

18. To endorse the Reformed Epistemologist approach is *not* to endorse the teachings of the Reformed tradition within Christendom or any other distinctively Christian doctrines. Rather, it's to say that belief in God (or other religious beliefs) can be properly basic.

19. This example is not meant to suggest that Jewish believers must or often do explain Christian and atheistic belief in this way. The point is just to give an illustration of how one *could* explain the beliefs of those with whom one disagrees on religious matters. Moreover, in explaining that Christian and atheistic belief involve cognitive malfunction, the Jewish believer needn't think the Christian and the atheist are insane or brain-damaged. Instead, the Jewish believer would just be saying that the sense of divinity isn't working property in the Christian or in the atheist.

20. An intuitive seeming that p is true is an experience of it seeming intuitively to you that p is true.

21. Again, the point isn't that your friend is insane or brain-damaged but just that the process by which her moral intuitions are formed is not working properly.

22. But won't the same hold for your moral nihilist friend? Won't the fact that you view her as externally irrational fail to show that she should give up her view that she, not you, is the one that is externally rational? That may be right. But if that's right, which of you *really is* externally rational? Presumably it could only be the one whose views on this matter are correct. Which one of you is

that? Unfortunately, that's a matter of dispute. But you (and many others) will sensibly think that your view (that Jack's behavior is morally wrong) is both true and externally rational. Questions parallel to those raised here can be raised in the case of disagreement over theistic belief and parallel answers can be given.

23. The main places to look for further discussion of these topics are Alston (1991) and Plantinga (2000).

24. Thanks to Jeffrey Brower and Michael Rea for helpful comments on earlier drafts of this paper.

REFERENCES

Alston, William, "Christian Experience and Christian Belief" pp. 103–34 in *Faith and Rationality*, eds. Alvin Plantinga and Nicholas Wolterstorff (Notre Dame: University of Notre Dame Press, 1983).

Alston, William, *Perceiving God* (Ithaca: Cornell University Press, 1991).

Alston, William, *The Reliability of Sense Perception* (Ithaca: Cornell University Press, 1993).

Barrett, Justin. *Why Would Anyone Believe in God?* (Lanham, MD: AltaMira Press, 2004).

Bergmann, Michael, "Rational Disagreement after Full Disclosure," *Episteme* 6(2009): 336–53.

Clark, Kelly James and Justin Barrett. "Reformed Epistemology and the Cognitive Science of Religion." *Faith and Philosophy* 27 (2010): 174–89.

Collins, Robin. "Evolution and Original Sin" pp. 469–501 in *Perspectives on an Evolving Creation*, ed. Keith B. Miller 2006, (Grand Rapids: Eerdmans Publishing Company, 2003).

Plantinga, Alvin, "Reason and Belief in God" pp. 16–93 in *Faith and Rationality*, eds. Alvin Plantinga and Nicholas Wolterstorff (Notre Dame: University of Notre Dame Press, 1983).

Plantinga, Alvin, *Warranted Christian Belief* (New York: Oxford University Press, 2000).

SUBJECTIVE TRUTH, INWARDNESS; TRUTH IS SUBJECTIVITY

SOREN KIERKEGAARD

W hether truth is defined more empirically as the agreement of thinking with being or more idealistically as the agreement of being with thinking, the point in each case is to pay scrupulous attention to what is understood by being and also to pay attention to whether the knowing human spirit might not be lured out into the indefinite and fantastically become something such as no *existing* human being has ever been or can be, a phantom with which the individual busies himself on occasion, yet without ever making it explicit to himself by means of dialectical middle terms how he gets out into this fantastical realm, what meaning it has for him to be there, whether the entire endeavor out there might not dissolve into a tautology within a rash, fantastical venture.

If, in the two definitions given, being [*Væren*] is understood as empirical being, then truth itself is transformed into a *desideratum* [something wanted] and everything is placed in the process of becoming [*Vorden*], because the empirical object is not finished, and the existing knowing spirit is itself in the process of becoming. Thus truth is an approximating whose beginning cannot be established absolutely, because there is no conclusion that has retroactive power. On the other hand, every beginning, when it is *made* (if it is not arbitrariness by not being conscious of this), does not occur by virtue of immanental thinking but *is made* by virtue of a resolution, essentially by virtue of faith. That the knowing spirit is an existing spirit, and that every human being is such a spirit existing for himself,[1] I cannot repeat often enough, because the fantastical disregard of this has been the cause of much confusion. May VII
158 no one misunderstand me. I am indeed a poor existing spirit like all other human beings, but if in a legitimate and honest way I could be assisted in becoming something extraordinary, the pure *I-I*, I would always be willing to give thanks for the gift and the good deed. If, however, it can occur only in the way mentioned

---

[1] On the phrase "for himself," see *Sickness unto Death*, p. 14 and note 6, *KW* XIX (*SV* XI 128).

---

earlier, by saying *eins, zwei, drei, kokolorum* or by tying a ribbon around the little finger and throwing it away in some remote place when the moon is full—then I would rather remain what I am, a poor existing individual human being.

The term "being" in those definitions must, then, be understood much more abstractly as the abstract rendition or the abstract prototype of what being *in concreto* is as empirical being. If it is understood in this way, nothing stands in the way of abstractly defining truth as something finished, because, viewed abstractly, the agreement between thinking and being is always finished, inasmuch as the beginning of the process of becoming lies precisely in the concretion that abstraction abstractly disregards.

But if being is understood in this way, the formula is a tautology; that is, thinking and being signify one and the same, and the agreement spoken of is only an abstract identity with itself. Therefore, none of the formulas says more than that truth is, if this is understood in such a way that the copula is accentuated—truth *is*—that is, truth is a redoubling [*Fordoblelse*].[2] Truth is the first, but truth's other, that it is, *is* the same as the first; this, its being, is the abstract form of truth. In this way it is expressed that truth is not something simple but in an entirely abstract sense a redoubling, which is nevertheless canceled at the very same moment.

Abstraction may go on by paraphrasing this as much as it pleases—it will never come any further. As soon as the being of truth becomes empirically concrete, truth itself is in the process of becoming and is indeed in turn, by intimation, the agreement between thinking and being, and is indeed actually that way for God, but it is not that way for any existing spirit, because this spirit, itself existing, is in the process of becoming.

For the existing spirit *qua* existing spirit, the question about truth persists, because the abstract answer is only for that *abstractum* which an existing spirit becomes by abstracting from himself *qua* existing, which he can do only momentarily, although at such moments he still pays his debt to existence by existing nevertheless. Consequently, it is an existing spirit who asks about truth, presumably because he wants to exist in it, but in any case the questioner is conscious of being an existing individual human being. In this way I believe I am able to make myself understandable to every Greek and to every rational human being. If a German philosopher follows his inclination to put on an act [*skabe sig*] and first transforms himself [*skabe sig om*] into a superrational something, just as alchemists and sorcerers bedizen themselves fantastically, in order to answer the question about truth in an extremely satisfying way, this is of no more concern to me than his satisfying answer, which no doubt is extremely satisfying—if one is fantastically dressed up. But whether a German philosopher is or is not doing this can easily be ascertained by anyone who with enthusiasm concentrates his soul on willing to allow himself to be guided by a sage of that kind, and uncritically just uses his guidance compliantly by willing to form his existence according to it. When a person as a learner enthusiastically relates in this way to such a German professor, he accomplishes the most superb epigram upon him, because a speculator of that sort is anything but

2 On this important concept, see *JP* III 3660–64 and pp. 908–09, also 3665–96 and pp. 910–11; VII, p. 80.

served by a learner's honest and enthusiastic zeal for expressing and accomplishing, for existentially appropriating his wisdom, since this wisdom is something that the Herr Professor himself has imagined and has written books about but has never attempted himself. It has not even occurred to him that it should be done. Like the customs clerk who, in the belief that his business was merely to write, wrote what he himself could not read,[3] so there are speculative thinkers who merely write, and write that which, if it is to be read with the aid of action, if I may put it that way, proves to be nonsense, unless it is perhaps intended only for fantastical beings.

When for the existing spirit *qua* existing there is a question about truth, that abstract reduplication [*Reduplikation*] of truth recurs; but existence itself, existence itself in the questioner, who does indeed exist, holds the two factors apart, one from the other, and reflection shows two relations. To objective reflection, truth becomes something objective, an object, and the point is to disregard the subject. To subjective reflection, truth becomes appropriation, inwardness, subjectivity, and the point is to immerse oneself, existing, in subjectivity.

But what then? Are we to remain in this disjunction, or does mediation offer its kind assistance here, so that truth becomes subject-object? Why not? But can mediation then help the existing person so that he himself, as long as he is existing, becomes mediation, which is, after all, *sub specie aeterni,* whereas the poor existing one is existing? It certainly does not help to make a fool of a person, to entice him with the subject-object when he himself is prevented from entering into the state in which he can relate himself to it, prevented because he himself, by virtue of existing, is in the process of becoming. Of what help is it to explain how the eternal truth is to be understood eternally when the one to use the explanation is prevented from understanding it in this way because he is existing and is merely a fantast if he fancies himself to be *sub specie aeterni,* consequently when he must avail himself precisely of the explanation of how the eternal truth is to be understood in the category of time by someone who by existing is himself in time, something the honored professor himself admits, if not always, then every three months when he draws his salary.

With the subject-object of mediation, we have merely reverted to abstraction, inasmuch as the definition of truth as subject-object is exactly the same as: the truth *is*, that is, the truth is a redoubling [*Fordoblelse*]. Consequently, the exalted wisdom has again been absentminded enough to forget that it was an existing spirit who asked about truth. Or is perhaps the existing spirit himself the subject-object? In that case, I am obliged to ask: Where is such an existing human being who is also a subject-object? Or shall we perhaps here again first transmute the existing spirit into a something in general and then explain everything except what was asked about: How an existing subject *in concreto* relates himself to the truth, or what then must be asked about: How the individual existing subject then relates himself to this something that seems to have not a little in common with a paper kite or with the lump of sugar that the Dutch used to hang from the ceiling and everyone would lick.

We return, then, to the two ways of reflection and have not forgotten that it is an existing spirit who is asking, simply an individual human being, and are not able to

---

3 See *Adler, KW* XXIV (*Pap.* VII² B 235, p. 73); *JP* III 3170; IV 4539 (*Pap.* X⁵ A 10; VI A 64).

forget, either, that his existing is precisely what will prevent him from going both ways at once, and his concerned questions will prevent him from light-mindedly and fantastically becoming a subject-object. Now, then, which of the ways is the way of truth for the existing spirit? Only the fantastical *I-I* is simultaneously finished with both ways or advances methodically along both ways simultaneously, which for an existing human being is such an inhuman way of walking that I dare not recommend it.

Since the questioner specifically emphasizes that he is an existing person, the way to be commended is naturally the one that especially accentuates what it means to exist.

The way of objective reflection turns the subjective individual into something accidental and thereby turns existence into an indifferent, vanishing something. The way to the objective truth goes away from the subject, and while the subject and subjectivity become indifferent [*ligegyldig*], the truth also becomes indifferent, and that is precisely its objective validity [*Gyldighed*], because the interest, just like the decision, is subjectivity. The way of objective reflection now leads to abstract thinking, to mathematics, to historical knowledge of various kinds, and always leads away from the subjective individual, whose existence or nonexistence becomes, from an objective point of view, altogether properly, infinitely indifferent, altogether properly, because, as Hamlet says, existence and nonexistence have only subjective significance.[4] At its maximum, this way will lead to a contradiction, and to the extent that the subject does not become totally indifferent to himself, this is merely an indication that his objective striving is not objective enough. At its maximum, it will lead to the contradiction that only objectivity has come about, whereas subjectivity has gone out, that is, the existing subjectivity that has made an attempt to become what in the abstract sense is called subjectivity, the abstract form of an abstract objectivity. And yet, viewed subjectively, the objectivity that has come about is at its maximum either a hypothesis or an approximation, because all eternal decision is rooted specifically in subjectivity.

But the objective way is of the opinion that it has a security that the subjective way does not have (of course, existence, what it means to exist, and objective security cannot be thought together). It is of the opinion that it avoids a danger that lies in wait for the subjective way, and at its maximum this danger is madness. In a solely subjective definition of truth, lunacy and truth are ultimately indistinguishable, because they may both have inwardness.[5] But one does not become lunatic by becoming objective. At this point I might perhaps add a little comment that does not seem superfluous in an objective age. Is the absence of inwardness also lunacy? The

---

4 See Shakespeare, *Hamlet*, III, 1, 56; Foersome and Wulff, I, p. 97; Ortlepp, I, p. 289; Schlegel and Tieck, VI, p. 63; Kittredge, p. 1167: "To be, or not to be—that is the question . . .."

5 Even this is not true, however, because madness never has the inwardness of infinity. Its fixed idea is a kind of objective something, and the contradiction of madness lies in wanting to embrace it with passion. The decisive factor in madness is thus not the subjective, but the little finitude that becomes fixed, something the infinite can never become.

objective truth as such does not at all decide that the one stating it is sensible; on the contrary, it can even betray that the man is lunatic, although what he says is entirely true and especially objectively true.

I shall here allow myself to relate an incident that, without any modification whatever by me, comes directly from a madhouse. A patient in such an institution wants to run away and actually carries out his plan by jumping through a window. He now finds himself in the garden of the institution and wishes to take to the road of freedom. Then it occurs to him (shall I say that he was sagacious enough or lunatic enough to have this whimsical idea?): When you arrive in the city, you will be recognized and will very likely be taken back right away. What you need to do, then, is to convince everyone completely, by the objective truth of what you say, that all is well as far as your sanity is concerned. As he is walking along and pondering this, he sees a skittle ball lying on the ground. He picks it up and puts it in the tail of his coat. At every step he takes, this ball bumps him, if you please, on his r—, and every time it bumps him he says, "Boom! The earth is round." He arrives in the capital city and immediately visits one of his friends. He wants to convince him that he is not lunatic and therefore paces up and down the floor and continually says, "Boom! The earth is round!" But is the earth not round? Does the madhouse demand yet another sacrifice on account of this assumption, as in those days when everyone assumed it to be as flat as a pancake? Or is he lunatic, the man who hopes to prove that he is not lunatic by stating a truth universally accepted and universally regarded as objective? And yet, precisely by this it became clear to the physician that the patient was not yet cured, although the cure certainly could not revolve around getting him to assume that the earth is flat. But not everyone is a physician, and the demand of the times has considerable influence on the question of lunacy. Now and then, one would indeed almost be tempted to assume that the modem age, which has modernized Christianity, has also modernized Pilate's question,[6] and that the need of the age to find something in which to repose declares itself in the question: What is lunacy? When an assistant professor, every time his coattail reminds him to say something, says *de omnibus dubitandum est* [everything must be doubted][7] and

6 John 18:38, "What is truth?"
7 An allusion to Descartes, *A Discourse on Method*, II, IV; *Renati DesCartes opera philosophica* (Amsterdam: 1685; *ASKB* 473 [1678]), pp. 7, 20; *A Discourse on Method and Selected Writings*, tr. John Veitch (New York: Dutton, 1951), pp. 9, 27:

I was then in Germany, attracted thither by the wars in that country, which have not yet been brought to a termination; and as I was returning to the army from the coronation of the emperor, the setting in of winter arrested me in a locality where, as I found no society to interest me, and was besides fortunately undisturbed by any cares or passions, I remained the whole day in seclusion[1] with full opportunity to occupy my attention with my own thoughts. . . I had long before remarked that, in relation to practice, it is sometimes necessary to adopt, as if above doubt, opinions which we discern to be highly uncertain, as has been already said; but as I then desired to give my attention solely to search after truth, I thought that a procedure exactly the opposite was called for, and that I ought to reject as absolutely false all opinions in regard to which I could suppose the least ground for doubt, in order to ascertain whether after that there remained aught in my belief that was wholly indubitable.
[1]Literally, in a room heated by means of a stove.—Tr.

briskly writes away on a system in which there is sufficient internal evidence in every other sentence that the man has never doubted anything—he is not considered lunatic.

Don Quixote is the prototype of the subjective lunacy in which the passion of inwardness grasps a particular fixed finite idea. But when inwardness is absent, parroting lunacy sets in, which is just as comic, and it would be desirable for an imaginatively constructing psychologist to depict it by taking a handful of such philosophers and putting them together. When the insanity is a delirium of inwardness, the tragic and the comic are that the something that infinitely pertains to the unfortunate person is a fixed detail that pertains to no one else. But when the insanity is the absence of inwardness, the comic is that the something known by the blissful person is the truth, truth that pertains to the whole human race but does not in the least pertain to the highly honored parroter. This kind of insanity is more inhuman than the other. One shrinks from looking the first one in the eye, lest one discover the depth of his frantic state, but one does not dare to look at the other at all for fear of discovering that he does not have proper eyes but glass eyes and hair made from a floor mat, in short, that he is an artificial product. If one happens to meet a mentally deranged person of that sort, whose illness is simply that he has no mind, one listens to him in cold horror. One does not know whether one dares to believe that it is a human being with whom one is speaking, or perhaps a "walking stick,"[8] an artificial contrivance of Døbler[9] that conceals in itself a barrel organ [*Positiv*].[10] To drink *Dus* with the executioner[11] can indeed be unpleasant for a self-respecting man, but to get into a rational and speculative conversation with a walking stick—now that is almost enough to drive one crazy.

Subjective reflection turns inward toward subjectivity and in this inward deepening will be of the truth, and in such a way that, just as in the preceding, when objectivity was advanced, subjectivity vanished, here subjectivity as such becomes the final factor and objectivity the vanishing. Here it is not forgotten, even for a single moment, that the subject is existing, and that existing is a becoming, and that truth as the identity of thought and being is therefore a chimera of abstraction and truly only a longing of creation,[12] not because truth is not an identity, but because the knower is an existing person, and thus truth cannot be an identity for him as long as he exists. If this is not held fast, then with the aid of speculative thought we promptly

---

See, for example, *Johannes Climacus*, pp. 133–59, *KW* VII (*Pap.* IV B 1, pp. 116–41); *Fear and Trembling*, pp. 5–6, *KW* VI (*SV* III 57–58).

8 See Supplement, p. 2.45 (*Pap.* VI B 40:21).

9 *Døbler* in the text may be the name of the maker of a walking stick that talks, or it may be Danish for "dowels" or "pins," which in a barrel organ are the parts that actuate the valves. See note 266 below. The first is perhaps the case here, but verification has not been found.

10 For continuation of the sentence and with reference to the following sentence, see Supplement, p. 2.45 (*Pap.* VI B 40:21). The Danish word for a barrel organ, "*et Positiv*," contains a double entendre in alluding to the positive. "*det Positive*." See pp. 1.80–81.

11 Holberg, *Mester Gert Westphaler eller Den meget talende Barbeer*, 8, *Danske Skue-Plads*, I, no pagination; *Seven One-Act Plays*, pp. 29–30.

12 Cf Romans 8:19.

enter into the fantastical *I-I* that recent speculative thought certainly has used but without explaining how a particular individual relates himself to it, and, good Lord, of course no human being is more than a particular individual.

If the existing person could actually be outside himself, the truth would be something concluded for him. But where is this point? The *I-I* is a mathematical point that does not exist at all; accordingly anyone can readily take up this stand-point—no one stands in the way of anyone else. Only momentarily can a particular individual, existing, be in a unity of the infinite and the finite that transcends existing. This instant is the moment of passion. Modern speculative thought has mustered everything to enable the individual to transcend himself objectively, but this just cannot be done. Existence exercises its constraint, and if philosophers nowadays had not become pencil-pushers serving the trifling busyness of fantastical thinking, it would have discerned that suicide is the only somewhat practical interpretation of its attempt. But pencil-pushing modern speculative thought takes a dim view of passion, and yet, for the existing person, passion is existence at its very highest—and we are, after all, existing persons. In passion, the existing subject is infinitized in the eternity of imagination and yet is also most definitely himself. The fantastical *I-I* is not infinitude and finitude in identity, since neither the one nor the other is actual; it is a fantastical union with a cloud,[13] an unfruitful embrace, and the relation of the individual *I* to this mirage is never stated.[14]

All essential knowing pertains to existence, or only the knowing whose relation to existence is essential is essential knowing. Essentially viewed, the knowing that does not inwardly in the reflection of inwardness pertain to existence is accidental knowing, and its degree and scope, essentially viewed, are a matter of indifference. That essential knowing is essentially related to existence does not, however, signify the above—mentioned abstract identity between thinking and being, nor does it signify that the knowledge is objectively related to something existent [*Tilværende*] as its object, but it means that the knowledge is related to the knower, who is essentially an existing person [*Existerende*], and that all essential knowing is therefore essentially related to existence and to existing. Therefore, only ethical and ethicalrefigious knowing is essential knowing. But all ethical and all ethicalreligious knowing is essentiafly a relating to the existing of the knower.

Mediation is a mirage, just as the *I-I* is. Viewed abstractly, everything is and nothing becomes. Mediation cannot possibly find its place in abstraction, since it has *movement* as its presupposition. Objective knowledge can certainly have the existent [*Tilværende*] as its object, but since the knowing subject is existing [*existerende*] and himself in the process of becoming by existing, speculative thought must first explain how a particular existing subject relates himself to the knowledge of mediation, what he is at the moment, whether, for example, he is not at that very moment rather

13 In Greek mythology, Zeus punished Ixion for making love to Hera (Roman Juno) by sending him a cloud resembling Hera. From this union came the centaurs. See Paul Friedrich A. Nitsch, *neues mythologisches Wörterbuch* I–II, rev. Friedrich Gotthilf Klopfer (Leipzig, Sorau: 1821; *ASKB* 1944–45), II, pp. 122–23. See also Faust's attempted union with Helena, *Faust*, ll, 3, 9939–54, *Werke*, XLI, pp. 244–45; Taylor, p. 183.

14 For continuation of the sentence and paragraph, see Supplement, pp. 2.45–46 (*Pap.* VI B 40:22).

absentminded, and where he is, whether he is not on the moon. There is this continual talk about mediation and mediation. Is mediation, then, a human being, just as Per Degn assumes *Imprimatur* to be a human being? How does a human being go about becoming something of that sort? Is this dignity, this great *philosophicum*,[15] attained by studying? Or does the magistrate give it away as he gives away sexton and gravedigger positions? Just try to become involved with these and other similar simple questions raised by a simple human being, who would so very much like to be mediation if he could become that in a legitimate and honorable manner, and not either by saying *eins, zwei, drei, kokolorum* or by forgetting that he himself is an existing human being, for whom existing is consequently something essential, and for whom existing ethically-religiously is a suitable *quantum satis* [sufficient amount]. To a speculative thinker it may seem *abgeschmackt* [in bad taste] to ask questions in this way, but it is especially important not to polemicize in the wrong place and hence not to begin fantastically-objectively a *pro* and *contra* as to whether or not there is mediation, but firmly to maintain what it means to be a human being.

VII
166

[16]In order to clarify the divergence of objective and subjective reflection, I shall now describe subjective reflection in its search back and inward into inwardness. At its highest, inwardness in an existing subject is passion; truth as a paradox corresponds to passion, and that truth becomes a paradox is grounded precisely in its relation to an existing subject. In this way the one corresponds to the other. In forgetting that one is an existing subject, one loses passion, and in return, truth does not become a paradox; but the knowing subject shifts from being human to being a fantastical something, and truth becomes a fantastical object for its knowing.

[17]*When the question about truth is asked objectively, truth is reflected upon objectively as an object to which the knower relates himself. What is reflected upon is not the relation but that what he relates himself to is the truth, the true. If only that to which he relates himself is the truth, the true, then the subject is in the truth. When the question about truth is asked subjectively, the individual's relation is reflected upon subjectively. If only the how of this relation is in truth, the individual is in truth, even if he in this way were to relate himself to untruth.*[18]

Let us take the knowledge of God as an example. Objectively, what is reflected upon is that this is the true God; subjectively, that the individual relates himself to a something *in such a way* that his relation is in truth a God-relation. Now, on which side is the truth? Alas, must we not at this point resort to mediation and say: It is on neither side; it is in the mediation? Superbly stated, if only someone could say how an existing person goes about being in mediation, because to be in mediation is to be

VII
167

---

15 In Kierkegaard's time, matriculating university students took the *Examen Artium*, or "first examination." After a semester they took the "second examination," frequently called the great *Philosophicum* of which Part One covered Latin, Greek, history, and mathematics. Part Two, taken after an additional semester, covered physics, advanced mathematics, and philosophy.

16 With reference to the following paragraph, see Supplement, p. 2.46 (*Pap.* VI B 19:6).

17 With reference to the following paragraph, see Supplement, p. 2.46 (*Pap.* VI B 19:7,8).

18 The reader will note that what is being discussed here is essential truth, or the truth that is related essentially to existence, and that it is specifically in order to clarify it as inwardness or as subjectivity that the contrast is pointed out.

finished; to exist is to become. An existing person cannot be in two places at the same time, cannot be subject-object. When he is closest to being in two places at the same time, he is in passion; but passion is only momentary, and passion is the highest pitch of subjectivity.

The existing person who chooses the objective way now enters upon all approximating deliberation intended to bring forth God objectively, which is not achieved in all eternity, because God is a subject and hence only for subjectivity in inwardness. The existing person who chooses the subjective way instantly comprehends the whole dialectical difficulty because he must use some time, perhaps a long time, to find God objectively. He comprehends this dialectical difficulty in all its pain, because he must resort to God at that very moment, because every moment in which he does not have God is wasted.[19] At that very moment he has God, not by virtue of any objective deliberation but by virtue of the infinite passion of inwardness. The objective person is not bothered by dialectical difficulties such as what it means to put a whole research period into finding God, since it is indeed possible that the researcher would die tomorrow, and if he goes on living, he cannot very well regard God as something to be taken along at his convenience, since God is something one takes along *à tout prix* [at any price], which, in passion's understanding, is the true relationship of inwardness with God.

It is at this point, dialectically so very difficult, that the road swings off for the person who knows what it means to think dialectically and, existing, to think dialectically, which is quite different from sitting as a fantastical being at a desk and writing about something one has never done oneself, quite different from writing *de omnibus dubitandum* and then as an existing person being just as credulous as the most sensate human being. It is here that the road swings off, and the change is this: whereas objective knowledge goes along leisurely on the long road of approximation, itself not actuated by passion, to subjective knowledge every delay is a deadly peril and the decision so infinitely important that it is immediately urgent, as if the opportunity had already passed by unused.

Now, if the problem is to calculate where there is more truth (and, as stated, simultaneously to be on both sides equally is not granted to an existing person but is only a beatifying delusion for a deluded *I-I*), whether on the side of the person who only objectively seeks the true God and the approximating truth of the God-idea or on the side of the person who is infinitely concerned that he in truth relate himself to God with the infinite passion of need—then there can be no doubt about the answer for anyone who is not totally botched by scholarship and science. If someone who lives in the midst of Christianity enters, with knowledge of the true idea of God, the house of God, the house of the true God, and prays, but prays in untruth, and if

---

19 [20]In this way God is indeed a postulate, but not in the loose sense in which it is ordinarily taken. Instead, it becomes clear that this is the only way an existing person enters into a relationship with God: when the dialectical contradiction brings passion to despair and assists him in grasping God with "the category of despair" (faith),[21] so that the postulate, far from being the arbitrary, is in fact *necessary* defense [*N ø d værge*], self-defense; in this way God is not a postulate, but the existing person's postulating of God is—a necessity [*Nödvendighed*].

20 With reference to the following note, see Supplement, p. 2,46 (*Pap.* VI B 40:23).

21 See, for example, *Sickness unto Death*, pp. 67, 116 fn., *KW* XIX *(SV* XI 178, 226).

someone lives in an idolatrous land but prays with all the passion of infinity, although his eyes are resting upon the image of an idol—where, then, is there more truth? The one prays in truth to God although he is worshiping an idol; the other prays in untruth to the true God and is therefore in truth worshiping an idol.

If someone objectively inquires into immortality, and someone else stakes the passion of the infinite on the uncertainty—where, then, is there more truth, and who has more certainty? The one has once and for all entered upon an approximation that never ends, because the certainty of immortality is rooted in subjectivity; the other is immortal and therefore struggles by contending with the uncertainty.

Let us consider Socrates. These days everyone is dabbling in a few proofs or demonstrations—one has many, another fewer. But Socrates! He poses the question objectively, problematically: if there is an immortality.[22] So, compared with one of the modern thinkers with the three demonstrations, was he a doubter? Not at all. He stakes his whole life on this "if"; he dares to die, and with the passion of the infinite he has so ordered his whole life that it might be acceptable—*if* there is an immortality. Is there any better demonstration for the immortality of the soul? But those who have the three demonstrations do not order their lives accordingly. If there is an immortality, it must be nauseated by their way of living—is there any better counterdemonstration to the three demonstrations? The "fragment", of uncertainty helped Socrates, because he himself helped with the passion of infinity. The three demonstrations are of no benefit whatever to those others, because they are and remain slugs and, failing to demonstrate anything else, have demonstrated it by their three demonstrations.

In the same way a girl has perhaps possessed all the sweetness of being in love through a weak hope of being loved by the beloved, because she herself staked

22 See, for example, Plato, *Apology*, 40 c–41 a; *Opera*, VIII, pp. 154–55; *Dialogues*, p. 25; *Phaedo*, 91 b; *Opera*, I, pp. 554–55; Heise, I, pp. 69–70; *Dialogues*, p. 73:

> Death is one of two things. Either it is annihilation, and the dead have no consciousness of anything, or, as we are told, it is really a change—a migration of the soul from this place to another. Now if there is no consciousness but only a dreamless steep, death must be a marvelous gain. I suppose that if anyone were told to pick out the night on which he slept so soundly as not even to dream, and then to compare it with all the other nights and days of his life, and then were told to say, after due consideration, how many better and happier days and nights than this he had spent in the course of his life—well, I think that the Great King himself, to say nothing of any private person, would find these days and nights easy to count in comparison with the rest. If death is like this, then, I call it gain, because the whole of time, if you look at it in this way, can be regarded as no more than one single night. If on the other hand death is a removal from here to some other place, and if what we are told is true, that all the dead are there, what greater blessing could there be than this, gentlemen? If on arrival in the other world, beyond the reach of our so-called justice, one will find there the true judges who are said to preside in those courts, Minos and Rhadamanthus and Aeacus and Triptolemus and all those other half-divinities who were upright in their earthly life, would that be an unrewarding journey? Put it in this way. How much would one of you give to meet Orpheus and Musaeus, Hesiod and Homer? I am willing to die ten times over if this account is true.
>
> If my theory is really true, it is right to believe it, while, even if death is extinction, at any rate during this time before my death I shall be less likely to distress my companions by giving way to self-pity, and this folly of-mine will not live on with me—which would be a calamity—but will shortly come to an end.

everything on this weak hope;[23] on the other hand, many a wedded matron, who more than once has submitted to the strongest expression of erotic love, has certainly had demonstrations and yet, strangely enough, has not possessed *quod erat demonstrandum* [that which was to be demonstrated]. The Socratic ignorance was thus the expression, firmly maintained with all the passion of inwardness, of the relation of the eternal truth to an existing person, and therefore it must remain for him a paradox as long as he exists. Yet it is possible that in the Socratic ignorance there was more truth in Socrates than in the objective truth of the entire system that flirts with the demands of the times and adapts itself to assistant professors.

[24]*Objectively the emphasis is on **what** is said; subjectively the emphasis is on **how** it is said.* This distinction applies even esthetically and is specifically expressed when we say that in the mouth of this or that person something that is truth can become untruth. Particular attention should be paid to this distinction in our day, for if one were to express in a single sentence the difference between ancient times and our time, one would no doubt have to say: In ancient times there were only a few individuals who knew the truth; now everyone knows it, but inwardness has an inverse relation to it.[25] Viewed esthetically, the contradiction that emerges when truth becomes untruth in this and that person's mouth is best interpreted comically. Ethically-religiously, the emphasis is again on: *how.* But this is not to be understood as manner, modulation of voice, oral delivery, etc., but it is to be understood as the relation of the existing person, in his very existence, to what is said. Objectively, the question is only about categories of thought; subjectively, about inwardness. At its maximum, this "how" is the passion of the infinite, and the passion of the infinite is the very truth. But the passion of the infinite is precisely subjectivity, and thus subjectivity is truth. From the objective point of view, there is no infinite decision, and thus it is objectively correct that the distinction between good and evil is canceled, along with the principle of contradiction, and thereby also the infinite distinction between truth and falsehood. Only in subjectivity is there decision, whereas wanting to become objective is untruth. The passion of the infinite, not its content, is the deciding factor, for its content is precisely itself. In this way the subjective "how" and subjectivity are the truth.

[27]But precisely because the subject is existing, the "how" that is subjectively emphasized is dialectical also with regard to time. In the moment of the decision of passion, where the road swings off from objective knowledge, it looks as if the infinite decision were thereby finished. But at the same moment, the existing person is in the temporal realm, and the subjective "how" is transformed into a striving that is motivated and repeatedly refreshed by the decisive passion of the infinite, but it is nevertheless a striving.

When subjectivity is truth, the definition of truth must also contain in itself an expression of the antithesis to objectivity, a memento of that fork in the road, and this

23 With reference to the remainder of the paragraph, see Supplement, p. 2.47 (*Pap.* VI B 40:24).
24 With reference to the following sentence, see Supplement, p. 2.11 (*Pap.* VI B 17).
25 See *Stages on Life's Way*, p. 366 fn.[26]
26 *Stages*, pp. 471–72, *KW* XI (*SV* VI 438).
27 With reference to the following three paragraphs, see Supplement, p. 2.47 (*Pap.* VI B 18).

expression will at the same time indicate the resilience of the inwardness. Here is such a definition of truth: *An objective uncertainty, held fast through appropriation with the most passionate inwardness, is the truth*, the highest truth there is for an *existing* person. At the point where the road swings off (and where that is cannot be stated objectively, since it is precisely subjectivity), objective knowledge is suspended. Objectively he then has only uncertainty, but this is precisely what intensifies the infinite passion of inwardness, and truth is precisely the daring venture of choosing the objective uncertainty with the passion of the infinite. I observe nature in order to find God, and I do indeed see omnipotence and wisdom, but I also see much that troubles and disturbs. The *summa summarum* [sum total] of this is an objective uncertainty, but the inwardness is so very great, precisely because it grasps this objective uncertainty with all the passion of the infinite. In a mathematical proposition, for example, the objectivity is given, but therefore its truth is also an indifferent truth.

But the definition of truth stated above is a paraphrasing of faith. Without risk, no faith.[28] Faith is the contradiction between the infinite passion of inwardness and the objective uncertainty. If I am able to apprehend God objectively, I do not have faith; but because I cannot do this, I must have faith. If I want to keep myself in faith, I

must continually see to it that I hold fast the objective uncertainty, see to it that in the objective uncertainty I am "out on 70,000 fathoms of water" and still have faith.

[29]The thesis that subjectivity, inwardness, is truth contains the Socratic wisdom, the undying merit of which is to have paid attention to the essential meaning of existing, of the knower's being an existing person. That is why, in his ignorance, Socrates was in the truth in the highest sense within paganism. To comprehend this, that the misfortune of speculative thought is simply that it forgets again and again that the knower is an existing person, can already be rather difficult in our objective age. "But to go beyond Socrates when one has not even comprehended the Socratic—that, at least, is not Socratic." See "The Moral" in *Fragments*.[30]

Just as in *Fragments,* let us from this point try a category of thought that actually does go beyond. Whether it is true or false is of no concern to me, since I am only imaginatively constructing, but this much is required, that it be clear that, the Socratic is presupposed in it, so that I at least do not end up behind Socrates again.

When subjectivity, inwardness, is truth, then truth, objectively defined, is a paradox; and that truth is objectively a paradox shows precisely that subjectivity is truth, since the objectivity does indeed thrust away, and the objectivity's repulsion, or the expression for the objectivity's repulsion, is the resilience and dynamometer of inwardness. The paradox is the objective uncertainty that is the expression for the passion of inwardness that is truth. So much for the Socratic. The eternal, essential truth, that is, the truth that is related essentially to the existing person by pertaining essentially to what it means to exist (viewed Socratically, all other knowledge is accidental, its degree and scope indifferent), is a paradox. Nevertheless the eternal,

---

28 With reference to the remainder of the paragraph, see Supplement, pp. 2.47–48 (*Pap.* VI B 18, 19:3, 10).

29 With reference to the following fourteen pages, see Supplement, pp. 2.48–51 (*Pap.* VI B 40:26).

30 Cf. *Fragments*, p. 111, *KW* VII (*SV* IV 272).

essential truth is itself not at all a paradox, but it is a paradox by being related to an existing person. Socratic ignorance is an expression of the objective uncertainty; the inwardness of the existing person is truth. In anticipation of what will be discussed later, the following comment is made here: Socratic ignorance is an analogue to the category of the absurd, except that there is even less objective certainty in the repulsion exerted by the absurd, since there is only the certainty that it is absurd, and for that very reason there is infinitely greater resilience in the inwardness. The Socratic inwardness in existing is an analogue to faith, except that the inwardness of faith, corresponding not to the repulsion exerted by ignorance but to the repulsion exerted by the absurd, is infinitely deeper.

Viewed Socratically, the eternal essential truth is not at all paradoxical in itself, but only by being related to an existing person. This is expressed in another Socratic thesis: that all knowing is a recollecting. This thesis is an intimation of the beginning of speculative thought, but for that very reason Socrates did not pursue it; essentially it became Platonic. This is where the road swings off,[31] and Socrates essentially emphasizes existing, whereas Plato, forgetting this, loses himself in speculative thought. Socrates' infinite merit is precisely that of being an *existing* thinker, not a speculative thinker who forgets what it means to exist. To Socrates, therefore, the thesis that all knowing is a recollecting has, at the moment of parting and as a continually annulled possibility of speculating, a double significance: (1) that the knower is essentially *integer* [uncorrupted] and that for him there is no other dubiousness with regard to knowledge of the eternal truth than this, that he exists, a dubiousness so essential and decisive to him that it signifies that existing, the inward deepening in and through existing, is truth; (2) that existence in temporarality has no decisive significance, because there is continually the possibility of taking oneself back into eternity by recollecting, even though this possibility is continually annulled because the inward deepening in existing fills up time.[32]

---

31 See Supplement, p. 2.51 (*Pap.* VII[1] A 31).

32 This may be the proper place to elucidate a dubiousness in the design of *Fragments*, a dubiousness that was due to my not wanting immediately to make the matter as dialectically difficult as it is, because in our day terminologies and the like are so muddled that it is almost impossible to safeguard oneself against confusion. In order, if possible, to elucidate properly the difference between the Socratic (which was supposed to be the philosophical, the pagan philosophical position) and the category of imaginatively constructed thought, which actually goes beyond the Socratic, I carried the Socratic back to the thesis that all knowing is a recollecting.[33] It is commonly accepted as such, and only for the person who with a very special interest devotes himself to the Socratic, always returning to the sources, only for him will it be important to distinguish between Socrates and Plato on this point. The thesis certainly belongs to both of them, but Socrates continually parts with it because he wants to exist. By holding Socrates to the thesis that all knowing is recollecting, one turns him into a speculative philosopher instead of what he was, an existing thinker who understood existing as the essential. The thesis that all knowing is recollecting belongs to speculative thought, and recollecting is immanence, and from the point of view of speculation and the eternal there is no paradox. The difficulty, however, is that no human being is speculation, but the speculating person is an existing human being, subject to the claims of existence. To forget this is no merit, but to hold this fast is indeed a merit, and that is precisely what Socrates did. To emphasize existence, which contains within it the qualification of inwardness, is the Socratic, whereas the Platonic is to pursue recollection and immanence. Basically Socrates is thereby beyond all speculation, because he does not have a fantastical beginning where the

The great merit of the Socratic was precisely to emphasize that the knower is an existing person and that to exist is the essential. To go beyond Socrates by failing to understand this is nothing but a mediocre merit. This we must keep *in mente* [in mind] and then see whether the formula cannot be changed in such a way that one actually does go beyond the Socratic.

So, then, subjectivity, inwardness, is truth. Is there *a more inward* expression for it? Yes, if the discussion about "Subjectivity, inwardness, is truth" begins in this way: "Subjectivity is untruth." But let us not be in a hurry. Speculative thought also says that subjectivity is untruth but says it in the very opposite direction, namely, that objectivity is truth. Speculative thought defines subjectivity negatively in the direction of objectivity. The other definition, however, puts barriers in its own way at the very moment it wants to begin, which makes the inwardness so much more inward. Viewed Socratically, subjectivity is untruth if it refuses to comprehend that subjectivity is truth but wants, for example, to be objective. Here, on the other hand, in wanting to begin to become truth by becoming subjective, subjectivity is in the predicament of being untruth. Thus the work goes backward, that is, backward in inwardness. The way is so far from being in the direction of the objective that the beginning only lies even deeper in subjectivity.

But the subject cannot be untruth eternally or be presupposed to have been untruth eternally; he must have become that in time or he becomes that in time.[35] The Socratic paradox consisted in this, that the eternal truth was related to an existing person. But now existence has accentuated the existing person a second time; a change so essential has taken place in him that he in no way can take himself back into eternity by Socratically recollecting. To do this is to speculate; to be able to do

speculating person changes clothes and then goes on and on and speculates, forgetting the most important thing, to exist. But precisely because Socrates is in this way beyond speculative thought, he acquires, when rightly depicted, a certain analogous likeness to what the imaginary construction set forth as that which truly goes beyond the Socratic: the truth as paradox is an analog to the paradox *sensu eminentiori* [in the more eminent sense]; the passion of inwardness in existing is then an analog to faith *sensu eminentiori*. That the difference is infinite nevertheless, that the designations in *Fragments* of that which truly goes beyond the Socratic are unchanged, I can easily show, but I was afraid to make complications by promptly using what seem to be the same designations, at least the same words, about the different things when the imaginary construction was to be presented as different from these.

Now, I think there would be no objection to speaking of the paradox in connection with Socrates and faith, since it is quite correct to do so, provided that it is understood correctly. Besides, the ancient Greeks also use the word πέστιζ [faith], although by no means in the sense of the imaginary construction, and use it so as to make possible some very illuminating observations bearing upon its dissimilarity to faith *sensu eminentiori*, especially with reference to one of Aristotle's works where the term is employed.[34]

33 See *Fragments*, pp. 9–14, *KW* VII (*SV* IV 179–84).

34 See, for example, Aristotle, *On the Soul*, 428 a; *Rhetoric*, 1355 a; *Aristoteles graece*, I–II, ed. Immanuel Bekker (Berlin: 1831; *ASKB* 1074–75), I, p. 428; II, p. 1355; *The Complete Works of Aristotle*, I–II, ed. Jonathan Barnes (rev. Oxford tr., Princeton: Princeton University Press, 1984), I, p. 681; II, p. 2153: "But opinion involves belief [πέστιζ] (for without belief in what we opine we cannot have an opinion), and in the brutes though we often find imagination we never find belief." "It is clear, then, that the technical study of rhetoric is concerned with the modes of persuasion. Now persuasion [πέστιζ] is a sort of demonstration . . .." See also *JP* I 628; III 3300; IV 4107; V 5779 (*Pap.* VI A 19; V A 98; VI A 1, C 2).

35 See *Fragments*, p. 15, *KW* VII (*SV* IV 184–85).

this but, by grasping the inward deepening in existence, to annul the possibility of doing it is the Socratic. But *now* the difficulty is that what accompanied Socrates as an annulled possibility has become an impossibility. If speculating was already of dubious merit in connection with the Socratic, it is now only confusion.

The paradox emerges when the eternal truth and existing are placed together, but each time existing is accentuated, the paradox becomes clearer and clearer. Viewed Socratically, the knower was an existing person, but now the existing person is accentuated in such a way that existence has made an essential change in him.

Let us now call the individual's untruth *sin*. Viewed eternally, he cannot be in sin or be presupposed to have been eternally in sin. Therefore, by coming into existence (for the beginning was that subjectivity is untruth), he becomes a sinner. He is not born as a sinner in the sense that he is presupposed to be a sinner before he is born, but he is born in sin and as a sinner. Indeed, we could call this *hereditary sin*.[36] But if existence has in this way obtained power over him, he is prevented from taking himself back into eternity through recollection. If it is already paradoxical that the eternal truth is related to an existing person, now it is absolutely paradoxical that it is related to such an existing person. But the more difficult it is made for him, recollecting, to take himself out of existence, the more inward his existing can become in existence; and when it is made impossible for him, when he is lodged in existence in such a way that the back door of recollection is forever closed, then the inwardness becomes the deepest. But let us never forget that the Socratic merit was precisely to emphasize that the knower is existing, because the more difficult the matter becomes, the more one is tempted to rush along the easy road of speculative thought, away from terrors and decisions, to fame, honor, a life of ease, etc. If even Socrates comprehended the dubiousness of taking himself speculatively out of existence back into eternity, when there was no dubiousness for the existing person except that he existed and, of course, that existing was the essential—now it is impossible. He must go forward; to go backward is impossible.

Subjectivity is truth. The paradox came into existence through the relating of the eternal, essential truth to the existing person. Let us now go further; let us assume that the eternal, essential truth is itself the paradox. How does the paradox emerge? By placing the eternal, essential truth together with existing. Consequently, if we place it together in the truth itself, the truth becomes a paradox. The eternal truth has come into existence in time. That is the paradox. If the subject just mentioned was prevented by sin from taking himself back into eternity, now he is not to concern himself with this, because now the eternal, essential truth is not behind him but has come in front of him by existing itself or by having existed, so that if the individual, existing, does not lay hold of the truth in existence, he will never have it.

Existence can never be accentuated more sharply than it has been here. The fraud of speculative thought in wanting to recollect itself out of existence has been made impossible. This is the only point to be comprehended here, and every speculation that insists on being speculation shows *eo ipso* [precisely thereby] that it has not comprehended this. The individual can thrust all this away and resort to speculation,

36 See, for example, *Anxiety*, pp. 25–51, *KW* VIII (*SV* IV 297–322).

but to accept it and then want to cancel it through speculation is impossible, because it is specifically designed to prevent speculation.

When the eternal truth relates itself to an existing person, it becomes the paradox. Through the objective uncertainty and ignorance, the paradox thrusts away in the inwardness of the existing person. But since the paradox is not in itself the paradox, it does not thrust away intensely enough, for without risk, no faith; the more risk, the more faith; the more objective reliability, the less inwardness (since inwardness is subjectivity); the less objective reliability, the deeper is the possible inwardness. When the paradox itself is the paradox, it thrusts away by virtue of the absurd, and the corresponding passion of inwardness is faith.

But subjectivity, inwardness, is truth; if not, we have forgotten the Socratic merit. But when the retreat out of existence into eternity by way of recollection has been made impossible, then, with the truth facing one as the paradox, in the anxiety of sin and its pain, with the tremendous risk of objectivity, there is no stronger expression for inwardness than to have faith. But without risk, no faith, not even the Socratic faith, to say nothing of the kind we are discussing here.

When Socrates believed that God is,[37] he held fast the objective uncertainty with the entire passion of inwardness, and faith is precisely in this contradiction, in this risk. Now it is otherwise. Instead of the objective uncertainty, there is here the certainty that, viewed objectively, it is the absurd, and this absurdity, held fast in the passion of inwardness, is faith. Compared with the earnestness of the absurd, the Socratic ignorance is like a witty jest, and compared with the strenuousness of faith, the Socratic existential inwardness resembles Greek nonchalance.

What, then, is the absurd? The absurd is that the eternal truth has come into existence in time, that God has come into existence, has been born, has grown up, etc., has come into existence exactly as an individual human being, indistinguishable from any other human being, inasmuch as all immediate recognizability is pre-Socratic paganism and from the Jewish point of view is idolatry.[38] Every qualification of that which actually goes beyond the Socratic must essentially have a mark of standing in relation to the god's having come into existence, because faith, *sensu strictissimo* [in the strictest sense], as explicated in *Fragments*,[39] refers to coming into existence. When Socrates believed that God is [*er til*], he no doubt perceived that where the road swings off there is a road of objective approximation, for example, the observation of nature, world history, etc. His merit was precisely to shun this road, where the quantifying siren song spellbinds and tricks the existing person.[40] In

---

37 Danish: *er til*. Although the English translation is usually "exists," the meaning here is simply "is" or "has being" but not in the sense of temporal-spatial historical existence. See, for example, *Fragments*, p. 87, *KW* VII (*SV* IV 250–51).

38 For continuation of the sentence, see Supplement, pp. 2.51–52 (*Pap.* VI B 98:43).

39 See *Fragments*, pp. 81–82, *KW* VII (*SV* IV 245).

40 With reference to the remainder of the paragraph and the five following paragraphs, see Supplement, p. 2.52 (*Pap.* VI B 42).

relation to the absurd, the objective approximation resembles the comedy *Mis-forstaaelse paa Misforstaaelse* [Misunderstanding upon Misunderstanding],[41] which ordinarily is played by assistant professors and speculative thinkers.

It is by way of the objective repulsion that the absurd is the dynamometer of faith in inwardness. So, then, there is a man who wants to have faith; well, let the comedy begin. He wants to have faith, but he wants to assure himself with the aid of objective deliberation and approximation. What happens? With the aid of approximation, the absurd becomes something else; it becomes probable, it becomes more probable, it may become to a high degree and exceedingly probable. Now he is all set to believe it, and he dares to say of himself that he does not believe as shoemakers and tailors and simple folk do, but only after long deliberation. Now he is all set to believe it, but, lo and behold, now it has indeed become impossible to believe it. The almost probable, the probable, the to-a-high-degree and exceedingly probable—that he can almost know, or as good as know, to a higher degree and exceedingly almost *know*—but *believe* it, that cannot be done, for the absurd is precisely the object of faith and only that can be believed.

Or there is a man who says he has faith, but now he wants to make his faith clear to himself; he wants to understand himself in his faith. Now the comedy begins again. The object of faith becomes almost probable, it becomes as good as probable, it becomes probable, it becomes to a high degree and exceedingly probable. He has finished; he dares to say of himself that he does not believe as shoemakers and tailors or other simple folk do but that he has also understood himself in his believing. What wondrous understanding! On the contrary, he has learned to know something different about faith than he believed and has learned to know that he no longer has faith, since he almost knows, as good as knows, to a high degree and exceedingly almost knows.

Inasmuch as the absurd contains the element of coming into existence, the road of approximation will also be that which confuses the absurd fact of coming into existence, which is the object of faith, with a simple historical fact, and then seeks historical certainty for that which is absurd precisely because it contains the contradiction that something that can become historical only in direct opposition to all human understanding has become historical. This contradiction is the absurd, which can only be believed. If a historical certainty is obtained, one obtains merely the certainty that what is certain is not what is the point in question. A witness can testify that he has believed it and then testify that, far from being a historical certainty, it is in direct opposition to his understanding, but such a witness repels in the same sense as the absurd repels, and a witness who does not repel in this way is *eo ipso* a deceiver or a man who is talking about something altogether different; and such a witness can be of no help except in obtaining certainty about something altogether different. One hundred thousand individual witnesses, who by the special nature of their testimony (that they have believed the absurd) remain individual witnesses, do not become something else *en masse* so that the absurd becomes less

---

[41] A play (1828) by Thomas Overskou (1798–1873), *Comedier*, I–V (Copenhagen: 1850–51), II, pp. 135–80.

absurd. Why? Because one hundred thousand people individually have believed that it was absurd? Quite the contrary, those one hundred thousand witnesses repel exactly as the absurd does.

But I do not need to develop this further here. In *Fragments* (especially where the difference between the follower at first hand and the follower at second hand is annulled[42]) and in Part One of this book, I have with sufficient care shown that all approximation is futile, since the point is rather to do away with introductory observations, reliabilities, demonstrations from effects, and the whole mob of pawnbrokers and guarantors, in order to get the absurd clear—so that one can believe if one will—I merely say that this must be extremely strenuous.

If speculative thought wants to become involved in this and, as always, say: From the point of view of the eternal, the divine, the theocentric, there is no paradox—I shall not be able to decide whether the speculative thinker is right, because I am only a poor existing human being who neither eternally nor divinely nor theocentrically is able to observe the eternal but must be content with existing. This much, however, is certain, that with speculative thought everything goes backward, back past the Socratic, which at least comprehended that for an existing person existing is the essential; and much less has speculative thought taken the time to comprehend what it means to be *situated* in existence the way the existing person is in the imaginary construction.

The difference between the Socratic position and the position that goes beyond the Socratic is clear enough and is essentially the same as in *Fragments,* for in the latter nothing has changed, and in the former the matter has only been made somewhat more difficult, but nevertheless not more difficult than it is. It has also become somewhat more difficult because, whereas in *Fragments* I set forth the thought-category of the paradox only in an imaginary construction, here I have also latently made an attempt to make clear the necessity of the paradox, and even though the attempt is somewhat weak, it is still something different from speculatively canceling the paradox.

[43]Christianity has itself proclaimed itself to be the eternal, essential truth that has come into existence in time; it has proclaimed itself as *the paradox* and has required the inwardness of faith with regard to what is an offense to the Jews, foolishness to the Greeks[44]—and an absurdity to the understanding. It cannot be expressed more strongly that subjectivity is truth and that objectivity only thrusts away, precisely by virtue of the absurd, and it seems strange that Christianity should have come into the world in order to be explained, alas, as if it were itself puzzled about itself and therefore came into the world to seek out the wise man, the speculative thinker, who can aid with the explanation. It cannot be expressed more inwardly that subjectivity is truth than when subjectivity is at first untruth,[45] and yet subjectivity is truth.

Suppose that Christianity was and wants to be a mystery, an utter mystery, not a theatrical mystery that is revealed in the fifth act, although the clever spectator

42 See *Fragments*, pp. 66–71, 89–105, *KW* VII (*SV* IV 230–34, 252–67).
43 With reference to the following four paragraphs, see Supplement, pp. 2.52–53 (*Pap.* VI B 43),
44 See I Corinthians 1:23.
45 See, for example, *Fragments*, pp. 13–16, 51–52, *KW* VII (*SV* IV 183–85, 218).

[*Tilskuer*] already sees through [*gennemskue*] it in the course of the exposition. Suppose that a revelation *sensu strictissimo* [in the strictest sense] must be a mystery and be recognizable just by its being a mystery, whereas a revelation *sensu laxiori* [in the broader sense], the withdrawing into the eternal through recollection, is a revelation in the direct sense. Suppose that the difference in intellectual endowment is the difference in being able to state more and more clearly that it is and remains a mystery for existing human beings. Suppose that the intellectual endowment in relation to misunderstanding differs according to the individual's ability more and more deceptively to give the appearance of having understood the mystery. Suppose that it is nevertheless a blessing that, situated at the extremity of existence, one relates oneself to this mystery without understanding it, only having faith. Suppose that Christianity does not at all want to be understood; suppose that, in order to express this and to prevent anyone, misguided, from taking the road of objectivity, it has proclaimed itself to be the paradox. Suppose that it wants to be only for existing persons and essentially for persons existing in inwardness, in the inwardness of faith, which cannot be expressed more definitely than this: it is the absurd, adhered to firmly with the passion of the infinite. Suppose that it does not want to be understood and that the maximum of any eventual understanding is to understand that it cannot be understood. Suppose that it so decisively accentuates existing that the single individual becomes a sinner, Christianity the paradox, and existence the time of decision. Suppose that speculating is a temptation, the most precarious of all. Suppose that the speculator is not the prodigal son, for this is what the concerned God presumably would call the offended one whom he continues to love nevertheless, but the naughty child who refuses to stay where existing human beings belong, in the children's nursery and the education room of existence where one becomes adult only through inwardness in existing, but who instead wants to enter God's council, continually screaming that, from the point of view of the eternal, the divine, the theocentric, there is no paradox. Suppose that the speculative thinker is the restless resident who, although it is obvious that he is a renter, yet in view of the abstract truth that, eternally and divinely perceived, all property is in common, wants to be the owner, so that there is nothing to do except to send for a police officer, who would presumably say, just as the subpoena servers say to Gert Westphaler: We are sorry to have to come on this errand.[46]

Has being human now become something different from what it was in the old days, is the condition not the same: to be an individual *existing* being, and is not existing the essential as long as one is in existence? "But people know so much more now." "Quite right, but suppose that Christianity is not a matter of knowing; then much knowledge is of no benefit, except to ease a person more readily into the confusion of regarding Christianity as a matter of knowledge." And if people do know more now—and we are not speaking of the knowledge of railroads, machines, and kaleidoscopes, but of knowing more of the religious—how have they come to

---

46 See Holberg, *Mester Gert Westphaler Eller Den meget talende Barbeer* (original five–act play), IV, 10; *Hans Mikkelsens Comoedier Sammenskrefne for Den nye oprettede Danske Skue-Plads*, I–II (n.p.: 1723–24), I, no pagination.

know more? Presumably, through Christianity. So this is how Christianity is rewarded. One learns something from Christianity, misunderstands it, and in new misunderstanding uses it against Christianity.

If the terror in the old days was that one could be offended, the terror these days is that there is no terror, that one, two, three, before looking around, one becomes a speculative thinker who speculates about faith. About what faith? Is it about the faith that he has and especially about whether he does or does not have it? Alas, no, that is too little for an objective speculator. Consequently, he speculates about objective faith. What does that mean—objective faith? It means a sum of tenets. But suppose Christianity is nothing of the kind; suppose that, on the contrary, it is inwardness, and

therefore the paradox, in order to thrust away objectively, so that it can be for the existing person in the inwardness of existence by placing him decisively, more decisively than any judge can place the accused, between time and eternity in time, between heaven and hell in the time of salvation. Objective faith—it is indeed as if Christianity had also been proclaimed as a little system of sorts, although presumably not as good as the Hegelian system. It is as if Christ—it is not my fault that I say it—as if Christ had been a professor and as if the apostles had formed a little professional society of scholars. Truly, if at one time it was difficult to become a Christian, I believe now it becomes more difficult year by year, because it has now become so easy to become one; there is a bit of competition only in becoming a speculative thinker. And yet the speculator is perhaps furthest removed from Christianity, and perhaps it is preferable by far to be someone who takes offense but still continually relates himself to Christianity, whereas the speculator has understood it. To that extent there is hope that there still remains a similarity between a Christian now and in those early days and that wanting to become a Christian will once again become foolishness. In those early days, a Christian was a fool in the eyes of the world.[47] To the pagans and Jews it was foolishness for him to want to become one. Now one is a Christian as a matter of course. If someone wants to be a Christian with infinite passion, he is a fool, just as it is always foolishness to will to exert oneself with infinite passion in order to become what one is as a matter of course, as if someone would give all his fortune to purchase a precious gem[48]—which he owned. Formerly a Christian was a fool in the eyes of the world; now all people are Christians, but he nevertheless becomes a fool—in the eyes of Christians.

Suppose that it is this way. I say merely "suppose," and more I do not say. But since we are now admittedly growing weary of speculative thinkers who examine one another in print in the systematic rigmarole, it may at least be a change to go through the question in another way.

"But from the eternal, divine, and especially theocentric point of view, there is no paradox. True speculative thought, therefore, does not stop with the paradox but goes further and explains it." "May I now ask for a little peace and request that he not begin again? After all, I did say that I cannot become involved with the suprater-restrial and the subterranean." "The beginning and the consummation of the

47 See I Corinthians 1:23, 4: 10.
48 See Matthew 13:45–46.

explanation are with me, and it is for this explanation that the eternal truth has been waiting; it is quite correct that it entered into time, but the first edition was only an imperfect attempt. Because the eternal truth required an explanation, it entered into the world and anticipated this by occasioning a discussion. Similarly, a professor publishes the outline of a system,[49] assuming that the work, by being reviewed and debated, will come out sooner or later in a new and totally revised form. Only this second edition, when it has waited for the advice and judgment of experts, is the truth, and thus speculative thought is the true and only satisfactory edition of the provisional truth of Christianity."

By means of a few examples, we shall now illustrate how speculative thought, for the very reason that it refuses to comprehend that subjectivity is truth, has earned the gratitude of Christianity, which once and for all is the paradox[50] and is paradoxical at every point, whereas speculative thought, remaining in immanence, which is recollection's removal of itself from existence, at every point produces a volatilization. By means of the tour de force of not thinking anything decisive about what is most decisive (which, through the decision, is specifically designed to forestall immanence) but utilizing the expression of decision as a locution, the volatilization becomes a pagan reminiscence, to which there is nothing to object if it breaks directly with Christianity but much to object if it is supposed to be Christianity.

The thesis that God has existed in human form, was born, grew up, etc. is certainly the paradox *sensu strictissimo,* the absolute paradox. But as the absolute paradox it cannot be related to a relative difference. A relative paradox is related to a relative difference between more or less sagacious people. But the absolute paradox, precisely because it is absolute, can be related only to the absolute difference by which a human being differs from God;[51] it cannot be related to relative bickering between one human being and another about whether one is a little smarter than the other. But the absolute difference between God and a human being is simply this, that a human being is an individual existing being (and this holds for the best brain just as fully as for the most obtuse), whose essential task therefore cannot be to think *sub specie aeterni,* because as long as he exists, he himself, although eternal, is essentially an existing person and the essential for him must therefore be inwardness in existence; God, however, is the infinite one, who is eternal. As soon as I make the understanding of the paradox commensurate with the difference between being more or less intellectually endowed (a difference that still does not ever transcend being human, unless someone were to become so brilliant that he became not only a human being but also God), my discussion of understanding *eo ipso* demonstrates that what

49 Possibly an allusion to Hans Lassen Martensen, *Grundrids til Moralphilosophiens System* (Copenhagen: 1841; *ASKB* 650), or to Rasmus Nielsen, *Den speculative Logik i dens Grandtræk,* fascicles 1–4 (Copenhagen: 1841–44, incomplete), which begins with ¶ 11. The overleaf reads: "This outline is to be regarded as a fragment of a philosophical methodology." See also "Public Confession," Corsair *Affair*, p. 8, *KW* XIII (*SV* XIII 402–03).

50 With reference to the remainder of the paragraph and the following paragraph, see Supplement, p. 2.53 (*Pap.* VI B 40:27)

51 See, for example, *Sickness unto Death,* pp. 99, 117, 121–22, 126, 127–28, and Supplement, p. 143, *KW* XIX (*SV* Xl 209–10, 227, 231, 235, 237; *Pap.* VIII^2 B 168:2); *JP* III 3645–50; VII, p. 78,

I have understood is not the absolute paradox but a relative paradox, because the only possible understanding of the absolute paradox is that it cannot be understood. "But then speculative thought cannot ever grasp it." "Entirely correct, this is just what is said by the paradox, which thrusts away only in the direction of inwardness in existence." Perhaps this is so because objectively there is no truth for existing beings, but only approximations, whereas subjectively truth for them is in inwardness, because the decision of truth is in subjectivity.

The modern mythical allegorizing trend[52] summarily declares Christianity to be a myth. Such a procedure is at least forthright behavior, and everyone can easily form a judgment about it. The friendship of speculative thought is of another kind. To be on the safe side, speculative thought opposes the ungodly mythical allegorizing trend and then goes on to say, "Speculative thought, on the other hand, accepts the paradox, but it does not stop with it." "Nor is there any need for that, because when a person in faith continues to adhere firmly to it, in his existence deepening himself in the inwardness of faith, he does not stop either." Speculative thought does not stop—what does that mean? Does it mean that Messrs. Speculators cease to be human beings, individual existing human beings, and *en famille* [as a family] become all sorts of things? If not, one is certainly obliged to stop with the paradox, since it is grounded in and is the expression for precisely this, that the eternal, essential truth relates itself to existing individuals with the summons that they go further and further in the inwardness of faith.

What on the whole does it mean to *explain* something? Does explaining mean to show that the obscure something in question is not this but something else? That would be a strange explanation. I should think that by the explanation it would become clear that the something in question is this definite something, so that the explanation would remove not the thing in question but the obscurity. Otherwise the explanation is something other than an explanation; it is a correction. An explanation of the paradox makes clear what the paradox is and removes the obscurity; a correction removes the paradox and makes clear that there is no paradox. But the latter is certainly no explanation of the paradox but rather an explanation that there is no paradox. But if the paradox emerges from the placing together of the eternal and an existing individual human being, does the explanation, in removing the paradox, then also remove existing from the existing person? And if on his own, or with the assistance of another, an existing person has arrived at or has been brought almost to the point where it seems to him as if he did not exist, what is he then? Then he is absentminded. Consequently, the explanation of the absolute paradox that declares there is no paradox except to a certain degree, in other words, that there are only relative paradoxes, is an explanation not for existing individuals but for the absentminded. Well, then everything is in order. The explanation is that the paradox is the paradox only to a certain degree, and it is quite in order that it, namely, the

---

52 Possibly an allusion to, for example, David Friedrich Strauss, *Das Leben Jesu, kritisch bearbeitet,* I–II (Tüebingen: 1835), and to Andreas Frederik Beck, *Begrebet Mythus eller den religiøse Form* (Copenhagen: 1843; *ASKB* 424).

explanation, is for an existing person who is an existing person only to a certain degree, since he forgets it every other moment, and an existing person of that kind is simply absentminded.

Then when someone speaks of the absolute paradox, which is an offense to the Jews, foolishness to the Greeks, and the absurd to the understanding, and addresses his words to speculative thought, it is not so impolite as to tell him bluntly that he is a fool but rather gives an explanation that contains a correction and thus indirectly gives him to understand that he was in error. This is the way a humane, superior intellect always behaves toward the more limited. The procedure is altogether Socratic; there would be an un-Socratic element only if the one speaking is indeed closer to the truth than the speculative explanation, for then there remains the dissimilarity that Socrates politely and indirectly took the untruth away from the learner and gave him the truth, whereas speculative thought politely and indirectly takes the truth away from the learner and gives him the untruth. But politeness still remains the common denominator. And when Christianity declares itself to be the paradox, the speculative explanation is not an explanation but a correction, a polite and indirect correction, such as befits a superior intellect in relation to the more limited.

Does *explaining* the paradox mean to turn the expression "paradox" into a *rhetorical* expression, into something the honorable speculative thinker indeed says has its validity—but then in turn does not have its validity? In that case, the *summa summarum* [sum total] is indeed that there is no paradox. Honor be to the Herr Professor! I say this not to take his honor away from him, as if I, too, could cancel [*hæve*] the paradox. Not at all. But if the professor has canceled it, then it is of course canceled; in that case I dare say that it is canceled—unless the annulment [*Ophævelse*] pertains to the professor more than to the paradox, so that he, instead of canceling the paradox, himself becomes an alarming, fantastical swelling [*Hævelse*].[53] In other cases, one assumes that explaining something means to have it become clear in its significance, that it is this and not something else. To explain the paradox would then be to comprehend ever more deeply what a paradox is and that the paradox is the paradox.

Thus God is a supreme conception that cannot be explained by anything else[54] but is explainable only by immersing oneself in the conception itself. The highest principles for all thinking can be demonstrated only indirectly (negatively).[55] Suppose that the paradox is the boundary for an *existing person's* relation to an

53 In addition to a play on *Aufhebung* [raising, annulment] in Hegel's writings, there is a play on the action of yeast in dough. See p. 1.220.

54 Spinoza, *Ethics*, I, prop. III, XIV, Appendix; *Opera*, pp. 288, 293, 305; *Works*, pp. 410, 420, 439: *"If things have nothing in common with one another, one* of *them cannot be the cause of the other." "Except God, no substance can be or be conceived."* "With these [demonstrations] I have explained God's nature and properties; that he exists necessarily; that he is unique; that he is and acts from the necessity alone of his nature; that (and how) he is the free cause of all things; that all things are in God and so depend on him that without him they can neither be nor be conceived; and finally, that all things have been predetermined by God, not from freedom of the will *or* absolute good pleasure, but from God's absolute nature, *or* infinite power."

55 See *JP* III 2341 *(Pap. V A 74).*

eternal, essential truth—in that case the paradox will not be explainable by anything else if the explanation is supposed to be for existing persons. But understood speculatively, even the absolute paradox (because speculative thought is not afraid of using decisive terms; the only thing it fears is thinking something decisive with them) expresses only a relative difference between more and less gifted and educated people. In this way the shape of the world will gradually be changed. When Christianity entered into the world, there were no professors or assistant professors whatever—then it was a paradox for all. It can be assumed that in the present generation every tenth person is an assistant professor; consequently it is a paradox for only nine out of ten. And when the fullness of time[56] finally comes, that matchless future, when a generation of assistant professors, male and female, will live on the earth—then Christianity will have ceased to be a paradox.

On the other hand, the person who takes it upon himself to explain the paradox, on the assumption that he knows what he wants, will focus directly upon showing that it must be a paradox. To explain the unutterable joy[57]—what does that mean? Does it mean to explain that it is this and that? In that case, the predicate "unutterable" becomes just a rhetorical predicate, a strong expression, and the like. The explaining jack-of-all-trades has everything in readiness before the beginning of the performance, and now it begins. He dupes the listener; he calls the joy unutterable, and then a new surprise, a truly surprising surprise[58]—he utters it. Suppose that the unutterable joy is based upon the contradiction that an existing human being is composed of the infinite and the finite, is situated in time, so that the joy of the eternal in him becomes unutterable because he is existing; it becomes a supreme drawing of breath that cannot take shape, because the existing person is existing. In that case, the explanation would be that it is unutterable; it cannot be anything else—no nonsense. If, however, a profound person first condemns someone or other who denies that there is an unutterable joy and then says: No, I assume that there is an unutterable joy, but I go further and utter it, then he is only making a fool of himself, and the only difference between him and the other whom he condemns is that the other is more honest and direct and says what the profound person is also saying, since they both are saying essentially the same thing.

[59]Does explaining what is decisive mean to transform the expression into a rhetorical locution, so that one does not, like the light-minded person, deny all decision, but assumes it, yet assumes it only to a certain degree? What does it mean to assert that, a decision is to a certain degree? It means to deny decision. Decision is designed specifically to put an end to that perpetual prattle about "to a certain degree." So the decision is assumed—but, lo and behold, assumed only to a certain degree. Speculative thought is not afraid to use expressions of decision; the only thing it fears is thinking something decisive with them. And when Christianity wants to be the eternal decision for the existing subject and speculative thought explains

56 Cf. Galatians 4:4.
57 See I Peter 1:8.
58 See J. L. Heiberg, *Recensenten og Dyret,* 15, *Skuespil,* 111, p. 239; *JP* V 5831, p. 285 (*Pap.* VI B 233, p. 287).
59 With reference to the following two paragraphs, see Supplement, p. 2.53 (*Pap.* VI B 40:29).

that the decision is relative, it is not explaining Christianity but correcting it. Whether speculative thought is in the right is an entirely different question; here the question is only how its explanation of Christianity is related to the Christianity that it explains.

Does explaining something mean to *annul* it? I do know that the word *aufheben* has various, indeed opposite, meanings in the German language. It has often been noted that the word can mean both *tollere* [annul, annihilate] and *conservare* [preserve]. I am not aware that the Danish word *ophæve* [annul] allows any such equivocation, but I do know that our German-Danish philosophers use it like the German word. Whether it is a good quality in a word to have opposite meanings, I do not know, but anyone who wants to express himself with precision usually avoids the use of such a word in decisive places. There is a simple folk saying that humorously denotes the impossible: to have one's mouth full of crackers and to whistle at the same time. Speculative thought accomplishes a tour de force somewhat like that by using a word that also denotes the very opposite. In order to denote very clearly that speculation knows nothing of any decision, it itself uses an ambiguous word in order to denote the kind of understanding that is speculative understanding. Upon closer inspection, the confusion becomes more evident. *Aufheben* in the sense of *tollere* means to annihilate; in the sense of *conservare*, it means to preserve [*bevare*] in altogether unaltered condition, to do nothing at all to what is being preserved. If the government dissolves [*ophæve*] a political society, it abolishes it; if a man keeps or preserves something for me, it is of particular importance to me that he make no change whatever in it. Neither of these meanings is the philosophical *aufheben*. So speculation annuls all difficulty and then leaves me with the difficulty of understanding just what it is doing with this *aufheben*. But now let this *aufheben* mean reducing something to a relative factor, which it does mean when what is decisive, the paradox, is reduced to a relative factor, which means that there is no paradox, no decision, since the paradox and the decisive are what they are just because of their unyielding resistance. Whether speculative thought is in the right is a different question, but here what is asked is only how its explanation of Christianity is related to the Christianity that it explains.

By no means does speculative thought say that Christianity is untruth; on the contrary, it specifically says that speculation comprehends the truth of Christianity. More could certainly not be asked for. His Christianity ever asked to be more than the truth? And when speculation comprehends it, everything is as it should be. And yet, no, that is not how it is. In relation to Christianity, systematic speculation is only a bit cunning in the use of all kinds of diplomatic locutions that bedazzle the credulous. Christianity as it is understood by the speculative thinker is something different from what is presented to the simple. To them it is the paradox, but the speculative thinker knows how to cancel the paradox. Then it is not Christianity that is and was and remains the truth,[60] and the speculative thinker's understanding is not the understanding that Christianity is the truth—no, it is the speculative thinker's understanding of Christianity that is the truth of Christianity. The understanding is

VII
187

60 Cf., for example, John 14:6; I Timothy 2:4; I John 1; Revelation 1:8.

thus something other than the truth, It is not the case that the truth is understood only when the understanding has understood everything implied in the truth, but it is rather the case that only when that χατὰ δύναμιν [potential] truth is understood in the way a speculative thinker understands it, only then—well, then it is not speculation that has become true, but it is the truth that has come into existence. Consequently, the truth is not a given and the understanding is not what is awaited, but what is awaited is that speculation's understanding will be finished, because only then has truth come into existence. Thus speculative knowledge is not as knowledge usually is, something indifferent in relation to what is known, so that this is not changed by being known but remains the same. No, speculative knowledge is itself the object of knowing, so that the latter is no longer the same as it was but has come into existence simultaneously with speculation as the truth.

Whether speculative thought is in the right is a different question. What is asked here is only how its explanation of Christianity is related to the Christianity that it explains. And how should they be related? Speculative thought is objective, and objectively there is no truth for an existing individual but only an approximation, since by existing he is prevented from becoming entirely objective. Christianity, on the other hand, is subjective; the inwardness of faith in the believer is the truth's eternal decision. Objectively there is no truth; an objective knowledge about the truth or the truths of Christianity is precisely untruth. To know a creed by rote is paganism, because Christianity is inwardness.

[61]Let us take the paradox of the forgiveness of sins. Socratically, the forgiveness of sins is a paradox, inasmuch as the eternal truth relates itself to an existing person, *sensu strictiori* [in the stricter sense], because the existing person is a sinner, a qualification by which existence is accentuated a second time, because it wants to be an eternal decision in time with retroactive power to annul the past, and because it is bound up with God's having existed in time. The individual existing human being has to feel himself a sinner (not objectively, which is nonsense, but subjectively, and this is the deepest pain). With all his understanding to the very last turn (if one person has a little more understanding than the other, it makes no essential difference, and to appeal to one's great understanding is merely to betray one's deficient inwardness, or else it runs out very soon), he must want to understand the forgiveness of sins—and then despair of understanding. With the understanding in direct opposition, the inwardness of faith must grasp the paradox, and that faith battles in just this way, as the Romans once did, blinded by the light of the sun, is the resilience of inwardness.[62] If any other understanding ever forces itself upon him, he sees that he

61 With reference to the following paragraph, see Supplement, pp. 2.53–54 (*Pap.* VI B 45).

62 That one can battle in this way, blinded by the sun, and yet see to battle, the Romans demonstrated at Zama. That one can battle in this way, blinded, and yet see to conquer, the Romans demonstrated at Zama.[63] And now the battle of faith, is that supposed to be tomfoolery, a staged swordplay of gallantry, this battle that is longer than a Thirty Years' War, because one does not fight merely to acquire but fights even more vehemently to preserve, this battle in which every day is just as hot as the day of battle at Zama! While the understanding despairs, faith presses forward victoriously in the passion of inwardness. But when the believer uses all his understanding, every last turn of despair, just to discover the difficulty of the paradox, then truly no part is left with which to explain the paradox—but for all

is about to lose his faith, just as a girl, when she has become the beloved's wife, upon discovering that it is easy to understand that she became this man's chosen one, ought to see that this explanation is easily understood as an indication that she is no longer in love.

But a speculative thinker goes about it in a different way. He appears before an esteemed public and says, "Ladies and gentlemen, for that is how I must address you. To a congregation of believers, the paradox can be proclaimed only by a believer, but to an esteemed public the truth can be proclaimed by a speculative thinker. Therefore the forgiveness of sins is a paradox (general excitement). The pantheistic line is a fallacy that speculative thought opposes, but speculative thought does not stop with the paradox; it explains and annuls it." The highly esteemed speculative thinker did not, then, stake all his understanding when he despaired; his despair was only to a certain degree, a simulated movement; he reserved part of his understanding—for the explanation. This can be called: deriving benefit from one's understanding. The believer derives no benefit whatever from his; he uses up all of it in despair. But the speculator knows how to stretch it out sufficiently; he takes one-half of it for despairing (as if it were not nonsense to despair by halves) and the other half for perceiving that there is no reason for the understanding to despair. Well, of course, then the matter becomes something different; so where is the error? In the deceitfulness of the first movement, of course, and therefore not actually in his not stopping with faith but in his never reaching it.

Now, suppose that the basis of the paradox of the forgiveness of sins is that the poor existing human being is existing, that he is half-godforsaken even when in the

that, there can indeed be the ample firmness of faith in the passion of inwardness. Sitting calmly on a ship in fair weather is not a metaphor for having faith; but when the ship has sprung a leak, then enthusiastically to keep the ship afloat by pumping and not to seek the harbor—that is the metaphor for having faith. Even if the image ultimately contains an impossibility, this is merely the imperfection of the image, but faith holds out. While the understanding, like a desperate passenger, stretches its arms toward land, but in vain, faith works vigorously in the depths—joyful and victorious, against the understanding it rescues the soul. To exist in faith is that kind of contradiction; to an existing person, compromise is a mirage, since it is a contradiction that an eternal spirit exists. Whether anyone has done this, whether anyone is doing it—of what concern is that to me, if this is indeed what it is to have faith? Although I am still far from having fully understood the difficulty of Christianity (and an explanation that makes the difficulty easy must be regarded as a temptation), I nevertheless perceive that the battle of faith is not a topic for vaudeville poets and its strenuousness is not a divertissement for assistant professors.

63 The Romans, under Cornelius Scipio Africanus, were victorious over Hannibal's army at Zama in northern Africa (202 B.C.) in the Second Punic War. Climacus apparently confuses the report of this battle and conditions with some other account, perhaps that of the battle at Cannae in South Italy (216 B.C.), where, however, the Romans were defeated by Hannibal's army. See, for example, Livy, *From the Founding of the City* (*History of Rome*), XXII, 46; *T. Livii Patavini historiarum libri*, I–V, ed. August Wilhelm Ernesti (Leipzig: 1801–04, *ASKB* 1251–55), II, pp. 111–12; *Livy*, I–XIV, tr. B. O. Foster et al. (Loeb, Cambridge: Harvard University Press, 1935–67), V, pp. 352–53: "The sun—whether they had so placed themselves on purpose or stood as they did by accident—was, very conveniently for both sides, on their flanks, the Romans looking south, the Phoenicians north. A wind—which those who live in those parts call Volturnus—beginning to blow against the Romans carried clouds of dust right into their faces and prevented them from seeing anything."

inwardness of faith he is victorious against the understanding. Suppose that only eternity can give an eternal certainty, whereas existence has to be satisfied with a struggling certainty, which is gained not as the battle becomes easier or more illusory but only as it becomes harder. In that case, the explanation is indeed that it is and remains a paradox, and all is lost only when one thinks that there is no paradox or only to a certain degree. But, the esteemed public may say, if the forgiveness of sins is anything like that, how, then, can one *believe* it? Answer: If it is not anything like that, how, then, can one believe it?

[64]Whether Christianity is in the right is another question. Here the question is only how the speculative explanation is related to the Christianity that it explains. But if Christianity is perhaps in the wrong, this much is certain: speculative thought is definitely in the wrong, because the only consistency outside Christianity is that of pantheism, the taking of oneself out of existence back into the eternal through recollection, whereby all existence-decisions become only shadow play compared with what is eternally decided from behind. Like all *simulated* decision, the simulated decision of speculative thought is nonsense, because decision is the eternal protest against fictions. The pantheist is eternally reassured backward; the moment that is the moment of existence in time, the seventy years, is something vanishing. The speculative thinker, on the other hand, wants to be an existing person, but an existing person who is not subjective, not in passion, indeed, is existing *sub specie aeterni*—in short, he is absentminded. But what is explained in absentmindedness must not be trusted absolutely—such an explanation, and here I agree with speculative thought, is an explanation only to a certain degree.

If the speculative thinker explains the paradox in such a way that he cancels it and now consciously knows that it is canceled, that consequently the paradox is not the essential relation of eternal essential truth to an existing person in the extremities of existence, but only an accidental relative relation to limited minds—then there is an essential difference between the speculative thinker and the simple person, whereby all existence is fundamentally confused. God is insulted by obtaining a group of hangers-on, a support staff of good minds, and humankind is vexed because there is not an equal relationship with God for all human beings. The religious formula set forth above for the difference between the simple person's knowledge and the simple wise person's knowledge of the simple, that the difference is a meaningless trifle, that the wise person knows that he knows or knows that he does not know what the simple person knows—speculative thought does not respect this formula at all. Nor does it respect the equality implicit in the difference between the wise person and the simple person—that they know the same thing. That is, the speculator and the simple person in no way know the same thing when the simple person believes the paradox and the speculator knows that it is annulled. According, however, to the formula just cited, which honors God and loves human beings, the difference will be that the wise person also knows that it must be a paradox, the paradox he himself believes. Consequently, they do indeed know essentially the same thing; the wise person does not know anything else about the paradox, but he knows that he knows this about the

64 With reference to the following paragraph, see Supplement, p. 2.54 (*Pap.* VI B 40:31).

paradox. The simple wise person will then immerse himself in comprehending the paradox as paradox and will not become involved in explaining the paradox by understanding that it is not a paradox.

If, for example, the simple wise person spoke with a simple person about the forgiveness of sins, the simple person would most likely say, "But I still cannot comprehend the divine mercy that can forgive sins; the more intensely I believe it, the less I am able to understand it." (Thus probability does not seem to increase as the inwardness of faith is augmented, rather the opposite.) But the simple wise person will most likely say, "It is the same with me. You know I have had the opportunity to be able to devote much time to research and reflection, and yet the *summa summarum* of all this is at most that I comprehend that it cannot be otherwise, that it must be incomprehensible. Look, this difference certainly cannot distress you or make you think wistfully about your own more laborious circumstances in life or about your perhaps more modest capabilities, as if I had some advantage over you. My advantage, when regarded as the fruit of study, is something both to laugh at and to weep over. Yet you are never to scorn this study, just as I myself do not regret it, since on the contrary it pleases me most when I smile at it, and just then enthusiastically resume the effort of thinking."

Such a confession is made in all sincerity, and it is not present in the wise person merely once in a while but is essentially present in him whenever he is occupied in thinking. Once a year to consider that one ought always to thank God would hardly be a proper understanding of these words. Similarly, once in a while, on a great occasion, to consider, deeply moved, that before God all human beings are essentially equal is not truly to understand this equality, particularly if one's daily work and striving in more than one way consign it to oblivion. But to comprehend equality most earnestly just when one is most earnestly aware of what differentiates—that is the noble piety of the simple wise person.

Much that is strange has been said about Christianity, much that is lamentable, much that is outrageous, but the most obtuse thing ever said is that it is true to a certain degree. Much that is strange has been said about enthusiasm, much that is lamentable, much that is outrageous, but the most obtuse thing said about it is that it is to a certain degree. Much that is strange has been said about erotic love, much that is lamentable, much that is outrageous, but the most obtuse thing said about it is that it is to a certain degree. When a person has prostituted himself by speaking in this way about enthusiasm and love, has betrayed his obtuseness, which is not, however, a matter of the understanding, since the cause of it is just that the understanding has become too large, in the same sense as the cause of liver disease is that the liver has become too large, and therefore, as another author has remarked, "It is the dumbness the salt takes on when it loses its strength"[65]—then one phenomenon still remains, and that is Christianity. If enthusiasm's vision has been incapable of helping him break with the understanding, if love has been incapable of snatching him from bondage, let him look at Christianity. Let him be offended; even

---

[65] Vigilius Haufniensis, pseudonymous author of *Anxiety*. See p. 95, *KW* VIII (*SV* IV 365). The line from *Anxiety* is freely quoted. See Matthew 5:13; Luke 14:14.

so, he is a human being. Let him despair of ever becoming a Christian himself, even so, he may be closer than he thinks. Let him to his very last drop of blood work to root out Christianity; even so, he is a human being—but if here he also has it in him to say, "It is true to a certain degree," then he is obtuse.[66]

Perhaps someone thinks that I shudder in saying this, that I must be prepared for a terrible chastisement from the speculative thinker. Not at all. The speculator will here again be consistent and say, "What the man is saying is true to a certain degree, except that one must not stop there." It would indeed also be strange if an insignificant person like me were to succeed in what not even Christianity has succeeded—bringing the speculative thinker into passion. And if that should happen, well, then my fragment of philosophy[67] would suddenly take on a significance of which I had scarcely ever dreamed. But the person who is neither cold nor hot[68] is an abomination, and God is no more served by dud individualities than a rifleman is served by a rifle that in the moment of decision clicks instead of firing. If Pilate had not asked objectively what truth is,[69] he would never have let Christ be crucified. If he had asked the question subjectively, then the passion of inwardness regarding *what he in truth had to do* about the decision facing him would have prevented him from doing an injustice. In that case, not only his wife would have been troubled by her frightening dream,[70] but Pilate himself would have become sleepless. But when a person has before his eyes something as immensely big as the objective truth, he can easily cross out his fragment of subjectivity and what he as a subjective individual has to do. Then the approximation-process of the objective truth is symbolically expressed by washing one's hands,[71] because objectively there is no decision, whereas the subjective decision demonstrates that one was nevertheless in untruth by not comprehending that the decision is indeed rooted in subjectivity.

If, however, subjectivity[72] is truth and subjectivity is the existing subjectivity, then, if I may put it this way, Christianity is a perfect fit. Subjectivity culminates in passion, Christianity is paradox; paradox and passion fit each other perfectly, and paradox perfectly fits a person situated in the extremity of existence. Indeed, in the whole wide world there are not to be found two lovers who fit each other as do paradox and passion, and their quarrel is only like the lovers' quarrel when the quarrel is about whether it was he who awakened her passion or it was she who awakened his—and similarly here, the existing person has been situated in the extremity of existence by the paradox itself. And what is more glorious for lovers than to be granted a long time together without the occurrence of any change in the relationship except that it becomes more inward? And this is indeed granted to that very unspeculative understanding between passion and paradox, for they have been granted all of time, and not until eternity is there a change.

66 See Supplement, p. 2.54 (*Pap.* VI B 98:44).
67 The subtitle of *Fragments.*
68 See Revelation 3:15–16.
69 See John 18:38.
70 See Matthew 27:19.
71 Cf. Matthew 27:24.
72 See Supplement, pp. 2.54–55 (*Pap.* VI B 40:32).

The speculative thinker, however, behaves differently; he believes only to a certain degree—he puts his hand to the plow and looks around[73] in order to find something to know. In a Christian sense, what he finds to know is hardly anything good. Even if it were not the case that it cannot be otherwise, something a simple wise person seeking to understand the paradox will endeavor to show, even if there were a little remnant of divine willfulness in the paradox, God, I daresay, is certainly one who is allowed to attach importance to his person, and therefore he is not constrained to reduce the price of the God-relationship because of a religious slackness (and this term is much more suitable here than when we speak of a slack grain market). And even if God were willing, the passionate one would never want it. It never occurs to a girl truly in love that she has purchased her happiness at too high a price,[74] but rather that she has not purchased it at a price high enough. And just as the passion of the infinite is itself the truth, so it is also the case with the highest that you get what you pay for, and that a low price merely signifies poor business acumen, whereas in relation to God the highest price is no merit, since the highest price is precisely to will to do everything and yet know that this is nothing (for if it is something, the price is lower) and yet to will it.

Since I am not totally unfamiliar with what has been said and written about Christianity, I could presumably say a thing or two about it. I shall, however, not do so here but merely repeat that there is one thing I shall beware of saying about it: that it is true to a certain degree. It is indeed just possible that Christianity is the truth; it is indeed just possible that someday there will be a judgment[75] in which the separation will hinge on the relation of inwardness to Christianity. Suppose that someone stepped forward who had to say, "Admittedly I have not believed, but I have so honored Christianity that I have spent every hour of my life pondering it." Or suppose that someone came forward of whom the accuser had to say, "He has persecuted the Christians," and the accused one responded, "Yes, I acknowledge it; Christianity has so inflamed my soul that, simply because I realized its terrible power, I have wanted nothing else than to root it out of the world." Or suppose that someone came forward of whom the accuser had to say, "He has renounced Christianity," and the accused one responded, "Yes, it is true, for I perceived that Christianity was such a power that if I gave it one finger it would take all of me, and I could not belong to it completely." But suppose, now, that eventually an active assistant professor came along at a hurried and bustling pace and said something like this, "I am not like those three;[76] I have not only believed but have even explained Christianity and have shown that what was proclaimed by the apostles and appropriated in the first centuries is true only to a certain degree. On the other hand, through speculative understanding I have shown how it is the true truth, and for that reason I must request suitable remuneration for my meritorious services to Christianity."

---

73 Cf. Luke 9:62.
74 Cf. I Corinthians 6:20, 7:23.
75 Cf. Matthew 25:31–33.
76 Cf. Luke 18:11.

Of these four, which position would be the most terrible? It is indeed just possible that Christianity is the truth. Suppose that its ungrateful children want to have it declared incapable of managing its own affairs and placed under the guardianship of speculative thought. Suppose, then, that Christianity, like that Greek poet whose children also insisted that their aged father be declared incompetent but who amazed the judges and the people by writing one of his most beautiful tragedies to show that he was still competent[77]—suppose that Christianity in like manner rose rejuvenated to its feet—there would still be no one whose position would become as awkward as that of the assistant professors.

I do not deny that it is prestigious to stand so high above Christianity. I do not deny that it is comfortable to be a Christian and yet to be exempted from the martyrdom that always remains even if no external persecution is inflicted, and even if a Christian remains unnoticed as if he had never lived at all—the martyrdom of believing against the understanding, the mortal danger of lying out on 70,000 fathoms of water, and only there finding God. See, the wader feels his way with his foot, lest he go out so far that he cannot touch bottom. In the same way, with his understanding, the sensible person feels his way in probability and finds God where probability suffices and thanks him on the great festival days of probability when he has obtained a really good job and there is the probability of quick advancement to boot. And he thanks him when for a wife he finds a girl both beautiful and congenial, and even Councilor of War Marcussen says that it will be a happy marriage, that the girl has the kind of beauty that in all probability will last a long time, and that she is built in such a way that in all probability she will bear healthy and strong children. To believe against the understanding is something else, and to believe with the understanding cannot be done at all, because the person who believes with the understanding talks only about job and wife and fields and oxen and the like,[78] which are in no way the object of faith, since faith *always* thanks God, is *always* in mortal danger in that collision of the infinite and the finite that is precisely a mortal danger for one who is composed of both. The believer cares so little for probability that he fears it most of all, since he knows very well that with it he is beginning to lose his faith.

Faith has, namely, two tasks: to watch for and at every moment to make the discovery of improbability, the paradox, in order then to hold it fast with the passion

VII
196

---

77 Sophocles. See Cicero, *On Old Age,* VII, 22–23; *Opera,* IV, pp, 938–39; *Cicero,* XX, *De Senectute, De Amicitia, De Divinatione,* tr. William Armistead Falconer (Loeb, Cambridge: Harvard University Press, 1979), pp. 30–31:

> Sophocles composed tragedies to extreme old age; and when, because of his absorption in literary work, he was thought to be neglecting his business affairs, his sons haled him into court in order to secure a verdict removing him from the control of his property on the ground of imbecility, under a law similar to ours, whereby it is customary to restrain heads of families from wasting their estates. Thereupon, it is said, the old man read to the jury his play, *Oedipus at Colonus,* which he had just written and was revising, and inquired: "Does that poem seem to you to be the work of an imbecile?" When he had finished he was acquitted by the verdict of the jury.

See also Lessing, *"Leben des Sophokles," Zur Geschichte, Sprache, Litteratur und Kritik,* XVI, *Schriften,* X. pp. 133–34.

78 See Luke 14:16–20.

of inwardness. The improbable, the paradox, is ordinarily conceived of as something to which faith is related only passively; one will have to be satisfied temporarily with this situation, but little by little things will improve—indeed, this is probable. What wondrous confusion-compounding in speaking about faith! One is supposed to begin to believe on the basis of a confidence that there is the probability that things will surely improve. When that is done, one still manages to smuggle in probability and to keep oneself from believing. When that is done, it is easy to understand that the fruit of having had faith for a long time is that one ceases to have faith rather than, as one might think, that the fruit would be to have faith ever more inwardly. No, faith, self-active, relates itself to the improbable and the paradox, is self-active in discovering it and in holding it fast at every moment—in order to be able to believe. It already takes all the passion of the infinite and its concentration to stop with the improbable, inasmuch as the improbable and the paradox are not to be reached by the understanding's quantifying of the more and more difficult. Where understanding despairs, faith is already present in order to make the despair properly decisive, lest the movement of faith become a transaction within the haggling territory of the understanding. But to believe against the understanding is a martyrdom; to begin to enlist the understanding a little is a temptation and retrogression. The speculative thinker is exempted from this martyrdom. That he must pursue his studies and especially that he must read many of the modern books, I am willing to admit, is onerous, but the martyrdom of faith is indeed something else.

What I recoil from, then, even more than from dying or from losing my dearest treasure, is to say of Christianity that it is true to a certain degree. Even if I live to be seventy years old, even if I from year to year shorten the night's sleep and lengthen the day's work, pondering over Christianity—what is such little study but a trifle if it is supposed to justify me in judging so superiorly of Christianity! It would be much more pardonable, much more human, for me to become so embittered toward Christianity on the basis of a superficial acquaintance with it that I would declare it to be untruth. But superiority seems to me to be the real perdition that makes every saving relationship impossible—and it is indeed just possible that Christianity is the truth.[79]

This almost seems to be earnestness. If I now dared to proclaim stridently that I had come into the world and was called to counteract speculative thought,[80] that this was my judging mission, whereas my prophetic mission[81] was to herald a matchless future, and that therefore, on the basis of my being strident and called, people could safely depend on what I said—there would presumably be many who, failing to regard the whole thing as a fantastical reminiscence in the head of a silly person,

---

79 See Supplement, p. 2.55 (*Pap.* VI B 98:45).

80 With reference to the remainder of the sentence up to the dash, see Supplement, pp. 2.55–56 (*Pap.* VI B 40:33).

81 Possibly a double allusion: to Grundtvig ("prophetic," "matchless future" [see p. 1.36 and note 44]) and to the distinctions among Christ's three offices (prophet, priest, and king [judge]). See Karl Hase, *Hutterus redivivus oder Dogmatik der evangelisch-lutherschen Kirche* (Leipzig: 1839; *ASKB* 581), 99–102, pp. 241–56; *Hutterus redivivus eller den Evangelisk-Lutherske Kirkes Dogmatik,* tr. Andreas Lauritz Carl Listow (Copenhagen: 1841), pp. 249–65; Supplement, pp. 55–56 (Pap. VI B 40:33).

would regard it as earnestness. But I can say nothing like that about myself.[82] The resolution with which I began may rather be considered a whim. In any case, it is so far from being a call to me, even remotely so, that on the contrary the call that I did follow came not to me, if you please, but to someone else; and even for him it was very far from being anything like a call in the stricter sense. But even if a call did come to him, I am still uncalled when I follow it.

The event is quite simple. It was four years ago, on a Sunday—well, perhaps no one will believe me, because once again it is a Sunday, but it is nevertheless quite certain that it was a Sunday, about two months after the Sunday mentioned previously. It was rather late, toward evening.[83] Evening's taking leave of day and of the person who has experienced the day is enigmatic speech; its warning is like the caring mother's instruction to the child to come home in good time. But its invitation, even though the leave-taking is without fault in thus being misunderstood, is an inexplicable beckoning, as if rest were to be found only if one remained out for a nocturnal rendezvous, not with a woman but, womanlike, with the infinite, persuaded by the night wind as it monotonously repeats itself, as it searches forest and field and sighs as if looking for something, persuaded by the distant echo of stillness within oneself, as if it had a presentiment of something, persuaded by the sublime tranquillity of heaven, as if it had been found, persuaded by the audible soundlessness of the dew, as if this were the explanation and the refreshment of infinitude, like the fruitfulness of the quiet night, only half-understood like the semitransparency of the nocturnal mist.

Contrary to my usual practice, I had come out to that garden called the garden of the dead, where the visitor's leave-taking is again doubly difficult, since it is meaningless to say "once more," because the last time is already past, and since there is no reason to cease taking leave when the beginning is made after the last time is past. Most of the visitors had already gone home. Just one person disappeared among the trees. Not caring to meet anyone, he avoided me, since he was seeking the dead, not the living. In this garden there is always the beautiful agreement among the visitors that one does not go out there in order to see and to be seen, but each visitor avoids the other. One does not need company either, least of all a talkative friend, here where everything is eloquence, where the dead person calls out the brief word placed upon his grave, not as a pastor does, who preaches widely and broadly on the word, but as a silent man does, who says only this word, but says it with a passion as if the dead might burst the grave—or is it not odd to place upon his grave "We shall meet again" and then to remain down there? And yet what inwardness there is in the words just because of the contradiction. That someone who is coming tomorrow says, "We shall meet again," is not startling. But for someone to have everything against him, to have no direct expression for his inwardness, none, and yet to stand by his word—that is true inwardness. Inwardness is untrue in direct proportion to the ready availability of external expressions in countenance and

---

82 With reference to the remainder of the paragraph and the following paragraph, see Supplement, p. 256
  (*Pap.* VI B 40:34).
83 With reference to the remainder of the paragraph, see Supplement, pp. 256–57 (*Pap.* VI 13 49).

bearing, in words and assuring protestations—not just because the expression itself is untrue, but because the untruth is that the inwardness was merely an element. The dead person remains completely quiet while time passes. The famous warrior's sword has been laid upon his grave, and shamelessness has torn down the picket fence surrounding it, but the dead one did not rise up and draw his sword to defend himself and his resting place. He does not gesticulate, he does not protest, he does not flare up in a moment of inwardness, but, silent as the grave and quiet as a dead person, he maintains his inwardness and stands by his word. Praised be the living person who externally relates himself as a dead person to his inwardness and thereby maintains it, not as the excitement of a moment and as a woman's infatuation, but as the eternal, which has been gained through death. Such a person is a man. It is not unlovely for a woman to bubble over in momentary inwardness, nor is it unlovely for her to forget it again very soon—the one corresponds to the other, and both correspond to the feminine nature and to what is ordinarily understood by inwardness.

Tired from walking, I sat down on a bench, a marveling witness of how that proud ruler who now for thousands of years has been the hero of the day and will continue to be that until the last day, of how the sun in its brilliant departure cast a transfiguring glow over the entire surroundings, while my eyes gazed beyond the wall enclosing the garden into that eternal symbol of eternity—the infinite horizon. What sleep is for the body, rest such as this is for the soul, so that it can exhale properly. At that very moment, I discovered to my surprise that the trees that hid me from the eyes of others had hidden others from mine, for I heard a voice just beside me. It has always wounded my modesty to witness the expression of the kind of feeling that another person surrenders himself to only when he thinks he is not being observed, because there is an inwardness of feeling that out of decency is hidden and is manifest only to God, just as a woman's beauty will be concealed from everyone and disclosed only to the beloved—therefore I decided to move away. But the first words I heard held me captive, and since I feared that the noise of my leaving might disturb more than my staying there quietly, I chose the latter and then became a witness of a situation that, however solemn it was, suffered no infringement because of my presence.

Through the leaves I saw that there were two: an old man with chalk-white hair and a child, a boy of about ten years. Both were in mourning clothes and sat beside a freshly covered grave, from which it was easy to conclude that it was a recent loss that occupied them. The old man's august form became even more solemn in the transfiguring glow of twilight, and his voice, calm and yet fervent, rendered the words clearly and distinctly with the inwardness they had in the speaker, who paused now and then when his voice choked with weeping or his mood ended in a sigh. Mood is like the Niger River[84] in Africa; no one knows its source, no one knows its outlet—only its reach is known! From the conversation I learned that the little boy was the old man's grandson and the person whose grave they were visiting was the boy's father. Presumably all the others in the family were dead, since no one was

---

84 The source of the Niger River, near the Sierra Leone frontier, was not discovered until 1879.

mentioned. On a later visit I verified this by reading the name on the gravestone and the names of the many dead.[85] As they talked, the old man told the child that he no longer had a father, had no one to cling to except an old man, who was too old for him and who himself longed to leave the world, but that there was a God in heaven after whom all fatherliness in heaven and on earth is called, that there was one name in which there was salvation, the name of Jesus Christ. He paused for a moment and then said half-aloud to himself: That this consolation should become for me a terror, that he, my son, who now he's buried in the grave, could abandon it! For what purpose all my hope, for what purpose all my concern, for what purpose all his wisdom, now that his death in the midst of his error makes a believer's soul uncertain about his salvation, brings my gray hair in sorrow to the grave,[86] makes a believer leave the world in apprehensiveness, makes an old man hurry like a doubter after a certainty and look back dejected for the surviving one.

Then he spoke again with the child and told him that there was a wisdom that wanted to fly past faith, that on the other side of faith there was a wide range like the blue mountains, a specious continent, which to the mortal eye looked like a certainty greater than that of faith, but the believer feared this mirage as the skipper fears a similar mirage at sea, feared that it was a sham eternity in which a mortal cannot live, but in which, if he steadily stares into it, he will lose his faith. He became silent again, and then said to himself half-aloud: That he, my unhappy son, should have allowed himself to be deceived! For what purpose, then, all his learning, so that he could not even make himself intelligible to me, so that I could not speak with him about his error because it was too elevated for me! Then he rose and led the child to the grave, and in a voice the impression of which I shall never forget he said, "Poor boy, you are just a child, and yet you will soon be alone in the world. Do you promise me by the memory of your dead father, who, if he could speak to you now, would speak in this way and now speaks with my voice; do you promise by the sight of my old age and my gray hair; do you promise by the solemnity of this hallowed place, by the God whose name I trust you have learned to call upon, by the name of Jesus Christ, in whom alone there is salvation—do you promise me that you will hold fast to this faith in life and in death, that you will not let yourself be deceived by any phantom, no matter how the shape of the world is changed—do you promise me that?" Overcome by the impression, the little one dropped to his knees, but the old man raised him up and pressed him to his breast.

I owe it to the truth to confess that this was the most heartrending scene I have ever witnessed. What may momentarily make someone or other inclined to consider the whole thing a fiction—that an old man speaks this way with a child—was precisely what shook me most: the unhappy old man who had become solitary in the world with a child and had no one with whom to speak about his concern except a child, and had only one person to save, a child, and yet could not presuppose the

---

85 With reference to the following sentence, see Supplement, p. 2.57 (*Pap.* VI B 40:35).
86 Cf. Genesis 42:38.

maturity to understand, and yet did not dare to wait for the advent of maturity,[87] because he himself was an old man. It is beautiful to be an old person, gratifying for the old man to see the generation growing up around him, a joyous arithmetical task to add to the sum every time the number is increased. But if it becomes his lot to have to recalculate, if the arithmetical task becomes that of having to subtract every time death takes away and takes away, until quits [qvit] is called and the old man is left behind to give the receipt [qvittere]—what then is as hard as being an old person! Just as need can bring a person to extremities, so it seems to me that the old man's suffering found its strongest expression in what poetically might be called an improbability—that an old person has his one and only confidant in a child, and that a sacred promise, an oath, is required of a child.

Although only a spectator and a witness, I was deeply affected. At one moment it seemed to me as if I myself were the young man whom the father had buried in terror. At the next moment, it seemed to me as if I were the child who was bound by the sacred promise. But I felt no urge to rush forward and emotionally express my sympathy to the old man, assuring him with tears and quivering voice that I would never forget this scene, or perhaps even beseeching him to put me under oath. Only for rash [overilede] people, barren clouds, and bursts of passing showers [Ilinger] is nothing more precipitous [ilsom] than to take an oath, because, being unable to keep it, they must keep on taking it. In my opinion, "to want never to forget this impression" is different from saying once in a solemn moment, "I will never forget this." The former is inwardness, the latter perhaps only momentary inwardness. And if one never forgets it, the solemnity with which it was said does not seem so important, since the sustained solemnity with which one day by day keeps oneself from forgetting it is a truer solemnity. The feminine approach is always dangerous.[88] A tender handshake, a passionate embrace, a tear in the eye are still not exactly the same as the quiet dedication of resolution. Inwardness of spirit is indeed always like a stranger and foreigner in a body—why, then, gesticulations? What Shakespeare's Brutus says when the conspirators want to bind themselves by an oath to the enterprise is so true: "No, not an oath . . . . . let priests and cowards and rogues, marrowless oldsters and crushed souls swear . . . . . but do not weaken the quiet strength of our purpose, our inner invincible fire, by thinking that our cause, our performance, needs an oath [Eed]."[89] The momentary outpouring of inwardness

[87] With reference to the remainder of the paragraph and the following two paragraphs, see Supplement, pp. 2.57–59 (Pap, VI B 40:36).
[88] See Supplement, p. 2.59 (Pap. VI B 98:46).
[89] Shakespeare, Julius Caesar, II, 1, 114–36; Foersom and Wulff, I, p. 42. Cf. Kittredge, p. 1089:

No, not an oath. . . .
Swear priests and cowards and men cautelous,
Old feeble carrions and such suffering souls
That welcome wrongs; unto bad causes swear
Such creatures as men doubt; but do not stain
The even virtue of our enterprise,
Nor th' insuppressive mettle of our spirits,
To think that or our cause or our performance
Did need an oath. . . .

frequently leaves behind a lethargy [*Mathed*] that is dangerous. Furthermore, in yet another way a simple observation has taught me circumspection with regard to making oaths and promises, so that true inwardness is even constrained to express itself with the opposite. There is nothing that hasty and easily excited people are more inclined to do than to require sacred promises, because the inner weakness needs the powerful stimulation of the moment. Having to make a sacred promise to such a person is very dubious, and therefore it is much better to forestall this solemn scene and at the same time to bind oneself with a little *reservatio mentalis* [mental reservation], that is, if the requirement of a promise is justified at all. One thereby benefits the other person, prevents profanation of the sacred, prevents him from becoming bound by an oath—it would all end with his breaking the oath anyway. For example, if Brutus, in view of the fact that the conspirators, with hardly a single exception, were no doubt excitable fellows and therefore precipitous in making oaths and sacred promises and requesting sacred promises, had pushed them aside and had for that reason prevented the making of a promise, and if at the same time he quietly dedicated himself, since he regarded it as a just cause and their turning to him as also somewhat justified—then it appears to me that his inwardness would have been even greater. Now he is a bit bombastic, and although there is truth in what he says,[90] there is still a little untruth in his saying it to the conspirators without really making clear to himself to whom he is speaking.

Then I, too, went home. I basically understood the old man right away, because in many ways my studies had led me to notice a dubious relation between modern Christian speculative thought and Christianity, but it had not occupied me in any decisive way. Now the matter had its significance. The august old man with his faith seemed to me a totally justified individuality whom existence had wronged, inasmuch as modern speculative thought, like a monetary reform, made doubtful the property title of faith. The august old man's pain over losing his son, not only through death but, as he understood it, even more terribly through speculative thought, moved me deeply, and at the same time the contradiction in his situation, that he could not even explain how the enemy force was operating, became for me a decisive summons to find a definite clue. The whole thing appealed to me like a complicated

criminal case in which the very convoluted circumstances have made it difficult to track down the truth. This was something for me. I thought as follows: You are quite bored with life's diversions, bored with girls, whom you love only in passing; you must have something that can totally occupy your time. Here it is: find out where the misunderstanding between speculative thought and Christianity lies. This, then, was my resolution. I have not spoken about it to anyone at all, and I am sure that my landlady has detected no change in me, neither the same evening nor the next day.

"But," I said to myself, "since you are not a genius and by no means have the mission of making all humankind blissfully happy at any cost, and since you have not promised anyone anything either, you can undertake the matter entirely *con amore*

---

90 The final copy, in Kierkegaard's handwriting, reads; *"det er Sandhed i ham hvad han siger* [what he says is truth in him]"; and the first Danish edition reads: *"der er Sandhed i hvad han siger* [there is truth in what he says]."

[with love] and proceed altogether *methodice* [methodically], as if a poet and a dialectician kept your every step under surveillance, now that you have gained a more definite understanding of your own whimsical idea that you must try to make something difficult." My studies, which had already in a sense led me to my goal, now became more definitely organized, but the old gentleman's august figure always hovered before my thoughts every time I wanted to transform my deliberations into learned knowledge. But primarily I sought through my own reflection to pick up a clue to the ultimate misunderstanding. I need not report my many mistakes, but it finally became clear to me that the deviation of speculative thought and, based thereupon, its presumed faith to reduce faith to a factor might not be something accidental, might be located far deeper in the orientation of the whole age—most likely in this, that because of much knowledge people have entirely forgotten what it means to *exist* and what *inwardness* is.

When I had comprehended this, it also became clear to me that if I wanted to communicate anything about this, the main point must be that my presentation would be made in *indirect* form. That is, if inwardness is truth, results are nothing but junk with which we should not bother one another, and wanting to communicate results is an unnatural association of one person with another, inasmuch as every human being is spirit and truth is the self-activity of appropriation, which a result hinders. Suppose that the teacher, in regard to essential truth (for otherwise the direct relation between teacher and learner is entirely in order), has much inwardness and would like, as people say, to proclaim his teaching day in and day out. If he assumes that there is a direct relation between him and the learner, then his inwardness is not inwardness but a spontaneous outpouring, because respect for the learner, that he in himself is his own inwardness, is the teacher's inwardness. Suppose that a learner is enthusiastic and in the strongest terms proclaims his praise of the teacher and thus, as we say, lays bare his inwardness; his inwardness is not inwardness but a spontaneous devotedness, because the pious, silent agreement, according to which the learner personally appropriates what is taught, distancing himself from the teacher because he turns inward into himself—precisely that is inwardness. Pathos is certainly inwardness, but it is spontaneous inwardness and therefore can be expressed. But pathos in the form of contrast is inwardness; it remains with the communicator even when expressed, and it cannot be appropriated directly except through the other's *self*-activity, and the contrastive form is the dynamometer of inwardness. The more consummate the contrastive form, the greater the inwardness; and the less it is present, to the point of being direct communication, the less the inwardness. For an enthusiastic genius who would like to make all humankind blissfully happy and lead them to the truth, it can be difficult enough to learn to constrain himself in this way and to grasp the *N.B.* [*nota bene*, note well] of reduplication, because truth is not like a circular letter on which signatures are collected, but is in the *valore intrinseco* [intrinsic worth] of inwardness. Understanding this comes more naturally to a vagabond and frivolous person. As soon as truth, the essential truth, can be assumed to be known by everyone, appropriation and inwardness must be worked for, and here can be worked for only in an indirect form.

The position of the apostle[91] is something else, because he must proclaim an unknown truth, and therefore direct communication can always have its validity temporarily.

Oddly enough, although there is so much clamoring for the positive and for the direct communication of results, it does not occur to anyone to complain about God, who as the eternal spirit, as the source of derived spirits, would seem to be able in the communication of truth to relate himself directly to the derived spirit in a quite different sense than when the relation is between derived spirits who, viewed *essentially*, are equals within a common derivation from God. No anonymous author can more slyly hide himself, and no maieutic can more carefully recede from a direct relation than God can. He is in the creation, everywhere in the creation, but he is not there directly, and only when the single individual turns inward into himself (consequently only in the inwardness of self-activity) does he become aware and capable of seeing God.

The direct relationship with God is simply paganism, and only when the break has taken place, only then can there be a true God-relationship. But this break is indeed the first act of inwardness oriented to the definition that truth is inwardness. Nature is certainly the work of God, but only the work is directly present, not God. With regard to the individual human being, is this not acting like an illusive author, who nowhere sets forth his result in block letters or provides it beforehand in a preface? And why is God illusive? Precisely because he is truth and in being illusive seeks to keep a person from untruth. The observer does not glide directly to the result but on his own must concern himself with finding it and thereby break the direct relation. But this break is the actual breakthrough of inwardness, an act of self-activity, the first designation of truth as inwardness.

Or is it not the case that God is so unnoticeable, so hidden yet present in his work, that a person might very well live on, marry, be respected and esteemed as husband, father, and captain of the popinjay shooting club,[92] without discovering God in his work, without ever receiving any impression of the infinitude of the ethical, because he managed with an analogy to the speculative confusion of the ethical and the world-historical by managing with custom and tradition in the city where he lived? Just as a mother admonishes her child who is about to attend a party, "Now, mind your manners and watch the other polite children and behave as they do," so he, too, could live on and behave as he saw others behave. He would never do anything first and would never have any opinion unless he first knew that others had it, because "the others" would be his very first. On special occasions he would act like someone who does not know how to eat a course that is served at a banquet; he would reconnoiter until he saw how the others did it etc. Such a person could perhaps know ever so much, perhaps even know the system by rote; he could perhaps live in a Christian country, know how to bow his head every time God's name was mentioned, perhaps also see God in nature if he was in the company of others who saw God; in

91 See, for example, "The Difference between a Genius and an Apostle," under the pseudonym of H. H., in *Without Authority, KW* XVIII (*SV* XI 93–109).
92 Danish: *Fuglekonge,* literally, "bird king."

short, well, he could be a congenial partygoer—and yet he would be deceived by the direct relation to truth, to the ethical, to God.

If one were to portray such a person in an imaginary construction, he would be a satire on what it is to be a human being. It is really the God-relationship that makes a human being a human being, but this is what he would lack. Yet no one would hesitate to consider him an actual human being (for the absence of inwardness is not seen directly), although he would be more like a puppet character that very deceptively imitates all the human externalities—would even have children with his wife. At the end of his life, one would have to say that one thing had escaped him: he had not become aware of God. If God could have permitted a direct relationship, he would certainly have become aware. If God had taken the form, for example, of a rare, enormously large green bird, with a red beak, that perched in a tree on the embankment and perhaps even whistled in an unprecedented manner—then our partygoing man would surely have had his eyes opened; for the first time in his life he would have been able to be the first.

All paganism consists in this, that God is related directly to a human being, as the remarkably striking to the amazed. But the spiritual relationship with God in truth, that is, inwardness, is first conditioned by the actual breakthrough of inward deepening that corresponds to the divine cunning that God has nothing remarkable, nothing at all remarkable, about him—indeed, he is so far from being remarkable that he is invisible, and thus one does not suspect that he is there [*er til*], although his invisibility is in turn his omnipresence. But an omnipresent being is the very one who is seen everywhere, for example, as a police officer is—how illusive, then, that an omnipresent being is cognizable precisely by his being invisible,[93] simply and solely by this, because his very visibility would annul his omnipresence. This relation between omnipresence and invisibility is like the relation between mystery and revelation, that the mystery expresses that the revelation is revelation in the stricter sense, that the mystery is the one and only mark by which it can be known, since otherwise a revelation becomes something like a police officer's omnipresence.

If God [*Gud*] wants to reveal himself in human form and provide a direct relation by taking, for example, the form of a man who is twelve feet tall, then that imaginatively constructed partygoer and captain of the popinjay shooting club will surely become aware. But since God is unwilling to deceive, the spiritual relation in

93 In order to indicate how illusive the rhetorical can be, I shall show here how one could perhaps produce an effect upon a listener rhetorically, even though what was said would be a dialectical retrogression. Suppose a pagan religious orator says that here on earth the god's temple is actually empty, but (and here the rhetorical begins) in heaven, where everything is more perfect, where water is air, and air is ether, there are also temples and shrines for the gods, but the difference is that the gods actually dwell in these temples—that the god actually dwells in the temple is dialectical retrogression, because his not dwelling in the temple is an expression for the spiritual relation to the invisible. But rhetorically it produces the effect. —Incidentally, I had in mind a specific passage by a Greek author,[94] but I shall not quote him.

94 See Plato, *Phaedo,* 111 a–b; *Opera,* I, pp. 602–03; Heise, I. p. 110; *Dialogues,* p. 92: "In a word, as water and the sea are to us for our purposes, so is air to them, and as air is to us, so the æther is to them."

truth specifically requires that there be nothing at all remarkable about his form; then the partygoer must say: There is nothing to see, not the slightest. If the god [*Guden*] has nothing whatever that is remarkable about him, the partygoer is perhaps deceived in not becoming aware at all. But the god is without blame in this, and the actuality of this deception is continually also the possibility of the truth. But if the god has something remarkable about him, he deceives, inasmuch as a human being thus becomes aware of the untruth, and this awareness is also the impossibility of the truth.

In paganism, the direct relation is idolatry; in Christianity, everyone indeed knows that God cannot manifest himself in this way. But this knowledge is not inwardness at all, and in Christianity it can certainly happen with a rote knower that he becomes utterly "without God in the world,"[95] which was not the case in paganism, where there was still the untrue relation of idolatry. Idolatry is certainly a dismal substitute, but that the rubric "God" disappears completely is even more mistaken.

Accordingly, not even God relates himself directly to a derived spirit (and this is the wondrousness of creation: not to produce something that is nothing in relation to the Creator, but to produce something that is something and that in the true worship of God can use this something to become by itself nothing before God); even less can one human being relate himself in this way to another *in truth*. Nature, the totality of creation, is God's work, and yet God is not there, but within the individual human being there is a possibility (he is spirit according to his possibility) that in inwardness is awakened to a God-relationship, and then it is possible to see God everywhere.

Compared with the spiritual relationship in inwardness, the sensate distinctions of the great, the amazing, the most crying-to-heaven superlatives of a southern nation are a retrogression to idolatry. Is it not as if an author wrote 166 folio volumes and the reader read and read, just as when someone observes and observes nature but does not discover that the meaning of this enormous work lies in the reader himself, because amazement at the many volumes and the five hundred lines to the page, which is similar to amazement at how immense nature is and how innumerable the animal species are, is not understanding.

With regard to the essential truth, a direct relation between spirit and spirit is unthinkable. If such a relation is assumed, it actually means that one party has ceased to be spirit, something that is not borne in mind by many a genius who both assists people *en masse* into the truth and is good-natured enough to think that applause, willingness to listen, signatures, etc. mean accepting the truth. Just as important as the truth, and of the two the even more important one, is the mode in which the truth is accepted, and it is of slight help if one gets millions to accept the truth if by the very mode of their acceptance they are transposed into untruth. And therefore all good-naturedness, all persuasion, all bargaining, all direct attraction with the aid of one's own person in consideration of one's suffering so much for the cause, of one's weeping over humankind, of one's being so enthusiastic, etc.—all such things are a misunderstanding, in relation to the truth a forgery by which, according to one's ability, one helps any number of people to acquire a semblance of truth.

95 Ephesians 2:12.

Socrates was a teacher of the ethical, but he was aware that there is no direct relation between the teacher and the learner, because inwardness is truth, and inwardness in the two is precisely the path away from each other. Probably because he perceived this he was so very pleased with his advantageous appearance.[96] What was it? Well, guess again! In our day, we say of a clergyman that he has a very advantageous appearance; we are pleased about this and understand that he is a handsome man, that the clerical gown is very becoming to him, that he has a sonorous voice and a figure that every tailor—but what am I saying—that every listener must be pleased with. Ah, yes, when one is so equipped by nature and so dressed by the tailor, one can easily be a teacher of religion, even with success, because the conditions of teachers of religion vary greatly—indeed, more than one thinks when one hears complaints that some pastoral appointments are so opulent and others so meager. The difference is much greater—some teachers of religion are crucified—and yet the religion is fully the same! No one cares much about the reduplicated repetition of the substance of the teaching in the conception of how the teacher ought to be. Orthodoxy is set forth, and the teacher is prinked up in pagan-esthetic categories. Christ is presented in biblical expressions. That he bore the sin of the whole world[97] will not really move the congregation; yet the speaker proclaims it, and in order to make the contrast strong, he describes Christ's beauty (because the contrast between guiltlessness and sin is not strong enough), and the believing congregation is stirred by this totally pagan qualification of the god in human form: beauty.

But back to Socrates.[98] He did not have an appearance as advantageous as the one described. He was very ugly, had clumsy feet, and more than that, a number of bumps on his forehead and other places, which were bound to convince everyone that he was a depraved character. This, you see, was what Socrates understood by his advantageous appearance, and he was so pleased as Punch about it that he would have considered it chicanery on the part of the god if, in order to keep him from being a teacher of morals, he had been given the pleasing appearance of a sentimental zither player, the languishing look of a *Schäfer* [amorous swain], the small feet of a dance director in the Friendship Society,[99] and *in toto* as advantageous an appearance as a job seeker in *Adresseavisen* or a theological graduate who had set his hopes on a patronage appointment could possibly wish for himself Now, then, why was that old teacher so pleased with his advantageous appearance, unless it was because he perceived that it might help to place the learner at a distance so that he would not be caught in a direct relation to the teacher, perhaps would admire him, perhaps would have his clothes made in the same way, but might understand through the repulsion of opposition, which in turn was his irony in a higher sphere, that the learner

96 See Xenophon, *Symposium,* V; *Xenophontis opera graece et latine*, I–IV, ed. Carl August Thieme (Leipzig: 1801–04; *ASKB* 1207-10), IV, pp. 471-74; *Xenophon* I–VII, IV, *Symposium and Apology,* tr. O. J. Todd (Loeb, Cambridge: Harvard University Press, 1979), pp. 598–603,

97 See John 1:29.

98 See, for example, *JP* IV 4246 (*Pap.* III B 30).

99 The Friendship Society (Copenhagen), organized in 1783, held social events arranged by a dance director.

essentially has himself to deal with[100] and that the inwardness of truth is not the chummy inwardness with which two bosom friends walk arm in arm with each other but is the separation in which each person for himself is existing in what is true.

Thus I had fully realized that every direct communication with regard to truth as inwardness is a misunderstanding, even though it can vary according to the variety of that which is responsible for it, be it a lovable predilection, a nebulous sympathy, cryptic vanity, obtuseness, brashness, and other things. But just because I had become clear about the form of communication, it did not mean that I had something to communicate, although it was nevertheless entirely in order that the form first became clear to me, because the form is indeed the inwardness.

My main thought was that, because of the copiousness of knowledge, people in our day have forgotten what it means *to exist,* and what *inwardness* is, and that the misunderstanding between speculative thought and Christianity could be explained by that. I now resolved to go back as far as possible in order not to arrive too soon at what it means to exist religiously, not to mention existing Christianly-religiously, and in that way leave dubieties behind me. If people had forgotten what it means to exist religiously, they had probably also forgotten what it means to exist humanly; therefore this would have to be brought out.[101] But this must not on any account be done didactically, because then the misunderstanding would in a new misunderstanding instantly make capital of the explanatory attempt, as if existing consisted in coming to know something about a particular point. If this is communicated as knowledge, the recipient is mistakenly induced to understand that he is gaining something to know, and then we are back in knowledge again. Only the person who has an idea of a misunderstanding's tenacity in assimilating even the most rigorous attempt at explanation and yet remaining a misunderstanding, only he will be aware of the difficulty of an authorship in which care must be taken with every word, and every word must go through the process of double-reflection. Direct communication about what it means to exist and about inwardness will only have the result that the speculative thinker will benevolently take it in hand and let one slip in along with it. The system is hospitable! Just as a bourgeois-philistine, without regard to compatibility, takes along every Tom, Dick, and Harry when he goes on an excursion to the woods, inasmuch as there is room enough in the four-seated Holstein carriage, so also is the system hospitable—there is indeed plenty of room.

I will not conceal the, fact that I admire Hamann,[102] although I readily admit that, if he is supposed to have worked coherently, the elasticity of his thoughts lacks evenness and his preternatural resilience lacks self-control. But the originality of genius is there in his brief statements, and the pithiness of form corresponds completely to the desultory hurling forth of a thought. With heart and soul, down to his last drop of blood, he is concentrated in a single word, a highly gifted genius's passionate protest against a system of existence. But the system is hospitable. Poor

---

100 With reference to the remainder of the paragraph, see Supplement, pp. 2.57–60 (*Pap.* VI B 40:38).

101 With reference to the remainder of the paragraph and the following paragraph, see Supplement, pp. 2.60, 2.61–62 (*Pap.* VI B 40:39, 45).

102 On Hamann, see *JP* II 1539–60 and pp. 574–76; VII, pp. 43–44,

Hamann, you have been reduced to a subsection by Michelet.[103] Whether your grave has ever been marked, I do not know; whether it is now trampled upon, I do not know; but I do know that by hook or by crook you have been stuck into the subsection uniform and thrust into the ranks. I do not deny that Jacobi[104] has often inspired me, although I am well aware that his dialectical skill is not in proportion to his noble enthusiasm, but he is the eloquent protest of a noble, unadulterated, lovable, highly gifted mind against the systematic crimping of existence, a triumphant consciousness of and an inspired battling for the significance of existence as something longer and deeper than the few years during which one forgets oneself in studying the system. Poor Jacobi! Whether anyone visits your grave, I do not know; but I do know that the subsection-plow plows under all your eloquence, all your inwardness, while a few paltry words are being registered about your importance in the system. It is said of Jacobi that he represented feeling with enthusiasm; such a report ridicules both feeling and enthusiasm, which have precisely the secret that neither can be reported secondhand and therefore cannot in the form of a result conveniently make a rote parroter blissfully happy through a *satisfactio vicaria* [vicarious satisfaction].

So, then, I resolved to begin, and the first thing I wanted to do in order to start from the bottom was *to have the existence-relation between the esthetic and the ethical come into existence in an existing individuality.* The task was set, and I foresaw that the work would be copious enough, and above all that I would have to be prepared to remain still at times when the spirit would not support me with pathos. But what happened then I shall tell in an appendix to this chapter.

---

103 See Carl Ludwig Michelet, *Geschichte der letzten Systeme der Philosophie in Deutschland von Kant bis Hegel,* I–II (Berlin: 1837–38; *ASKB* 678–79), I, pp. 302–18.

104 Friedrich Heinrich Jacobi (1743–1819), German philosopher. See also *Fragments*, p. 84, *KW* VII (*SV* IV 247); *JP* I 810, 1033; II 1113; V 5728, 5733 (*Pap.* V A 35, 30, 40, 21, C 13).

III.1

Selections of Mystical Experiences

AN OLD TESTAMENT SELECTION: THE CALL OF ISAIAH

In the year of King Uzziah's death I saw the Lord seated on a throne, high and exalted, and the skirt of his robe filled the temple. About him were attendant seraphim, and each had six wings; one pair covered his face and one pair his feet, and one pair was spread inflight. They were calling ceaselessly to one another,

> *Holy, holy, holy is the Lord of Hosts:*
> *the whole earth is full of his glory.*

And, as each one called, the threshold shook to its foundations, while the house was filled with smoke. Then I cried,

> *Woe is me! I am lost,*
> *for I am. a man of unclean lips*
> *and I dwell among a people of unclean lips;*
> *yet with these eyes I have seen the King, the*
> LORD *of Hosts.*

Then one of the seraphim flew to me carrying in his hand a glowing coal which he had taken from the altar with a pair of tongs. He touched my mouth with it and said,

> *See, this has touched your lips;*
> *your iniquity is removed,*
> *and your sin is wiped away.*

Then I heard the Lord saying, Whom shall I send? Who will go for me? And I answered, Here am I; send me. He said, Go and tell this people:

> *You may listen and listen, but you will not*
> *understand.*
> *You may look and look again, but you will*
> *never know.*
> *This people's wits are dulled,*
> *their ears are deafened and their eyes*
> *blinded, so that they cannot see with their*
> *eyes nor listen with their ears nor under-*
> *stand with their wits, so that they may turn*
> *and be healed.*

ISAIAH, Chapter 6, New English Bible

THE CHRISTIAN MYSTIC, ST. TERESA OF ÁVILA

One day when I was at prayer... I saw Christ at my side—or, to put it better, I was conscious of Him, for I saw nothing with the eyes of the body or the eyes of the soul (the imagination). He seemed quite close to me and I saw that it was He. As I thought, He was speaking to me. Being completely ignorant that such visions were possible, I was very much afraid at first, and could do nothing but weep, though as soon as He spoke His first word of assurance to me, I regained my usual calm, and became cheerful and free from fear. All the time Jesus Christ seemed to be at my side, but as this was not an imaginary vision I could not see in what form. But I most clearly felt that He was all the time on my right, and was a witness of everything that I was doing... if I say that I do not see Him with the eyes of the body or the eyes of the soul, because this is no imaginary vision, how then can I know and affirm that he is beside me with greater certainty than if I saw Him? If one says that one is like a person in the dark who cannot see someone though he is beside him, or that one is like somebody who is blind, it is not right. There is some similarity here, but not much, because a person in the dark can perceive with the other senses, or hear his neighbor speak or move, or can touch him. Here this is not so, nor is there any feeling of darkness. On the contrary, He appears to the soul by a knowledge brighter than the sun. I do not mean that any sun is seen, or any brightness, but there is a light which, though unseen, illuminates the understanding.

J. M. Cohen, trans., *The Life of St. Teresa of Ávila*, London: Penguin, 1957

A HINDU EXAMPLE

The Ego has disappeared. I have realized my identity with Brahman and so all my desires have melted away. I have arisen above my ignorance and my knowledge of this seeming universe. What is this joy I feel? Who shall measure it? I know nothing but joy, limitless, unbounded! The treasure I have found there cannot be described in words. The mind cannot conceive of it. My mind fell like a hailstone into that vast expanse of Brahman's ocean. Touching one drop of it, I melted away and became

one with Brahman. Where is this universe? Who took it away? Has it merged into something else? A while ago, I beheld it—now it exists no longer. Is there anything apart or distinct from Brahman? Now, finally and clearly, I know that I am the Atman [the soul identified with Brahman], whose nature is eternal joy. I see nothing, I hear nothing, I know nothing that is separate from me.

Swami Prabhavandanda, trans., *Shankara's Crest-Jewel of Discrimination*, New York: Mentor Books, 1970

A BUDDHIST MEDITATION

Of one who has entered the first trance the voice has ceased; of one who has entered the second trance reasoning and reflection have ceased; of one who has entered the third trance joy has ceased; of one who has entered the fourth trance the inspiration and expiration have ceased; of one who has entered the realm of the infinity of space the perception of form has ceased; of one who has entered the realm of the infinity of consciousness the perception of the realm of the infinity of space has ceased; of one who has entered the realm of nothingness the perception of the realm of the infinity of consciousness has ceased.

HENRY WARREN, ed., SAMYUTTA-NIKAYA, in *Buddhism in Translation*, New York: Atheneum, 1973

III.2

Mysticism

WILLIAM JAMES

William James (1842–1910), American philosopher and psychologist, was one of the most influential thinkers of his time. He taught at Harvard University and is considered, along with C. S. Peirce, one of the fathers of pragmatism. The Varieties of Religious Experience *(1902) is his classic study of*

From William James, *The Varieties of Religious Experience* (Longman, Green & Co.: New York, 1902). Some footnotes deleted.

religious experience. In this selection James describes mystical experience, which he considers to be the deepest kind of religious experience it is something that transcends our ordinary, sensory experience and that cannot be described in terms of our normal concepts and language.

Over and over again in these lectures I have raised points and left them open and unfinished until we should have come to the subject of Mysticism. Some of you, I fear, may have smiled as you noted my reiterated postponements. But now the hour has come when mysticism must be faced in good earnest, and those broken threads wound up together. One may say truly, I think, that personal religious experience has its root and centre in mystical states of consciousness; so for us, who in these lectures are treating personal experience as the exclusive subject of our study, such states of consciousness ought to form the vital chapter from which the other chapters get their light. Whether my treatment of mystical states will shed more light or darkness, I do not know, for my own constitution shuts me out from their enjoyment almost entirely, and I can speak of them only at second hand. But though forced to look upon the subject so externally, I will be as objective and receptive as I can; and I think I shall at least succeed in convincing you of the reality of the states in question, and of the paramount importance of their function.

First of all, then, I ask, What does the expression "mystical states of consciousness" mean? How do we part off mystical states from other states?

The words "mysticism" and "mystical" are often used as terms of mere reproach, to throw at any opinion which we regard as vague and vast and sentimental, and without a base in either facts or logic. For some writers a "mystic" is any person who believes in thought-transference, or spirit-return. Employed in this way the word has little value: there are too many less ambiguous synonyms. So, to keep it useful by restricting it, I will do what I did in the case of the word "religion," and simply propose to you four marks which, when an experience has them, may justify us in calling it mystical for the purpose of the present lectures. In this way we shall save verbal disputation, and the recriminations that generally go therewith.

1. Ineffability   The handiest of the marks by which I classify a state of mind as mystical is negative. The subject of it immediately says that it defies expression, that no adequate report of its contents can be given in words. It follows from this that its quality must be directly experienced; it cannot be imparted or transferred to others. In this peculiarity mystical states are more like states of feeling than like states of intellect. No one can make clear to another who has never had a certain feeling, in what the quality or worth of it consists. One must have musical ears to know the value of a symphony; one must have been in love one's self to understand a lover's state of mind. Lacking the heart or ear, we cannot interpret the musician or the lover justly, and are even likely to consider him weak-minded or absurd. The mystic finds that most of us accord to his experiences an equally incompetent treatment.

2. Noetic quality   Although so similar to states of feeling, mystical states seem to those who experience them to be also states of knowledge. They are states of insight into depths of truth unplumbed by the discursive intellect. They are illuminations, revelations, full of significance and importance, all inarticulate though they remain; and as a rule they carry with them a curious sense of authority for aftertime.

These two characters will entitle any state to be called mystical, in the sense in which I use the word. Two other qualities are less sharply marked, but are usually found. These are:—

3. Transiency   Mystical states cannot be sustained for long. Except in rare instances, half an hour, or at most an hour or two, seems to be the limit beyond which they fade into the light of common day. Often, when faded, their quality can but imperfectly be reproduced in memory; but when they recur it is recognized; and from one recurrence to another it is susceptible of continuous development in what is felt as inner richness and importance.

4. Passivity   Although the oncoming of mystical states may be facilitated by preliminary voluntary operations, as by fixing the attention, or going through certain bodily performances, or in other ways which manuals of mysticism prescribe; yet when the characteristic sort of consciousness once has set in, the mystic feels as if his own will were in abeyance, and indeed sometimes as if he were grasped and held by a superior power. This latter peculiarity connects mystical states with certain definite phenomena of secondary or alternative personality, such as prophetic speech, automatic writing, or the mediumistic trance. When these latter conditions are well pronounced, however, there may be no recollection whatever of the phenomenon, and it may have no significance for the subject's usual inner life, to which, as it were, it makes a mere interruption. Mystical states, strictly so-called, are never merely interruptive. Some memory of their content always remains, and a profound sense of their importance. They modify the inner life of the subject between the times of their recurrence. Sharp divisions in this region are, however, difficult to make, and we find all sorts of gradations and mixtures.

These four characteristics are sufficient to mark out a group of states of consciousness peculiar enough to deserve a special name and to call for careful study. Let it then be called the mystical group.

Our next step should be to gain acquaintance with some typical examples. Professional mystics at the height of their development have often elaborately organized experiences and a philosophy based thereupon. But you remember what I said in my first lecture: phenomena are best understood when placed within their series, studied in their germ and in their over-ripe decay, and compared with their exaggerated and degenerated kindred. The range of mystical experience is very wide, much too wide for us to cover in the time at our disposal. Yet the method of serial study is so essential for interpretation that if we really wish to reach conclusions we must use it. I will begin, therefore, with phenomena which claim no special religious significance, and end with those of which the religious pretensions are extreme.

The simplest rudiment of mystical experience would seem to be that deepened sense of the significance of a maxim or formula which occasionally sweeps over one. "I've heard that said all my life," we exclaim, "but I never realized its full meaning until now." "When a fellow-monk," said Luther, "one day repeated the words of the Creed: I believe in the forgiveness of sins,' I saw the Scripture in an entirely new light; and straightway I felt as if I were born anew. It was as if I had found the door of paradise thrown wide open." This sense of deeper significance is not confined to rational propositions. Single words, and conjunctions of words, effects of light on land and sea, odors and musical sounds, all bring it when the mind is tuned aright. Most of us can remember the strangely moving power of passages in certain poems read when we were young, irrational doorways as they were through which the mystery of fact, the wildness and the pang of life, stole into our hearts and thrilled them. The words have now perhaps become mere polished surfaces for us; but lyric poetry and music are alive and significant only in proportion as they fetch these vague vistas of a life continuous with our own, beckoning and inviting, yet ever eluding our pursuit. We are alive or dead to the eternal inner message of the arts according as we have kept or lost this mystical susceptibility....

....

[An] incommunicableness of the transport is the keynote of all mysticism. Mystical truth exists for the individual who has the transport, but for no one else. In this, as I have said, it resembles the knowledge given to us in sensations more than that given by conceptual thought. Thought, with its remoteness and abstractness, has often enough in the history of philosophy been contrasted unfavorably with sensation. It is a commonplace of metaphysics that God's knowledge cannot be discursive but must be intuitive, that is, must be constructed more after the pattern of what in ourselves is called immediate feeling, than after that of proposition and judgment. But *our* immediate feelings have no content but what the five senses supply; and we have seen and shall see again that mystics may emphatically deny that the senses play any part in the very highest type of knowledge which their transports yield.

In the Christian church there have always been mystics. Although many of them have been viewed with suspicion, some have gained favor in the eyes of the authorities. The experiences of these have been treated as precedents, and a codified system of mystical theology has been based upon them, in which everything legitimate finds its place. The basis of the system is "orison" or meditation, the methodical elevation of the soul towards God. Through the practice of orison the higher levels of mystical experience may be attained. It is odd that Protestantism, especially evangelical Protestantism, should seemingly have abandoned everything methodical in this line. Apart from what prayer may lead to, Protestant mystical experience appears to have been almost exclusively sporadic. It has been left to our mind-curers to reintroduce methodical meditation into our religious life.

The first thing to be aimed at in orison is the mind's detachment from outer sensations for these interfere with its concentration upon ideal things. Such manuals as Saint Ignatius's *Spiritual Exercises* recommend the disciple to expel sensation by a graduated series of efforts to imagine holy scenes. The acme of this kind of discipline would be a semi-hallucinatory mono-ideism—an imaginary figure of Christ, for example, coming fully to occupy the mind. Sensorial images of this sort, whether literal or symbolic, play an enormous part in mysticism. But in certain cases imagery may fall away entirely, and in the very highest raptures it tends to do so. The state of consciousness becomes then insusceptible of any verbal description. Mystical teachers are unanimous as to this. Saint John of the Cross, for instance, one of the best of them, thus describes the condition called the "union of love," which, he says, is reached by "dark contemplation." In this the Deity compensates the soul, but in such a hidden way that the soul—

> finds no terms, no means, no comparison whereby to render the sublimity of the wisdom and the delicacy of the spiritual feeling with which she is filled…We receive this mystical knowledge of God clothed in none of the kinds of images, in none of the sensible representations, which our mind makes use of in other circumstances. Accordingly in this knowledge, since the senses and the imagination are not employed, we get neither form nor impression, nor can we give any account or furnish any likeness, although the mysterious and sweet-tasting wisdom comes home so clearly to the inmost parts of our soul. Fancy a man seeing a certain kind of thing for the first time in his life. He can understand it, use and enjoy it, but he cannot apply a name to it, nor communicate any idea of it, even though all the while it be a mere thing of sense. How much greater will be his powerlessness when it goes beyond the senses! This is the peculiarity of the divine language. The more infused, intimate, spiritual, and supersensible it is, the more does it exceed the senses, both inner and outer, and impose silence upon them.
>
> …The soul then feels as if placed in a vast and profound solitude, to which no created thing has access, in an immense and boundless desert, desert the more delicious the more solitary it is. There, in this abyss of wisdom, the soul grows by what it drinks in from the wellsprings of the comprehension of love,… and recognizes, however sublime and learned may be the terms we employ, how utterly vile, insignificant, and improper they are, when we seek to discourse of divine things by their means.

I cannot pretend to detail to you the sundry stages of the Christian mystical life. Our time would not suffice, for one thing; and moreover, I confess that the subdivisions and names which we find in the Catholic books seem to me to represent nothing objectively distinct. So many men, so many minds; I imagine that these experiences can be as infinitely varied as are the idiosyncrasies of individuals.

The cognitive aspects of them, their value in the way of revelation, is what we are directly concerned with, and it is easy to show by citation how strong an impression they leave of being revelations of new depths of truth. Saint Teresa is the expert of experts in describing such conditions, so I will turn immediately to what she says of one of the highest of them, the "orison of union."

In the orison of union (says Saint Teresa) the soul is fully awake as regards God, but wholly asleep as regards things of this world and in respect of herself. During the short time the union lasts, she is as it were deprived of every feeling, and even if she would, she could not think of any single thing. Thus she needs to employ no artifice in order to arrest the use of her understanding: it remains so stricken with inactivity that she neither knows what she loves, nor in what manner she loves, nor what she wills. In short, she is utterly dead to the things of the world and lives solely in God.... I do not even know whether in this state she has enough life left to breathe. It seems to me she has not; or at least that if she does breathe, she is unaware of it. Her intellect would fain understand something of what is going on within her, but it has so little force now that it can act in no way whatsoever. So a person who falls into a deep faint appears as if dead...

Thus does God, when he raises a soul to union with himself, suspend the natural action of all her faculties. She neither sees, hears, nor understands, so long as she is united with God. But this time is always short, and it seems even shorter than it is. God establishes himself in the interior of this soul in such a way, that when she returns to herself, it is wholly impossible for her to doubt that she has been in God, and God in her. This truth remains so strongly impressed on her that,

even though many years should pass without the condition returning, she can neither forget the favor she received, nor doubt of its reality. If you, nevertheless, ask how it is possible that the soul can see and understand that she has been in God, since during the union she has neither sight nor understanding, I reply that she does not see it then, but that she sees it clearly later, after she has returned to herself, not by any vision, but by a certitude which abides with her and which God alone can give her. I knew a person who was ignorant of the truth that God's mode of being in everything must be either by presence, by power, or by essence, but who, after having received the grace of which I am speaking, believed this truth in the most unshakable manner. So much so that, having consulted a half-learned man who was as ignorant on this point as she had been before she was enlightened, when he replied that God is in us only by "grace," she disbelieved his reply, so sure she was of the true answer; and when she came to ask wiser doctors, they confirmed her in her belief, which much consoled her...

But how, you will repeat, can one have such certainty in respect to what one does not see? This question, I am powerless to answer. These are secrets of God's omnipotence which it does not appertain to me to penetrate. All that I know is that I tell the truth; and I shall never believe that any soul who does not possess this certainty has ever been really united to God.

The kinds of truth communicable in mystical ways, whether these be sensible or supersensible, are various. Some of them relate to this world—visions of the future, the reading of hearts, the sudden understanding of texts, the knowledge of distant events, for example; but the most important revelations are theological or metaphysical.

Saint Ignatius confessed one day to Father Laynez that a single hour of meditation at Manresa had taught him more truths about heavenly things than all the teachings of all the doctors put together could have taught him.... One day in orison, on the steps of the choir of the Dominican church, he saw in a distinct manner the plan of divine wisdom in the creation of the world. On another occasion, during a procession, his spirit was ravished in God, and it was given him to contemplate, in a form and images fitted to the weak understanding of a dweller on the earth, the deep mystery of the holy Trinity. This last vision flooded his heart with such sweetness, that the mere memory of it in after times made him shed abundant tears.

Similarly with Saint Teresa.

One day, being in orison (she writes), it was granted me to perceive in one instant how all things are seen and contained in God. I did not perceive them in their proper form, and nevertheless the view I had of them was of a sovereign clearness, and has remained vividly impressed upon my soul. It is one of the most signal of all the graces which the Lord has granted me.... The view was so subtle and delicate that the understanding cannot grasp it.

She goes on to tell how it was as if the Deity were an enormous and sovereignly limpid diamond, in which all our actions were contained in such a way their full sinfulness appeared evident as never before. On another day, she relates, while she was reciting the Athanasian Creed—

Our Lord made me comprehend in what way it is that one God can be in three persons. He made me see it so clearly that I remained as extremely surprised as I was comforted,... and now, when I think of the holy Trinity, or hear It spoken of, I understand how the three adorable Persons form only one God and I experience an unspeakable happiness.

On still another occasion it was given to Saint Teresa to see and understand in what wise the Mother of God had been assumed into her place in Heaven.

The deliciousness of some of these states seems to be beyond anything known in ordinary consciousness. It evidently involves organic sensibilities, for it is spoken of as something too extreme to be borne, and as verging on bodily pain. But it is too subtle and piercing a delight for ordinary words to denote. God's touches, the wounds of his spear, references to ebriety and to nuptial union have to figure in the phraseology by which it is shadowed forth. Intellect and senses both swoon away in these highest states of ecstasy. "If our understanding comprehends," says Saint Teresa, "it is in a mode which remains unknown to it, and it can understand nothing of what it comprehends. For my own part, I do not believe that it does comprehend, because, as I said, it does not understand itself to do so. I confess that it is all a mystery in which I am lost." In the condition called *raptus* or ravishment by theologians, breathing and circulation are so depressed that it is a question among the doctors whether the soul be or be not temporarily dissevered from the body. One must read Saint Teresa's descriptions and the very exact distinctions which she makes, to persuade one's self that one is dealing, not with imaginary experiences, but with phenomena which, however rare, follow perfectly definite psychological types.

To the medical mind these ecstasies signify nothing but suggested and imitated hypnoid states, on an intellectual basis of superstition, and a corporeal one of degeneration and hysteria. Undoubtedly these pathological conditions have existed in many and possibly in all the cases, but that fact tells us nothing about the value for knowledge of the consciousness which they induce. To pass a spiritual judgment upon these states, we must not content ourselves with superficial medical talk, but inquire into their fruits for life.

Their fruits appear to have been various. Stupefaction, for one thing, seems not to have been altogether absent as a result. You may remember the helplessness in the kitchen and schoolroom of poor Margaret Mary Alacoque. Many other ecstatics would have perished but for the care taken of them by admiring followers. The "other-worldliness" encouraged by the mystical consciousness makes this over-abstraction from practical life peculiarly liable to befall mystics in whom the character is naturally passive and the intellect feeble; but in natively strong minds and characters we find quite opposite results. The great Spanish mystics, who carried the habit of ecstasy as far as it has often carried, appear for the most part to have shown indomitable spirit and energy, and all the more so for the trances in which they indulged.

Saint Ignatius was a mystic, but his mysticism made him assuredly one of the most powerfully practical human engines that ever lived. Saint John of the Cross, writing of the intuitions and "touches" by which God reaches the substance of the soul, tells us that—

> They enrich it marvelously. A single one of them may be sufficient to abolish at a stroke certain imperfections of which the soul during its whole life had vainly tried to rid itself, and to leave it adorned with virtues and loaded with supernatural gifts. A single one of these intoxicating consolations may reward it for all the labors undergone in its life—even were they numberless. Invested with an invincible courage, filled with an impassioned desire to suffer for its God, the soul then is seized with a strange torment—that of not being allowed to suffer enough.

Saint Teresa is as emphatic, and much more detailed. You may perhaps remember a passage I quoted from her in my first lecture. There are many similar pages in her autobiography. Where in literature is a more evidently veracious account of the formation of a new centre of spiritual energy, than is given in her description of the effects of certain ecstasies which in departing leave the soul upon a higher level of emotional excitement?

Often, infirm and wrought upon with dreadful pains before the ecstasy, the soul emerges from it full of health and admirably disposed for action... as if God had willed that the body itself, already obedient to the soul's desires, should share in the soul's happiness... The soul after such a favor is animated with a degree of courage so great that if at that moment its body should be torn to pieces for the cause of God, it would feel nothing but the liveliest comfort. Then it is that promises and heroic resolutions spring up in profusion in us, soaring desires, horror of the world, and the clear perception of our proper nothingness... .What empire is comparable to that of a soul who, from this sublime summit to which God has raised her, sees all the things of earth beneath her feet, and is captivated by no one of them? How ashamed she is of her former attachments! How amazed at her blindness! What lively pity she feels for those whom she recognizes still shrouded in the darkness!... She groans at having ever been sensitive to points of honor, at the illusion that made her ever see as honor what the world calls by that name. Now she sees in this name nothing more than an immense lie of which the world remains a victim. She discovers, in the new light from above, that in genuine honor there is nothing spurious, that to be faithful to this honor is to give our respect to what deserves to be respected really, and to consider as nothing, or as less than nothing, whatsoever perishes and is not agreeable to God. ...She laughs when she sees grave persons, persons of orison, caring for points of honor for which she now feels profoundest contempt. It is suitable to the dignity of their rank to act thus, they pretend, and it makes them more useful to others. But she knows that in despising the dignity of their rank for the pure love of God they would do more good in a single day than they would effect in ten years by preserving it…She laughs at herself that there should ever have been a time in her life when she made any case of money, when she ever desired it…Oh! if human beings might only agree together to regard it as so much useless mud, what harmony would then reign in the world! With what friendship we would all treat each other if our interest in honor and in money could but disappear from earth! For my own part, I feel as if it would be a remedy for all our ills.

Mystical conditions may, therefore, render the soul more energetic in the lines which their inspiration favors. But this could be reckoned an advantage only in case the inspiration were a true one. If the inspiration were erroneous, the energy would be all the more mistaken and misbegotten. So we stand once more before the problem of truth which confronted us at the end of the lectures on saintliness. You will remember that we turned to mysticism precisely to get some light on truth. Do mystical states establish the truth of those theological affections in which the saintly life has its root?

In spite of their repudiation of articulate self-description, mystical states in general assert a pretty distinct theoretic drift. It is possible to give the outcome of the majority of them in terms that point in definite philosophical directions. One of these directions is optimism, and the other is monism. We pass into mystical states from out of ordinary consciousness as from a less into a more, as from a smallness into a vastness, and at the same time as from an unrest to a rest. We feel them as reconciling, unifying states. They appeal to the yes-function more than to the no-function in us. In them the unlimited absorbs the limits and peacefully closes the account. Their very denial of every adjective you may propose as applicable to the ultimate truth—He, the Self, the Atman, is to be described by "No! no!": only, say the Upanishads—though it seems on the surface to be a no-function, is a denial made on

behalf of a deeper yes. Whoso calls the Absolute anything in particular, or says that it is this, seems implicitly to shut it off from being *that*—it is as if he lessened it. So we deny the "this," negating the negation which it seems to us to imply, in the interests of the higher affirmative attitude by which we are possessed. The fountain-head of Christian mysticism is Dionysius the Are-opagite. He describes the absolute truth by negatives exclusively.

> The cause of all things is neither soul nor intellect; nor has it imagination, opinion, or reason, or intelligence; nor is it reason or intelligence; nor is it spoken or thought. It is neither number, nor order, nor magnitude, nor littleness, nor equality, nor inequality, nor similarity, nor dissimilarity. It neither stands, nor moves, nor rests…. It is neither essence, nor eternity, nor time. Even intellectual contact does not belong to it. It is neither science nor truth. It is not even royalty or wisdom; not one; not unity; not divinity or goodness; nor even spirit as we know it (etc., *ad libitum*).

But these qualifications are denied by Dionysius, not because the truth falls short of them, but because it so infinitely excels them. It is above them. It is super-lucent, *super*-splendent, *super*-essential, *super*-sublime, *super* everything that can be named. Like Hegel in his logic, mystics journey towards the positive pole of truth only by the "Methode der Absoluten Negativität."

Thus comes the paradoxical expressions that so abound in mystical writings. As when Eckhart tells of the still desert of the Godhead, "where never was seen difference, neither Father, Son, nor Holy Ghost, where there is no one at home, yet where the spark of the soul is more at peace than in itself." As when Boehme writes of the Primal Love, that "it may fitly be compared to Nothing, for it is deeper than any Thing, and is as nothing with respect to all things, forasmuch as it is not comprehensible by any of them. And because it is nothing respectively, it is therefore free from all things, and is that only good, which a man cannot express or utter what it is, there being nothing to which it may be compared, to express it by." Or as when Angelus Silesius sings:—

[God is pure Nothing. Neither Now
nor Here affects Him.
But the more you grasp him,
the more He disappears"] (Ed. trans.)

To this dialectical use, by the intellect, of negation as a mode of passage towards a higher kind of affirmation, there is correlated the subtlest of moral counterparts in the sphere of the personal will. Since denial of the finite self and its wants, since asceticism of some sort, is found in religious experience to be the only doorway to the larger and more blessed life, this moral mystery intertwines and combines with the intellectual mystery in all mystical writings.

> Love (continues Boehme) [is Nothing, for] when thou art gone forth wholly from the Creature and from that which is visible, and art become Nothing to all that is Nature and Creature, then thou art in that eternal One, which is God himself, and then thou shalt feel within thee the highest virtue of Love....The treasure of treasures for the soul is where she goeth out of the Somewhat into that Nothing out of which all things may be made. The soul here saith, *I have nothing*, for I am utterly stripped and naked; *I can do nothing*, for I have no manner of power, but am as water poured out; *I am nothing*, for all that I am is no more than an image of Being, and only God is to me I AM; and so, sitting down in my own Nothingness, I give glory to the eternal Being, and *will nothing* of myself, that so God may will all in me, being unto me my God and all things.

In Paul's language, I live, yet not I, but Christ liveth in me. Only when I become as nothing can God enter in and no difference between his life and mine remain outstanding.

This overcoming of all the usual barriers between the individual and the Absolute is the great mystic achievement. In mystic states we both become one with the Absolute and we become aware of our oneness. This is the everlasting and triumphant mystical tradition, hardly altered by differences of clime or creed. In Hinduism, in Neoplatonism, in Sufism, in Christian mysticism, in Whitmanism, we find the same recurring note, so that there is about mystical utterances an eternal unanimity which ought to make a critic stop and think, and which brings it about that the mystical classics have, as has been said, neither birthday nor native land. Perpetually telling of the unity of man with God, their speech antedates languages, and they do not grow old.

"That are Thou!" says the Upanishads, and the Vedantists add: "Not a part, nor a mode of That, but identically That, that absolute Spirit of the World." "As pure water poured into pure water remains the same, thus, O Gautama, is the Self of a thinker who knows. Water in water, fire in fire, ether in ether, no one can distinguish them: likewise a man whose mind has entered into the self." "Everyman," says the Sufi Gulshan-Raz, "whose heart is no longer shaken by any doubts, knows with certainty that there is no being save only One...In his divine majesty the me, and we, the thou, are not found, for in the One there can be no distinction. Every being who is annulled and entirely separated from himself, hears resound outside of him this voice and this echo: *I am God*: he has an eternal way of existing, and is no longer subject to death." In the vision of God, says Plotinus, "what sees is not our reason, but something prior and superior to our reason— He who thus sees does not properly see, does not distinguish or imagine two things. He changes, he ceases to be himself, preserves nothing of himself. Absorbed in God, he makes but one with him, like a Centre of a circle coinciding with another centre." "Here," writes Suso, "the spirit dies, and yet is all alive in the marvels of the Godhead... and is lost in the stillness of the glorious dazzling obscurity and of the naked simple unity. It is in this modeless *where* that the highest bliss is to be found." ["I am as great as God,"] sings Angelus Silesius again, ["He is as small as I. He cannot be above me, nor I under Him."] (Ed. trans.)

In mystical literature such self-contradictory phrases as "dazzling obscurity," "whispering silence," "teeming desert," are continually met with. They prove that not conceptual speech, but music rather, is the element through which we are best spoken to by mystical truth. Many mystical scriptures are indeed little more than musical compositions.

> He who would hear the voice of Nada, "the Soundless Sound," and comprehend it, he has to learn the nature of Dhâranâ... When to him-self his form appears unreal, as do on waking all the forms he sees in dreams; when he has ceased to hear the many, he may discern the ONE—the inner sound which kills the outer. ... For then the soul will hear, and will remember. And then to the inner ear will speak THE VOICE OF THE SILENCE....And now thy *Self* is lost in SELF, *thyself* unto THYSELF, merged in that SELF from which thou first didst radiate...Behold! thou hast become the Light, thou hast become the Sound, thou art thy Master and thy God. Thou art THYSELF the object of thy search: the VOICE unbroken, that resounds through-out eternities, exempt from change, from sin exempt, the seven sounds in one, the VOICE OF THE SILENCE. *Om tat Sat.*

These words, if they do not awaken laughter as you receive them, probably stir chords within you which music and language touch in common. Music gives us ontological messages which non-musical criticism is unable to contradict, though it may laugh at our foolishness in minding them. There is a verge of the mind which these things haunt; and whispers there-from mingle with the operations of our understanding, even as the waters of the infinite ocean send their waves to break among the pebbles that he upon our shores.

> *Here begins the sea that ends not till the*
> *world's end. Where we stand,*
> *Could we know the next high sea-mark set*
> *beyond these waves that gleam,*

> *We should know what never man hath known,*
> *nor eye of man hath scanned.*

> ...

> *Ah, but here man's heart leaps, yearning*
> *towards the gloom with venturous glee,*
> *From the shore that hath no shore beyond it,*
> *set in all the sea.*

That doctrine, for example, that eternity is timeless, that our "immortality," if we live in the eternal, is not so much future as already now and here, which we find so often expressed today in certain philosophical circles, finds its support in a "hear, hear!" or an "amen," which floats up from that mysteriously deeper level. We recognize the passwords to the mystical region as we hear them, but we cannot use them ourselves; it alone has the keeping of "the password primeval."

I have now sketched with extreme brevity and insufficiency, but as fairly as I am able in the time allowed, the general traits of the mystic range of consciousness. *It is on the whole pantheistic and optimistic, or at least the opposite of pessimistic. It is anti-naturalistic, and harmonizes best with twice-bornness and so-called other-worldly states of mind.*

My next task is to inquire whether we can invoke it as authoritative. Does it furnish any *warrant for the truth* of the twice-bornness and supernaturality and pantheism which it favors? I must give my answer to this question as concisely as I can.

In brief my answer is this—and I will divide it into three parts:—

1. Mystical states, when well developed, usually are, and have the right to be, absolutely authoritative over the individuals to whom they come.

2. No authority emanates from them which should make it a duty for those who stand outside of them to accept their revelations uncritically.

3. They break down the authority of the non-mystical or rationalistic consciousness, based upon the understanding and the senses alone.

They show it to be only one kind of consciousness. They open out the possibility of other orders of truth, in which, so far as anything in us vitally responds to them, we may freely continue to have faith.

I will take up these points one by one.

1. As a matter of psychological fact, mystical states of a well-pronounced and emphatic sort are usually authoritative over those who have them. They have been "there," and know. It is vain for rationalism to grumble about this. If the mystical truth that comes to a man proves to be a force that he can live by, what mandate have we of the majority to order him to live in another way? We can throw him into a prison or a madhouse, but we cannot change his mind—we commonly attach it only the more stubbornly to its beliefs. It mocks our utmost efforts, as a matter of fact, and in point of logic it absolutely escapes our jurisdiction. Our own more "rational" beliefs are based on evidence exactly similar in nature to that which mystics quote for theirs. Our senses, namely, have assured us of certain states of fact; but mystical experiences are as direct perceptions of fact for those who have them as any sensations ever were for us. The records show that even though the five senses be in abeyance in them, they are absolutely sensational in their epistemological quality, if I may be pardoned the barbarous expression—that is, they are face to face presentations of what seems immediately to exist.

The mystic is, in short, *invulnerable*, and must be left, whether we relish it or not, in undisturbed enjoyment of his creed. Faith, says Tolstoy, is that by which men live. And faith-state and mystic state are practically convertible terms.

2. But I now proceed to add that mystics have no right to claim that we ought to accept the deliverance of their peculiar experiences, if we are ourselves outsiders and feel no private call thereto. The utmost they can ever ask of us in this life is to admit that they establish a presumption. They form a consensus and have an unequivocal outcome; and it would be odd, mystics might say, if such a unanimous type of experience should prove to be altogether wrong. At bottom, however, this would only be an appeal to numbers, like the appeal of rationalism the other way; and the appeal to numbers has no logical force. If we acknowledge it, it is for "suggestive," not for logical reasons: we follow the majority because to do so suits our life.

But even this presumption from the unanimity of mystics is far from being strong. In characterizing mystic states as pantheistic, optimistic, etc., I am afraid I over-simplified the truth. I did so for expository reasons, and to keep the closer to the classic mystical tradition. The classic religious mysticism, it now must be confessed, is only a "privileged case." It is an *extract*, kept true to type by the selection of the fittest specimens and their preservation in "schools." It is carved out from a much larger mass; and if we take the larger mass as seriously as religious mysticism has historically taken itself, we find that the supposed unanimity largely disappears. To begin with, even religious mysticism itself, the kind that accumulates traditions and makes schools, is much less unanimous than I have allowed. It has been both ascetic and antinomianly self-indulgent within the Christian church. It is dualistic in Sankhya, and monistic in Vedanta philosophy. I called it pantheistic; but the great Spanish mystics are anything but pantheists. They are with few exceptions non-metaphysical minds, for whom "the category of personality" is absolute. The "union" of man with God is for them much more like an occasional miracle than like an original identity. How different again, apart from the happiness common to all, is the mysticism of Walt Whitman, Edward Carpenter, Richard Jefferies, and other naturalistic pantheists, from the more distinctively Christian sort. The fact is that the mystical feeling of enlargement, union, and emancipation has no specific intellectual content whatever of its own. It is capable of forming matrimonial alliances with material furnished by the most diverse philosophies and theologies, provided only they can find a place in their framework for its peculiar emotional mood. We have no right, therefore, to invoke its prestige as distinctively in favor of any special belief, such as that in absolute idealism, or in the absolute monistic identity, or in the absolute goodness, of the world. It is only relatively in favor of all these things—it passes out of common human consciousness in the direction in which they lie.

So much for religious mysticism proper. But more remains to be told, for religious mysticism is only one half of mysticism. The other half has no accumulated traditions except those which the textbooks on insanity supply. Open any one of these and you will find abundant cases in which "mystical ideas" are cited as characteristic symptoms of enfeebled or deluded states of mind. In delusional insanity, paranoia, as they sometimes call it, we may have a *diabolical* mysticism, a sort of religious mysticism turned upside down. The same sense of ineffable importance in the smallest events, the same texts and words coming with new meanings, the same voices and visions and leadings and missions, the same controlling by extraneous powers; only this time the emotion is pessimistic: instead of consolations we have desolations; the meanings are dreadful; and the powers are enemies to life. It is evident from the point of view of their psychological mechanism, the classic mysticism and these lower mysticisms spring from the same mental level, from that great subliminal or transmarginal region of which science is beginning to admit the existence, but of which so little is really known. That region contains every kind of matter: "seraph and snake" abide there side by side. To come from thence is no infallible credential. What comes must be sifted and tested, and run the gauntlet of confrontation with the total context of experience, just like what comes from the outer world of sense. Its value must be ascertained by empirical methods, so long as we are not mystics ourselves.

Once more, then, I repeat that non-mystics are under no obligation to acknowledge in mystical states a superior authority conferred on them by their intrinsic nature.

3. Yet, I repeat once more, the existence of mystical states absolutely overthrows the pretension of non-mystical states to be the sole and ultimate dictators of what we may believe. As a rule, mystical states merely add a supersensuous meaning to the ordinary outward data of consciousness. They are excitements like the emotions of love or ambition, gifts to our spirit by means of which facts already objectively before us fall into a new expressiveness and make a new connection with our active life. They do not contradict these facts as such, or deny anything that our senses have immediately seized. It is the rationalistic critic rather who plays the part of denier in the controversy, and his denials have no strength, for there never can be a state of facts to which new meaning may not truthfully be added, provided the mind ascend to a more enveloping point of view. It must always remain an open question whether mystical states may not possibly be such superior points of view, windows through which the mind looks out upon a more extensive and inclusive world. The difference of the views seen from the different mystical windows need not prevent us from entertaining this supposition. The wider world would in that case prove to have a mixed constitution like that of this world, that is all. It would have its celestial and its infernal regions, its tempting and its saving moments, its valid experiences and its counterfeit ones, just as our world has them; but it would be a wider world all the same. We should have to use its experiences by selecting and. subordinating and substituting just as is our custom in this ordinary naturalistic world; we should be liable to error just as we are now; yet the counting in of that wider world of meanings, and the serious dealing with it, might, in spite of all the perplexity, be indispensable stages in our approach to the final fullness of the truth.

In this shape, I think, we have to leave the subject. Mystical states indeed wield no authority due simply to their being mystical states. But the higher ones among them point in directions to which the religious sentiments even of non-mystical men incline. They tell of the supremacy of the ideal, of vastness, of union, of safety, and of rest. They offer us *hypotheses*, hypotheses which we may voluntarily ignore, but which as thinkers we cannot possibly upset. The supernaturalism and optimism to which they would persuade us may, interpreted in one way or another, be after all the truest of insights into the meaning of this life.

"Oh, the little more, and how much it is; and the little less, and what worlds away!" It may be that possibility and permission of this sort are all that our religious consciousness requires to live on. In my last lecture I shall have to try to persuade you that this is the case. Meanwhile, however, I am sure that for many of my readers this diet is too slender. If supernaturalism and inner union with the divine are true, you think, then not so much permission, as compulsion to believe, ought to be found. Philosophy has always professed to prove religious truth by coercive argument; and the construction of philosophies of this kind has always been one favorite function of the religious life, if we use this term in the large historic sense. But religious philosophy is an enormous subject, and in my next lecture I can only give that brief glance at it which my limits will allow.

CONCLUSIONS ON RELIGIOUS EXPERIENCE

Let us agree, then, that Religion, occupying her-self with personal destinies and keeping thus in contact with the only absolute realities which we know, must necessarily play an eternal part in human history. The next thing to decide is what she reveals about those destinies, or whether indeed she reveals anything distinct enough to be considered a general message to mankind. We have done as you see, with our preliminaries, and our final summing up can now begin…

Both thought and feeling are determinants of conduct, and the same conduct may be determined either by feeling or by thought. When we survey the whole field of religion, we find a great variety in the thoughts that have prevailed there; but the feelings on the one hand and the conduct on the other are almost always the same, for Stoic, Christian, and Buddhist saints are practically indistinguishable in their lives. The theories which Religion generates, being thus variable, are secondary; and if you wish to grasp her essence, you must look to the feelings and the conduct as being the more constant elements. It is between these two

elements that the short circuit exists on which she carries on her principal business, while the ideas and symbols and other institutions form loop-lines which may be perfections and improvements, and may even some day all be united into one harmonious system, but which are not to be regarded as organs with an indispensable function, necessary at all times for religious life to go on. This seems to me the first conclusion which we are entitled to draw from the phenomena we have passed in review.

The next step is to characterize the feelings. To what psychological order do they belong?

The resultant outcome of them is in any case what Kant calls "sthenic" affection, an excitement of the cheerful, expansive, "dynamogenic" order which, like any tonic, freshens our vital powers. In almost every lecture, but especially in the lectures on Conversion and on Saintliness, we have seen how this emotion overcomes temperamental melancholy and imparts endurance to the Subject, or a zest, or a meaning, or an enchantment and glory to the common objects of life. The name of "faith state," by which Professor Leuba designates it, is a good one. It is a biological as well as a psychological condition, and Tolstoy is absolutely accurate in classing faith among the forces *by which men live*. The total absence of it, anhedonia, means collapse.

The faith-state may hold a very minimum of intellectual content. We saw examples of this in those sudden raptures of the divine presence, or in such mystical seizures as Dr. Bucke described. It may be a mere vague enthusiasm, half spiritual, half vital, a courage, and a feeling that great and wondrous things are in the air.

When, however, a positive intellectual content is associated with a faith-state, it gets invincibly stamped in upon belief, and this explains the passionate loyalty of religious persons everywhere to the minutest details of their so widely differing creeds. Taking creeds and faith-state together, as forming "religions," and treating these as purely subjective phenomena, without regard to the question of their "truth," we are obliged, on account of their extraordinary influence upon action and endurance, to class them amongst the most important biological functions of mankind. Their stimulant and anaesthetic effect is so great that Professor Leuba, in a recent article, goes so far as to say that so long as men can use their God, they care very little who he is, or even whether he is at all. "The truth of the matter can be put," says Leuba, "in this way: *God is not known, he is not understood; he is used*—sometimes as meat-purveyor, sometimes as moral support, sometimes as friend, sometimes as an object of love. If he proves himself useful, the religious consciousness asks for no more than that. Does God really exist? How does he exist? What is he? are so many irrelevant questions. Not God, but life, more life, a larger, richer, more satisfying life is, in the last analysis, the end of religion. The love of life, at any and every level of development, is the religious impulse."

At this purely subjective rating, therefore, Religion must be considered vindicated in a certain way from the attacks of her critics. It would seem that she cannot be a mere anachronism and survival, but must exert a permanent function, whether she be with or without intellectual content, and whether, if she have any, it be true or false.

We must next pass beyond the point of view of merely subjective utility, and make inquiry into the intellectual content itself.

First, is there, under all the discrepancies of the creeds, a common nucleus to which they bear their testimony unanimously?

And second, ought we to consider the testimony true?

I will take up the first question first, and answer it immediately in the affirmative. The warring gods and formulas of the various religions do indeed cancel each other, but there is a certain uniform deliverance in which religions all appear to meet. It consists of two parts:—

1. An uneasiness; and

2. Its solution.

1. The uneasiness, reduced to its simplest terms, is a sense that there is *something wrong about us* as we naturally stand.

2. The solution is a sense that *we are saved from the wrongness* by making proper connection with the higher powers.

In those more developed minds, which alone we are studying, the wrongness takes a moral character, and the salvation takes a mystical tinge. I think we shall keep well within the limits of what is common to all such minds if we formulate the essence of their religious experience in terms like these:—

The individual, so far as he suffers from his wrongness and criticizes it, is to that extent consciously beyond it, and in at least possible touch with something higher, if anything higher exist. Along with the wrong part there is thus a better part of him, even though it may be but a most helpless germ. With which part he should identify his real being is by no means obvious at this stage; but when stage 2 (the stage of solution or salvation) arrives, the man identifies his real being with the germinal higher part of himself; and does so in the following way. *He becomes conscious that this higher part is conterminous and continuous with a more of the same quality, which is operative in the universe outside of him, and which he can keep in working touch with, and in a fashion get on board of and save himself when all his lower being has gone to pieces in the wreck.*

It seems to me that all the phenomena are accurately describable in these very simple general terms. They allow for the divided self and the struggle; they involve the change of personal centre and the surrender of the lower self; they express the appearance of exteriority of the helping power and yet account for our sense of union with it; and they fully justify our feelings of security and joy. There is probably no autobiographic document, among all those which I have quoted, to which the description will not well apply. One need only add such specific details as will adapt it to various theologies and various personal temperaments, and one will then have the various experiences reconstructed in their individual forms.

So far, however, as this analysis goes, the experiences are only psychological phenomena. They possess, it is true, enormous biological worth. Spiritual strength really increases in the subject when he has them, a new life opens for him, and they seem to him a place of conflux where the forces of two universes meet; and yet this may be nothing but his subjective way of feeling things, a mood of his own fancy, in spite of the effects produced. I now turn to my second question: What is the objective "truth" of their content?

The part of the content concerning which the question of truth most pertinently arises is that "MORE of the same quality" with which our own higher self appears in the experience to come into harmonious working relation. Is such a "more" merely our own notion, or does it really exist? If so, in what shape does it exist? Does it act, as well as exist? And in what form should we conceive of that "union" with it of which religious geniuses are so convinced?

It is in answering these questions that the various theologies perform their theoretic work, and that their divergencies most come to light. They all agree that the "more" really exists; though some of them hold it to exist in the shape of a personal god or gods, while others are satisfied to conceive it as a stream of ideal tendency embedded in the eternal structure of the world. They all agree, moreover, that it acts as well as exists, and that something really is effected for the better when you throw your life into its hands. It is when they treat of the experience of "union" with it that their speculative differences appear most clearly. Over this point pantheism and theism, nature and second birth, works and grace and karma, immortality and reincarnation, rationalism and mysticism, carry on inveterate disputes.

At the end of my lecture on Philosophy I held out the notion that an impartial science of religions might sift out from the midst of their discrepancies a common body of doctrine which she might also formulate in terms to which physical science need not object. This, I said, she might adopt as her own reconciling hypothesis, and recommend it for general belief. I also said that in my last lecture I should have to try my own hand at framing such an hypothesis.

The time has now come for this attempt. Who says "hypothesis" renounces the ambition to be coercive in his arguments. The most I can do is, accordingly, to offer something that may fit the facts so easily that your scientific logic will find no plausible pretext for vetoing your impulse to welcome it as true.

The "more," as we called it, and the meaning of our "union" with it, form the nucleus of our inquiry. Into what definite description can these words be translated, and for what definite facts do they stand? It would never do for us to place ourselves offhand at the position of a particular theology, the Christian theology, for example, and proceed immediately to define the "more" as Jehovah, and the "union" as his imputation to us of the righteousness of Christ. That would be unfair to other religions, and from our present standpoint at least, would be an over-belief.

We must begin by using less particularized terms; and, since one of the duties of the science of religions is to keep religion in connection with the rest of science, we shall do well to seek first of all a way of describing the "more," which psychologists may also recognize as real. The *subconscious self* is nowadays a well-accredited psychological entity; and I believe that in it we have exactly the mediating term required. Apart from all religious considerations, there is actually and literally more life in our total soul than we are at any time aware of. The exploration of the transmarginal field has hardly yet been seriously undertaken, but what Mr. Myers said in 1892 in his essay on the Subliminal Consciousness is as true as when it was first written: "Each of us is in reality an abiding psychical entity far more extensive than he knows—an individuality which can never express itself completely through any corporeal manifestation. The Self manifests through the organism; but there is always some part of the Self unmanifested; and always, as it seems, some power of organic expression in abeyance or reserve." Much of the content of this larger background against which our conscious being stands out in relief is insignificant. Imperfect memories, silly jingles, inhibitive timidities, "dissolutive" phenomena of various sorts, as Myers calls them, enter into it for a large part. But in it many of the performances of genius seem also to have their origin; and in our study of conversion, of mystical experiences, and of prayer, we have seen how striking a part invasions from this region play in the religious life.

Let me then propose, as an hypothesis, that whatever it may be on its *further* side, the "more" with which in religious experience we feel ourselves connected is on its *hither* side the subconscious continuation of our conscious life. Starting thus with a recognized psychological fact as our basis, we seem to preserve a contact with "science" which the ordinary theologian lacks. At the same time the theologian's contention that the religious man is moved by an external power is vindicated, for it is one of the peculiarities of invasions from the subconscious region to take on objective appearances, and to suggest to the Subject an external control. In the religious life the control is felt as "higher"; but since on our hypothesis it is primarily the higher faculties of our own hidden mind which are controlling, the sense of union with the power beyond us is a sense of something, not merely apparently, but literally true.

This doorway into the subject seems to me the best one for a science of religions, for it mediates between a number of different points of view. Yet it is only a doorway, and difficulties present themselves as soon as we step through it, and ask how far our transmarginal consciousness carries us if we follow it on its remoter side. Here the over-beliefs begin: here mysticism and the conversion-rapture and Vedantism and transcendental idealism bring in their monistic interpretations and tell us that the finite self rejoins the absolute self, for it was always one with God and identical with the soul of the world. Here the prophets of all the different religions come with their visions, voices, raptures, and other openings, supposed by each to authenticate his own peculiar faith.

Those of us who are not personally favored with such specific revelations must stand outside of them altogether and, for the present at least, decide that, since they corroborate incompatible theological doctrines, they neutralize one another and leave no fixed result. If we follow any one of them, or if we follow philosophical theory and embrace monistic pantheism on non-mystical grounds, we do so in the exercise of our individual freedom, and build out our religion in the way most congruous with our personal susceptibilities. Among these susceptibilities intellectual ones play a decisive part. Although the religious question is primarily a question of life, of living or not living in the higher union which opens itself to us as a gift, yet the spiritual excitement in which the gift appears a real one will often fail to be aroused in an individual until certain particular intellectual beliefs or ideas which, as we say, come home to him, are touched. These ideas will thus be essential to that individual's religion;—which is as much as to say that overbeliefs in various directions are absolutely indispensable, and that we should treat them with tenderness and tolerance so long as they are not intolerant themselves. As I have elsewhere written, the most interesting and valuable things about a man are usually his over-beliefs.

Disregarding the over-beliefs, and confining ourselves to what is common and generic, we have in *the fact that the conscious person is continuous with a wider self through which saving experiences come,* a positive content of religious experience which, it seems to me, *is literally and objectively true as far as it goes.* If I now proceed to state my own hypothesis about the farther limits of this extension of our personality, I shall be offering my own overbelief—though I know it will appear a sorry under-belief to some of you—for which I can only bespeak the same indulgence which in a converse case I should accord to yours.

The further limits of our being plunge, it seems to me, into an altogether other dimension of existence from the sensible and merely "understandable" world. Name it the mystical region, or the supernatural region, whichever you choose. So far as our ideal impulses originate in this region (and most of them do originate in it, for we find them possessing us in a way for which we cannot articulately account), we belong to it in a more intimate sense than that in which we belong to the visible world, for we belong in the most intimate sense wherever our ideals belong. Yet the unseen region in question is not merely ideal, for it produces effects in this world. When we commune with it, work is actually done upon our finite personality, for we are turned into new men, and consequences in the way of conduct follow in the natural world upon our regenerative change. But that which produces effects within another reality must be termed a reality itself, so I feel as if we had no philosophic excuse for calling the unseen or mystical world unreal.

God is the natural appellation, for us Christians at least, for the supreme reality, so I will call this higher part of the universe by the name of God. We and God have business with each other; and in opening ourselves to his influence our deepest destiny is fulfilled. The universe, at those parts of it which our personal being constitutes, takes a turn genuinely for the worse or for the better in proportion as each one of us fulfills or evades God's demands. As far as this goes I probably have you with me, for I only translate into schematic language what I may call the instinctive belief of mankind: God is real since he produces real effects.

The real effects in question, so far as I have as yet admitted them, are exerted on the personal centres of energy of the various subjects, but the spontaneous faith of most of the subjects is that they embrace a wider sphere than this. Most religious men believe (or "know," if they be mystical) that not only they themselves, but the whole universe of beings to whom the God is present, are secure in his parental hands. There is a sense, a dimension, they are sure, in which we are *all* saved, in spite of the gates of hell and all adverse terrestrial appearances. God's existence is the guarantee of an ideal order that shall be permanently preserved. This world may indeed, as science assures us, some day burn up or freeze; but if it is part of his order, the old ideals are sure to be brought elsewhere to fruition, so that where God is, tragedy is only provisional and partial, and shipwreck and dissolution are not the absolutely final things. Only when this further step of faith concerning God is taken, and remote objective consequences are predicted, does religion, as it seems to me, get wholly free from the first immediate subjective experience, and bring a *real hypothesis* into play. A good hypothesis in science must have other properties than those of the phenomenon it is immediately invoked to explain, otherwise it is not prolific enough. God, meaning only what enters into the religious man's experience of union, falls short of being an hypothesis of this more useful order. He needs to enter into wider cosmic relations in order to justify the subject's absolute confidence and peace.

That the God with whom, starting from the hither side of our own extra-marginal self, we come at its remoter margin into commerce should be the absolute world-ruler, is of course a very considerable over-belief. Over-belief as it is, though, it is an article of almost every one's religion. Most of us pretend in some way to prop it up upon our philosophy, but the philosophy itself is really propped upon this faith. What is this but to say that Religion, in her fullest exercise of function, is not a mere illumination of facts already elsewhere given, not a mere passion, like love, which views things in a rosier light. It is indeed that, as we have seen abundantly. But it is something more, namely, a postulator of new *facts* as well. The world interpreted religiously is not the materialistic world over again, with an altered expression; it must have, over and above the altered expression, a *natural constitution* different at some point from that which a materialistic world would have. It must be such that different events can be expected in it, different conduct must be required.

This thoroughly "pragmatic" view of religion has usually been taken as a matter of course by common men. They have interpolated divine miracles into the field of nature, they have built a heaven out beyond the grave. It is only transcendentalist metaphysicians who think that, without adding any concrete details to Nature, or subtracting any, but by simply calling it the expression of absolute spirit, you make it more divine just as it stands. I believe the pragmatic way of taking religion to be the deeper way. It gives it body as well as soul, it makes it claim, as everything real must claim, some characteristic realm of fact as its very own. What the more characteristically divine facts are, apart from the actual inflow of energy in the faith-state and the prayer-state, I know not. But the over-belief on which I am ready to make my personal venture is that they exist. The whole drift of my education goes to persuade me that the world of our present consciousness is only one out of many worlds of consciousness that exist, and that those other worlds must contain experiences which have a meaning for our life also; and that although in the main their experiences and those of this world keep discrete, yet the two become continuous at certain points, and higher energies filter in. By being faithful in my poor measure to this over-belief, I seem to myself to keep more sane and true. I can, of course, put myself into the sectarian scientist's attitude, and imagine vividly that the world of sensations and of scientific laws and objects may be all. But whenever I do this, I hear that inward monitor of which W. K. Clifford once wrote, whispering the word "bosh!" Humbug is humbug, even though it bear the scientific name, and the total expression of human experience, as I view it objectively, invincibly urges me beyond the narrow "scientific" bounds. Assuredly, the real world is of a different temperament more intricately built than physical science allows. So my objective and my subjective conscience both hold me to the over-belief which I express. Who knows whether the faithfulness of individuals here below to their own poor over-beliefs may not actually help God in turn to be more effectively faithful to his own greater tasks? ...

III.3

Perceiving God

WILLIAM P. ALSTON

William P. Alston (1921–2009) was a professor of philosophy at Syracuse University and one of the leading figures in the fields of epistemology and philosophy of religion throughout the past fifty years. In this selection, he argues that religious experience plays a role with respect to beliefs about God that is analogous to the role played by sense perception with respect to beliefs about the external world. On his view, religious experience may be thought of as perception *of God, and it is a source of justified belief about God.*

I want to explore and defend the idea that the experience, or, as I shall say, the *perception*, of God plays an epistemic role with respect to beliefs about God importantly analogous to that played by sense perception with respect to beliefs about the physical world. The nature of that latter role is, of course, a matter of controversy, and I have no time here to go into those controversies. It is admitted, however, on (almost) all hands that sense perception provides us with knowledge (justified belief) about current states of affairs in the immediate environment of the perceiver and that knowledge of this sort is somehow required for any further knowledge of the physical world. The possibility I wish to explore is that what a person takes to be an experience of God can provide him/her with knowledge (justified beliefs) about what God is doing, or how God is "situated," vis-á-vis that subject at that moment. Thus, by experiencing the presence and activity of God, *S* can come to know (justifiably believe) that God is sustaining her in being, filling her with His love, strengthening her, or communicating a certain message to her. Let's call beliefs as to how God is currently related to the subject *M-beliefs* ("M" for manifestation); these are the "perceptual beliefs" of the theological sphere. I shall suppose that here too the "perceptual" knowledge one acquires from experience is crucial for whatever else we can learn about God, though I won't have time to explore and defend

Reprinted from William P. Alston, "Perceiving God?", *The Journal of Philosophy* LXXXII (1986): 655–65. Used with permission.

that part of the position; I will have my hands full defending the claim that M-beliefs are justified. I will just make two quick points about the role of M-beliefs in the larger scheme. First, just as with our knowledge of the physical world, the recognition of a crucial role for perceptual knowledge is compatible with a wide variety of views as to just how it figures in the total system and as to what else is involved. Second, an important difference between the two spheres is that in the theological sphere perceptual beliefs as to what God has "said" (communicated, revealed) to one or another person play a major role.

I have been speaking alternatively of perceptual *knowledge* and of the *justification* of perceptual beliefs. In this paper I shall concentrate on justification, leaving to one side whatever else is involved in knowledge. It will be my contention that (putative) experience of God is a source of justification for M-beliefs, somewhat in the way that sense experience is a source of justification for perceptual beliefs. Again, it is quite controversial what this latter way is. I shall be thinking of it in terms of a direct-realist construal of sense perception, according to which I can be justified in supposing that my dog is wagging his tail just because something is visually presenting itself to me as (looks like) my dog wagging his tail; that is, it looks to me in such a way that I am thereby justified in thereby supposing it to be my dog wagging his tail. Analogously I think of the "experience of God" as a matter of something's presenting itself to one's experience as God (doing so and so); so that here too the subject is justified in believing that God is present to her, or is doing so and so vis-a-vis her, just because that is the way in which the object is presented to her experience. (For the purposes of this paper let's focus on those cases in which this presentation is not via any *sensory* qualities or *sensorily* perceivable objects. The experience involved will be nonsensory in character.) It is because I think of the experience of God as having basically the same structure as the sense perception of physical objects that I feel entitled to speak of "perceiving God." But though I construe the matter in direct-realist terms, most of what I have to say here will be relevant to a defense of the more general claim that the experiential justification of M-beliefs is importantly parallel to

the experiential justification of perceptual beliefs about the physical environment, on any halfway plausible construal of the latter, at least on any halfway plausible realist construal.

I shall develop the position by way of responding to a number of objections. This procedure reflects my conviction that the very considerable incidence of putative perceptions of God creates a certain initial presumption that these experiences are what they seem to be and that something can thereby be learned about God.

Objection I. What reason do we have for supposing that anyone ever does really perceive God? In order for *S* to perceive God it would have to be the case that (1) God exists, and (2) God is related to *S* or to his experience in such a way as to be perceivable by him. Only after we have seen reason to accept all that will we take seriously any claim to perceive God.

Answer. It all depends on what you will take as a reason. What you have in mind, presumably, are reasons drawn from some source other than perceptions of God, e.g., metaphysical arguments for the existence and nature of God. But why do you think you are justified in that restriction? We don't proceed in this way with respect to sense perception. Although in determining whether a particular alleged perception was genuine we don't make use of the results of *that* perception, we do utilize what has been observed in many other cases. And what alternative is there? The conditions of veridical sense perception have to do with states of affairs and causal interactions in the physical world, matters to which we have no cognitive access that is not based on sense perception. In like fashion, if there is a divine reality why suppose that the conditions of veridically perceiving it could be ascertained without relying on perceptions of *it*? In requiring external validation in this case but not the other you are arbitrarily imposing a double standard.

Objection II. There are many contradictions in the body of M-beliefs. In particular, persons report communications from God that contradict other reported communications. How, then, can one claim that all M-beliefs are justified?

Answer. What is (should be) claimed is only *prima facie* justification. When a person believes that God is experientially present to him, that belief is justified *unless* the subject has sufficient reasons to suppose it to be false or to suppose that the experience is not, in these circumstances, sufficiently indicative of the truth of the belief. This is, of course, precisely the status of individual perceptual beliefs about the physical environment. When, seeming to see a lake, I believe there to be a lake in front of me, my belief is thereby justified unless I have sufficient reason to suppose it false or to suppose that, in these circumstances, the experience is not sufficiently indicative of the truth of the belief.

Objection III. It is rational to form beliefs about the physical environment on the basis of the way that environment appears to us in sense experience (call this practice of belief formation SP) because that is a generally reliable mode of belief formation. And it is reliable just because, in normal conditions, sense experience varies concomitantly with variations in what we take ourselves to be perceiving. But we have no reason to suppose any such regular covariation for putative perception of God. And hence we lack reason for regarding as rational the parallel practice of forming M-beliefs on the basis of what is taken to be a perception of God (call that practice RE).

Answer. This is another use of a double standard. How do we know that normal sense experience varies concomitantly with perceived objects? We don't know this a priori. Rather, we have strong empirical evidence for it. That is, by relying on sense perception for our data we have piled up evidence for the reliability of SP. Let's call the kind of circularity exhibited here *epistemic circularity*. It is involved whenever the premises in an argument for the reliability or rationality of a belief-forming practice have themselves been acquired by that practice.[2] If we allow epistemically circular arguments, the reliability of RE can be supported in the same way. Among the things people have claimed to learn from RE is that God will enable people to experience His presence and activity from time to time in a veridical way. By relying on what one learns from the practice of RE, one can show that RE is a reliable belief-forming practice. On the other hand, if epistemically circular arguments are not countenanced, there can be no significant basis for a reliability claim in either case.

Objection IV. A claim to perceive X, and so to form reliable perceptual beliefs about X on the basis of this, presupposes that the experience involved is best explained by the activity of X, *inter alia*. But it seems that we can give adequate explanations of putative experiences of God in purely naturalistic terms, without bringing God into the explanation at all. Whereas we can't give adequate explanations of normal sense experience without bringing the experienced external objects into the explanation. Hence RE, but not SP, is discredited by these considerations.

Answer. I do not believe that much of a case can be made for the adequacy of any naturalistic explanation of experiences of God. But for present purposes I want to concentrate on the way in which this objection once more depends on a double standard. You will have no case at all for your claim unless you, question-beggingly, restrict yourself to sources of evidence that exclude RE. For from RE and systems built up on its output we learn that God is involved in the explanation of every fact whatever. But you would not proceed in that way with SP. If it is a question of determining the best explanation of sense experience you will, of course, make use of what you think you have learned from SP. Again, you have arbitrarily applied different standards to the two practices.

Here is another point. Suppose that one could give a purely psychological or physiological explanation of the experiences in question. That is quite compatible with God's figuring among their causes and, hence, coming into an ideally complete explanation. After all, it is presumably possible to give an adequate causal explanation of sense experience in terms of what goes on within the skull, but that is quite compatible with the external perceived objects' figuring further back along the causal chain.

Objection V. You have been accusing me of *arbitrarily* employing a double standard. But I maintain that RE differs from SP in ways that make different standards appropriate. SP is a pervasive and inescapable feature of our lives. Sense experience is insistent, omnipresent, vivid, and richly detailed.

We use it as a source of information during all our waking hours. RE, by contrast, is not universally shared; and even for its devotees its practice is relatively infrequent. Moreover, its deliverances are, by comparison, meager, obscure, and uncertain. Thus when an output of RE does pop up, it is naturally greeted with more skepticism, and one properly demands more for its validation than in the case of so regular and central part of our lives as SP.

Answer. I don't want to deny either the existence or the importance of these differences. I want to deny only that they have the alleged bearing on the epistemic situation. Why should we suppose that a cognitive access enjoyed only by a part of the population is less likely to be reliable than one that is universally distributed? Why should we suppose that a source that yields less detailed and less fully understood beliefs is more suspect than a richer source? A priori it would seem just as likely that some aspects of reality are accessible only to persons that satisfy certain conditions not satisfied by all human beings as that some aspects are equally accessible to all. A priori it would seem just as likely that some aspects of reality are humanly graspable only in a fragmentary and opaque manner as that some aspects are graspable in a more nearly complete and pellucid fashion. Why view the one sort of cognitive claim with more suspicion than the other? I will agree that the spotty distribution of RE calls for explanation, as does the various cognitively unsatisfactory features of its output. But, for that matter, so does the universal distribution and cognitive richness of SP. And in both cases explanations are forthcoming, though in both cases the outputs of the practices are utilized in order to achieve those explanations. As for RE, the limited distribution may be explained by the fact that many persons are not prepared to meet the moral and other "way of life" conditions that God has set for awareness of Himself. And the cognitively unsatisfactory features of the doxastic output are explained by the fact that God infinitely exceeds our cognitive powers.

Objection VI. When someone claims to see a spruce tree in a certain spot, the claim is checkable. Other people can take a look, photographs can be taken, the subject's condition can be diagnosed, and so on. But there are no comparable checks and tests available in RE. And how can we take seriously a claim to have perceived an objective state of affairs if there is, in principle, no intersubjective way of determining whether that claim is correct?

Answer. The answer to this objection is implicit in a point made earlier, viz., that putative experience of God yields only prima facie justification, justification (unqualifiedly) provided there are no sufficient overriding considerations. This notion has a significant application only where there is what we may call an *overrider system*, i.e., ways of determining whether the facts are such as to indicate a belief from the range in question to be false and ways of determining whether conditions are such that the basis of the belief is sufficiently indicative of its truth. SP does contain such a system. What about RE? Here we must confront a salient difference between the two spheres. If we consider the way in which a body of beliefs has been developed on the basis of SP we find pretty much the same system across all cultures. But our encounters with God have spawned a number of different religious communities with beliefs and practices of worship which are quite different, though with some considerable overlap. These differences carry with them differences in overrider systems. But it remains true that if we consider any particular religious community which exhibits a significant commonality in doctrine and worship it will feature a more or less definite overrider system. For concreteness let's think of what I will call the *mainline Christian community*. (From this point onward I will use the term "RE" for the practice of forming M-beliefs as it goes on in this community.) In that community a body of doctrine has developed concerning the nature of God, His purposes, and His interactions with mankind, including His appearances to us. If an M-belief contradicts this system that is a reason for deeming it false. Moreover there is a long and varied history of experiential encounters with God, embodied in written accounts as well as oral transmission. This provides bases for regarding particular experiences as more or less likely to be veridical, given the conditions, psychological or otherwise, in which they occurred, the character of the subject, and the effects in the life of the subject. Thus a socially established religious doxastic practice like RE will contain a rich system of overriders that provides resources for checking the acceptability of any particular M-belief.

But perhaps your point is rather that there are no *external* checks on a particular report, none that do not rely on other claims of the same sort. Let's agree that this is the case. But why suppose that to be any black mark against RE? Here is the double standard again. After all, particular claims within SP cannot be checked without relying on what we have learned from SP. Suppose I claim to see a fir tree in a certain spot. To check on this one would have to rely on other persons' perceptual reports as to what is at that spot, our general empirical knowledge of the likelihood of a fir tree in that locality, and so on. Apart from what we take ourselves to have learned from SP, we would have nothing to go on. One can hardly determine whether my report was accurate by intuiting self-evident truths or by consulting divine revelation. But if SP counts as having a system of checks even though this system involves relying on some outputs of the practice in order to put others to the test, why should RE be deemed to have no such system when its procedures exhibit the same structure? Once more you are, arbitrarily, setting quite different requirements for different practices.

Perhaps your point was that RE's system of checks is unlike SP's. In particular, the following difference can be discerned. Suppose I report seeing a morel at a certain spot in the forest. Now suppose that a number of qualified observers take a good look at that spot at that time and report that no morel is to be seen. In that case my report would have been decisively disconfirmed. But nothing like that is possible in RE. We can't lay down any conditions (of a sort the satisfaction of which we can determine) under which a properly qualified person will experience the presence of God if God is "there" to be experienced. Hence a particular report cannot be decisively disconfirmed by the experience of others.

But what epistemic relevance does this difference have? Why should we suppose that RE is rendered dubious for lacking check ability of this sort? Let's consider what makes this kind of intersubjective test possible for SP. Clearly it is that we have discovered fairly firm regularities in the behavior of physical things, including human sense perception. Since there are stable regularities in the ways in which physical objects disclose themselves to our perception, we can be assured that if X exists at a certain time and place and if S satisfies appropriate conditions then S is sure to perceive X. But no such tight regularities are discoverable in God's appearances to our experience. We can say something about the way in which such matters as the distribution of attention and the moral and spiritual state of the subject are conducive to such appearances; but these most emphatically do not add up to the sort of lawlike connections we get with SP. Now what about this difference? Is it to the epistemic discredit of RE that it does not enable us to discover such regularities? Well, that all depends on what it would be reasonable to expect if RE does put us into effective cognitive contact with God. Given what we have learned about God and our relations to Him (from RE, supplemented by whatever other sources there be), should we expect to be able to discover such realities if God really exists? Clearly not. There are several important points here, but the most important is that it is contrary to God's plans for us to give us that much control, cognitive and practical. Hence it is quite understandable, if God exists and is as RE leads us to suppose, that we should not be able to ascertain the kinds of regularities that would make possible the kinds of intersubjective tests exhibited by SP. Hence, the epistemic status of RE is in no way diminished by its lack of such tests. Once more RE is subjected to an inappropriate standard. This time, however, it is not a double standard, but rather an inappropriate single standard. RE is being graded down for lacking positive features of other practices, where these features cannot reasonably be supposed to be generally necessary conditions of epistemic excellence, even for experiential practices. Thus my critic is exhibiting what we might term *epistemic chauvinism*, judging alien forms of life according to whether they conform to the home situation, a procedure as much to be deplored in the epistemic as in the political sphere.

Objection VII. How can it be rational to take RE as a sorce of justification when there are incompatible rivals that can lay claim to that status on exactly the same grounds? M-beliefs of different religious communities conflict to a considerable extent, particularly those concerning alleged divine messages, and the bodies of doctrine they support conflict even more. We get incompatible accounts of God's plans for us and requirements on us, of the conditions of salvation, and so on. This being the case, how can we pick out just one of these communal practices as yielding justified belief?

Answer. I take this to be by far the most serious difficulty with my position. I have chosen to concentrate on what I take to be less serious problems, partly because their consideration brings out better the main lineaments of the position, and partly because any serious treatment of this last problem would spill beyond the confines of this paper.[2] Here I shall have to content myself with making one basic point. We are not faced with the necessity of choosing only one such practice as yielding prima facie justified M-beliefs. The fact that there are incompatibilities between systems of religious beliefs, in M-beliefs and elsewhere, shows that not all M-beliefs can be true, but not that they cannot all be prima facie justified. After all, incompatible beliefs *within* a system can all be prima facie justified; that's the point of the prima facie qualification. When we are faced with a situation like that, the hope is that the overrider system and other winnowing devices will weed out the inconsistencies. To be sure, inter-system winnowing devices are hazier and more meager than those which are available within a system; but consistency, consonance with other well-entrenched beliefs and doxastic practices, and general reasonability and plausibility give us something to go on. Moreover, it may be that some religious ways of life fulfill their own promises more fully than others. Of course, there is never any guarantee that a unique way of resolving incompatibilities will present itself, even with a system. But where there are established practices of forming beliefs on the basis of experience, I believe the rational course is to regard each such belief as thereby prima facie justified, hoping that future developments, perhaps unforeseeable at present, will resolve fundamental incompatibilities.

In conclusion I will make explicit the general epistemological orientation I have been presupposing in my defense of RE. I take our human situation to be such that we engage in a plurality of basic doxastic practices, each of which involves a distinctive sort of input to belief-forming "mechanisms," a distinctive

range of belief contents (a "subject matter" and ways of conceiving it), and a set of functions that determine belief contents as a function of input features. Each practice is socially established: socially shared, inculcated, reinforced, and propagated. In addition to experiential practices, with which we have been concerned in this paper, there are, e.g., inferential practices, the input of which consists of beliefs, and the practice of forming memory beliefs. A doxastic practice is not restricted to the formation of first-level beliefs; it will also typically involve criteria and procedures of criticism of the beliefs thus formed; here we will find the "overrider systems" of which we were speaking earlier. In general, we learn these practices and engage in them long before we arrive at the stage of explicitly formulating their principles and subjecting them to critical reflection. Theory is deeply rooted in practice.

Nor, having arrived at the age of reason, can we turn our back on all that and take a fresh start, in the Cartesian spirit, choosing our epistemic procedures and criteria anew, on a purely "rational" basis.

Apart from reliance on doxastic tendencies with which we find ourselves, we literally have nothing to go on. Indeed, what Descartes did, as Thomas Reid trenchantly pointed out, was arbitrarily to pick one doxastic practice he found himself engaged in—accepting propositions that seem self-evident—and set that as a judge over all the others, with what results we are all too familiar. This is not to say that we must acquiesce in our pre-reflective doxastic tendencies in every respect. We can tidy things up, modify our established practices so as to make each more internally consistent and more consistent with the others. But, on the whole and for the most part, we have no choice but to continue to form beliefs in accordance with these practices and to take these ways of forming beliefs as paradigmatically conferring epistemic justification. And this is the way that epistemology has in fact gone, except for some arbitrary partiality. Of course it would be satisfying to economize our basic commitments by taking one or a few of these practices as basic and using them to validate the others; but we have made little progress in this enterprise over the centuries. It is not self-evident that sense perception is reliable, nor can we establish its reliability if we restrict ourselves to premises drawn from introspection; we cannot show that deductive reasoning is valid without using deductive reasoning to do so; and so on. We are endowed with strong tendencies to engage in a number of distinct doxastic practices, none of which can be warranted on the basis of others. It is clearly the better part of wisdom to recognize beliefs that emerge from these practices to be rational and justified, at least once they are properly sifted and refined.

In this paper I have undertaken to extend this account to doxastic practices that are not universally practiced. Except for that matter of distribution and the other peripheral matters mentioned in Objection V and except for being faced with actually existing rivals, a religious experiential doxastic practice like RE seems to me to be on all fours with SP and other universal practices. It too involves a distinctive range of inputs, a range of belief contents, and functions that map features of the former onto contents of the latter. It is socially established within a certain community. It involves higher-level procedures of correction and modification of its first-level beliefs. Though it *may* be acquired in a deliberate and self-conscious fashion, it is more typically acquired in a practical, prereflective form. Though it is obviously evitable in a way SP, e.g., is not, for many of its practitioners it is just about as firmly entrenched.

These similarities lead me to the conclusion that if, as it seems we must concede, a belief is prima facie justified by virtue of emerging from one of the universal basic practices, we should also concede the same status to the products of RE. I have sought to show that various plausible-sounding objections to this position depend on the use of a double standard or reflect arbitrary epistemic chauvinism. They involve subjecting RE to inappropriate standards. Once we appreciate these points, we can see the strength of the case for RE as one more epistemically autonomous practice of belief formation and source of justification.

NOTES

1. See my "Epistemic Circularity," Philosophy and Phenomenological Research, XLVII, 1 (September 1986): 1–30.

2. For an extended treatment of this issue, see my "Religious Experience and Religious Diversity," forthcoming in Christian Scholars' Review.

Reprinted from *Zygon* 33 (1998): 187–201, by permission of John Wiley & Sons.

IX.4

Buddhism, Christianity, and the Prospects for World Religion

DALAI LAMA

Dalai Lama, originally Tenzin Gyatso (1935–), the spiritual and temporal head of Tibet, was born in China. In 1937 he was designated the fourteenth Dalai Lama, but his right to rule was delayed until 1950. An ardent advocate of nonviolent liberation, he was awarded the Nobel Prize for Peace in 1989. In this selection he responds to questions from José

Reprinted from *The Bodhgaya Interviews*, ed. Jose Ignacio Cabezon (Snow Lion Publications, 1988) by permission.

Ignacio Cabezon on the possibility of a religious integration of Buddhism and Christianity. The Dalai Lama (referred to as "His Holiness") doesn't think such an integration is possible, for there are unique features in these religions that cannot be compromised without loss of identity. But he argues that all the major religions have much in common. They aim at the same goal of permanent happiness, and all encourage moral integrity. These common concerns should enable people of all faiths to find common ground in building a better world of peace and justice.

Question: Do you see any possibility of an integration of Christianity and Buddhism in the West? An overall religion for Western society?

His Holiness: It depends upon what you mean by integration. If you mean by this the possibility of the integration of Buddhism and Christianity within a society, where they co-exist side by side, then I would answer affirmatively. If, however, your view of integration envisions all of society following some sort of composite religion which is neither pure Buddhism nor pure Christianity, then I would have to consider this form of integration implausible.

It is, of course, quite possible for a country to be predominantly Christian, and yet that some of the people of that country choose to follow Buddhism. I think it is quite possible that a person who is basically a Christian, who accepts the idea of a God, who believes in God, could at the same time incorporate certain Buddhist ideas and techniques into his/her practice. The teachings of love, compassion, and kindness are present in Christianity and also in Buddhism. Particularly in the Bodhisattva vehicle there are many techniques which focus on developing compassion, kindness, etc. These are things which can be practiced at the same time by Christians and by Buddhists. While remaining committed to Christianity it is quite conceivable that a person may choose to undergo training in meditation, concentration, and onepointedness of mind, that, while remaining a Christian, one may choose to practice Buddhist ideas. This is another possible and very viable kind of integration.

Question: Is there any conflict between the Buddhist teachings and the idea of a creator God who exists independently from us?

His Holiness: If we view the world's religions from the widest possible viewpoint, and examine their ultimate goal, we find that all of the major world religions, whether Christianity or Islam, Hinduism or Buddhism, are directed to the achievement of permanent human happiness. They are all directed toward that goal. All religions emphasize the fact that the true follower must be honest and gentle, in other words, that a truly religious person must always strive to be a better human being. To this end, the different world's religions teach different doctrines which will help transform the person. In this regard, all religions are the same, there is no conflict. This is something we must emphasize. We must consider the question of religious diversity from *this* viewpoint. And when we do, we find no conflict.

Now from the philosophical point of view, the theory that God is the creator, is almighty and permanent, is in contradiction to the Buddhist teachings. From this point of view there is disagreement. For Buddhists, the universe has no first cause and hence no creator, nor can there be such a thing as a permanent, primordially pure being. So, of course, doctrinally, there is conflict. The views are opposite to one another. But if we consider the purpose of these different philosophies, then we see that they are the same. This is my belief.

Different kinds of food have different tastes: one may be very hot, one may be very sour, and one very sweet. They are opposite tastes, they conflict. But whether a dish is concocted to taste sweet, sour or hot, it is nonetheless made in this way so as to taste good. Some people prefer very spicy hot foods with a lot of chili peppers. Many Indians and Tibetans have a liking for such dishes. Others are very fond of bland tasting foods. It is a wonderful thing to have variety. It is an expression of individuality; it is a personal thing.

Likewise, the variety of the different world religious philosophies is a very useful and beautiful thing. For certain people, the idea of God as creator and of everything depending on his will is beneficial and soothing, and so for that person such a doctrine is worthwhile. For someone else, the idea that there is no creator, that ultimately, one is oneself the creator—in that everything depends upon oneself—is more appropriate. For certain people, it may be a more effective method of spiritual growth, it may be more beneficial. For such persons, this idea is better and for the other type of person, the other idea is more suitable. You see, there is no conflict, no problem. This is my belief.

Now conflicting doctrines are something which is not unknown even within Buddhism itself. The Mādhyamikas and Cittāmtrins, two Buddhist philosophical subschools, accept the theory of emptiness. The Vaibhṣikas and Sautṝntikas, two others, accept another theory, the theory of selflessness, which, strictly speaking, is not the same as the doctrine of emptiness as posited by the two higher schools. So there exists this difference, some schools accepting the emptiness of phenomena and others not. There also exists a difference as regards the way in which the two upper schools explain the doctrine of emptiness. For the Cittāmtrinsāmtrins, emptiness is set forth in terms of the non-duality of subject and object. The Mādhyamikas, however, repudiate the notion that emptiness is tantamount to idealism, the claim that everything is of the nature of mind. So you see, even within Buddhism, the Mādhyamikas and Cittāmtrins schools are in conflict. The Mādhyamikas are again divided into Prṣangikas and Sv̄tantrikas, and between these two sub-schools there is also conflict. The latter accept that things exist by virtue of an inherent characteristic, while the former do not.

So you see, conflict in the philosophical field is nothing to be surprised at. It exists within Buddhism itself....

Question: I would like to know the role that consciousness plays in the process of reincarnation.

His Holiness: In general, there are different levels of consciousness. The more rough or gross levels of consciousness are very heavily dependent upon the physical or material sphere. Since one's own physical aggregate (the body) changes from birth to birth, so too do these gross levels of consciousness. The more subtle the level of consciousness, however, the more independent of the physical sphere and hence the more likely that it will remain from one life to the next. But in general, whether more subtle or more gross, all levels of consciousness are of the same nature.

Question: It is generally said that teachers of other religions, no matter how great, cannot attain liberation without turning to the Buddhist path. Now suppose there is a great teacher, say he is a Śaivite, and suppose he upholds very strict discipline and is totally dedicated to other people all of the time, always giving of himself. Is this person, simply because he follows Śiva, incapable of attaining liberation, and if so, what can be done to help him?

His Holiness: During the Buddha's own time, there were many non-Buddhist teachers whom the Buddha could not help, for whom he could do nothing. So he just let them be.

The Buddha Śkyamuni was an extraordinary being, he was the manifestation (*nirm̄nakya*), the physical appearance, of an already enlightened being. But while some people recognized him as a Buddha, others regarded him as a black magician with strange and evil powers. So, you see, even the Buddha Śkyamuni himself was not accepted as an enlightened being by all of his contemporaries. Different human beings have different mental predispositions, and there are cases when even the Buddha himself could not do much to overcome these—there was a limit.

Now today, the followers of Śiva have their own religious practices and they reap some benefit from engaging in their own forms of worship. Through this, their life will gradually change. Now my own position on this question is that Śivaji's followers should practice according to their own beliefs and traditions, Christians must genuinely and sincerely follow what they believe, and so forth. That is sufficient.

Question: But they will not attain liberation!

His Holiness: We Buddhists ourselves will not be liberated at once. In our own case, it will take time. Gradually we will be able to reach *mokṣa* or *nirvna*, but the majority of Buddhists will not achieve this within their own lifetimes. So there's no hurry. If Buddhists themselves have to wait, perhaps many lifetimes, for their goal, why should we expect that it be different for non-Buddhists? So, you see, nothing much can be done.

Suppose, for example, you try to convert someone from another religion to the Buddhist religion, and you argue with them trying to convince them of the inferiority of their position. And suppose you do not succeed, suppose they do not become Buddhist. On the one hand, you have failed in your task, and on the other hand, you may have weakened the trust they have in their own religion, so that they may come to doubt their own faith. What have you accomplished by all this? It is of no use. When we come into contact with the followers of different religions, we should not argue. Instead, we should advise them to follow their own beliefs as sincerely and as truthfully as possible. For if they do so, they will no doubt reap certain benefit. Of this there is no doubt. Even in the immediate future they will be able to achieve more happiness and more satisfaction. Do you agree?

This is the way I usually act in such matters, it is my belief. When I meet the followers of different religions, I always praise them, for it is enough, it is sufficient, that they are following the moral teachings that are emphasized in every religion. It is enough, as I mentioned earlier, that they are trying to become better human beings. This in itself is very good and worthy of praise.

Question: But is it only the Buddha who can be the ultimate source of refuge?

His Holiness: Here, you see, it is necessary to examine what is meant by liberation or salvation. Liberation in which "a mind that understands the sphere of reality annihilates all defilements in the sphere of reality" is a state that only Buddhists can accomplish. This kind of *mokṣa* or *nirvna* is only explained in the Buddhist scriptures, and is achieved only through Buddhist practice. According to certain religions, however, salvation is a place, a beautiful paradise, like a peaceful valley. To attain such a state as this, to achieve such a state of *mokṣa*, does not require the practice of emptiness, the understanding of reality. In Buddhism itself, we believe that through the accumulation of merit one can obtain rebirth in heavenly paradises like Tuṣita....

Question: Could you please give us some brief advice which we can take with us into our daily lives?

His Holiness: I don't know, I don't really have that much to say—I'll simply say this. We are all human beings, and from this point of view we are the same. We all want happiness, and we do not want suffering. If we consider this point, we will find that there are no differences between people of different faiths, races, color or cultures. We all have this common wish for happiness.

Actually, we Buddhists are supposed to save all sentient beings, but practically speaking, this may be too broad a notion for most people. In any case, we must at least think in terms of helping all human beings. This is very important. Even if we cannot think in terms of sentient beings inhabiting different worlds, we should nonetheless think in terms of the human beings on our own planet. To do this is to take a practical approach to the problem. It is necessary to help others, not only in our prayers, but in our daily lives. If we find we cannot help another, the least we can do is to desist from harming them. We must not cheat others or lie to them. We must be honest human beings, sincere human beings.

On a very practical level, such attitudes are things which we need. Whether one is a believer, a religious person, or not, is another matter. Simply as an inhabitant of the world, as a member of the human family, we need this kind of attitude. It is through such an attitude that real and lasting world peace and harmony can be achieved. Through harmony, friendship, and respecting one another, we can solve many problems. Through such means, it is possible to overcome problems in the right way, without difficulties.

This is what I believe, and wherever I go, whether it be to a communist country like the Soviet Union or Mongolia, or to a capitalist and democratic country like the United States and the countries of Western Europe, I express this same message. This is my advice, my suggestion. It is what I feel. I myself practice this as much as I can. If you find you agree with me, and you find some value in what I have said, then it has been worthwhile.

You see, sometimes religious persons, people who are genuinely engaged in the practice of religion, withdraw from the sphere of human activity. In my opinion, this is not good. It is not right. But I should qualify this. In certain cases, when a person genuinely wishes to engage in intensive meditation, for example when someone wishes to attain *śamatha*, then it is alright to seek isolation for certain limited periods of time. But such cases are by far the exception, and the vast majority of us must work out a genuine religious practice within the context of human society.

In Buddhism, both learning and practice are extremely important and they must go hand in hand. Without knowledge, just to rely on faith, faith and more faith is good but not sufficient. So the intellectual part must definitely be present. At the same time, strictly intellectual development without faith and practice, is also of no use. It is necessary to combine knowledge born from study with sincere practice in our daily lives. These two must go together....

Question: The Christian notion of God is that He is omniscient, all-compassionate, all-powerful, and the creator. The Buddhist notion of Buddha is the same, except that He is not the Creator. To what extent does the Buddha exist apart from our minds, as the Christians believe their God to?

His Holiness: There are two ways of interpreting this question. The general question is whether the Buddha is a separate thing from mind. Now in one sense, this could be asking whether or not the Buddha is a phenomenon imputed or labelled by mind, and of course all phenomena in this sense must be said to be labelled by name and conceptual thought. The Buddha is not a separate phenomenon from mind because our minds impute or label Him by means of words and conceptual thought.

In another sense, the question could be asking about the relationship of buddhahood to our own minds, and in this sense we must say that buddhahood, or the state of a buddha, is the object to be attained by us. Buddhahood is the resultant object of refuge. Our minds are related to buddhahood (they are not separate from buddhahood) in the sense that this is something that we will gradually attain by the systematic purification of our minds. Hence, by purifying our minds step by step, we will eventually attain the state of buddhahood. And that buddha which we will eventually become is of the same continuity as ourselves. But that buddha which we will become is different, for example, from Śkyamuni Buddha. They are two distinct persons. We cannot attain Śkyamuni Buddha's enlightenment, because that is His own individual thing.

If instead the question is referring to whether or not our minds are separate from the state of buddhahood, and if we take buddhahood to refer to the essential purity of the mind, then of course this is something which we possess even now. Even today, our minds have the nature of essential purity. This is something called the "buddha nature." The very nature of the mind, the mere quality of knowledge and clarity without being affected by conceptual thoughts, that too we may call "buddha nature." To be exact, it is the innermost clear light mind which is called the "buddha nature."

Question: When creating merit, one must acknowledge that Christians create merit as well as Buddhists, so that the whole source of merit cannot reside solely in the object, i.e., Buddha or God, to which one is making offerings. This leads me to think that the source of merit is in our own minds. Could you please comment on this?

His Holiness: The main thing is motivation, but probably there is some difference in regard to the object to which one makes offering and so forth. The pure motivation must, however, be based on reasoning, that is, it must be verified by valid cognition; it must be unmistaken. But no doubt that the main point is the motivation.

For example, when we generate great compassion we take as our object sentient beings. But it is not due to anything on the side of sentient beings, on the part of sentient beings, that great compassion is special. It is not due to any blessing from sentient beings that great compassion is special. Nonetheless, when we meditate in this way on great compassion and we generate it from our hearts, we know that there is a tremendous amount of benefit that results from this. This is not, however, due to anything from the side of sentient beings, from the object of the great compassion. It is simply by thinking of the kindness of sentient beings and so forth that we generate great compassion and that benefit comes, but not due to the blessing of (or anything inherent in) sentient beings themselves. So strictly from the point of view of motivation, from one's own motivation, a great amount of benefit can result, isn't it so?

Likewise, when we take the Buddha as our object, if our motivation is that of great faith, of very strong faith, and we make offerings and so forth, then again, great benefit can result from this. Although a suitable object is necessary, that is, an object which, for example, has limitless good qualities, nonetheless the principal thing is our motivation, i.e., the strong faith. Still there is probably some difference as regards the kind of object to which one is making these offerings.

From one point of view, were sentient beings not to exist, then we could not take them as our object, and great compassion could not arise. So from this perspective, the object is, once again, very important. If suffering sentient beings did not exist, compassion could never arise. So from that point of view, the object, sentient beings, is a special one....

Question: To what do you attribute the growing fascination in the West, especially in America, with Eastern religions. I include many, many cults and practices which are becoming extremely strong in America. To what do you attribute, in this particular age, the reasons for this fascination, and would you encourage people who are dissatisfied with their own Western way of life, having been brought up in the Mosaic religions (Christianity, Judaism and Islam), dissatisfied with their lack of spiritual refreshment, would you encourage them to search further in their own religions or to look into Buddhism as an alternative?

His Holiness: That's a tricky question. Of course, from the Buddhist viewpoint, we are all human beings and we all have every right to investigate either one's own religion or another religion. This is our right. I think that on the whole a comparative study of different religious traditions is useful.

I generally believe that every major religion has the potential for giving any human being good advice; there is no question that this is so. But we must always keep in mind that different individuals have different mental predispositions. This means that for some individuals one religious system or philosophy will be more suitable than another. The only way one can come to a proper conclusion as to what is most suitable for *oneself* is through comparative study. Hence, we look and study, and we find a teaching that is most suitable to our own taste. This, you see, is my feeling.

I cannot advise everyone to practice Buddhism. That I cannot do. Certainly, for some people the Buddhist religion or ideology is most suitable, most effective. But that does not mean it is suitable for *all*.

IX.1

Religious Pluralism and Ultimate Reality

JOHN HICK

Biographical remarks about John Hick precede selection IV.C.2. In this essay from his path-breaking work God and the Universe of Faiths *(1973), Hick sets forth the thesis that God historically revealed himself (or itself) through various individuals in various situations where geographic isolation prevented a common revelation to all humanity. Each major religion has a different interpretation of the same ultimate reality, to the same salvation. Now the time has come to engage in interreligious dialogue so that we may discover our common bonds and realize that other religious people participate in ultimate reality as validly as we do within our religion, "for all these exist in time, as ways through time to eternity."*

Let me begin by proposing a working definition of religion as an understanding of the universe, together with an appropriate way of living within it, which involves reference beyond the natural world to God or gods or to the Absolute or to a transcendent order or process. Such a definition includes such theistic faiths as Judaism, Christianity, Islam, Sikhism; the theistic Hinduism of the Bhagavad Gītā; the semi-theistic faith of Mahayana Buddhism and the non-theistic faiths of Theravada Buddhism and non-theistic Hinduism. It does not however include purely naturalistic systems of belief, such as communism and humanism, immensely important though these are today as alternatives to religious life.

When we look back into the past we find that religion has been a virtually universal dimension of

Reprinted from John Hick, *God and the Universe of Faiths*, published 1973 (St. Martin's Press, New York). Reproduced with permission of Palgrave MacMillan. Notes deleted.

human life—so much so that man has been defined as the religious animal. For he has displayed an innate tendency to experience his environment as being religiously as well as naturally significant, and to feel required to live in it as such. To quote the anthropologist, Raymond Firth, "religion is universal in human societies." "In every human community on earth today," says Wilfred Cantwell Smith, "there exists something that we, as sophisticated observers, may term religion, or a religion. And we are able to see it in each case as the latest development in a continuous tradition that goes back, we can now affirm, for at least one hundred thousand years." In the life of primitive man this religious tendency is expressed in a belief in sacred objects endowed with *mana*, and in a multitude of natural and ancestral spirits needing to be carefully propitiated. The divine was here crudely apprehended as a plurality of quasianimal forces which could to some extent be controlled by ritualistic and magical procedures. This represents the simplest beginning of man's awareness of the transcendent in the infancy of the human race—an infancy which is also to some extent still available for study in the life of primitive tribes today.

The development of religion and religions begins to emerge into the light of recorded history as the third millennium B.C. moves towards the period around 2000 B.C. There are two main regions of the earth in which civilisation seems first to have arisen and in which religions first took a shape that is at least dimly discernible to us as we peer back through the mists of time—these being Mesopotamia in the Near East and the Indus valley of northern India. In Mesopotamia men lived in nomadic shepherd tribes, each worshipping its own god. Then the tribes gradually coalesced into nation states, the former tribal gods becoming ranked in hierarchies (some however being lost by amalgamation in the process) dominated by great national deities such as Marduk of Babylon, the Sumerian Ishtar, Amon of Thebes, Jahweh of Israel, the Greek Zeus, and so on. Further east in the Indus valley there was likewise a wealth of gods and goddesses, though apparently not so much tribal or national in character as expressive of the basic forces of nature, above all fertility. The many deities of the Near East and of India expressed man's awareness of the divine at the dawn of documentary history, some four thousand years ago. It is perhaps worth stressing that the picture was by no means a wholly pleasant one. The tribal and national gods were often martial and cruel, sometimes requiring human sacrifices. And although rather little is known about the very early, pre-Aryan Indian deities, it is certain that later Indian deities have vividly symbolised the cruel and destructive as well as the beneficent aspects of nature.

These early developments in the two cradles of civilisation, Mesopotamia and the Indus valley, can be described as the growth of natural religion, prior to any special intrusions of divine revelation or illumination. Primitive spirit-worship expressed man's fears of unknown forces; his reverence for nature deities expressed his sense of dependence upon realities greater than himself; and his tribal gods expressed the unity and continuity of his group over against other groups. One can in fact discern all sorts of causal connections between the forms which early religion took and the material circumstances of man's life, indicating the large part played by the human element within the history of religion. For example, Trevor Ling points out that life in ancient India (apart from the Punjab immediately prior to the Aryan invasions) was agricultural and was organised in small village units; and suggests that "among agricultural peoples, aware of the fertile earth which brings forth from itself and nourishes its progeny upon its broad bosom, it is the mother-principle which seems important." Accordingly God the Mother, and a variety of more specialised female deities, have always held a prominent place in Indian religious thought and mythology. This contrasts with the characteristically male expression of deity in the Semitic religions, which had their origins among nomadic, pastoral, herd-keeping peoples in the Near East. The divine was known to the desert-dwelling herdsmen who founded the Israelite tradition as God the King and Father; and this conception has continued both in later Judaism and in Christianity, and was renewed out of the desert experience of Mohammed in the Islamic religion. Such regional variations in our human ways of conceiving the divine have persisted through time into the developed world faiths that we know today. The typical western conception of God is still predominantly in terms of the male principle of power and authority; and in the typical Indian conceptions of deity the female principle still plays a distinctly larger part than in the west.

Here then was the natural condition of man's religious life: religion without revelation. But sometime around 800 B.C. there began what has been called the golden age of religious creativity. This consisted in a remarkable series of revelatory experiences occurring during the next five hundred or so years in different parts of the world, experiences which deepened and purified men's conception of the ultimate, and which religious faith can only attribute to the pressure of the divine Spirit upon the human spirit. First came the early Jewish prophets, Amos, Hosea and first Isaiah, declaring that they had heard the Word of the Lord claiming their obedience and demanding a new level of righteousness and justice in the life of Israel. Then in Persia the great prophet Zoroaster appeared; China produced Lao-tzu and then Confucius; in India the Upanishads were written, and Gotama the Buddha lived, and Mahavira, the founder of the Jain religion and, probably about the end of this period, the writing of the Bhagavad Gītā, and Greece produced Pythagoras and then, ending this golden age, Socrates and Plato. Then after the gap of some three hundred years came Jesus of Nazareth and the emergence of Christianity; and after another gap the prophet Mohammed and the rise of Islam.

The suggestion that we must consider is that these were all moments of divine revelation. But let us ask, in order to test this thought, whether we should not expect God to make his revelation in a single mighty act, rather than to produce a number of different, and therefore presumably partial, revelations at different times and places? I think that in seeing the answer to this question we receive an important clue to the place of the religions of the world in the divine purpose. For when we remember the facts of history and geography we realise that in the period we are speaking of, between two and three thousand years ago, it was not possible for God

to reveal himself through any human mediation to all mankind. A world-wide revelation might be possible today, thanks to the inventions of printing, and even more of radio, TV and communication satellites. But in the technology of the ancient world this was not possible. Although on a time scale of centuries and millennia there has been a slow diffusion and interaction of cultures, particularly within the vast Euro-Asian land mass, yet the more striking fact for our present purpose is the fragmented character of the ancient world. Communications between the different groups of humanity was then so limited and slow that for all practical purposes men inhabited different worlds. For the most part people in Europe, in India, in Arabia, in Africa, in China were unaware of the others' existence. And as the world was fragmented, so was its religious life. If there was to be a revelation of the divine reality to mankind it had to be a pluriform revelation, a series of revealing experiences occurring independently within the different streams of human history. And since religion and culture were one, the great creative moments of revelation and illumination have influenced the development of the various cultures, giving them the coherence and impetus to expand into larger units, thus creating the vast, many-sided historical entities which we call the world religions.

Each of these religio-cultural complexes has expanded until it touched the boundaries of another such complex spreading out from another centre. Thus each major occasion of divine revelation has slowly transformed the primitive and national religions within the sphere of its influence into what we now know as the world faiths. The early Dravidian and Aryan polytheisms of India were drawn through the religious experience and thought of the Brahmins into what the west calls Hinduism. The national and mystery cults of the Mediterranean world and then of northern Europe were drawn by influences stemming from the life and teaching of Christ into what has become Christianity. The early polytheism of the Arab peoples has been transformed under the influence of Mohammed and his message into Islam. Great areas of Southeast Asia, of China, Tibet and Japan were drawn into the spreading Buddhist movement.

None of these expansions from different centres of revelation has of course been simple and uncontested, and a number of alternatives which proved less durable have perished or been absorbed in the process—for example, Mithraism has disappeared altogether; and Zoroastrianism, whilst it greatly influenced the development of the Judaic-Christian tradition, and has to that extent been absorbed, only survives directly today on a small scale in Parseeism.

Seen in this historical context these movements of faith—the Judaic-Christian, the Buddhist, the Hindu, the Muslim—are not essentially rivals. They began at different times and in different places, and each expanded outwards into the surrounding world of primitive natural religion until most of the world was drawn up into one or other of the great revealed faiths. And once this global pattern had become established it has ever since remained fairly stable. It is true that the process of establishment involved conflict in the case of Islam's entry into India and the virtual expulsion of Buddhism from India in the medieval period, and in the case of Islam's advance into Europe and then its retreat at the end of the medieval period. But since the frontiers of the different world faiths became more or less fixed there has been little penetration of one faith into societies moulded by another. The most successful missionary efforts of the great faiths continue to this day to be "downwards" into the remaining world of relatively primitive religions rather than "sideways" into territories dominated by another world faith. For example, as between Christianity and Islam there has been little more than rather rare individual conversions; but both faiths have successful missions in Africa. Again, the Christian population of the Indian subcontinent, after more than two centuries of missionary effort, is only about 2.7 percent; but on the other hand the Christian missions in the South Pacific are fairly successful. Thus the general picture, so far as the great world religions is concerned, is that each has gone through an early period of geographical expansion, converting a region of the world from its more primitive religious state, and has thereafter continued in a comparatively settled condition within more or less stable boundaries.

Now it is of course possible to see this entire development from the primitive forms of religion up to and including the great world faiths as the history of man's most persistent illusion, growing from crude fantasies into sophisticated metaphysical speculations. But from the standpoint of religious faith the only reasonable hypothesis is that this historical picture represents a movement of divine self-revelation to mankind. This hypothesis offers a general answer to the question of the relation between the different world religions and of the truths which they embody. It suggests to us that the same divine reality has always been self-revealingly active towards mankind, and that the differences of human response are related to different human circumstances. These circumstances—ethnic, geographical, climatic, economic, sociological, historical—have produced the existing differentiations of human culture, and within each main cultural region the response to the divine has taken its own characteristic forms. In each case the post-primitive response has been initiated by some spiritually outstanding individual or succession of individuals, developing in the course of time into one of the great religio-cultural phenomena which we call the world religions. Thus Islam embodies the main response of the Arabic peoples to the divine reality; Hinduism, the main (though not the only) response of the peoples of India; Buddhism, the main response of the peoples of South-east Asia and parts of northern Asia; Christianity, the main response of the European peoples, both within Europe itself and in their emigrations to the Americas and Australasia.

Thus it is, I think, intelligible historically why the revelation of the divine reality to man, and the disclosure of the divine will for human life, had to occur separately within the different streams of human life. We can see how these revelations took different forms related to the different mentalities of the peoples to whom they came and developed within these different cultures into the vast and many-sided historical phenomena of the world religions.

But let us now ask whether this is intelligible theologically. What about the conflicting truth claims of the different faiths? Is the divine nature personal or non-personal; does deity become incarnate in the world; are human beings born again and again on earth; is the Bible, or the Koran, or the Bhagavad Gītā the Word of God? If what Christianity says in answer to these questions is true, must not what Hinduism says be to a large extent false? If what Buddhism says is true, must not what Islam says be largely false?

Let us begin with the recognition, which is made in all the main religious traditions, that the ultimate divine reality is infinite and as such transcends the grasp of the human mind. God, to use our Christian term, is infinite. He is not a thing, a part of the universe, existing alongside other things; nor is he a being falling under a certain kind. And therefore he cannot be defined or encompassed by human thought. We cannot draw boundaries around his nature and say that he is this and no more. If we could fully define God, describing his inner being and his outer limits, this would not be God. The God whom our minds can penetrate and whom our thoughts can circumnavigate is merely a finite and partial image of God.

From this it follows that the different encounters with the transcendent within the different religious traditions may all be encounters with the one infinite reality; though with partially different and overlapping aspects of that reality. This is a very familiar thought in Indian religious literature. We read, for example, in the ancient Rig-Vedas, dating back to perhaps as much as a thousand years before Christ:

> They call it Indra, Mitra, Varuna, and Agni
> And also heavenly, beautiful Garutman:
> The real is one, though sages name it variously.

We might translate this thought into the terms of the faiths represented today in Britain:

> They call it Jahweh, Allah, Krishna, Param
>   Atma,
> And also holy, blessed Trinity:
> The real is one, though sages name it
>   differently.

And in the Bhagavad Gītā the Lord Krishna, the personal God of love, says, "However men approach me, even so do I accept them: for, on all sides, whatever path they may choose is mine."

Again, there is the parable of the blind men and the elephant, said to have been told by the Buddha. An elephant was brought to a group of blind men who had never encountered such an animal before. One felt a leg and reported that an elephant is a great living pillar. Another felt the trunk and reported that an elephant is a great snake. Another felt the tusk and reported that an elephant is like a sharp ploughshare. And so on. And then they all quarrelled together, each claiming that his own account was the truth and therefore all the others false. In fact of course they were all true, but each referring only to one aspect of the total reality and all expressed in very imperfect analogies.

Now the possibility, indeed the probability, that we have seriously to consider is that many different accounts of the divine reality may be true, though all expressed in imperfect human analogies, but that none is "the truth, the whole truth, and nothing but the truth." May it not be that the different concepts of God, as Jahweh, Allah, Krishna, Param Atma, Holy Trinity, and so on; and likewise the different concepts of the hidden structure of reality, as the eternal emanation of Brahman or as an immense cosmic process culminating in Nirvana, are all images of the divine, each expressing some aspect or range of aspects and yet none by itself fully and exhaustively corresponding to the infinite nature of the ultimate reality?

Two immediate qualifications however to this hypothesis. First, the idea that we are considering is not that any and every conception of God or of the transcendent is valid, still less all equally valid; but that every conception of the divine which has come out of a great revelatory religious experience and has been tested though a long tradition of worship, and has sustained human faith over centuries of time and in millions of lives, is likely to represent a genuine encounter with the divine reality. And second, the parable of the blind men and the elephant is of course only a parable and like most parables it is designed to make one point and must not be pressed as an analogy at other points. The suggestion is not that the different encounters with the divine which lie at the basis of the great religious traditions are responses to different *parts* of the divine. They are rather encounters from different historical and cultural standpoints with the same infinite divine reality and as such they lead to differently focused awareness of the reality. The indications of this are most evident in worship and prayer. What is said about God in the theological treatises of the different faiths is indeed often widely different. But it is in prayer that a belief in God comes alive and does its main work. And when we turn from abstract theology to the living stuff of worship we meet again and again the overlap and confluence of faiths.

Here, for example, is a Muslim prayer at the feast of Ramadan:

> Praise be to God, Lord of creation, Source of all livelihood, who orders the morning, Lord of majesty and honour, of grace and beneficence. He who is so far that he may not be seen and so near that he witnesses the secret things. Blessed be he and for ever exalted.

And here is a Sikh creed used at the morning prayer:

> There is but one God. He is all that is.
> He is the Creator of all things and He is all
>   pervasive.
> He is without fear and without enmity.
> He is timeless, unborn and self-existent.
>   He is the Enlightener
> And can be realised by grace of Himself
>   alone. He was in the beginning; He was
>   in all ages.
> The True One is, was, O Nanak, and shall
>   for ever be.

And here again is a verse from the Koran:

> To God belongs the praise. Lord of the heavens and Lord of the earth, the Lord of all being. His is the dominion in the heavens and in the earth: he is the Almighty, the All-wise.

Turning now to the Hindu idea of the many incarnations of God, here is a verse from the Rāmāyana:

> Seers and sages, saints and hermits, fix on
>   Him their reverent gaze,

> And in faint and trembling accents, holy
>   scripture hymns His praise.
> He the omnipresent spirit, lord of heaven
>   and earth and hell,
> To redeem His people, freely has vouch-
>   safed with men to dwell.

And from the rich literature of devotional song here is a Bhakti hymn of the Vaishnavite branch of Hinduism:

> Now all my days with joy I'll fill, full to
>   the brim
> With all my heart to Vitthal cling, and
>   only Him.
> He will sweep utterly away all dole and care;
> And all in sunder shall I rend illusion's snare.
> O altogether dear is He, and He alone,
> For all my burden He will take to be His own.
> Lo, all the sorrow of the world will straight
>   way cease,
> And all unending now shall be the reign of
>   peace.

And a Muslim mystical verse:

> Love came a guest
> Within my breast,
> My soul was spread,
> Love banqueted.

And finally another Hindu (Vaishnavite) devotional hymn:

> O save me, save me, Mightiest, Save me
>   and set me free.
> O let the love that fills my breast Cling to
>   thee lovingly.
> Grant me to taste how sweet thou art;
>   Grant me but this, I pray.
> And never shall my love depart Or turn
>   from thee away.
> Then I thy name shall magnify And tell thy
>   praise abroad,
> For very love and gladness I Shall dance
>   before my God.

Such prayers and hymns as these must express, surely, diverse encounters with the same divine reality. These encounters have taken place within different human cultures by people of different ways of thought and feeling, with different histories and different frameworks of philosophical thought, and have developed into different systems of theology embodied in different religious structures and organisations. These resulting large-scale religio-cultural phenomena are what we call the religions of the world. But must there not lie behind them the same infinite divine reality, and may not our divisions into Christian, Hindu, Muslim, Jew, and so on, and all that goes with them, accordingly represent secondary, human, historical developments?

There is a further problem, however, which now arises. I have been speaking so far of the ultimate reality in a variety of terms—the Father, Son and Spirit of Christianity, the Jahweh of Judaism, the Allah of Islam, and so on—but always thus far in theistic terms, as a personal God under one name or another. But what of the non-theistic religions? What of the non-theistic Hinduism according to which the ultimate reality, Brahman, is not He but It; and what about Buddhism, which in one form is agnostic concerning the existence of God even though in another form it has come to worship the Buddha himself? Can these non-theistic faiths be seen as encounters with the same divine reality that is encountered in theistic religion?

Speaking very tentatively, I think it is possible that the sense of the divine as non-personal may indeed reflect an aspect of the same infinite reality that is encountered as personal in theistic religious experience. The question can be pursued both as a matter of pure theology and in relation to religious experience. Theologically, the Hindu distinction between Nirguna Brahman and Saguna Brahman is important and should be adopted into western religious thought. Detaching the distinction, then from its Hindu context we may say that Nirguna God is the eternal self-existent divine reality, beyond the scope of all human categories, including personality; and Saguna God is God in relation to his creation and with the attributes which express this relationship, such as personality, omnipotence, goodness, love and omniscience. Thus the one ultimate reality is both Nirguna and non-personal,

and Saguna and personal, in a duality which is in principle acceptable to human understanding. When we turn to men's religious awareness of God we are speaking of Saguna God, God in relation to man. And here the larger traditions of both east and west report a dual experience of the divine as personal and as other than personal. It will be a sufficient reminder of the strand of personal relationship with the divine in Hinduism to mention Iswaru, the personal God who represents the Absolute as known and worshipped by finite persons. It should also be remembered that the characterisation of Brahman as *satcitananda*, absolute being, consciousness and bliss, is not far from the conception of infinitely transcendent personal life. Thus there is both the thought and the experience of the personal divine within Hinduism. But there is likewise the thought and the experience of God as other than personal within Christianity. Rudolph Otto describes this strand in the mysticism of Meister Eckhart. He says:

> The divine, which on the one hand is conceived in symbols taken from the social sphere, as Lord, King, Father, Judge—a person in relation to persons—is on the other hand denoted in dynamic symbols as the power of life, as light and life, as spirit ebbing and flowing, as truth, knowledge, essential justice and holiness, a glowing fire that penetrates and pervades. It is characterized as the principle of a renewed, supernatural Life, mediating and giving itself, breaking forth in the living man as his nova vita, as the content of his life and being. What is here insisted upon is not so much an immanent God, as an "experienced" God, known as an inward principle of the power of new being and life. Eckhart knows this *deuteros theos* besides the personal God ...

Let me now try to draw the threads together and to project them into the future. I have been suggesting that Christianity is a way of salvation which, beginning some two thousand years ago, has become the principal way of salvation in three continents. The other great faiths are likewise of salvation, providing the principal path to the divine reality for other large sections of humanity. I have also suggested that the idea that Jesus proclaimed himself as God incarnate, and as the sole point of saving contact between God and man, is without adequate historical foundation and represents a doctrine developed by the church. We should therefore not infer, from the christian experience of redemption through Christ, that salvation cannot be experienced in any other way. The alternative possibility is that the ultimate divine reality—in our christian terms, God—has always been pressing in upon the human spirit, but in ways which leave men free to open or close themselves to the divine presence. Human life has developed along characteristically different lines in the main areas of civilisation, and these differences have naturally entered into the ways in which men have apprehended and responded to God. For the great religious figures through whose experience divine revelation has come have each been conditioned by a particular history and culture. One can hardly imagine Gotama the Buddha except in the setting of the India of his time, or Jesus the Christ except against the background of Old Testament Judaism, or Mohammed except in the setting of Arabia. And human history and culture have likewise shaped the development of the webs of religious creeds, practices and organisations which we know as the great world faiths.

It is thus possible to consider the hypothesis that they are all, at their experiential roots, in contact with the same ultimate reality, but that their differing experiences of that reality, interacting over the centuries with the different thought-forms of different cultures, have led to increasing differentiation and contrasting elaboration—so that Hinduism, for example, is a very different phenomenon from Christianity, and very different ways of conceiving and experiencing the divine occur within them.

However, now that the religious traditions are consciously interacting with each other in the "one world" of today, in mutual observation and dialogue, it is possible that their future developments may be on gradually converging courses. For during the next few centuries they will no doubt continue to change, and it may be that they will grow closer together, and even that one day such names as "Christianity," "Buddhism," "Islam," "Hinduism," will no longer describe the then current configurations of men's religious experience and belief. I am not here thinking of the extinction of human religiousness in a universal wave of secularisation. This is of course a possible future; and indeed many think it the most likely future to come about. But if man is an indelibly religious animal he will always, even in his secular cultures, experience a sense of the transcendent by which he will be both troubled and uplifted. The future I am thinking of is accordingly one in which what we now call the different religions will constitute the past history of different emphases and variations within a global religious life. I do not mean that all men everywhere will be overtly religious, any more than they are today. I mean rather that the discoveries now taking place by men of different faiths of central common ground, hitherto largely concealed by the variety of cultural forms in which it was expressed, may eventually render obsolete the sense of belonging to rival ideological communities. Not that all religious men will think alike, or worship in the same way or experience the divine identically. On the contrary, so long as there is a rich variety of human cultures—and let us hope there will always be this—we should expect there to be correspondingly different forms of religious cult, ritual and organisation, conceptualised in different theological doctrines. And so long as there is a wide spectrum of human psychological types—and again let us hope that there will always be this—we should expect there to be correspondingly different emphases between, for example, the sense of the divine as just and as merciful, between *karma* and *bhakti*; or between worship as formal and communal and worship as free and personal. Thus we may expect the different world faiths to continue as religio-cultural phenomena, though phenomena which are increasingly influencing one another's development. The relation between them will then perhaps be somewhat like that now obtaining between the different denominations of Christianity in Europe or the United States. That is to say, there will in most countries be a dominant religious tradition, with other traditions present in varying strengths, but with considerable awareness on all hands of what they have in common; with some degree of osmosis of membership through their institutional walls; with a large degree of practical cooperation; and even conceivably with some interchange of ministry.

Beyond this the ultimate unity of faiths will be an eschatological unity in which each is both fulfilled and transcended—fulfilled in so far as it is true, transcended in so far as it is less than the whole truth. And indeed even such fulfilling must be a transcending;

for the function of a religion is to bring us to a right relationship with the ultimate divine reality, to awareness of our true nature and our place in the Whole, into the presence of God. In the eternal life there is no longer any place for religions; the pilgrim has no need of a way after he has finally arrived. In St. John's vision of the heavenly city at the end of our christian scriptures it is said that there is no temple—no christian church or chapel, no jewish synagogue, no hindu or buddhist temple, no muslim mosque, no sikh gurdwara.... For all these exist in time, as ways through time to eternity.

This essay appeared in print for the first time in an earlier edition of this text. Used with permission. Endnotes edited.

IX.2

A Defense of Religious Exclusivism

ALVIN PLANTINGA

Biographical remarks about Alvin Plantinga appear before selection I.B.8. In this selection, Plantinga argues for three theses: (1) The religious exclusivist is not necessarily guilty of any moral wrongdoing; (2) the religious exclusivist is not necessarily guilty of any epistemic fault; (3) some exclusivism in our beliefs is inevitable. If a person truly believes his or her creed, it may be wrong to expect him or her to treat all religions as equally good ways to God, or even as ways to God simpliciter. Nevertheless, Plantinga agrees that the knowledge of other religions is something to be sought, and that this may lessen our assurance in our own belief.

When I was a graduate student at Yale, the philosophy department prided itself on diversity, and it was indeed diverse. There were idealists, pragmatists, phenomenologists, existentialists, Whiteheadians, historians of philosophy, a token positivist, and what could only be described as observers of the passing intellectual scene. In some ways, this was indeed something to take pride in; a student could behold and encounter real, live representatives of many of the main traditions in philosophy. However, it also had an unintended and unhappy side effect. If anyone raised a philosophical question inside, but particularly

This essay appeared in print for the first time in an earlier edition of this text. Used with permission. Endnotes edited.

outside, of class, the typical response would be to catalog some of the various different answers the world has seen: There is the Aristotelian answer, the existentialist answer, the Cartesian answer, Heidegger's answer, perhaps the Buddhist answer, and so on. But the question "What is the truth about this matter?" was often greeted with disdain as unduly naive. There are all these different answers, all endorsed by people of great intellectual power and great dedication to philosophy; for every argument *for* one of these positions, there is another *against* it; would it not be excessively naive, or perhaps arbitrary, to suppose that one of these is in fact true, the others being false? Or, if even there really is a truth of the matter, so that one of them is true and conflicting ones false, wouldn't it be merely arbitrary, in the face of this embarrassment of riches, to *endorse* one of them as the truth, consigning the others to falsehood? How could you possibly know which was true?

A similar attitude is sometimes urged with respect to the impressive variety of religions the world displays. There are theistic religions but also at least some nontheistic religions (or perhaps nontheistic strands) among the enormous variety of religions going under the names Hinduism and Buddhism; among the theistic religions, there are strands of Hinduism and Buddhism and American Indian religion as well as Islam, Judaism, and Christianity; and all differ significantly from each other. Isn't it somehow arbitrary, or irrational, or unjustified, or unwarranted, or even oppressive and imperialistic to endorse one of these as opposed to all the others? According to Jean Bodin, "each is refuted by all";[1] must we not agree? It is in this neighborhood that the so-called problem of pluralism arises. Of course, many concerns and problems can come under this rubric; the specific problem I mean to discuss can be thought of as follows. To put it in an internal and personal way, I find myself with religious beliefs, and religious beliefs that I realize aren't shared by nearly everyone else. For example, I believe both

(1)   The world was created by God, an almighty, all-knowing, and perfectly good personal being (one that holds beliefs; has aims, plans,

and intentions; and can act to accomplish these aims).

(2)   Human beings require salvation, and God has provided a unique way of salvation through the incarnation, life, sacrificial death, and resurrection of his divine son.

Now there are many who do not believe these things. First, there are those who agree with me on (1) but not (2): They are non-Christian theistic religions. Second, there are those who don't accept either (1) or (2) but nonetheless do believe that there is something beyond the natural world, a something such that human well-being and salvation depend upon standing in a right relation to it. Third, in the West and since the Enlightenment, anyway, there are people—*naturalists*, we may call them—who don't believe any of these three things. And my problem is this: When I become really aware of these other ways of looking at the world, these other ways of responding religiously to the world, what must or should I do? What is the right sort of attitude to take? What sort of impact should this awareness have on the beliefs I hold and the strength with which I hold them? My question is this: How should I think about the great religious diversity the world in fact displays? Can I sensibly remain an adherent of just one of these religions, rejecting the others? And here I am thinking specifically of *beliefs*. Of course, there is a great deal more to any religion or religious practice than just belief, and I don't for a moment mean to deny it. But belief is a crucially important part of most religions; it is a crucially important part of *my* religion; and the question I mean to ask here is, What does the awareness of religious diversity mean or should mean for my religious beliefs?

Some speak here of a *new* awareness of religious diversity and speak of this new awareness as constituting (for us in the West) a crisis, a revolution, an intellectual development of the same magnitude as the Copernican revolution of the sixteenth century and the alleged discovery of evolution and our animal origins in the nineteenth.[2] No doubt there is at least some truth to this. Of course, the fact is all along many Western Christians and Jews have known that there are other religions and that not nearly everyone shares *their* religion. The ancient Israelites—some of the prophets, say—were clearly aware of Canaanite religion; and the apostle Paul said that he preached "Christ crucified, a stumbling block to Jews and folly to the Greeks" (1 Corinthians 1:23). Other early Christians, the Christian martyrs, say, must have suspected that not everyone believed as they did; and the church fathers, in offering defenses of Christianity, were certainly apprised of this fact. Thomas Aquinas, again, was clearly aware of those to whom he addressed the *Summa Contra Gentiles*; and the fact that there are non-Christian religions would have come as no surprise to the Jesuit missionaries of the sixteenth and seventeenth centuries or to the Methodist missionaries of the nineteenth. To come to more recent times, when I was a child, *The Banner*, the official publication of my church, contained a small column for children; it was written by "Uncle Dick" who exhorted us to save our nickels and send them to our Indian cousins at the Navaho mission in New Mexico. Both we and our elders knew that the Navahos had or had had a religion different from Christianity, and part of the point of sending the nickels was to try to rectify that situation.

Still, in recent years, probably more of us Christian Westerners have become aware of the world's religious diversity; we have probably learned more about people of other religious persuasions, and we have come to see that they display what looks like real piety, devoutness, and spirituality. What is new, perhaps, is a more widespread sympathy for other religions, a tendency to see them as more valuable, as containing more by way of truth, and a new feeling of solidarity with their practitioners.

Now there are several possible reactions to awareness of religious diversity. One is to continue to believe—what you have all along believed; you learn about this diversity but continue to believe that is, take to be true—such propositions as (1) and (2) above, consequently taking to be false any beliefs, religious or otherwise, that are incompatible with (1) and (2). Following current practice, I will call this *exclusivism*; the exclusivist holds that the tenets or some of the tenets of *one* religion—Christianity, let's say—are in fact true; he adds, naturally

enough, that any propositions, including other religious beliefs, that are incompatible with those tenets are false. And there is a fairly widespread apprehension that there is something seriously wrong with exclusivism. It is irrational, or egotistical and unjustified,[3] or intellectually arrogant,[4] or elitist,[5] or a manifestation of harmful pride,[6] or even oppressive and imperialistic.[7] The claim is that exclusivism as such is or involves a vice of some sort: It is wrong or deplorable. It is this claim I want to examine. I propose to argue that exclusivism need not involve either epistemic or moral failure and that, furthermore, something like it is wholly unavoidable, given our human condition.

These objections, of course, are not to the *truth* of (1) or (2) or any other proposition someone might accept in this exclusivist way (although objections of that sort are also put forward); they are instead directed to the *propriety or rightness* of exclusivism. There are initially two different kinds of indictments of exclusivism: broadly moral, or ethical, indictments and other broadly intellectual, or epistemic, indictments. These overlap in interesting ways as we will see below. But initially, anyway, we can take some of the complaints about exclusivism as *intellectual* criticisms: It is *irrational* or *unjustified* to think in an exclusivistic way. The other large body of complaint is moral: There is something *morally* suspect about exclusivism—it is arbitrary, or intellectually arrogant, or imperialistic. As Joseph Runzo suggests, exclusivism is "neither tolerable nor any longer intellectually honest in the context of our contemporary knowledge of other faiths."[8] I want to consider both kinds of claims or criticisms; I propose to argue that the exclusivist as such is not necessarily guilty of any of these charges.

MORAL OBJECTIONS TO EXCLUSIVISM

I turn to the moral complaints: that the exclusivist is intellectually arrogant, or egotistical or self-servingly arbitrary, or dishonest, or imperialistic, or oppressive. But first, I provide three qualifications. An exclusivist, like anyone else, will probably be guilty of some or of all of these things to at least some degree, perhaps particularly the first two. The question, however, is whether she is guilty of these things just by virtue of being an exclusivist. Second, I will use the term *exclusivism* in such a way that you don't count as an exclusivist unless you are rather fully aware of other faiths, have had their existence and their claims called to your attention with some force and perhaps fairly frequently, and have to some degree reflected on the problem of pluralism, asking yourself such questions as whether it is or could be really true that the Lord has revealed Himself and His programs to us Christians, say, in a way in which He hasn't revealed Himself to those of other faiths. Thus, my grandmother, for example, would not have counted as an exclusivist. She had, of course, *heard* of the heathen, as she called them, but the idea that perhaps Christians could learn from them, and learn from them with respect to religious matters, had not so much as entered her head; and the fact that it *hadn't* entered her head, I take it, was not a matter of moral dereliction on her part. This same would go for a Buddhist or Hindu peasant. These people are not, I think, properly charged with arrogance or other moral flaws in believing as they do.

Third, suppose I am an exclusivist with respect to (1), for example, but nonculpably believe, like Aquinas, say, that I have a knock-down, drag-out argument, a demonstration or conclusive proof of the proposition that there is such a person as God; and suppose I think further (and nonculpably) that if those who don't believe (1) were to be apprised of this argument (and had the ability and training necessary to grasp it and were to think about the argument fairly and reflectively), *they* too would come to believe (1)? Then I could hardly be charged with these moral faults. My condition would be like that of Gödel, let's say, upon having recognized that he had a proof for the incompleteness of arithmetic. True, many of his colleagues and peers didn't believe that arithmetic was incomplete, and some believed that it was complete; but presumably Gödel wasn't arbitrary or egotistical in believing that arithmetic is in fact incomplete.

Furthermore, he would not have been at fault had he nonculpably but *mistakenly* believed that he had found such a proof. Accordingly, I will use the term *exclusivist* in such a way that you don't count as an exclusivist if you nonculpably think you know of a demonstration or conclusive argument for the beliefs with respect to which you are an exclusivist, or even if you nonculpably think you know of an argument that would convince all or most intelligent and honest people of the truth of that proposition. So an exclusivist, as I use the term, not only believes something like (1) or (2) and thinks false any proposition incompatible with it; she also meets a further condition *C* that is hard to state precisely and in detail (and in fact any attempt to do so would involve a long and presently irrelevant discussion of *ceteris paribus* clauses). Suffice it to say that *C* includes (a) being rather fully aware of other religions, (b) knowing that there is much that at the least looks like genuine piety and devoutness in them, and (c) believing that you know of no arguments that would necessarily convince all or most honest and intelligent dissenters.

Given these qualifications then, why should we think that an exclusivist is properly charged with these moral faults? I will deal first and most briefly with charges of oppression and imperialism: I think we must say that they are on the face of it wholly implausible. I daresay there are some among you who reject some of the things I believe; I do not believe that you are thereby oppressing me, even if you do not believe you have an argument that would convince me. It is conceivable that exclusivism might in some way *contribute* to oppression, but it isn't in itself oppressive.

The more important moral charge is that there is a sort of self-serving arbitrariness, an arrogance or egotism, in accepting such propositions as (1) or (2) under condition *C*; exclusivism is guilty of some serious moral fault or flaw. According to Wilfred Cantwell Smith, "…except at the cost of insensitivity or delinquency, it is morally not possible actually to go out into the world and say to devout, intelligent, fellow human beings: '… we believe that we know God and we are right; you believe that you know God, and you are totally wrong.'"[9]

So what can the exclusivist have to say for himself Well, it must be conceded immediately that if he believes (1) or (2), then he must also believe that those who believe something incompatible with them are mistaken and believe what is false. That's no more than simple logic. Furthermore, he must also believe that those who do not believe as he does—those who believe neither (1) nor (2), whether or not they believe their negations—*fail* to believe something that is deep and important and that he *does* believe. He must therefore see himself as *privileged* with respect to those others—those others of both kinds. There is something of great value, he must think, that *he* has and *they* lack. They are ignorant of something—something of great importance—of which he has knowledge. But does this make him properly subject to the above censure?

I think the answer must be no. Or if the answer is yes, then I think we have here a genuine moral dilemma; for in our earthly life here below, as my Sunday School teacher used to say, there is no real alternative; there is no reflective attitude that is not open to the same strictures. These charges of arrogance are a philosophical tar baby: Get close enough to them to use them against the exclusivist and you are likely to find them stuck fast to yourself. How so? Well, as an exclusivist, I realize that I can't convince others that they should believe as I do, but I nonetheless continue to believe as I do. The charge is that I am, as a result, arrogant or egotistical, arbitrarily preferring my way of doing things to other ways.[10] But what are my alternatives with respect to a proposition like (1)? There seem to be three choices. I can continue to hold it; I can withhold it, in Roderick Chisholm's sense, believing neither it nor its denial, and I can accept its denial. Consider the third way, a way taken by those pluralists who, like John Hick, hold that such propositions as (1) and (2) and their colleagues from other faiths are literally false, although in some way still valid responses to the Real. This seems to me to be no advance at all with respect to the arrogance or egotism problem; this is not a way out. For if I do this, I will then be in the very same condition as I am now: I will believe many propositions others don't believe and will be in condition C with respect to those propositions. For I will then

believe the denials of (1) and (2) (as well as the denials of many other propositions explicitly accepted by those of other faiths). Many others, of course, do not believe the denials of (1) and (2) and in fact believe (1) and (2). Further, I will not know of any arguments that can be counted on to persuade those who do believe (1) or (2) (or propositions accepted by the adherents of other religions). I am therefore in the condition of believing propositions that many others do not believe and furthermore am in condition C. If, in the case of those who believe (1) and (2), that is sufficient for intellectual arrogance or egotism, the same goes for those who believe their denials.

So consider the second option: I can instead *withhold* the proposition in question. I can say to myself: "The right course here, given that I can't or couldn't convince these others of what I believe, is to believe neither these propositions nor their denials." The pluralist objector to exclusivism can say that the right course, under condition C, is to abstain from believing the offending proposition and also abstain from believing its denial; call him, therefore, "the abstemious pluralist." But does he thus really avoid the condition that, on the part of the exclusivist, leads to the charges of egotism and arrogance in this way? Think, for a moment, about disagreement. Disagreement, fundamentally, is a matter of adopting conflicting propositional attitudes with respect to a given proposition. In the simplest and most familiar case, I disagree with you if there is some proposition p such that I believe p and you believe $-p$. But that's just the simplest case; there are also others. The one that is presently of interest is this: I believe p and you withhold it, fail to believe it. Call the first kind of disagreement "contradicting"; call the second "dissenting."

My claim is that if contradicting others (under the condition C spelled out above) is arrogant and egotistical, so is dissenting (under that same condition). Suppose you believe some proposition p but I don't; perhaps you believe that it is wrong to discriminate against people simply on the grounds of race, but I, recognizing that there are many people who disagree with you, do not believe this proposition. I don't disbelieve it either, of course, but in the circumstances I think the right thing to do is to abstain from belief. Then am I not implicitly condemning your attitude, your *believing* the proposition, as somehow improper—naive, perhaps, or unjustified, or in some other way less than optimal? I am implicitly saying that my attitude is the superior one; I think my course of action here is the right one and yours somehow wrong, inadequate, improper, in the circumstances at best second-rate. Of course, I realize that there is no question, here, of *showing* you that your attitude is wrong or improper or naive; so am I not guilty of intellectual arrogance? Of a sort of egotism, thinking I know better than you, arrogating to myself a privileged status with respect to you? The problem for the exclusivist was that she was obliged to think she possessed a truth missed by many others; the problem for the abstemious pluralist is that he is obliged to think that he possesses a virtue others don't or acts rightly where others don't. If, in condition *C*, one is arrogant by way of believing a proposition others don't, isn't one equally, under those reflective conditions, arrogant by way of withholding a proposition others don't?

Perhaps you will respond by saying that the abstemious pluralist gets into trouble, falls into arrogance, by way of implicitly saying or believing that his way of proceeding is better or wiser than other ways pursued by other people; and perhaps he can escape by abstaining from *that* view as well. Can't he escape the problem by refraining from believing that racial bigotry is wrong and also refraining from holding the view that it is *better*, under the conditions that obtain, to withhold that proposition than to assert and believe it? Well, yes he can; then he has no *reason* for his abstention; he doesn't believe that abstention is better or more appropriate; he simply does abstain. Does this get him off the egotistical hook? Perhaps. But then he can't, in consistency, also hold that there is something wrong with *not* abstaining, with coming right out and *believing* that bigotry is wrong; he loses his objection to the exclusivist. Accordingly, this way out is not available for the abstemious pluralist who accuses the exclusivist of arrogance and egotism.

Indeed, I think we can show that the abstemious pluralist who brings charges of intellectual arrogance against exclusivism is hoist with his own petard, holds a position that in a certain way is self-referentially inconsistent in the circumstances. For he believes

(3) If S knows that others don't believe *p* and that he is in condition *C* with respect to *p*, then *S* should not believe *p*.

This or something like it is the ground of the charges he brings against the exclusivist. But the abstemious pluralist realizes that many do not accept (3); and I suppose he also realizes that it is unlikely that he can find arguments for (3) that will convince them; hence, he knows that condition obtains. Given his acceptance of (3), therefore, the right course for him is to abstain from believing (3). Under the conditions that do in fact obtain—namely, his knowledge that others don't accept it and that condition *C* obtains—he can't properly accept it.

I am therefore inclined to think that one can't, in the circumstances, properly hold (3) or any other proposition that will do the job. One can't find here some principle on the basis of which to hold that the exclusivist is doing the wrong thing, suffers from some moral fault—that is, one can't find such a principle that doesn't, as we might put it, fall victim to itself.

So the abstemious pluralist is hoist with his own petard; but even apart from this dialectical argument (which in any event some will think unduly cute), aren't the charges unconvincing and implausible? I must concede that there are a variety of ways in which I can be and have been intellectually arrogant and egotistic; I have certainly fallen into this vice in the past and no doubt am not free of it now. But am I really arrogant and egotistic just by virtue of believing what I know others don't believe, where I can't show them that I am right? Suppose I think the matter over, consider the objections as carefully as I can, realize that I am finite and furthermore a sinner, certainly no better than those with whom I disagree; but suppose it still seems clear to me that the proposition in question is true. Can I really be behaving immorally in continuing to believe it? I am dead sure that it is wrong to try to advance my career by telling lies about my colleagues; I realize there are those who disagree; I also realize that in all likelihood there is no way I can find to show them that they are wrong; nonetheless I think they are wrong. If I think this after careful reflection, if I consider the claims of those who disagree as sympathetically as I can, if I try my level best to ascertain the truth here, and it *still* seems to me sleazy, wrong, and despicable to lie about my colleagues to advance my career, could I really be doing what is immoral by continuing to believe as before? I can't see how. If, after careful reflection and thought, you find yourself convinced that the right propositional attitude to take to (1) and (2) in the face of the facts of religious pluralism is abstention from belief, how could you properly be taxed with egotism, either for so believing or for so abstaining? Even if you knew others did not agree with you?

EPISTEMIC OBJECTIONS TO EXCLUSIVISM

I turn now to *epistemic* objections to exclusivism. There are many different specifically epistemic virtues and a corresponding plethora of epistemic vices. The ones with which the exclusivist is most frequently charged, however, are *irrationality* and *lack of justification* in holding his exclusivist beliefs. The claim is that as an exclusivist he holds unjustified beliefs and/or irrational beliefs. Better, *he* is unjustified or irrational in holding these beliefs. I will therefore consider those two claims, and I will argue that the exclusivist views need not be either unjustified or irrational. I will then turn to the question whether his beliefs could have *warrant*—that property, whatever precisely it is, that distinguishes knowledge from mere true belief—and whether they could have enough warrant for knowledge.

Justification

The pluralist objector sometimes claims that to hold exclusivist views, in condition *C*, is *unjustified*—*epistemically* unjustified. Is this true? And what does he mean when he makes this claim? As even a brief glance at the contemporary epistemological literature will show, justification is a protean and multifarious

notion. There are, I think, substantially two possibilities as to what he means. The central core of the notion, its beating heart, the paradigmatic center to which most of the myriad contemporary variations are related by way of analogical extension and family resemblance, is the notion of *being within one's intellectual rights*, having violated no intellectual or cognitive duties or obligations in the formation and sustenance of the belief in question. This is the palimpsest, going back to Rene Descartes and especially John Locke, that underlies the multitudinous battery of contemporary inscriptions. There is no space to argue that point here; but chances are, when the pluralist objector to exclusivism claims that the latter is unjustified, it is some notion lying in this neighborhood that he has in mind. (Here we should note the very close connection between the moral objections to exclusivism and the objection that exclusivism is epistemically unjustified.)

The duties involved, naturally enough, would be specifically *epistemic* duties: perhaps a duty to proportion degree of belief to (propositional) evidence from what is *certain*, that is, self-evident or incorrigible, as with Locke, or perhaps to try one's best to get into and stay in the right relation to the truth, as with Chisholm, the leading contemporary champion of the justificationist tradition with respect to knowledge. But at present there is widespread (and as I see it, correct) agreement that there is no duty of the Lockean kind. Perhaps there is one of the Chisholmian kind; but isn't the exclusivist conforming to that duty if, after the sort of careful, indeed prayerful consideration I mentioned in the response to the moral objection, it still seems to him strongly that (1), say, is true and he accordingly still believes it? It is therefore very hard to see that the exclusivist is necessarily unjustified in this way.

The second possibility for understanding the charge—the charge that exclusivism is epistemically unjustified—has to do with the oft-repeated claim that exclusivism is intellectually *arbitrary*. Perhaps the idea is that there is an intellectual duty to treat similar cases similarly; the exclusivist violates this duty by arbitrarily choosing to believe (for the moment going along with the fiction that we *choose* beliefs of this sort) (1) and (2) in the face of the plurality of conflicting religious beliefs the world presents. But suppose there is such a duty. Clearly you do not violate it if you nonculpably think the beliefs in question are not on a par. And as an exclusivist, I *do* think (nonculpably, I hope) that they are not on a par: I think (1) and (2) *true* and those incompatible with either of them *false*.

The rejoinder, of course, will be that it is not alethic parity (their having the same truth value) that is at issue: it is *epistemic* parity that counts. What kind of epistemic parity? What would be relevant, here, I should think, would be *internal* or internalist epistemic parity: parity with respect to what is internally available to the believer. What is internally available to the believer includes, for example, detectable relationships between the belief in question and other beliefs you hold; so internal parity would include parity of propositional evidence. What is internally available to the believer also includes the *phenomenology* that goes with the beliefs in question: the *sensuous* phenomenology but also the nonsensuous phenomenology involved, for example, in the belief's just having the feel of being *right*. But once more, then, (1) and (2) are not on an internal par, for the exclusivist, with beliefs that are incompatible with them. (1) and (2), after all, seem to me to be true; they have for me the phenomenology that accompanies that seeming. The same cannot be said for propositions incompatible with them. If, furthermore, John Calvin is right in thinking that there is such a thing as the *Sensus Divinitatis* and the Internal Testimony of the Holy Spirit, then perhaps (1) and (2) are produced in me by those belief-producing processes and have for me the phenomenology that goes with them; the same is not true for propositions incompatible with them.

But then the next rejoinder: Isn't it probably true that those who reject (1) and (2) in favor of other beliefs have propositional evidence for their beliefs that is on a par with mine for my beliefs? And isn't it also probably true that the same or similar phenomenology accompanies their beliefs as accompanies mine? So that those beliefs really are epistemically and internally on a par with (1) and (2), and the exclusivist is still treating like cases differently? I don't think so; I think there really are arguments

available for (1), at least, that are not available for its competitors. And as for similar phenomenology, this is not easy to say; it is not easy to look into the breast of another; the secrets of the human heart are hard to fathom; it is hard indeed to discover this sort of thing even with respect to someone you know really well. I am prepared, however, to stipulate both sorts of parity. Let's agree for purposes of argument that these beliefs are on an epistemic par in the sense that those of a different religious tradition have the same sort of internally available markers—evidence, phenomenology and the like—for their beliefs as I have for (1) and (2). What follows?

Return to the case of moral belief. King David took Bathsheba, made her pregnant, and then, after the failure of various stratagems to get her husband Uriah to think the baby was his, arranged for him to be killed. The prophet Nathan came to David and told him a story about a rich man and a poor man. The rich man had many flocks and herds; the poor man had only a single ewe lamb, which grew up with his children, "ate at his table, drank from his cup, lay in his bosom, and was like a daughter to him." The rich man had unexpected guests. Rather than slaughter one of his own sheep, he took the poor man's single ewe lamb, slaughtered it, and served it to his guests. David exploded in anger: "The man who did this deserves to die!" Then, in one of the most riveting passages in all the Bible, Nathan turns to David and declares, "You are that man!" And then David sees what he has done.

My interest here is in David's reaction to the story. I agree with David: Such injustice is utterly and despicably wrong; there are really no words for it. I believe that such an action is wrong, and I believe that the proposition that it *isn't* wrong—either because really *nothing* is wrong, or because even if some things are wrong, *this* isn't—is false. As a matter of fact, there isn't a lot I believe more strongly. I recognize, however, that there are those who disagree with me; and once more, I doubt that I could find an argument to show them that I am right and they wrong. Further, for all I know, their conflicting beliefs have for them the same internally available epistemic markers, the same phenomenology, as mine have for me. Am I then being arbitrary, treating similar cases differently in continuing to hold, as I do, that in fact that kind of behavior *is* dreadfully wrong? I don't think so. Am I wrong in thinking racial bigotry despicable, even though I know that there are others who disagree, and even if I think they have the same internal markers for their beliefs as I have for mine? I don't think so. I believe in serious actualism, the view that no objects have properties in worlds in which they do not exist, not even nonexistence. Others do not believe this, and perhaps the internal markers of their dissenting views have for them the same quality as my views have for me. Am I being arbitrary in continuing to think as I do? I can't see how.

And the reason here is this: in each of these cases, the believer in question doesn't really think the beliefs in question *are* on a relevant epistemic par. She may agree that she and those who dissent are equally convinced of the truth of their belief and even that they are internally on a par, that the internally available markers are similar, or relevantly similar. But she must still think that there is an important epistemic difference, she thinks that somehow the other person has *made a mistake,* or *has a blind spot*, or hasn't been wholly attentive, or hasn't received some grace she has, or is in some way epistemically less fortunate. And, of course, the pluralist critic is in no better case. He thinks the thing to do when there is internal epistemic parity is to withhold judgment; he knows that there are others who don't think so, and for all he knows that belief has internal parity with his; if he continues in that belief, therefore, he will be in the same condition as the exclusivist; and if he doesn't continue in this belief, he no longer has an objection to the exclusivist.

But couldn't I be wrong? Of course I could! But I don't avoid that risk by withholding all religious (or philosophical or moral) beliefs; I can go wrong that way as well as any other, treating all religions, or all philosophical thoughts, or all moral views as on a par. Again, there is no safe haven here, no way to avoid risk. In particular, you won't reach a safe haven by trying to take the same attitude toward all the historically available patterns of belief and withholding; for in so doing, you adopt a particular pattern of belief and withholding, one incompatible with some adopted by others. "You

pays your money and you takes your choice," realizing that you, like anyone else, can be desperately wrong. But what else can you do? You don't really have an alternative. And how can you do better than believe and withhold according to what, after serious and responsible consideration, seems to you to be the right pattern of belief and withholding?

Irrationality

I therefore can't see how it can be sensibly maintained that the exclusivist is unjustified in his exclusivist views; but perhaps, as is sometimes claimed, he or his view is *irrational*. Irrationality, however, is many things to many people; so there is a prior question: What is it to be irrational? More exactly, precisely what quality is it that the objector is attributing to the exclusivist (in condition *C*) when the former says the latter's exclusivist beliefs are irrational? Since the charge is never developed at all fully, it isn't easy to say. So suppose we simply consider the main varieties of irrationality (or, if you prefer, the main senses of "irrational") and ask whether any of them attach to the exclusivist just by virtue of being an exclusivist. I believe there are substantially five varieties of rationality, five distinct but analogically connected senses of the term *rational*; fortunately not all of them require detailed consideration.

Aristotelian Rationality   This is the sense in which man is a rational animal, one that has *ratio*, one that can look before and after, can hold beliefs, make inferences and is capable of knowledge. This is perhaps the basic sense, the one of which the others are analogical extensions. It is also, presumably irrelevant in the present context; at any rate I hope the objector does not mean to hold that an exclusivist will by that token no longer be a rational animal.

The Deliverances of Reason   To be rational in the Aristotelian sense is to possess reason: the power or thinking, believing, inferring, reasoning, knowing. Aristotelian rationality is thus *generic*. But there is an important more specific sense lurking in the neighborhood; this is the sense that goes with reason taken more narrowly, as the source of a priori knowledge and belief. An important use of *rational* analogically connected with the first has to do with reason taken in this more narrow way. It is by reason thus construed that we know *self-evident* beliefs —beliefs so obvious that you can't so much as grasp them without seeing that they couldn't be false. These will be among the *deliverances of reason*. Of course there are other beliefs—38 × 39 = 1482, for example—that are not self-evident but are a consequence of self-evident beliefs by way of arguments that are self-evidently valid; these too are among the deliverances of reason. So say that the deliverances of reason is the set of those propositions that are self-evident for us human beings, closed under self-evident consequence. This yields another sense of rationality: a belief is *rational* if it is among the deliverances of reason and *irrational* if it is contrary to the deliverances of reason. (A belief can therefore be neither rational nor irrational, in this sense.) This sense of *rational* is an analogical extension of the fundamental sense, but it is itself extended by analogy to still other senses. Thus, we can broaden the category of reason to include memory, experience, induction, probability, and whatever else goes into science; this is the sense of the term when reason is sometimes contrasted with faith. And we can also soften the requirement for self-evidence, recognizing both that self-evidence or a priori warrant is a matter of degree and that there are many propositions that have a priori warrant, but are not such that no one who understands them can fail to believe them.[11]

Is the exclusivist irrational in *these* senses? I think not; at any rate, the question whether he is isn't the question at issue. His exclusivist beliefs are irrational in these senses only if there is a good argument from the deliverances of reason (taken broadly) to the denials of what he believes. I do not believe that there are any such arguments. Presumably, the same goes for the pluralist objector: at any rate, his objection is not that (1) and (2) are demonstrably false or even that there are good arguments against them from the deliverances of reason; his objection is instead that there is something wrong or subpar with believing them in condition *C*. This sense too, then, is irrelevant to our present concerns.

The Deontological Sense This sense of the term has to do with intellectual *requirement*, or *duty*, or *obligation*; a person's belief is irrational in this sense if in forming or holding it she violates such a duty. This is the sense of *irrational* in which according to many contemporary evidentialist objectors to theistic belief, those who believe in God without propositional evidence are irrational. Irrationality in this sense is a matter of failing to conform to intellectual or epistemic duties; the analogical connection with the first, Aristotelian sense is that these duties are thought to be among the deliverances of reason (and hence among the deliverances of the power by virtue of which human beings are rational in the Aristotelian sense). But we have already considered whether the exclusivist is flouting duties; we need say no more about the matter here. As we say, the exclusivist is not necessarily irrational in this sense either.

Zweckrationalität A common and very important notion of rationality is *means-end rationality*— what our continental cousins, following Max Weber, sometimes call *Zweckrationalität*, the sort of rationality displayed by your actions if they are well calculated to achieve your goals. (Again, the analogical connection with the first sense is clear: The calculation in question requires the power by virtue of which we are rational in Aristotle's sense.) Clearly, there is a whole constellation of notions lurking in the nearby bushes: What would *in fact* contribute to your goals? What you *take* it would contribute to your goals? What you *would* take it would contribute to your goals if you were sufficiently acute, or knew enough, or weren't distracted by lust, greed, pride, ambition, and the like? What you would take it would contribute to your goals if you weren't thus distracted and were also to reflect sufficiently? and so on. This notion of rationality has assumed enormous importance in the last 150 years or so. (Among its laurels, for example, is the complete domination of the development of the discipline of economics.) Rationality thus construed is a matter of knowing how to get what you want; it is the cunning of reason. Is the exclusivist properly charged with irrationality in this sense? Does his believing in the way he does interfere with his attaining some of his goals, or is it a markedly inferior way of attaining those goals?

An initial *caveat*: It isn't clear that this notion of rationality applies to belief at all. It isn't clear that in *believing* something, I am acting to achieve some goal. If believing is an action at all, it is very far from being the paradigmatic kind of action taken to achieve some end; we don't have a choice as to whether to have beliefs, and we don't have a lot of choice with respect to which beliefs we have. But suppose we set this *caveat* aside and stipulate for purposes of argument that we have sufficient control over our beliefs for them to qualify as actions. Would the exclusivist's beliefs then be irrational in this sense? Well, that depends upon what his goals are; if among his goals for religious belief is, for example, not believing anything not believed by someone else, then indeed it would be. But, of course, he needn't have that goal. If I do have an end or goal in holding such beliefs as (1) and (2), it would presumably be that of believing the truth on this exceedingly important matter or perhaps that of trying to get in touch as adequately as possible with God, or more broadly with the deepest reality. And if (1) and (2) are *true*, believing them will be a way of doing exactly that. It is only if they are *not* true, then, that believing them could sensibly be thought to be irrational in this means-ends sense. Because the objector does not propose to take as a premise the proposition that (1) and (2) are false—he holds only that there is some flaw involved in *believing* them—this also is presumably not what he means.

Rationality as Sanity and Proper Function One in the grip of pathological confusion, or flight of ideas, or certain kinds of agnosia, or the manic phase of manic-depressive psychosis will often be said to be irrational; the episode may pass, after which he has regained rationality. Here *rationality* means absence of dysfunction, disorder, impairment, or pathology with respect to rational faculties. So this variety of rationality is again analogically related to Aristotelian rationality; a person is rational in this sense when no malfunction obstructs her use of the faculties by virtue of the possession of which she is rational in the Aristotelian sense. Rationality as sanity does not require possession of particularly exalted rational faculties; it

requires only normality (in the nonstatistical sense) or health, or proper function. This use of the term, naturally enough, is prominent in psychiatric discussions—Oliver Sacks's male patient who mistook his wife for a hat, for example, was thus irrational. This fifth and final sense of rationality is itself a family of analogically related senses. The fundamental sense here is that of sanity and proper function, but there are other closely related senses. Thus, we may say that a belief (in certain circumstances) is irrational, not because no sane person would hold it, but because no person who was sane and had also undergone a certain course of education would hold it or because no person who was sane and furthermore was as intelligent as we and our friends would hold it; alternatively and more briefly, the idea is not merely that no one who was functioning properly in those circumstances would hold it, but rather no one who was functioning *optimally*, as well or nearly as well as human beings ordinarily do (leaving aside the occasional great genius) would hold it. And this sense of rationality leads directly to the notion of *warrant*; I turn now to that notion; in treating it, we will also treat *ambulando*—this fifth kind of irrationality.

Warrant

So we come to the third version of the epistemic objection: that at any rate the exclusivist doesn't have warrant, or anyway *much* warrant (enough warrant for knowledge) for his exclusivistic views. Many pluralists—for example, Hick, Runzo, and Cantwell Smith—unite in declaring that, at any rate, the exclusivist certainly can't *know* that his exclusivistic views are true. But is this really true? I will argue briefly that it is not. At any rate, from the perspective of each of the major contemporary accounts of knowledge, it may very well be that the exclusivist knows (1) or (2) or both. First, consider the two main internalistic accounts of knowledge: the justified true belief accounts and the coherentist accounts. As I have already argued, it seems clear that a theist, a believer in (1) could certainly be *justified* (in the primary sense) in believing as she does: she could be flouting no intellectual or cognitive duties or obligations. But then on the most straightforward justified true belief account of knowledge, she can also *know* that it is true—if, that is, it *can* be true. More exactly, what must be possible is that both the exclusivist is justified in believing (1) and/or (2) and they be true. Presumably, the pluralist does not mean to dispute this possibility.

For concreteness, consider the account of justification given by the classical foundationalist Chisholm. On this view, a belief has warrant for me to the extent that accepting it is apt for the fulfillment of my epistemic duty, which (roughly speaking) is that of trying to get and remain in the right relation to the truth. But if after the most careful, thorough, open, and prayerful consideration, it still seems to me—perhaps more strongly than ever—that (1) and (2) are true, then clearly accepting them has great aptness for the fulfillment of that duty.

A similarly brief argument can be given with respect to *coherentism*, the view that what constitutes warrant is coherence with some body of belief. We must distinguish two varieties of coherentism. On the one hand, it might be held that what is required is coherence with some or all of the other beliefs I actually hold; on the other, that what is required is coherence with my *verific* noetic structure (Keith Lehrer's term): the set of beliefs that remains when all the false ones are deleted or replaced by their contradictories. But surely a coherent set of beliefs could include both (1) and (2) together with the beliefs involved in being in condition *C*, what would be required, perhaps, would be that the set of beliefs contain some explanation of why it is that others do not believe as I do. And if (1) and (2) are true, then surely (and a fortiori) there can be coherent verific noetic structures that include them. Hence, neither of these versions of coherentism rule out the possibility that the exclusivist in condition *C* could know (1) and/or (2).

And now consider the main externalist accounts. The most popular externalist account at present would be one or another version of *reliabilism*. And there is an oft-repeated pluralistic argument that seems to be designed to appeal to reliabilist intuitions. The conclusion of this argument is not always clear, but here is its premise, in Hick's words:

> For it is evident that in some ninety-nine percent of cases the religion which an individual professes and to which he or she adheres depends upon the accidents of birth.

Someone born to Buddhist parents in Thailand is very likely to be a Buddhist, someone born to Muslim parents in Saudi Arabia to be a Muslim, someone born to Christian parents in Mexico to be a Christian, and so on.

As a matter of sociological fact, this may be right. Furthermore, it can certainly produce a sense of intellectual vertigo. But what is one to do with this fact, if fact it is, and what follows from it? Does it follow, for example, that I ought not to accept the religious views that I have been brought up to accept, or the ones that I find myself inclined to accept, or the ones that seem to me to be true? Or that the belief-producing processes that have produced those beliefs in me are unreliable? Surely not. Furthermore, self-referential problems once more loom; this argument is another philosophical tar baby.

For suppose we concede that if I had been born of Muslim parents in Morocco rather than Christian parents in Michigan, my beliefs would have been quite different. (For one thing, I probably wouldn't believe that I was born in Michigan.) The same goes for the pluralist. Pluralism isn't and hasn't been widely popular in the world at large; if the pluralist had been born in Madagascar, or medieval France, he probably wouldn't have been a pluralist. Does it follow that he shouldn't be a pluralist or that his pluralist beliefs are produced in him by an unreliable belief-producing process? I doubt it. Suppose I hold the following, or something similar:

(4)   If *S*'s religious or philosophical beliefs are such that if *S* had been born elsewhere and else when, she wouldn't have held them, then those beliefs are produced by unreliable belief producing mechanisms and hence have no warrant.

Once more I will be hoist with my own petard. For in all probability, someone born in Mexico to Christian parents wouldn't believe (4) itself. No matter what philosophical and religious beliefs we hold and withhold (so it seems), there are places and times such that if we have been born there and then, then we would not have displayed the pattern of holding and withholding of religious and philosophical beliefs we *do* display. As I said, this can indeed be vertiginous; but what can we make of it? What can we infer from it about what has warrant and how we should conduct our intellectual lives? That's not easy to say. Can we infer *anything at all* about what has warrant or how we should conduct our intellectual lives? Not obviously.

To return to reliabilism then: For simplicity, let's take the version of reliabilism according to which S knows p if the belief that p is produced in S by a reliable belief producing mechanism or process. I don't have the space here to go into this matter in sufficient detail, but it seems pretty clear that if (1) and (2) are true, then it *could* be that the beliefs that (1) and (2) be produced in me by a reliable belief-producing process. For either we are thinking of *concrete* belief-producing processes, like your memory or John's powers of a priori reasoning (tokens as opposed to types), or else we are thinking of types of belief-producing processes (type reliabilism). The problem with the latter is that there are an enormous number of *different* types of belief-producing processes for any given belief, some of which are reliable and some of which are not; the problem (and a horrifying problem it is) is to say which of these is the type the reliability of which determines whether the belief in question has warrant. So the first (token reliabilism) is a better way of stating reliabilism. But then clearly enough if (1) or (2) are true, they could be produced in me by a reliable belief-producing process. Calvin's *Sensus Divinitatis*, for example, could be working in the exclusivist in such a way as to reliably produce the belief that (1) is true; Calvin's Internal Testimony of the Holy Spirit could do the same for (2). If (1) and (2) are true, therefore, then from a reliabilist perspective there is no reason whatever to think that the exclusivist might not know that they are true.

There is another brand of externalism which seems to me to be closer to the truth than reliabilism; call it (*faute de mieux*) "proper functionalism." This view can be stated to a first approximation as follows: S knows p if (1) the belief that p is produced in S by cognitive faculties that are functioning properly (working as they ought to work, suffering from no dysfunction), (2) the cognitive environment in which p is produced is appropriate for those faculties, (3) the purpose of the module of

the epistemic faculties producing the belief in question is to produce true beliefs (alternatively, the module of the design plan governing the production of p is aimed at the production of true beliefs), and (4) the objective probability of a belief's being true, given that it is produced under those conditions, is high. All of this needs explanation, of course; for present purposes, perhaps, we can collapse the account into the first condition. But then clearly it could be, if (1) and (2) are true, that they are produced in me by cognitive faculties functioning properly under condition C. For suppose (1) is true. Then it is surely possible that God has created us human beings with something like Calvin's *Sensus Divinitatis*, a belief-producing process that in a wide variety of circumstances functions properly to produce (1) or some very similar belief. Furthermore it is also possible that in response to the human condition of sin and misery, God has provided for us human beings a means of salvation, which he has revealed in the Bible. Still further, perhaps he has arranged for us to come to believe what he means to teach there by way of the operation of something like the Internal Testimony of the Holy Spirit of which Calvin speaks. So on this view, too, if (1) and (2) are true, it is certainly possible that the exclusivist know that they are. We can be sure that the exclusivist's views are irrational in this sense, then, only if they are false; but the pluralist objector does not mean to claim that they are false; this version of the objection, therefore, also fails. The exclusivist isn't necessarily irrational, and indeed might *know* that (1) and (2) are true, if indeed they *are* true.

All this seems right. But don't the realities of religious pluralism count for anything at all? Is there nothing at all to the claims of the pluralists? Could that really be right? Of course not. For many or most exclusivists, I think, an awareness of the enormous variety of human religious response functions as a *defeater* for such beliefs as (1) and (2)—an *undercutting defeater*, as opposed to a rebutting defeater. It calls into question, to some degree or other, the sources of one's belief in (1) or (2). It doesn't or needn't do so by way of an *argument*; and indeed there isn't a very powerful argument from the proposition that many apparently devout people around the world dissent from (1) and (2) to the conclusion that (1) and (2) are false. Instead, it works more directly; it directly reduces the level of confidence or degree of belief in the proposition in question. From a Christian perspective, this situation of religious pluralism and our awareness of it is itself a manifestation of our miserable human condition; and it may deprive us of some of the comfort and peace the Lord has promised his followers. It can also deprive the exclusivist of the *knowledge* that (1) and (2) *are* true, if even they are true and he *believes* that they are. Because degree of warrant depends in part on degree of belief, it is possible, though not necessary, that knowledge of the facts of religious pluralism should reduce an exclusivist's degree of belief and hence of warrant for (1) and (2) in such a way as to deprive him of knowledge of (1) and (2). He might be such that if he *hadn't* known the facts of pluralism, then he would have known (1) and (2), but now that he *does* know those facts, he doesn't know (1) and (2). In this way, he may come to know less by knowing more.

Things *could* go this way with the exclusivist. On the other hand, they *needn't* go this way. Consider once more the moral parallel. Perhaps you have always believed it deeply wrong for a counselor to use his position of trust to seduce a client. Perhaps you

discover that others disagree; they think it more like a minor peccadillo, like running a red light when there's no traffic; and you realize that possibly these people have the same internal markers for their beliefs that you have for yours. You think the matter over more fully, imaginatively recreate and rehearse such situations, become more aware of just what is involved in such a situation (the breach of trust, the breaking of implied promises, the injustice and unfairness, the nasty irony of a situation in which someone comes to a counselor seeking help but receives only hurt), and come to believe even more fully that such an action is wrong—and indeed to have more warrant for that belief. But something similar can happen in the case of religious beliefs. A fresh or heightened awareness of the facts of religious pluralism could bring about a reappraisal of one's religious life, a reawakening, a new or renewed and deepened grasp and apprehension of (1) and (2). From Calvin's perspective, it could serve as an occasion for a renewed and more powerful working of the belief-producing processes by which we come to apprehend (1) and (2). In that way, knowledge of the facts of pluralism could initially serve as a defeater, but in the long run have precisely the opposite effect.

NOTES

1. *Colloquium Heptaplomeres de Rerum Sublimium Arcanis Abditis*, written by 1593 but first published in 1857. English translation by Marion Kuntz (Princeton, N.J.: Princeton Univ. Press, 1975), p. 256.

2. Joseph Runzo: "Today, the impressive piety and evident rationality of the belief systems of other religious traditions, inescapably confronts Christians with a crisis and a potential revolution." "God, Commitment, and Other Faiths: Pluralism vs. Relativism," *Faith and Philosophy* 5, no. 4 (October 1988): 343f. (Reading IX.5 in this book.)

3. Gary Gutting: "Applying these considerations to religious belief, we seem led to the conclusion that, because believers have many epistemic peers who do not share their belief in God..., they have no right to maintain their belief without a justification. If they do so, they are guilty of epistemological

egoism." *Religious Belief and Religious Skepticism* (Notre Dame, Ind.: Univ. of Notre Dame Press, 1982), p. 90 (but see the following pages for an important qualification).

4. Wilfred Cantwell Smith: "Here my submission is that on this front the traditional doctrinal position of the Church has in fact militated against its traditional moral position, and has in fact encouraged Christians to approach other men immorally. Christ has taught us humility, but we have approached them with arrogance.... This charge of arrogance is a serious one." *Religious Diversity* (New York: Harper & Row, 1976), p. 13.

5. Runzo: "Ethically, Religious Exclusivism has the morally repugnant result of making those who have privileged knowledge, or who are intellectually astute, a religious elite, while penalizing those who

happen to have no access to the putatively correct religious view, or who are incapable of advanced understanding." Op. cit., p. 348.

6. John Hick: "But natural pride, despite its positive contribution to human life, becomes harmful when it is elevated to the level of dogma and is built into the belief system of a religious community. This happens when its sense of its own validity and worth is expressed in doctrines implying an exclusive or a decisively superior access to the truth or the power to save." "Religious Pluralism and Absolute Claims," *Religious Pluralism* (Notre Dame, Ind.: Univ. of Notre Dame Press, 1984), p. 197.

7. John Cobb: "I agree with the liberal theists that even in Pannenberg's case, the quest for an absolute as a basis for understanding reflects the long tradition of Christian imperialism and triumphalism rather than the pluralistic spirit." "The Meaning of Pluralism or Christian Self-Understanding," *Religious Pluralism*, ed. Leroy Rouner (Notre Dame, Ind.: Univ. of Notre Dame Press, 1984), p. 171.

8. "God, Commitment, and Other Faiths: Pluralism vs. Relativism" *Faith and Philosophy* 5, no. 4 (October 1988):357.

9. Smith, op. cit., p. 14.

10. John Hick: "... the only reason for treating one's tradition differently from others is the very human but not very cogent reason that it is one's own!" *An Interpretation of Religion*, loc. cit.

11. *An Interpretation of Religion* (New Haven, Conn.: Yale Univ. Press, 1989), p. 2.

IX.3

Hick's Religious Pluralism and "Reformed Epistemology"—A Middle Ground

DAVID BASINGER

David Basinger is professor of philosophy at Roberts Wesleyan College in Rochester, New York, and is the author of several works in the philosophy of religion. His goal in this article is to analyze comparatively the influential argument for religious pluralism offered by John Hick and the argument for religious exclusivism (sectarianism) that can be generated by proponents of what has come to be labeled "Reformed epistemology." He argues that while Hick and the Reformed exclusivist appear to be giving us incompatible responses to the same question about the true nature of "religious" reality, they are actually responding to related but distinct questions, each of which must be considered by those desiring to give a religious explanation for the phenomenon of religious diversity. Moreover, he concludes that the insights of neither ought to be emphasized at the expense of the other.

Reprinted from *Faith and Philosophy* 5 (1988): 421–32, by permission. Endnotes deleted.

No one denies that the basic tenets of many religious perspectives are, if taken literally, quite incompatible. The salvific claims of some forms of Judeo-Christian thought, for example, condemn the proponents of all other perspectives to hell, while the incompatible salvific claims of some forms of Islamic thought do the same.

Such incompatibility is normally explained in one of three basic ways. The nontheist argues that all religious claims are false, the product perhaps of wish fulfillment. The religious pluralist argues that the basic claims of at least all of the major world religions are more or less accurate descriptions of the same reality. Finally, the religious exclusivist argues that the tenets of only one religion (or some limited number of religions) are to any significant degree accurate descriptions of reality.

The purpose of this discussion is to analyze comparatively the influential argument for religious pluralism offered by John Hick and the argument for religious exclusivism which can be (and perhaps has been) generated by proponents of what has come to be labeled "Reformed Epistemology." I shall argue that while Hick and the Reformed epistemologist appear to be giving us incompatible responses to the same question about the true nature of "religious" reality, they are actually responding to related, but distinct questions, each of which must be considered by those desiring to give a religious explanation for the phenomenon of religious diversity. Moreover, I shall conclude that the insights offered by both Hick and the Reformed epistemologist are of value and, accordingly, that those of neither ought to be emphasized at the expense of the other.

JOHN HICK'S THEOLOGICAL PLURALISM

Hick's contention is not that different religions make no conflicting truth claims. In fact, he believes that "the differences of belief between (and within) the traditions are legion," and has often in great detail discussed them. His basic claim, rather, is that such differences are best seen as "different ways of conceiving and experiencing the one ultimate divine Reality."

However, if the various religions are really "responses to a single ultimate transcendent Reality," how then do we account for such significant differences? The best explanation, we are told, is the assumption that "the limitless divine reality has been thought and experienced by different human mentalities forming and formed by different intellectual frameworks and devotional techniques." Or, as Hick has stated the point elsewhere, the best explanation is the assumption that the correspondingly different ways of responding to divine reality "owe their differences to the modes of thinking, perceiving and feeling which have developed within the different patterns of human existence embodied in the various cultures of the earth." Each "constitutes a valid context of salvation/liberation; but none constitutes the one and only such context."

But why accept such a pluralistic explanation? Why not hold, rather, that there is no higher Reality beyond us and thus that all religious claims are false—i.e., why not opt for naturalism? Or why not adopt the exclusivistic contention that the religious claims of only one perspective are true?

Hick does not reject naturalism because he sees it to be an untenable position. It is certainly *possible*, he tells us, that the "entire realm of [religious] experience is delusory or hallucinatory, simply a human projection, and not in any way or degree a result of the presence of a greater divine reality." In fact, since the "universe of which we are part is religiously ambiguous," it is not even *unreasonable* or *implausible* "to interpret any aspect of it, including our religious experience, in non-religious as well as religious ways."

However, he is quick to add, "it is perfectly reasonable and sane for us to trust our experience"—including our religious experience—"as generally cognitive of reality except when we have some reason to doubt it." Moreover, "the mere theoretical possibility that any or all [religious experience] may be illusory does not count as a reason to doubt it." Nor is religious experience overturned by the fact that the great religious figures of the past, including Jesus, held a number of beliefs which we today reject as arising from the now outmoded science of their day, or by the fact that some people find "it impossible to accept that the profound dimension of pain and suffering is the measure of the cost of creation through creaturely freedom."

He acknowledges that those who have "no positive ground for religious belief within their own experience" often do see such factors as "insuperable barriers" to religious belief. But given the ambiguous nature of the evidence, he argues, it cannot be demonstrated that all rational people must see it this way. That is, belief in a supernatural realm can't be shown to be any less plausible than disbelief. Accordingly, he concludes, "those who actually participate in this field of religious experience are fully entitled, as sane and rational persons, to take the risk of trusting their own experience together with that of their tradition, and of proceeding to live and to believe on the basis of it, rather than taking the alternative risk of distrusting it and so—for the time being at least—turning their backs on God."

But why choose pluralism as the best religious hypothesis? Why does Hick believe we ought not be exclusivists? It is not because he sees exclusivism as incoherent. It is certainly possible, he grants, that "one particular 'Ptolemaic' religious vision does correspond uniquely with how things are." Nor does Hick claim to have some privileged "cosmic vantage point from which [he can] observe both the divine reality in itself and the different partial human awarenesses of that reality." But when we individually consider the evidence in the case, he argues, the result is less ambiguous. When "we start from the phenomenological fact of the various forms of religious experience, and we seek an hypothesis which will make sense of this realm of phenomena" from a religious point of view, "the theory that most naturally suggests itself postulates a divine Reality which is itself limitless, exceeding the scope of human conceptuality and language, but which is humanly thought and experienced in various conditioned and limited ways."

What is this evidence which makes the pluralistic hypothesis so "considerably more probable" than

exclusivism? For one thing, Hick informs us, a credible religious hypothesis must account for the fact, "evident to ordinary people (even though not always taken into account by theologians) that in the great majority of cases—say 98 to 99 percent—the religion in which a person believes and to which he adheres depends upon where he was born." Moreover, a credible hypothesis must account for the fact that within all of the major religious traditions, "basically the same salvific process is taking place, namely the transformation of human existence from self-centeredness to Reality-centeredness." And while pluralism "illuminates" these otherwise baffling facts, the strict exclusivist's view "has come to seem increasingly implausible and unrealistic."

But even more importantly, he maintains, a credible religious hypothesis must account for the fact, of which "we have become irreversibly aware in the present century, as the result of anthropological, sociological and psychological studies and the work of philosophy of language, that there is no one universal and invariable" pattern for interpreting human experience, but rather a range of significantly different patterns or conceptual schemes "which have developed within the major cultural streams." And when considered in light of this, Hick concludes, a "pluralistic theory becomes inevitable."

THE REFORMED OBJECTION

There are two basic ways in which Hick's pluralistic position can be critiqued. One "appropriate critical response," according to Hick himself, "would be to offer a better [religious] hypothesis." That is, one way to challenge Hick is to claim that the evidence he cites is better explained by some form of exclusivism.

But there is another, potentially more powerful type of objection, one which finds its roots in the currently popular "Reformed Epistemology" being championed by philosophers such as Alvin Plantinga. I will first briefly outline Plantinga's latest version of this epistemological approach and then discuss its impact on Hick's position.

According to Plantinga, it has been widely held since the Enlightenment that if theistic beliefs—e.g., religious hypotheses—are to be considered rational, they must be based on propositional evidence. It is not enough for the theist just to refute objections to any such belief. The theist "must also have something like an argument for the belief, or some positive reason to think that the belief is true." But this is incorrect, Plantinga maintains. There are beliefs which acquire their warrant propositionally—i.e., have warrant conferred on them by an evidential line of reasoning from other beliefs. And for such beliefs, it may well be true that proponents need something like an argument for their veridicality.

However, there are also, he tells us, *basic* beliefs which are not based on propositional evidence and, thus, do not require propositional warrant. In fact, *if* such beliefs can be affirmed "without either violating an epistemic duty or displaying some kind of noetic defect," they can be considered *properly* basic. And, according to Plantinga, many theistic beliefs can be properly basic: "Under widely realized conditions it is perfectly rational, reasonable, intellectually respectable and acceptable to believe [certain theistic tenets] without believing [them] on the basis of [propositional] evidence."

But what are such conditions? Under what conditions can a belief have positive epistemic status if it is not conferred by other propositions whose epistemic status is not in question? The answer, Plantinga informs us, lies in an analysis of belief formation.

[We have] cognitive faculties designed to enable us to achieve true beliefs with respect to a wide variety of propositions—propositions about our immediate environment, about our interior lives, about the thoughts and experiences of other persons, about our universe at large, about right and wrong, about the whole realm of *abstracta*—numbers, properties, propositions, states of affairs, possible worlds and their like, about modality—what is necessary and possible—and about [ourselves]. These faculties work in such a way that under the appropriate circumstances we form the appropriate belief. More exactly, the appropriate belief is *formed in us*; in the

typical case we do not *decide* to hold or form the belief in question, but simply find ourselves with it. Upon considering an instance of *modus ponens*, I find myself believing its corresponding conditional; upon being appeared to in the familiar way, I find myself holding the belief that there is a large tree before me; upon being asked what I had for breakfast, I reflect for a moment and find myself with the belief that what I had was eggs on toast. In these and other cases I do not *decide* what to believe; I don't total up the evidence (I'm being appeared to redly; on most occasions when thus appeared to I am in the presence of something red, so most probably in this case I am) and make a decision as to what seems best supported; I simply find myself believing.

And from a theistic point of view, Plantinga continues, the same is true in the religious realm. Just as it is true that when our senses or memory are functioning properly, "appropriate belief is formed in us," so it is that God has created us with faculties which will, "when they are working the way they were designed to work by the being who designed and created us and them," produce true theistic beliefs. Moreover, if these faculties are functioning properly, a basic belief thus formed has "positive epistemic status to the degree [the individual in question finds herself] inclined to accept it."

What, though, of the alleged counter-evidence to such theistic beliefs? What, for example, of all the arguments the conclusion of which is that God does not exist? Can they all be dismissed as irrelevant? Not immediately, answers Plantinga. We must seriously consider potential defeaters of our basic beliefs. With respect to the belief that God exists, for example, we must seriously consider the claim that religious belief is mere wish fulfillment and the claim that God's existence is incompatible with (or at least improbable given) the amount of evil in the world.

But to undercut such defeaters, he continues, we need not engage in positive apologetics: produce propositional evidence for our beliefs. We need only engage in negative apologetics: refute such arguments. Moreover, it is Plantinga's conviction that such defeaters do normally exist. "The non-propositional warrant enjoyed by [a person's] belief in God, for example, [seems] itself sufficient to turn back the challenge offered by some alleged defeaters"—e.g., the claim that theistic belief is mere wish fulfillment. And other defeaters such as the "problem of evil," he tells us, can be undercut by identifying validity or soundness problems or even by appealing to the fact that "experts think it unsound or that the experts are evenly divided as to its soundness."

Do Plantinga or other proponents of this Reformed epistemology maintain that their exclusivistic religious hypotheses are properly basic and can thus be "defended" in the manner just outlined? I am not *certain* that they do. However, when Plantinga, for example, claims that "God exists" is for most adult theists properly basic, he appears to have in mind a classical Christian conception of the divine—i.e., a being who is the triune, omnipotent, omniscient, perfectly good, *ex nihilo* creator of the universe. In fact, given his recent claim that "the internal testimony of the Holy Spirit… is a source of reliable and perfectly acceptable beliefs about what is communicated [by God] in Scripture," and the manner in which most who make such a claim view the truth claims of the other world religions, it would appear that Plantinga's "basic" conception of God is quite exclusive.

However, even if no Reformed epistemologist actually does affirm an exclusivistic hypothesis she claims is properly basic, it is obvious that the Reformed analysis of belief justification can be used to critique Hick's line of reasoning. Hick claims that an objective inductive assessment of the relevant evidence makes his pluralistic thesis a more plausible religious explanation than any of the competing exclusivistic hypotheses. But a Reformed exclusivist could easily argue that this approach to the issue is misguided. My affirmation of an exclusivistic Christian perspective, such an argument might begin, is not evidential in nature. It is, rather, simply a belief I have found formed in me, much like the belief that I am seeing a tree in front of me or the belief that killing innocent children is wrong.

Now, of course, I must seriously consider the allegedly formidable defeaters with which pluralists such as Hick have presented me. I must consider the fact, for example, that the exclusive beliefs simply formed in most people are not similar to mine, but rather tend to mirror those beliefs found in the cultures in which such people have been raised. But I do not agree with Hick that this fact is best explained by a pluralistic hypothesis. I attribute this phenomenon to other factors such as the epistemic blindness with which most of humanity has been plagued since the fall.

Moreover, to defend my position—to maintain justifiably (rationally) that I am right and Hick is wrong—I need not, as Hick seems to suggest, produce objective "proof" that his hypothesis is weaker than mine. That is, I need not produce "evidence" that would lead most rational people to agree with me. That would be to involve myself in Classical Foundationalism, which is increasingly being recognized as a bankrupt epistemological methodology. All I need do is undercut Hick's defeaters—i.e., show that his challenge does not require me to abandon my exclusivity thesis. And this I can easily do. For Hick has not demonstrated that my thesis is self-contradictory. And it is extremely doubtful that there exists any other non-question-begging criterion for plausibility by which he could even attempt to demonstrate that my thesis is less plausible (less probable) than his.

Hick, of course, believes firmly that his hypothesis makes the most sense. But why should this bother me? By his own admission, many individuals firmly believe that, given the amount of seemingly gratuitous evil in the world, God's nonexistence is by far most plausible. Yet this does not keep him from affirming theism. He simply reserves the right to see things differently and continues to believe. And there is no reason why I cannot do the same.

Moreover, even if what others believed were relevant, by Hick's own admission, the majority of theists doubt that his thesis is true. Or, at the very least, I could rightly maintain that "the experts are evenly divided as to its soundness." Thus, given the criteria for defeater assessment which we Reformed exclusivists affirm, Hick's defeaters are clearly undercut. And, accordingly, I remain perfectly justified in continuing to hold that my exclusivity thesis is correct and, therefore, that all incompatible competing hypotheses are false.

A MIDDLE GROUND

It is tempting to see Hick and the Reformed exclusivist as espousing incompatible approaches to the question of religious diversity. If Hick is correct—if the issue is primarily evidential in nature—then the Reformed exclusivist is misguided and vice versa. But this, I believe, is an inaccurate assessment of the situation. There are two equally important, but distinct, questions which arise in this context, and Hick and the Reformed exclusivist, it seems to me, each *primarily* address only one.

The Reformed exclusivist is primarily interested in the following question:

Q1. Under what conditions is an individual within her epistemic rights (is she rational) in affirming one of the many mutually exclusive religious diversity hypotheses?

In response, as we have seen, the Reformed exclusivist argues (or at least could argue) that a person need not grant that her religious hypothesis (belief) requires propositional (evidential) warrant. She is within her epistemic rights in maintaining that it is a *basic* belief. And if she does so, then to preserve rationality, she is not required to "prove" in some objective manner that her hypothesis is most plausible. She is fulfilling all epistemic requirements solely by defending her hypothesis against claims that it is less plausible than competitors.

It seems to me that the Reformed exclusivist is basically right on this point. I do believe, for reasons mentioned later in this essay, that attempts by any knowledgeable exclusivist to define her hypothesis will ultimately require her to enter the realm of positive apologetics—i.e., will require her to engage in a comparative analysis of her exclusivistic beliefs. But I wholeheartedly agree with the Reformed exclusivist's contention that to preserve rationality, she need not actually demonstrate that her hypothesis is most plausible. She need ultimately only defend herself against the claim that a

thoughtful assessment of the matter makes the affirmation of some incompatible perspective—i.e., pluralism or some incompatible exclusivistic perspective—the only rational option. And this, I believe, she can clearly do.

What this means, of course, is that if Hick is actually arguing that pluralism is the only rational option, then I think he is wrong. And his claim that pluralism "is considerably more probable" than exclusivism does, it must be granted, make it appear as if he believes pluralism to be the only hypothesis a knowledgeable theist can justifiably affirm.

But Hick never actually calls his opponents irrational in this context. That is, while Hick clearly believes that sincere, knowledgeable exclusivists are *wrong*, he has never to my knowledge claimed that they are guilty of violating the basic epistemic rules governing rational belief. Accordingly, it seems best to assume that Q1—a concern with what can be rationally affirmed—is not Hick's primary interest in this context.

But what then is it with which Hick is concerned? As we have seen, Q1 is defensive in nature. It asks for identification of conditions under which we can justifiably continue to affirm a belief we *already* hold. But *why* hold the specific religious beliefs we desire to defend? Why, specifically, choose to defend religious pluralism rather than exclusivism or vice versa? Or, to state this question of "belief origin" more formally:

Q2. Given that an individual can be within her epistemic rights (can be rational) in affirming either exclusivism or pluralism, upon what basis should her actual choice be made?

This is the type of question in which I believe Hick is primarily interested.

Now, it might be tempting for a Reformed exclusivist to contend that she is exempt from the consideration of Q2. As I see it, she might begin, this question is based on the assumption that individuals consciously choose their religious belief systems. But the exclusivistic hypothesis which I affirm was not the result of a conscious attempt to choose the most plausible option. I have simply discovered this exclusivistic hypothesis formed in me in much the same fashion I find my visual and moral beliefs just formed in me. And thus Hick's question is simply irrelevant to my position.

But such a response will not do. There is no reason to deny that Reformed exclusivists do have, let's say, a Calvinistic religious hypothesis just formed in them. However, although almost everyone in every culture does in the appropriate context have similar "tree-beliefs" just formed in them, there is no such unanimity within the religious realm. As Hick rightly points out, the religious belief that the overwhelming majority of people in any given culture find just formed in them is the dominant hypothesis of that culture or subculture. Moreover, the dominant religious hypotheses in most of these cultures are exclusivistic—i.e., incompatible with one another.

Accordingly, it seems to me that Hick can rightly be interpreted as offering the following challenge to the knowledgeable Reformed exclusivist (the exclusivist aware of pervasive religious diversity): I will grant that your exclusivistic beliefs were not originally the product of conscious deliberation. But given that most sincere theists initially go through a type of religious belief-forming process similar to yours and yet usually find formed in themselves the dominant exclusivistic hypotheses of their own culture, upon what basis can you justifiably continue to claim that the hypothesis you affirm has some special status just because you found it formed in you? Or, to state the question somewhat differently, Hick's analysis of religious diversity challenges knowledgeable Reformed exclusivists to ask themselves why they now believe that their religious belief-forming mechanisms are functioning properly while the analogous mechanisms in all others are faulty.

Some Reformed exclusivists, as we have seen, have a ready response. Because of "the fall," they maintain, most individuals suffer from religious epistemic blindness—i.e., do not possess properly functioning religious belief-forming mechanisms. Only our mechanisms are trustworthy. However, every exclusivistic religious tradition can—and many do—make such claims. Hence, an analogous Hickian question again faces knowledgeable Reformed exclusivists: Why do you believe that only those religious belief-forming mechanisms which produce exclusivistic beliefs compatible with yours do not suffer from epistemic blindness?

Reformed exclusivists cannot at this point argue that they have found this belief just formed in them for it is *now* the reliability of the belief-forming mechanism, itself, which is being questioned. Nor, since they are anti-foundationalists, can Reformed exclusivists argue that the evidence demonstrates conclusively that their religious position is correct. So upon what then can they base their crucial belief that their belief-forming mechanisms *alone* produce true beliefs?

They must, it seems to me, ultimately fall back on the contention that their belief-forming mechanisms can alone be trusted because that set of beliefs thus generated appears to them to form the most plausible religious explanatory hypothesis available. But to respond in this fashion brings them into basic methodological agreement with Hick's position on Q2. That is, it appears that knowledgeable Reformed exclusivists must ultimately maintain with Hick that when attempting to discover which of the many self-consistent hypotheses that *can* rationally be affirmed is the one that *ought* to be affirmed, a person must finally decide which hypothesis she believes best explains the phenomena. Or, to state this important point differently yet, what Hick's analysis of religious diversity demonstrates, I believe, is that even for those knowledgeable Reformed exclusivists who claim to find their religious perspectives just formed in them, a conscious choice among competing religious hypotheses is ultimately called for.

This is not to say, it must again be emphasized, that such Reformed exclusivists must attempt to "prove" their choice is best. But, given the culturally relative nature of religious belief-forming mechanisms, a simple appeal to such a mechanism seems inadequate as a basis for such exclusivists to continue to affirm their perspective. It seems rather that knowledgeable exclusivists must ultimately make a conscious decision whether to retain the religious hypothesis that has been formed in them or choose another. And it further appears that they should feel some prima facie obligation to consider the available options—consciously consider the nature